Praise for Voyageur

'This book is mesmerising from first page to last and deeply, unexpectedly moving'   *Sunday Telegraph*

'Twigger is a fine raconteur . . . [his] book is also an eloquent tribute to the melancholy surrealism of small settlements in the middle of empty space, and the severity and grandeur of wild places'   *Spectator*

'*Voyageur* is a compelling read that vividly brings to life an often overlooked historical achievement'   *Times Literary Supplement*

'*Voyageur* is a great read, brimming with intrepid adventure, close shaves and servings of pemmican. It is a grown-up *Swallows and Amazons*, Twigger prompting the same childish excitement I remember when reading Arthur Ransome's classic . . . Brilliant'   *Wanderlust*

'He combines a wonderful sense of romantic adventure, a desire to tap back into something primitive and elemental, with a knack of debunking any tendency in himself to be pompous'
The Herald

'The book is replete with fascinating details'   *Scotland on Sunday*

Robert Twigger won the Newdigate prize for poetry in 1985. He is the author of *Angry White Pyjamas*, winner of the Somerset Maugham Award and the William Hill Sports Book of the Year Award, *Big Snake*, *The Extinction Club* and *Being a Man*. Robert Twigger lives in Oxford.

Voyageur

Across the Rocky Mountains
in a Birchback Canoe

Robert Twigger

PHOENIX

A PHOENIX PAPERBACK

First published in Great Britain in 2006
by Weidenfeld & Nicolson
This paperback edition published in 2007
by Phoenix,
an imprint of Orion Books Ltd,
Orion House, 5 Upper St Martin's Lane,
London WC2H 9EA

1 3 5 7 9 10 8 6 4 2

A CIP catalogue record for this book
is available from the British Library.

ISBN-13 978-0-7538-2148-0

Printed and bound in Great Britain by
Clays Ltd, St Ives plc

The Orion Publishing Group's policy is to use papers that
are natural, renewable and recyclable products and
made from wood grown in sustainable forests. The logging
and manufacturing processes are expected to conform to
the environmental regulations of the country of origin.

www.orionbooks.co.uk

To Jean Twigger

Many people helped us. Even if it wasn't possible to mention them in the text I'd like to thank them all. Financial discounts were kindly provided by Debbie Marshall at Zoom airlines, Becky at Travel Alberta, the Sheridan Lawrence hotel in Fort Vermilion, the Ramada hotel in Prince George, and Derek McClintock at GAPC video-equipment hire in Ottawa. Great assistance was also provided by the Alexander Mackenzie Voyageur Route Association as well as the museum staff in Peace River, Fort Chipewyan and Bella Coola.

CONTENTS

'I have dined with Lords and Ladies, chatted with Queen Victoria and have been formally received by the Emperor Napoleon III, yet my most cherished memories come from a leaky tent, a bark canoe and the vast and mysterious wilderness of Canada.'

Sir William Logan, Founder of the
Geological Survey of Canada, 1842

PLATES

Section 1

p.1 Ben and John fit the ribs and cedar sheathing; Sota, the dog, rarely left the boat.

p.2 & 3 A rare burst of quiet paddling on the Peace.

p.4 A never-ending task: fixing one of the many leaks.

Section 2

p.5 Early morning and towing on the Peace.

p.6 & 7 Navigating the mighty curves of the Peace.

p.8 Dave and dragonfly; Joe never minded getting wet; author makes fire; Barney sketching.

Section 3

p.9 The new chief's ceremony.

p.10 & 11 It's amazing what you can get in a canoe.

p.12 Nigel's fresh fish were a welcome change from cinnamon porridge.

Section 4

p.13 Portaging the dam; Steve's thumb.

p.14 & 15 Nigel towing on the Parsnip; Arctic Lake.

p.16 The Bad River was bad; crossing the Inland Plateau; Alexander Mackenzie – no longer popular with the natives; Mackenzie's furthest point west – the end of the voyage; the trip takes its toll on (from left to right, before and after) Joe, Steve, Nigel, the author.

Part One

FIRST ATTEMPT

One

PITT RIVERS DREAMING

*'For most men, rest is stagnation,
activity madness.'* Epicurus

I

The canoe was not silvery like a silver birch but light golden brown. It sat on a vast mirror of water; a dark mirror you could also see through, down to the unknown depths, past the perfect reflection of the canoe, the trees and the sky. The intensity of the sky's blueness seemed necessary. It had something to do with the greenness of the pines. For some reason I was wearing a weatherbeaten buckskin jacket with fringes and a coonskin cap with its furry tail hanging down my neck. A collie dog panted in the bow of the boat and the sun glinted off the sights of my rifle. All my gear was in a canvas Duluth bag with a tumpline, a headband, to make the carrying easier. Was I alone? I couldn't tell. In this waking dream the most solid figure was the boat, fashioned from bark and just floating, floating in its quiet way.

Like the water the boat rested on, the dream had depth. It was made from memories and desire and was as real as anything else in my dreamlike suburban existence. I was a writer living on the edge of Oxford with a reliable Japanese car parked in my drive and a fistful of unpaid bills on my exquisite pine-block kitchen table. I was forever looking out of the window and seeing the wind in the eucalyptus trees that towered above everyone else's tiny gardens. Then one day the trees grew too tall and they cut the tops off, giving me a better view of everyone's satellite dishes

3

and TV antenna. At night I pissed in my back garden, and zipping up I'd try to recognise stars in the night sky through the sodium haze of the streetlights. By day I wrestled with earning a living for my small family. This involved large amounts of time not writing in a shed at the bottom of the garden.

The shed was home-built and on hot days smelled of pine resin and wood preservative. It encouraged the dream. I had once built a coracle as a child and floated inside it along a stream near my house. I can still remember the immense shock of the cold water as the thing capsized on its maiden voyage. I dragged with a friend an old war-surplus aluminium kayak along a wider river that was mostly too shallow for paddling. That took one day twenty-five years ago and it's still as sharp as everyday reality in my mind.

This dream of travel and adventure needed appeasement. I took to visiting the Pitt Rivers Ethnological Museum where native boats form part of the display. Modern museums with their worthy instructional aims bored me as a child. I only liked the Science Museum in London and the Pitt Rivers in Oxford. The Pitt Rivers was a magician's cave of artefacts, with Japanese *katana* and Chinese matchlocks on the walls and dugout canoes suspended from the high ceiling. In a central glass cabinet were shrunken heads from Peru, including, for comparison, a modern one shrunk for the tourist trade. Tourist shrunken heads have furry faces – real ones are shaved smooth. The Pitt Rivers has, thankfully, not changed in years. I went alone and stared deeply at Inuit anoraks made from chewed sealskin and Naga spears decorated with human hair. The exercise of walking to the museum helped too. I was forever trying to get my life into balance: good walk, weird exhibits, then back to the more mundane necessities of life – or so I half hoped.

In the museum bookshop I found a pamphlet entitled 'The Algonquin Birchbark Canoe'. At the cash till the woman said, 'You've seen our one, have you?'

The Pitt Rivers is famously dark. Those with poor eyesight have to squint at the labels penned in faded Indian ink. The corners of the museum are especially dark, and in twenty-five

4

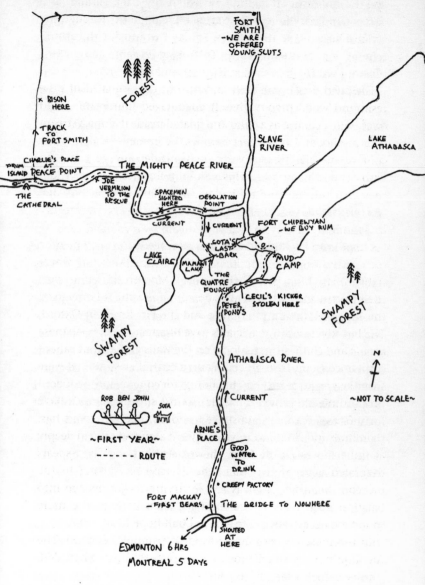

FORT
SMITH
—WE ARE
OFFERED
YOUNG SLUTS

FOREST

x BISON
HERE

TRACK
TO
FORT SMITH

SLAVE
RIVER

LAKE
ATHABASCA

DRUM   CHARLIE'S PLACE
  AT
ISLAND PEACE POINT

THE MIGHTY PEACE RIVER

THE
CATHEDRAL

JOE
VERMILION
TO THE
RESCUE

SPACEMEN
SIGHTED HERE

DESOLATION
POINT

CURRENT

CURRENT

FORT CHIPEWYAN
—WE BUY RUM

SOTA'S
LAST
BARK

LAKE
CLAIRE

MAMAWI
LAKE

MUD
CAMP

THE
QUATRE
FOURCHES

CECIL'S KICKER
STOLEN HERE

PETER
POND'S

SWAMPY
FOREST

SWAMPY
FOREST

ATHABASCA RIVER

N

~NOT TO SCALE~

ROB BEN JOHN   SOTA

~FIRST YEAR~

------ ROUTE

CURRENT

ARNIE'S
PLACE

GOOD
WATER
TO
DRINK

CREEPY FACTORY

FORT MACKAY
—FIRST BEARS

THE BRIDGE TO NOWHERE

SHOUTED
AT
HERE

EDMONTON 6 HRS
MONTREAL 5 DAYS

THE ROUTE OF DRAGONFLY AND
HER CREW
FROM FORT MACKAY TO PEACE POINT

years of visiting I had never really taken much notice of what treasures the corners hid. But armed with the pamphlet I went back. And there, high up on the wall of the darkest corner, was a birchbark canoe. It had been there all along, waiting to be discovered, dark brown with age, the seams sealed with blackened pitch or resin, the pine-root sewing fist-tight and reflecting the small amount of light there was. It was too high up to touch. I could see how I'd missed it all these years. It was set back over a display cabinet, hard to see unless you were looking for it. I took the pamphlet home and showed it to my son, who was three, and he gurgled with delight at the picture on the cover – a canoe on a blue lake floating on its exact reflection.

I thought the way to deal with dreams was to hand them on to your kids. Pass the buck as you earn the next one. I took my son to the woods for the first time to find a birch tree and its fabled bark. I had permission from the forest manager to fell a tree that needed felling anyway, and remove its bark. I was far more excited than my son, who, being tiny and not very steady on his feet, soon lost interest in the novelty of tripping over tree roots and falling into nettle patches. Never mind – I was introducing my son to the woods. This was how a lifelong passion might begin. He cheered up when we found the tree. I hoped it would provide enough bark for me to make a model of a canoe for my son. I was full of such good intentions and largely ignoring my son, who was prattling away: 'What's this in the hole? It's a buzzy fly. It's a big black fly. Go away, buzz-fly. Aaaaaaaaaggggghhhh.'

It's a sound no parent wants to hear. My son had just been stung on the finger by something black that buzzed. Maybe a hornet or a rare kind of killer bumblebee. He was sobbing and his finger was swelling mightily. He hated the woods, probably for life. I ran through the trees carrying him to the car and drove at high speed to the nearest pharmacy, obsessing about anaphylactic shock reactions and hyper-allergies. It was a hot day and warm in the car and when I came out of the pharmacist's with the drugs he was fast asleep in his special car seat, head drooped forward over the harness. His finger was already going down, looking normal again.

In my spare time I took to walking further, across the fields, and even wading through the Cherwell River to make things more exciting. Wading through rivers with your boots around your neck is immensely satisfying. I felt my range had suddenly increased. It was almost like having a boat. Then one day I was attacked by a black swan whilst I was midstream at a point where the riverbed was particularly rocky and not at all conducive to moving fast. I retreated with stubbed toes.

Beaten back by a mere bird! A rather large bully of a bird, I might add, but still? I was going soft at the edges.

The way dreams communicate with us is through coincidence. The coincidences keep piling up until you can't ignore them any longer. Out of the blue a friend sent me an anthology of travel writing. One of the pieces was an extract from the journal of Alexander Mackenzie. The first man to cross North America, fifteen years before Lewis and Clark. He travelled by birchbark canoe.

The journal was out of print and I almost forgot about it. A few weeks later, in a second-hand bookshop in a neighbouring town, I was looking through the Arctic/Antarctic collection when I came across Mackenzie's journals, with notes, expensive at £50, but they had to be bought.

I read the story of his expedition from Lake Athabasca to the Pacific Ocean that night at my pine-block kitchen table. It was a story involving compass directions, flies, attacks by Indians, mutinous French voyageurs (men employed to transport goods between trading posts), grizzly bears, pemmican, wrecked canoes rebuilt from trees at hand, deadly rapids, trade goods and beaver pelts, getting lost and seeing for the first time the aquatic jewel of the Pacific Ocean caught in the chink of two snow-capped mountains.

The dream had become something I could rely on. An unwarranted sense of certainty was growing and I thought, Maybe, just maybe, I will build a birchbark canoe and be the second person to cross North America in this way. In a flurry of research

I had discovered that Mackenzie had taken a route that was indirect and never repeated, not until the modern era of plastic boats and outboard motors. If I followed, or rather we followed – I'd need a team – the exact route in a birchbark canoe we'd be the first to retrace his route in a traditional craft since 1793.

II

Jean-François was my new friend, a telephone friend I spoke to each night from the junk room in my house, which had become the command centre of my 'expedition'. I use inverted commas not out of any sense of modesty but because at that time I was only able to think about my endeavours with a kind of ironical glee – I was bunking off, doing something only other people such as Thor Heyerdahl and Ranulph Fiennes did: going on an expedition. A part of me refused to take seriously the concept of 'expeditions' in an age that routinely expected to soon be sending people to Mars. Expeditions were for poor deluded fools who regretted being born in the late twentieth century. Expeditions were for people who couldn't accept the fact that the world was all explored. Expeditions were for wealthy nitwits looking for kicks in speedboats and balloons.

And another part of me, the part that insisted on using the word 'expedition' despite having to make the ironic concession, knew that all of the above was lies.

Anyway, I was talking to my new pal Jean-François, whom I had tracked down to the Yukon and who made birchbark canoes as part of an ongoing art project, when suddenly he turned nasty on me. 'You need someone like me on such a trip. You cross a lot of Indian reserves. They do a lot of drinking on the reserves and they don't like intruders, Europeans.' Despite his French accent the word carried the implication that Jean-François was somehow an honorary Indian. 'I speak their language. A leetle,' he added, a rare concession to modesty. 'I know how they think.

'And I never go anywhere in the bush without a gun.'

I had found him through the internet, and though he seemed promising at first, full of enthusiasm for building a canoe and travelling with me, he soon started imposing conditions and, when I resisted, dropping sinister hints.

'I know your type,' he said. 'You won't make eet.'

The internet was full of concerned advice. Another chance correspondent in a canoe chatroom told me: 'I stand in awe of the achievements of men like Mackenzie and John Rae. Alongside them our modern achievements look so puny. I have traveled some of the rivers they traveled and goodness knows how they did it. I counsel you strongly to have a four-wheel-drive back-up, satellite telephone and perhaps a small outboard motor for convenience.'

What put off most modern canoeists was that the journey went over a mountain range. And to climb that range meant paddling over a thousand miles against the current, largely along the inaccurately named Peace River. Against a current that could be wickedly powerful. Mackenzie wrote of the Peace: 'It was with the utmost difficulties that we could prevent the canoe from being dashed to pieces against the rocks by the violence of the eddies ... the river above us, as far as we could see, was one white sheet of foaming water.'

Another internet buddy was briefer. 'Do you want to drown? Because you will.'

III

In the late seventeenth century the Pacific coast of North America had been visited by European sailors. European fur traders had pushed from the Atlantic as far as Lake Athabasca in northern Canada. But, apart from the narrower isthmus of Mexico, no one had linked the two up and crossed the entire continent.

The impulse to cross America was not merely one of exploration. There was the possibility of great wealth in obtaining fur, needed in Europe for the 'beaver' hats everyone demanded.

9

There was also the political advantage of claiming territory.

In 1793, twelve years before Lewis and Clark's monumental expedition, which is often wrongly described as 'the first to cross America', Alexander Mackenzie, a Scotsman, with nine companions in a twenty-five-foot birchbark canoe, became the first person to cross North America.

Mackenzie was born sometime between 1762 and 1764 in Stornoway, the chief town of the Outer Hebrides. He grew up on a farm and his mother died when he was still a child. It is likely that his first language was Gaelic. At twelve years of age he emigrated with his family to New York and then Montreal. At sixteen he entered the fur trade as a clerk in a warehouse. At twenty-two he was offered a partnership, 'on condition that I would proceed to the Indian country in the following spring'.

He arrived at the Athabasca River, in what is now northern Alberta, in 1787 and spent the winter with Peter Pond, a fur trader who had killed a man in a duel in Detroit. Pond was notoriously tough and difficult but he had a dream: to expand the fur business as far as the Pacific Ocean. Mackenzie learned from Pond how to deal skilfully with native people. He also became inspired by Pond's dream. Before he was thirty he set out to achieve it.

Mackenzie's first attempt ended in failure. He reached the Arctic Ocean rather than the Pacific. Two years later, in 1792, he set out again, this time with better native information. They spoke of 'the stinking lake' across the mountains. He went from the fur-trading base of Fort Chipewyan, close to Peter Pond's original cabin, and ascended the Peace River to its junction with the Smoky River. Here he overwintered. This was the furthest west any white man had been.

The following summer he set out with ten companions: a twenty-two-year-old assistant called Mr Mackay, six French Canadian voyageurs, two Beaver Indian guides and a dog. To approach the mountains they had to travel continuously against the current of the mile-wide Peace River. It was a most physically gruelling task – day after day of paddling, towing, wading and poling against a strong current fed by glacier water from the Rockies. Slowly he clawed his way forward until he reached the Finlay River. Here he wanted to turn right, but was persuaded by an Indian guide to go left, again against the current of the Parsnip River. He entered the narrower and narrower confines of the Rocky Mountain Trench before reaching the dry land that separates the Arctic drainage system from the Pacific. It is a gap of only 817 paces, along a muddy, undulating path. After two more narrow lakes Mackenzie was now going downstream, on what he aptly named Bad River. He wrecked the fragile canoe and almost drowned. His men spent three days gathering birch-bark and pine resin and roots to fix it. They cut a trail through boggy forest to meet the Herrick, which is a vast tributary of the Fraser. From then on it was easy, until the terrible canyons of the river again wrecked the boat. They rebuilt it and hid it for the return journey and set out to walk to the ocean. Several guides had told Mackenzie of a 'grease trail' walked by natives who traded oolichan-fish oil with the coastal Nuxhalk Indians. They found the trail and in seventeen days walked 350 kilo-metres to the Pacific coast. There Mackenzie borrowed dugouts to go a further fifty kilometres up the fjord that leads from Bella Coola. Here he finally ran into truly belligerent Indians and was forced to retreat in a hurry. On a rock that is still there today he painted 'Alexander Mackenzie, from Canada, by land, the twenty-second of July, one thousand seven hundred and ninety-three'. As a commercial route his was a failure. But he was first, and for that he achieved glory, riches and a knighthood, though his health was ruined. He died in his native Scotland before he was fifty-eight.

One of the diseases of modernity is an inordinate longing for the primitive. I had fallen victim to that disease long ago. As a teenager I had loved the books of Thor Heyerdahl, which, despite their academic intention to test theories about long-distance travel by primitive raft, are really about re-experiencing the primitive and so finding adventure in a world that denies it. Building a primitive bark canoe, a design that had not changed for thousands of years, I could do, in my own small way, what

11

Heyerdahl had done. I could get back to the primitive and find adventure.

Instead of proving an academic theory, my alibi would be tracking Alexander Mackenzie and his voyageurs. The voyageurs were the men who paddled the fur-trade canoes across the lakes and rivers of North America. It was not surprising to discover that Mackenzie hadn't actually paddled a stroke himself – that was all done by the specialist voyageurs. Most of them were French. The ones who were good at singing were paid $5 a year more, as were the bowman and the steersman. They sat in great canoes up to thirty-six feet long, each with a waterproof bundle of belongings and a two-quart-capacity sponge at his feet. The sponge was for dealing with leaks. Voyageurs wore red caps and colourful cummerbunds and drank rum until they fell over and passed out. They swore in French and mocked anyone who couldn't carry at least two bundles of fur on a portage. A bundle weighed ninety pounds, and a portage (carrying boat and belongings between two pieces of water) could be anything from a hundred paces to twenty miles. Interestingly, it is possible to cross Canada by water making no portage longer than thirteen miles; the route is very circuitous, but it shows how much water there is in the place.

Mackenzie was a cut above the voyageurs in terms of ambition and self-education, though he was every bit as tough. He used a ratty old cloak as a sleeping bag; for a pillow he used the box containing his sextant. In eight days he traversed the return journey from the coast, 350 km of hard, mountainous terrain, in shoes that had fallen apart. Almost every day he had to deal with the mutinous voyageurs, who didn't mind hard work but objected to going up rivers that promised nothing except death in swirling water or at the hands of angry Indians.

I made a list on the back of a drawing my son gave me of a canoe. He had copied it from pictures in Edwin Tappan Adney's classic *Bark Canoes and Skin Boats of North America*. It wasn't a bad drawing but he had filled the boat with stick people. I didn't have any. I needed a team. I needed a boat. I needed training. The list went:

Qualifications?
Team?
Training?
Birchbark canoe?

Qualifications. My own experience of canoeing was negligible. I wasn't even sure of the right way to paddle a Canadian canoe, though I had some experience of kayaks. As a teenager I'd taken a course in Eskimo rolling at the local swimming pool. Eskimos always wear their anorak hoods up when they roll, as the Pitt Rivers exhibit demonstrates. Unfortunately in the swimming pool we had to roll again and again without wearing a hood. For days after my ears would be dribbling chlorinated water. Perhaps it was the shape of my ears, tailor-made for scooping up water. Whatever the reason, I was put off the Eskimo approach to canoeing.

But Canadian canoes were different. You can't roll them, for one thing, unless they're full of flotation material. They're bigger and more comfortable.

I'd done a lot of camping – but most of it in places like Hampshire. I'd also been on a survival course run by Ray Mears – but that was also in Hampshire. I had made several long trips in jungles in Indonesia – but always with guides and people who knew how to gut a civet cat or build a quick bamboo bridge. I had never been on my own in serious wilderness.

Team. My first thought for a companion was Ben. He was Australian, very tall and strong, and had learned to put up with me when we shared a tiny room with two others in Japan. Ben liked swimming in rivers and playing a tin whistle. He had the usual Australian expertise with the outback. His parents had been naked hippies in the 1970s and Ben had been toughened by the experience. He was able to exist on low-quality food whilst sustaining elevating conversation. He worked as a computer animator but was so keen he quit the job to come on the trip.

A team of one, or rather, two, as I would be paddling, unlike Mackenzie. At that stage I looked forward to the physical challenge and identified as much with the voyageurs as with

13

Mackenzie. I'd need others, at the very least one other. It would have to be someone with experience of paddling birchbark canoes in Canada – a skill that is not common. The chances of finding that person in Canada were greatest so I put off searching and concentrated instead on training.

Training. Every day I walked briskly down to Bardwell Road punt station and hired a plastic Canadian canoe. The punt-master, a large, underemployed man with goggle eyes, was something of a canoeing enthusiast. He gave me a few hints as to the right way to J stroke. This is a canoe-paddling stroke that is awkward to get used to – I'd have to go over five hundred miles before it felt even slightly natural – but there on the still, weedy calm of the Cherwell River I practised with avid concentration.

I went both with and against the current on the little Cherwell and found no difference between the two. This gave me a welcome but entirely false sense of optimism.

The google-eyed man watched me with increasing interest. 'You going on a trip somewhere?' he asked.

'Canada,' I replied. 'Across the Rocky Mountains in a birchbark canoe.'

He looked at me with disbelief. Then he realized I was serious. 'You do it, mate.' He gestured vaguely at the neat lawns of the houses that bordered the River Cherwell, as if dismissing them. 'You fuckin' do it.'

Now all I needed was a boat.

Two

SQUARE PEG IN A ROUND HOLE

'I was led, at an early period of life, by commercial views, to the country North-West of Lake Superior, in North America, and being endowed by Nature with an inquisitive mind and enterprising spirit; possessing also a constitution and frame of body equal to the most arduous undertakings, I not only contemplated the practicability of penetrating across the continent of America, but was confident in the qualifications, as I was animated by the desire, to undertake the perilous enterprise.' Alexander Mackenzie

I

'You know what we're looking for,' said John Zeitoun, mosquitoes crowding his bald head like a scraggly instant wig – he didn't seem to notice or care – 'what we're looking for is the perfect tree.'

'Perfect?'

'You have to have perfection in mind or you'll never even come close.' He reached up, wiped, and then stared at his bloody hand. All around us the high spruce, cedar and maple rose in tubular glory, higher and higher, carving the sunlight into great silver shards, spinning my head as I looked, vertigo at ground zero. Which way was north? I'd be lost in the forest, the great Canadian forest, without my new friend and mentor John Zeitoun, which means olive in Arabic, him being half Palestinian – not Indian, not native, but still one of the most

15

respected traditional-birchbark-canoe builders in the world. It was a small world, but it was my world now, the world of traditional craft, not plastic, steel, carbon fibre and Kevlar, not cedar strip, plywood, ferroconcrete and pine clinker, not inflated vinyl, fibreglass, aluminium or rubber. Birchbark. The real thing. Older than history. What the Red Indians used. What the fur traders, voyageurs and *coureurs du bois* used, what the first explorers like Alex Mackenzie used. What I would use. If only we could find that perfect tree.

'I found it once,' mused John. 'I mean I really found it. Absolutely perfect. Twenty-five-inch diameter. Straight for thirty feet or more. Bark without a blemish.'

'What did you do?'

'I marvelled. I think that's what you're supposed to do. And then I moved on. I wanted to come back to that tree, I wanted to keep it in reserve for the bad times. But you know what, Rob?'

'What?'

'It blew down and a year later I found it and all the bark was cut and damaged from the fall and it was useless.'

'I guess the lesson is, take perfection when you find it.'

'No. I don't think there is a lesson. Not that time.'

John waded on through the undergrowth, machete in hand like an explorer, his pastel purple T-shirt stained with sweat. John was a cabinetmaker, a canoe builder and a woodland philosopher. I was glad to be in his hands. His *big* hands. The only problem was John did not want to come on the trip.

II

Three weeks earlier I'd almost packed the whole thing in. I'd fallen during a drink-fuelled game of street football and cracked a bone in my wrist. The game had been in celebration of the diamond jubilee, the north side of the street against the south. If I needed evidence that living in suburbia had its dangers, here it was. With a plastic bag over my plaster cast I kept up my paddling practice. In the mild waters of the Cherwell I managed with just a twinge or two. The cast came off two days before I flew to Canada. I told no one about the injury in case they backed out, thinking, correctly, that I was unfit for the job. I practised lifting heavy bags, hooking the weight cunningly on my lower arm rather than using my hand.

At the beginning of a journey all my superstitions are engaged. I tend to look for signs. I'd found John on the internet when I'd all but given up hope of finding a traditional birchbark-canoe builder. Good sign. He could build it with Ben's and my help in a few weeks. Very good sign. But the injury had been a very bad sign and when my flight to Canada had been delayed it confirmed the bad omens. The fact that I'd been hauled over in Detroit for drug testing had been a further evil portent (carrying lots of $100 bills to pay for the canoe hadn't helped – 'You telling me a canoe made of *bark* costs that much?'). And the bad luck continued when I arrived at Ottawa airport at midnight sure that Ben and John would be there to meet me. They weren't. I waited and waited, as hoping turned to moping outside the glass enormity of the arrivals lounge. Taxis came and went and then dwindled away. The night was warm and I sat on a low protective metal bar smoking small cigars, knowing that I wasn't going to make it to John's that night. A workman with an intellectual's round glasses took in the implication of my rucksack and bright red waterproof kitbag.

'Guys finish late here, they just crash out in the chapel. Never a problem.'

I must have made a face. I was still moping. John wasn't answering the phone in his shop, the one I'd left all the messages on about the delay. They must have assumed I'd arrive the following day. Except I was here and alone and didn't know what to do. If the journey were a swim, I was now inching into a cold ocean in a genital-protecting crouch. All the bad signs.

'Hey,' said the tough, brainy cable cutter or whatever he was, cutting through to the real problem with a smile, 'it's all part of the trip, right?'

In a moment I had dived, head under; I was swimming – all part of the trip. The strange mysticism of travelling had taken over and would never be relinquished. Everything had a place and a meaning on the trip.

In the middle of the night a great fat boy wearing a plastic hard hat lay down next to me in the chapel. It was a small place, as impersonal as a crematorium chapel, but then I'd once crashed out in the grounds of a crematorium whilst hitch-hiking across France.

'Is it OK?' the boy asked in a high voice at odds with his great bulk. He took up a place sufficiently distant to convey that neither was he interested in that way, nor did he suspect me of being so. When I left in the morning he was still sleeping, his soft red face pressed against the hard fuzz of the industrial carpeting. On the lectern, I leafed through well-thumbed copies of the Koran and the Bible which sat side by side.

III

John and Ben were already firm friends. I wasn't surprised. Lanky and laid-back, Ben was good at worming his way into people's affections. When I arrived at John's place, which was a single-storey wooden house on the banks of the Gattineau River in Quebec, Ben appeared with his camera and John's big half-husky, half-collie dog, Sota. He looked even taller than I remembered. Maybe too tall. All the voyageurs were under five foot six. 'I'm videoing everything,' Ben grinned, 'just in case things go really wrong and we have to make a last-ditch message for friends and family. You know, when we're sunk and starving out in the bush somewhere.'

John didn't look like his voice suggested. He had a big drawl, a laid-back big man's voice. A bearded voice, I thought, grizzled beard. But John was medium height, clean shaven, wearing a mauve tie-dye T-shirt, almost completely bald, with the oval glasses of a French hitman. But his forearms were tanned and big with the tendons and veins only real work can give you.

Ben got me on one side as we went into the house. 'I've been trying to persuade him to come,' he whispered. Good old Ben, able to connect to the natural hippy in John that vied with the hard-headed Palestinian who knew how to make money. If Ben failed our plan was to try to recruit someone along the way, perhaps in Edmonton, the last major town before we hit the start of the journey.

We sipped our coffee and I handed over the duty-free bourbon I'd bought. 'Why thank you, Rob,' said John, 'let's hope we can drink some of this later.' He's got to come with us, I thought; the trip demanded it.

Ben, John and I spent two days in the woods near John's house gathering the bark and the roots. John took the bark off standing trees, without completely ringing them; that way they had a chance to keep growing. A two-foot-diameter tree gave a piece of bark six feet wide and perhaps eight or ten feet in length – any longer made it awkward to peel.

There is an Algonquin tradition that the reason good bark is so hard to find is because of a mythical being called Meso who could speak the language of all things. Meso knew that people would never be thrifty if every birch tree supplied a good piece of bark. They would cut down all the trees and that would be the end of the forest. Instead Meso climbed into trees and bent the branches and scarred the trunks with a balsam branch and only the ones he missed were any good for a canoe. That way men learned how to be grateful for the good bark they found.

We never did find that perfect tree, but we cut the bark off three pretty good specimens. John climbed the stepladder and chopped with a hand-axe the dimensions required. Then we peeled it off very slowly, taking especial care at the blobby-looking growths which were points of weakness in the bark. When it was on the ground John rolled it against its natural curl, silver on the inside.

We scooped with our hands for roots in the black mulchy swamp where the black spruce grew. When you got a good one you pulled it up, like tearing a cable from the ground. The roots were black and tangly but once the outer skin was peeled off and the splitting all done they looked as neat and serviceable as the weave of a rattan chair.

IV

The boat was to be twenty-one feet long, built to the design of a three-and-a-half-fathom trading canoe. It could carry an imperial ton of fur, that is twenty-five 'pieces' (ninety-pound packs), each one made of the compressed pelts of sixty beavers if they were trapped in the fall, half that number if caught in the spring. Mixed-fur packs were also common. In 1800 trader James Mackenzie, no relation to Alexander, wrote of a typical fur pack containing '44 beaver skins, 12 otters, 5 bears and 6 pichous (fishers)', a fisher being a kind of marten.

Ours was a north canoe as opposed to the bigger *canoe de maîtres* used to bring goods from Montreal to Grande Portage on Lake Superior. These boats, sometimes thirty-six feet in length, were too unwieldy for the interior. Mackenzie wrote of the north canoe: 'some of about half the size [of the big canoes] are procured from the natives, and are navigated by four, five, or six men according to the distance which they have to go'. Our north canoe would be slightly smaller than Mackenzie's craft which was twenty-five feet long and capable of carrying thirty-five pieces.

John sewed the outer skin together with split pine roots and laid it on the building table inside his workshop. We piled rocks on top to keep the central part flat. Long stakes, pushed deep into holes around the edge of the table, marked out the shape of the canoe. The stakes bent the bark upwards. John split two strips of ash to make the gunwhale, the oval-shaped rim of the deck. This was clamped around the bark. The canoe now had shape but no rigidity. We then made ribs from split cedar to force the bark outwards, making it drum-tight.

John hewed the rough shape of the ribs and then steamed them in a contraption made from a drainpipe and a metal paintpot on a stove. He then bent them quickly over his knee, by eye, breaking only two.

Ben was better at sewing the skin to the gunwhales than I. He had an insouciance that came from not knowing what we had ahead of us. I was too studied, thinking too hard about it. I took frequent small cigar breaks to restore my sense of calm. I knew Ben well, but a younger Ben. He was now twenty-eight, about the age of Mackenzie when he made his first voyage to the Arctic. The Ben I'd known, and written about in a book called *Angry White Pyjamas*, had been nineteen and prone to crying when things got tough. He didn't look like he cried any more, though he was harder to talk to than before. 'You've just got more uptight,' he said. 'Having kids has made you a worried man.'

John, too, was a picture of relaxation. He was about thirty but seemed older. It was hard to imagine him apologizing about anything, or, indeed, being in the situation of having to apologize about anything. When a hole in the gunwhale cracked he looked at my concerned face and said, 'Hey, Raab, there are plenty more, don't worry about it.' The way he stretched out the 'a' in Rob was reassuring, up to a point.

John looked at Ben and me sewing the seams of the boat and said, 'Now I'm going to prove to you that not only does a square peg fit in a round hole, it's actually better.'

The holes for holding the protective gunwhale strip were round, but the pegs John sawed up from pieces of oak were square and sharp-edged. The sharp edges bit into the round holes and gripped more tightly, much tighter than a round peg in a round hole. Ben and I became competitive about who could drill the best holes. John praised us like a teacher and drove in the pegs with two swift swipes of a mallet.

The traditional way of building a bark canoe was pretty much as near to perfection, considering the natural materials at hand, as one could get. Even the large fur-trade canoes had copied the original Algonquin Indian design, and, apart from being bigger, were built in the same way. It was the reason I chose the bark canoe over one made of fibreglass or metal. The materials for building and rebuilding my canoe would be all around me. The canoe was part of the environment it travelled through. It was part of a wholeness that a bright plastic canoe, nosing through the shallows, isn't. Machenzie had rebuilt his canoe twice, once after the horrible smash-up on the Bad River. Bits of the old canoe were salvaged and covered with new pieces of birchbark, sewn with split spruce root and sealed with pine pitch and resin.

Now everything was split and sewn and fitted together and the canoe looked like a real canoe, we only had to seal the seams and the 'gores'. The gores are the splits in the bark you make so that it can be folded around the compound curves of the bow and the stern. These are the sections that show up someone's skill or lack of it. On our boat they looked perfect.

With the workshop doors thrown back, the canoe caught the morning light on its rosy skin. The stringy silvery outside of the bark was on the inside. The canoe had a patchwork look: yellow in places, dull brown at one end, but predominantly rose-tinted along the middle, a light brown with a healthy pink tinge, like the glow under the tanned skin of someone beautiful. I was astonished at what had been achieved in two weeks. John was grinning, Ben excitedly examining the bits he'd sewn and comparing them to mine. I had expected to be disappointed, after all the expectation, but I wasn't. The boat was beautiful and straight with thwarts and gunwhales of ash. The only imperfection was a section of the bark near the bow which had a bubbly look. 'A layer has separated out, but you got thirty more,' said John. He was used to dealing with customers. He let me do the talking, except when I was wrong. Ben was busy filming us, pushing his long hair out of the viewfinder from time to time. Long hair suited him. It was what the voyageurs favoured, to keep the blackfly and mosquitoes away from their faces and necks.

John brought out a foul-smelling tar-like substance called Vulkem to seal the seams and gores. It was only traditional in the sense that it looked like the pine resin and melted animal fat that was originally used. It was one of the few innovations John agreed with; it was easier to apply to a dry boat than resin and didn't melt when the sun was too hot. John said I could always repair the boat with resin while on the trip. I did, and found the one advantage of this natural sealant: you can apply it while the bark is damp. Stinky, man-made Vulkem needs absolute dryness, which is pretty rare on the river.

We filled the boat with water to find out if it had any leaks. There were three tiny ones, mere pinholes. John looked pleased, as if all the omens were good. I fretted over the authenticity of the sealant and Ben manhandled Sota.

That night as we sat on the verandah John looked pensive. 'You ever read *Zen and the Art of Motorcycle Maintenance*?'

I admitted I had. John looked at me with expectation. 'Took that book on my Mississippi journey. Kind of went with the surroundings somehow.' John had made a six-week trip down the Mississippi in one of his birchbark canoes. He had all the experience we needed.

'Good title,' I said.

'Yeah, that book made an impression on me. Thought I might re-read it sometime.'

I refilled his glass. Hints had been dropped about our need for a third man. But John was the kind of guy you couldn't pressurize. He'd let us stay at his house. In fact it was his girlfriend Nat's house but she was just as relaxed as he was, so it seemed like John's house. We'd all got on together. It was the right time to ask. But John had other things on his mind.

'You know, Raab, I've never been separated from Sota. More to the point, he's never been separated from me.'

'I didn't know that. Even on your Mississippi trip?'

'Even then – he came for the whole six weeks.'

'Does that mean you're coming?'

'Yeah, if I'm welcome. But only as long as Sota comes.'

Three men and a dog. A big dog. A dog that was very much always around. I liked dogs, but I'd never been dog-camping or dog-canoeing. How did it work? What about food? Would it crap near the tents?

I asked none of these questions. It'll be fine, I thought. We needed John so that was that.

'I reckon Sota can last three, four days with you and Ben. He likes Ben, I can tell, so it should be okay. You drive with him and the canoe to Fort Chipewyan, or wherever, and I'll fly a few days later. That way I can make arrangements for all the work I'll have to miss.'

The trip demanded it. We needed John so he had to come. I banished all negative thoughts. In fact, I told myself, it was a real stroke of luck to have a dog – it made us more like Mackenzie, who also took one.

We spent a day shopping in Ottawa for more kit while the seams dried. John left his big van unlocked at the roadside, which struck me as too trusting, especially as our mound of shopping grew in the back. Would he be that careless in the bush? Now he had agreed I was looking for signs that might signal disaster. 'Calm down, Rob,' said Ben, 'everything'll be fine.' I felt the trip was just out of my control, just beyond my fingertips, that I was racing to keep up with it. But at the time it seemed like the only way. In a frenzy of spending we bought a large dome tent, quick-dry nylon trousers, a grill, mosquito headnets and numerous camping gadgets. In the store, a magic grotto strung with the beautiful man-made oddments of outdoor living, Ben became obsessed by candle lanterns.

'They're essential,' he said.

'Why?'

'It's too expensive to keep buying batteries.'

'But they're fifteen dollars each. That's a lot of batteries.'

'They kind of look good around the campfire,' suggested John, who'd appeared from behind a rack of Nalgene water bottles wearing a fetching stone-coloured bush hat with a wide brim. We bought two lanterns. Ben carried them.

In Canadian Tyre, the largest hardware chain in Canada, we bought a small axe, duct tape and a Leatherman 'Supertool' knife. We contemplated a row of red nylon lifejackets, gently swinging on the rail.

'The voyageurs never used them,' I said.

'I read that it's illegal not to have them on a small boat,' said Ben.

'I believe that's correct,' said John.

'We can always sit on them. Pad our bums.'

We bought lifejackets. The cheapest ones.

We spent a long time searching for a small aerosol airhorn

designed for yachts. The bearhorn, we christened it. Stephen Herrero, in his definitive *Bear Attacks – Their Causes and Avoidance*, had recommended using one to scare off ursine intruders. Ben gave the horn we eventually bought an experimental toot in the car park. Above the din and roar of the midday traffic it still made me flinch, a concentrated pipsqueak amplified to a deafening level.

The boat seams were dry. Ben and I shouldered it, me disguising the difficulty I had with lifting. All birchbark canoes are lighter than fibreglass ones of the same design. Mackenzie's *canoe du nord*, which was around twenty-five feet long, could be carried by two men. The plastic equivalent would need four. John's shop was across the road from the water. Ben and I carried the boat about a hundred yards to the launching spot. It seemed heavy and awkward to me but I said nothing, thinking about the ten- and twenty-kilometre carries we had ahead of us.

'I've been practising paddling in John's carbon-fibre canoe,' said Ben from in front.

'Bet it's not as light as this.'

'It is.'

'But ours is bigger. And better.'

We splashed happily along, making progress against the current, though I had to admit it was tiring, even for five minutes. Would the Peace River be faster than this sedate swirl?

'Can you do a J stroke?'

'What's that?' asked Ben.

I showed him.

'Can you do a ferry stroke?'

'Yes.'

Ben showed me all the same.

Ben learned fast, I had to admit, and the martial-arts training he did had made him strong. When we rested, the boat floated this way and that like something made of paper. Loaded, it would be a different matter. Sota jumped in and out of the water, chasing after beavers. When the beavers saw him they slapped the water with the great pancakes of their tails and dropped out of sight. Sota's blunt claws rattled on the gunwhales as he hauled himself aboard. It was like being with someone else's naughty child. Like a child, he sensed my antipathy and took to always shaking his water-loaded fur in my face. A husky, even a half-husky, can pack a lot of river water on his back.

Everyone was cheerful and that evening we ate with John's girlfriend Nat in a riverside restaurant plagued by mosquitoes, a can of repellent on the table along with the salt and pepper. Nat was competent and attractive; she even backed our truck up the drive when Ben got it stuck. She was French Canadian, maybe a descendant of a voyageur.

The next morning at five o'clock Ben and I set off in a truck with the canoe tied to the roof and Sota in the cab with us. We had found the truck through John's brother. It had been bought by a dealer and was a one-way delivery job from Montreal to Edmonton, Alberta. We even got $300 towards fuel costs. 'It'll take about twenty hours' driving to just cross Ontario,' John warned. He would fly in and meet us at Fort McMurray on the Athabasca River in five days' time. This was the nearest place, by road, we could get to Mackenzie's starting point. John gave us dry dog food and a water bowl for Sota, and ruffled the big dog's fur. Then he turned without a word and went up to his workshop as we drove off. It was the first time he had been separated from Sota in five years.

Three

THE BRIDGE TO NOWHERE

'It is not necessary for me to examine the cause, but experience proves that it requires much less time for a civilized people to deviate into the manners and customs of savage life, than for savages to rise into a state of civilization.' Alexander Mackenzie

I

It took four days.

Driving twenty hours a day.

Sleeping in the cab with the window a quarter down and the stinky dog between us.

We ate all-Canadian breakfast specials, $2.99 before 8 a.m., and walked the dog in the diesel-smelling area behind gas stations.

The first night we drove alongside Lake Superior and smelled the pines, as powerful and fragrant as . . . floor cleaner . . . without the floor. Pure scent of pine on the night air. Strong enough to smell it in the cab with the windows shut.

We spent another night in a lay-by surrounded by the shuddering hulks of great trucks. Their spotlights, which were never switched off, criss-crossed the cab with unwelcome light. Opening the door meant hopping over puddles, rainbow-hued with spilled diesel. The mud between the puddles was black and stinky. It was a horrible place but Sota drank, as always, from the groundwater, making me think, How come a dog, an animal like me, can do that and I can't, or won't? If I was going that way I had a long way to go.

In the day it was hot and sweaty in the cab. The roads were poor despite it being the Trans-Canada Highway. Some of the road workers we saw were women, in orange coats, holding Stop–Go signs. We drove on and on. The forests gave way to prairie, but far too slowly. The speed limit was always pitifully low, but I didn't mind, not with our precious canoe on the roof. At gas stations and coffee shops old guys and wiry men with tattoos would admire the boat. (We excited only blue-collar admiration.)

When we parked we always kept the top of the truck in view. Wouldn't do to lose it before we started. Ben and I talked about the lives we had interrupted. He had a new girlfriend who was older than him.

'She knows more about life than us.'

'How do you mean?' She wasn't older than me, after all.

'She knows how to get things done. She's streetwise.'

'Oh, that,' I said.

'She doesn't sit around all day. She gets things done.'

'Well, we're getting things done. *And* we're sitting around all day.'

'You know what I mean.'

'You know what I think? You're in love.'

But Ben wasn't listening. We were parked on a featureless stretch of highway with prairie on each side. He looked out of the open door at Sota's bowl on the ground. The rope we usually tied from his collar to the door handle was gone. Sota was nowhere to be seen.

'Oh, man,' said Ben. 'If we lose Sota John will go nuts.' We both ran up and down both sides of the road, looking into the shallow ditches beyond the crumbling edge of the asphalt. Shit. Where was he? Then I lay down on the ground and looked under the truck. Sota was asleep in the shade.

'So what would your new girlfriend have done in that situation?' I said as we bundled the dog back into the cab.

'Tied a better knot.'

More prairie – flat, of course – with huge co-operative silos by the side of the rail track which runs alongside the highway. At coffee shops in prairie towns the farmers are all up and drinking coffee by 7 a.m., discussing corn prices and machinery in Monsanto caps. Big old guys who don't like the look of Ben and me. We tip big and leave.

'You're getting a middle-aged spread,' quips Ben.

Some prairie goes by before I answer. I'm catching the pace of the place.

'It's not middle-aged spread, it's a money belt. And I'm losing weight all the time.'

Money always needed to be spent. We bought all our provisions for the next month in fifteen minutes before closing time at a Supersave just outside Regina, Saskatchewan. Don't ask me why. It was as if the insane hurry we put ourselves in would reduce the bill. I insisted on buying as much value-range produce as possible. Ben was remarkably quiescent – after all, I was paying. We bought mountains of cheap tuna and sardines in tins without keys. We bought lots of garlic as a substitute for vegetables. There was a sort of system, based around five hundred grams of pasta doing for four people for one meal.

In Edmonton I delivered the truck to a Ukrainian salesman who didn't want the big padlock we'd fitted to the back. We kept the padlock until it went rusty on the river. We stayed in a youth hostel and smuggled the dog into our dormitory at night. The night porter caught us leaving early with Sota, but Ben, with typical quick thinking, clapped his hands together and shooed the animal out. He complained to the startled porter, 'I don't know who keeps letting these strays in.'

Edmonton is south of Fort Chipewyan. Since it was impossible to fly in (the canoe was too big to fix to the strut of a floatplane) and impossible to motorboat in (too big for a jetboat, the only boats that go to Fort Chipewyan), we would have to paddle to our starting point. It was all taking time, eating into the short summer of the north, reducing our chances.

'This is a reconnaissance trip,' I kept telling Ben, just to cover myself. But inside I had every confidence we would successfully paddle a great distance. *Every confidence*. It was the travel high, when you move so fast and so far your mind starts working in a different way. Everyone you meet, it's like you know them already and they loom up so fast there's no time to be paranoid, you just reach out and connect to them.

Just getting to the place where we could start paddling from to get to the place where we could actually start our voyage required another truck. Roland, who worked in an outdoor-equipment store, agreed to drop us off at Fort McMurray on the Athabasca River, where we'd arranged to meet John, three hundred kilometres south of our start point but the nearest to Fort Chipewyan we could possibly get.

For hours we drove across grid systems of empty roads through more endless flat prairie. Sometimes there would be a small dip in one corner of a field, or a farmhouse would be ringed by planted pines as a windbreak. Almost unnoticeably there began to appear stands of aspen on each side of the road, ghostly white trunks and bright green shimmering leaves, catching the evening sun. We saw fewer and fewer farms.

Roland was tall and sat stooped over the wheel. Older-looking than his thirty years, but then his own travel business had gone bust owing $100,000 only the year before. That was why he worked in the store. He had blond hair and a nose that stretched upwards redly from the skin of his face. He was amenable and eager to be liked. We talked for hours (it was a six-hour drive) and he told us of his experiences with bears and Indians.

'What should we say?' I asked. 'First Nations Peoples sounds so bloody cumbersome.'

Roland grinned. 'Just use the band name [a band is a sub-group of a tribe]: Mikisew Cree people, Chipewyan people, Dene people. The more remote the area the less they worry what you call them.'

'I was told we should always carry cigarettes as a kind of peace offering.'

'Awesome,' said Roland, grinning. 'Kind of awkward if you don't smoke, though?'

When he had his tourist business Roland had organized sweatlodge-experience tours with a Stoney-tribe Indian called Frank Sitting Wind.

'You're kidding,' I said.

'It sounds better in Stoney language,' giggled Roland. 'The problem was I was making Frank so much money he lost interest. I was always calling him at the golf course and he'd be like, "I've got a lot riding on this shot, could you call me back later?"'

We were in a different country now. The pick-ups at the gas station were rusty and old with fenders at odd angles and stone-hit windscreens with cracks like a piece of bent wire stretching their full width. There were Indians and white men but they all looked rough. Inside the station was a small restaurant where the waitress was blonde and in a petulant mood. 'I suppose you'll be wanting food,' she said.

'If we may,' said Roland, smiling.

'If you're lucky,' she quipped. I could see the petulance was her style, her routine.

A man with a black moustache, perhaps metis, or half-Indian, of the indeterminate age men assume when they do hard phys-ical labour, politely engaged us in conversation about the canoe.

'How many miles a day you plan on doing?'

'Well, Mackenzie sometimes did thirty miles or more.'

The man nodded. 'That's pretty good. I reckon even fifteen miles against a current takes some doing.'

Roland, who remained vague and complimentary about our plans, said, 'They usually say four to one with a river like the Peace. It it takes one hour to go ten miles downstream it will take four hours to go ten miles upstream.'

'Really?' I said, but I was thinking, *No way*. We're going to be *way* faster than that.

'Where you putting in?' asked the man, his face hard but with no hint of a challenge. On the back of one hand he had five blue dots tattooed.

'Fort MacKay, just below McMurray.'

'I know it. You got the bridge to nowhere just before the town. There's a way down to the river each side. You can put in there.'

'Thanks,' said Roland.

'Why is it called the bridge to nowhere?' asked Ben.

'Because it goes fuckin' nowhere. The road just stops. After that it's three hundred miles of swamp between you and Fort Chip.'

Outside at the pumps were two Indians; an old man with a bootlace tie and a young girl, overweight, with see-through platform-soled shoes. As the old man climbed into the huge rusting pick-up he smiled once, perhaps to himself.

We drove on. It was night now, and raining. I was reminded of journeys back from the seaside with my parents, the sound of the wipers going, the way the night was a shiny black backing to the windscreen, contemplated from our own pool of cosy darkness lit by the illuminated ring of the speedometer. Ben was asleep. Roland spoke about the natural history of bears.

'Black bears charge but it's usually fake. When a grizzly charges then you could be in trouble.'

'There aren't any grizzlies until we get to the Rockies.'

'Actually they do say black bears are more aggressive than grizzlies. If in doubt climb a tree.'

'But can't bears climb?'

'There's no recorded case of a black bear climbing higher than thirty-three feet,' said Roland, quoting a passage from Herrero's book, one I'd committed to memory.

'And grizzly bears are too heavy to climb,' I added, showing I knew my stuff.

'They do say that, but I've seen a grizzly climb a silver fir with thick branches.'

'Great.'

'But usually they don't.'

'What's that about bears?' asked Ben, now awake and apprehensive.

'It's pretty simple – if a black bear attacks, fight back. If it's a grizzly, play dead.'

Roland laughed, enjoying our discomfort. 'One time a really big cinnamon bear, that's a brown black bear, charged me while I was eating some ice cream round the campfire. All I had was a spoon to defend myself.'

'What did you do?'

'The bear just kept huffing and puffing and it ran right up to me and I just didn't move. I knew if I turned my back to him he'd go for me. At the last minute I threw my spoon at his nose.'

'And?'

'He took fright and ran like anything.'

There was a silence like indigestion as Ben and I, for the first time, really contemplated the reality of a charging bear. *And we were going to be out there on our own!*

We told Roland about the bearhorn.

'Oh, you should be fine then,' he said, and then burst out laughing.

When he realized the joke was getting thin he said in a nice voice, 'Less people get killed by bears than are struck by lightning on golf courses.'

For some reason that did not make us feel any better. At all.

We could see a growing orange glow on the horizon and flames, as if in the sky: the flarestacks of Fort McMurray, the world's largest deposit of oilsand, enough they say to keep the whole of North America in petroleum for another five hundred years at present rates of consumption. Though at higher prices and producing huge amounts of waste silt. McMurray is like something out of *Bladerunner* – huge crate-like buildings fed by silver tubes bigger than a main sewer pipe. It was easy to imagine we were looking at a model, something made for *Thunderbirds*, but then a real car as small as a Matchbox toy would appear and the hugeness of everything would reassert itself. On a patch of waste ground outside of town our sense of scale was further warped by a stationary tipper truck that grew like something out of *Alice* as we approached. The van didn't even reach up to the middle of the massive wheels, shod with deep-tracked tyres that towered over me. A small plaque announced this giant's plaything as the biggest tipper in the world, recently retired, a Terex Titan 3319 50/90 six-wheeler, 350 tons, 67 feet long, 26 feet wide, with tyres 11 feet high. It was painted Tonka Toy yellow with reverse-angled glass on the cab, like the pilot house on a yacht, silent and empty. Surely no normal-sized man could drive such a thing?

33

'That is one hell of a big tipper,' said Ben. No one disagreed. We drove on, past the bandaged pipes and smoking refinery units laddered with gigantic zigzag girders, parts dull grey, parts shiny steel picking up the reflection of the dancing flames of the flarestacks. In the background there was a noise of clanking and hissing in the far distance, the sound of extraction, money being hewed from the earth by giant machines.

'Glad that's over,' said Ben, as the first trees reappeared again on either side of the road. We drove on, but not for much longer.

Without warning we were zooming across the great concrete span of a bridge. We weren't sure so we went another mile. The road ended abruptly in a concreted yard with a few old containers. The bridge to nowhere.

We drove back and forth over the bridge, which was a good half-kilometre wide and far too high above the river for us to see anything. Then Roland found a track that led off to one side, down the bank to a blackness we could only assume was the Athabasca.

The track was muddy, with deep ruts full of water that reflected our headlights. We came to a fork.

'Let's check it out on foot,' I said.

'Have you got a torch?' asked Ben.

'At the very bottom of my pack. What about the candle lanterns?'

'Here,' said Ben, showing me his two precious lanterns, no doubt kept close to hand for such an emergency. 'The trouble is the candles are right at the bottom of my pack.'

'Great.'

'I'll flip on the main beam,' said Roland, climbing back into the van.

'D'you hear that noise?' said Ben.

'What noise?'

'Voices.'

The light shot forward, harsh and rigorous, creating its own straight shadows. Now I could hear the voices.

'No disrespectin' motherfuckers ... Fuckin lights. Fuck! FUCK!'

I could see a figure a hundred yards away hiding his eyes behind his elbow. Two black trucks were visible by their darkness against the last grey of the night sky. Other heads appeared in our scorching light. The tirade of abuse increased.

'It's one in the morning,' I said. 'No one's down at the river at one in the morning.'

'They are,' said Ben. 'Let's go.'

Roland seemed to want to make peace, explain our position to the drunk men, perhaps Indians from nearby Fort MacKay, perhaps not.

'Let's go,' I said.

We reversed in a high-pitched whine up the track, skidding in the ruts. One figure lurched after us until we turned a corner and could go forward again. My last sight was of a man caught redly in the tail-lights as he jerked from staggering to hurl an empty beercan at our disappearing vehicle.

'Glad we didn't breakdown down there,' said Ben.

As we headed towards the Indian settlement of MacKay, Roland said, apropos of nothing, 'I'm thinking of seminary school, but I missed the applications for this year.'

'Really?' I said.

'You'd be a good priest,' said Ben. 'Helping people get to their destination, like us.'

'I'd like to think so, but hopefully this won't be your *final* destination,' said Roland, a little too quietly for my liking. 'Anyway,' he perked up. 'Looks like this is your village.'

It was. The small town or village of Fort Mackay was on a hillside above the Athabasca, the great river that we needed to descend just to get to our starting point in Fort Chipewyan.

II

The houses were the kind I had become used to. Single-storey, grey-and-white-painted, beaten-up vehicles half in and half out of garages full of rubber hoses, plastic crates of bolts and washers and the parts left over when a washing machine is repaired, as if all this mechanical detritus were trying to expel the pick-up from its rightful home. There were no European cars, very few cars at all: this was pick-up country, home of the Ford 150, 250, 350, the Dodge Ram dualie, the Chevy three-quarter-ton, vehicles that hadn't changed their names or basic design in thirty-five years, just thinner metal and bigger bulges. It was as if technological society had reached its zenith, run out of steam, imagination and zest. Nothing could be improved, except cosmetically; the North American model had triumphed, now it just sought to be endlessly reproduced and exported around the globe.

The village slept, unaware of such extravagant notions. Each house had a reasonable lawn, cast in shadow as we drove by. Down a bumpy track we found the river, dark, tiny crystal wavelets catching what light there was, very wide it seemed, now that we were level with it. The place smelled of dead fish and it was raining again. Roland switched on his high beams to give us hope and cheer as we gathered our forlorn mass of baggage on the wet, muddy ground by the river. I hoisted myself on to the van roof and fumbled with knots in the darkness.

We lumbered the canoe, now sheened with droplets of rain, down to the ground. There was rapid fruitless discussion about where to lay it. I remembered a famous Hopkins oil painting, *Bivouac of a Canoe Party*, where a merry group of voyageurs sit under their leaning canoe with long pipes, a crackling fire going and a coffeepot boiling. No fire, but I had my pipe, but of course the tobacco was deep in ... which bag? I had even brought a pipe for Ben, a very occasional smoker. It would be part of the fun of the thing, measuring out our distance in pipes, just as the voyageurs did. A pipe was smoked at the end of fifty-five minutes' paddling; one took five minutes to smoke it and then they were off again, often for as long as ten pipes in a day with food only at breakfast and supper.

Roland kindly prolonged the moment of departure. He helped put the tent up. He wrote out an elaborate receipt, 'for tax purposes'. Took a photo of Ben and me standing in front of the canoe and all the kit, blackness all around, our startled red-eyed look reminiscent of partygoers who have missed the party, fallen asleep and woken to find nothing but empty beer bottles, folded cigarette butts and all the taxis departed.

Finally he could stay no longer. He had a six-hour drive back to Edmonton and had to be at work by nine the next morning. He gave me his apologetic grin. 'I'll get an hour or two shuteye at the roadside,' he said.

We gratefully crept into the tent, accepting the thin excuse of security provided by the flysheet and tent inner. Sota, who had become more and more subdued, perhaps sensing our own mood, or missing John, curled up in the half-covered 'vestibule' of the tent.

'Wasn't that vestibule supposed to zip up?' asked Ben.

'Yes.'

'Well, it doesn't.'

'The tent we looked at had a closed vestibule for sure.'

'That girl must have given us a different model.'

'Bugger. I'm definitely taking it back when we ... finish.'

Dud goods on day one and a finish that seemed so far away I could hardly bring myself to mention it. The tent flapped and the rain drummed like someone beating a tattoo with knitting needles all over the flysheet. We lay on our foam mats and imitated sleep.

'What was that?'

'It's the wind. Go to sleep.'

'Shall I fire off the horn, just for good measure?'

'It'll wake people up.'

'Block your ears.'

I fired off the horn and its great powerful high-pitched parp dispelled all apprehension for a second. Then the tent flapped, in its own broken rhythm, the signature of a wind that wasn't yet through with us, not by a long way. The needles continued drumming. At three-thirty there was a scratching at the tent door. It was Sota, wet through and miserable.

'What d'you think?' said Ben.

'At the foot of the bed, at the very foot.'

'Tonight only.'

'Absolutely.'

Sota barged in and gratefully shook his wet fur in my face, then lay down to sleep between us.

III

By 5 a.m. we could stand no more of it and arose to scan the flat, uninviting greyness of the river. Four hundred yards or so across was a line of sullen dark green pines crowded right up to the undercut bank, some toppling over, as if the forest were pushing the front line of trees continuously into the water.

'Do you like canoeing?' I asked Ben.

'Don't know yet. Do you?'

'Love it,' I lied.

The smell of dead fish was strongest by the canoe, which we had laid on its side, facing down, against a verge of cow parsley and hazel. Beyond this lay the river.

'Ugh!' said Ben. He'd found the dead fish, something grey and unidentifiable rotting on its bone.

'Hey, not with the paddle.'

Ben flipped the remains over the foliage and back into the river. It was only spitting now and I saw we were at the taking-out point for boats that needed to be trailered in and out of the river. Skidmarks and deep tyre tracks led down to the water's edge. Either side sprouted hazels, scrub alders and willows, and further along the dark lines of spruce began.

Ben went a short way up the track, between the hazel hedges, and came back excitedly.

'Bear prints, just back there.'

I went to look with our bear-print id book (Ben Gadd's *Rocky Mountain Guide*, not a bad book but far too heavy).

'That's not the print I meant.' He came over and studied the ground. 'That's a dog print. And look, that's a dog turd.' He was right. 'The bear track is over there.'

When I saw what he was talking about I immediately knew it was a bear print because it was quite unlike any print I had ever seen, except for that of a human being. Bear prints look unnervingly human.

'Do you think it's a grizzly?' said Ben.

I measured the print with the ruler on the Leatherman, which I'd found after a long dive in my rucksack.

'No,' I said, 'too small. It's a bear, though. Maybe that was what we heard in the night.' We were full of the clever, poorly informed theories of the neophyte. It was a great comfort to us.

As Ben cooked up some porridge on our little gas stove (back-up only, we planned to cook on wood fires) I tried to balance the bearhorn on the curving top of the canoe. Eventually it stayed put. I wanted that horn within easy reach.

Ben went up to the town to scout around. I stayed with the canoe, repacking my bright red Ortlieb waterproof kitbag, of which I was extremely proud. I could hear dogs barking above me and see, jutting out from the hillside, homes overlooking the bluff.

Two young Indian men came down in their pick-ups. Their handshakes were as soft and perfunctory as a young child's. They said little for a long time. One was much fatter and more ebullient than the other, who was thin and unsmiling in surfer wraparound shades.

There was a little girl, maybe ten, playing with a Gameboy in the front of the fat Indian's pick-up, an old purple Chevy, virtually rust-coloured already. The girl gave up playing after a while but sat without complaint for as long as I talked to her father. Flies buzzed in and out of the open window but she never even looked our way.

The fat Indian, with one look, both acknowledged me and asked permission to look at the canoe. He carefully inspected the ribs and the stitching. He beckoned his friend over with a rapid hand gesture, but his friend only gave it a cool glance.

With something approaching excitement the fat one said, 'I never seen a real one of those before except on television.'

I told the Indian, whose whole diction, impassive flat face, silent friend seemed to gang up against any sort of verbal communication, that I had seen bear tracks. 'Oh yeah, more than likely, round here, yeah.' He spoke with a pronounced, unfamiliar accent. Something Irish or Romany about it, but an absence of any words of consolation or flattery. Also no challenge or hostility, no handholds or footholds for verbal grappling. I asked what they were up to around here. It seemed a suitably vague and indirect kind of question. I noticed they hadn't asked me any questions at all.

'We waiting for the call-up,' said the fat one. 'They got bad fires over to the north of here. Good work in the summer fire-fighting around here.'

'I saw stretches of burned-out forest as we drove down yesterday,' I said.

'There was fires around here five years ago. Bad fires. No one knew how they started.'

'Arson?'

'What's that?'

'It's when a fire is started to make trouble,' explained his friend, who didn't smile, but I could tell he was all right.

'Yes, maybe arson.'

They did not waste any small-talk saying goodbye. No 'good luck' or pat on the back, just a nod, at a moment seemingly known to both of them at the right time to leave.

IV

Ben came back from his explorations full of bounce, carrying some magazines.

'I met some Indians,' he said.

'So did I.'

'I went into the band office and asked if it was OK for us to stay here. I met the band secretary. She was nice and said no problem and gave me these. No one else'll read them, she said.'

We had had an earnest discussion with Roland about asking permission to stay at MacKay. All the guidebooks suggest, even demand, that you get permission before staying on reserve land.

'I don't think it matters too much,' said Ben. 'Not here anyway.'

A man in a smart shiny crewcab came by looking for places to fish. His name was Donald and he worked at Suncor, the big oilsand refinery in McMurray. He wore a smart fisherman's waistcoat, the kind favoured by foreign correspondents, but he carried no rod.

'Just looking around,' he said.

He'd worked twenty years at Suncor. He'd been there almost since it began this biggest, latest phase of production.

'I worked so many years in that place, guess I'll retire around here. Fishing is good. You go past Firebag Creek, that's good for jackfish and pickerel. You got a rod?'

We had.

'Athabasca's a tricky river. I've been all the way down it to the lake. Lots of sandbars. Lost a lot of prop shearpins in this river. What d'you draw in that canoe?'

'Six inches.'

'There's sandbars less than that. But the Athabasca ain't your problem – you got the current with you. It's the Peace River I'd be worried about. Seen it from a chopper once – that's one wide, fast motherfucker to go against. I'd want more'n a piece of bark on that sucker, I can tell you.'

He turned, almost with sadness, back to his spotless black Dodge, parked with its snout arrogantly raised, or so it seemed.

'Piece of bark?' said Ben, indignantly, as Donald gunned his five-litre engine.

John arrived sometime after lunch and we greeted him like a long-lost brother. Sota barked and jumped with happiness. The sun came out and stewed us with its heat as we loaded the boat. John being there made everything easy. He spoke about his journey down the Mississippi. We liked to hear such reminiscences: they were a touchstone, proof that such a journey could be made, at least *with the current*.

For the time being John would be the steersman, I would be

in the bow and Ben would be the powerhouse in the middle. With the current whipping us downstream to Fort Chipewyan I hoped my arm would rapidly heal and get stronger, ready for the difficult paddling ahead. There was plenty of room for our kit and stores in a three-and-a-half-fathom trading canoe, good for a ton of fur.

MacKay, the last town for two hundred miles or more, disappeared in a minute. Now the grey-green pines crowded down to the bank and the river washed past them. The roots, like tangled hairy cables, connected through from the overhanging lip to the narrow welt of shingle beneath. Behind the roots lay a continuous cave broken only by the hard-to-see outlet of creeks and the beaver lodges, which from a distance looked like the chewed-up remains of a wooden boat.

Sota jumped in the water after a beaver, the dog's dark head keeping pace with us, swirling along with the river long after the beaver had slapped his tail and gone. A bald eagle, with its snowy back and rough-fingered wings, flew from tall tree to tall tree along the bank, watching over us, I liked to think.

'Hey, what's that?' called John from the back. 'Is it a man?'

Three hundred yards away a black figure made its way up the beach opposite. He had a hurried, fugitive look.

'It's a bear,' said Ben. I strained to look, believing it would be my first and last chance to see one in the wild. And we'd only been going half an hour!

Ten minutes later Ben announced, 'I'm knackered.' I had to agree. Even paddling downstream wasn't as effortless as it promised, even in a five-mile-an-hour current like the Athabasca's. I thought about Mackenzie sitting back and being paddled but, short of paying people, I couldn't quite see modern adventurers agreeing to such an iniquitous arrangement. We coasted towards the bank and hung on to some roots. The current was less here, but even so you could see it piling up evenly against any obstruction, a smooth glassy bulge, the size telling you how fast the river was moving.

'You'll get tired,' said John, 'the first few days, but soon enough you'll be paddling eight hours a day and not really noticing.'

That might be true for you and Ben, I thought, but I'm going to have problems with this. I was glad he was at the back and not me. Steering as well as paddling would have been a double strain – or at least I imagined it would be. Everything I knew about canoeing could be written on a paddle blade. A narrow paddle blade, just like the voyageurs used. It had even been news to me, though eminently logical news, that you went downstream following the outside curves because that was where the current was fastest.

'What's that?' said Ben.

It looked like the head of a dog swimming but it was a bear, quite close, swimming across the river in front of us. At the bank it shuddered clear of the water, revealing a bulk belied by the swimming head. Two bears and we hadn't even been gone an hour!

At our first campsite I spent until nightfall trying to rig a device to keep our food clear of the ground and any bears sniffing around. The food was so heavy and the ground so uneven that it hardly worked. It was the last night we bothered to suspend our supplies. John had a plastic barrel which we used to seal all the half-open food and we stored it on the ground, a hundred yards downwind of the tents.

We lit a fire and I puffed on my voyageur pipe. Ben filmed the campfire embers forming tablet-shaped scales of charcoal. We had a tot of rum, as befitting voyageurs, who always carried a hogshead aboard the canoe, measured out by Mackenzie as a reward and a pacifier against mutiny.

The fire was close to the water's edge. Our tent was a hundred yards further along the narrow bank, a thin verge of sprouting willows that was all the open land available to us. Everywhere else was the dark overcrowded forest. It was full of rotting trunks suspended as if by invisible cotton between other trees. Super-light, often just a casing of bark, all the wood having rotted away, these logs sometimes just crashed to the ground with one push. It was possible to make a way back through the gloom, but not pleasant. There was no 'forest floor', just a succession of stumps, fallen logs, some huge, and spruce, straight, scaly-barked, crammed together like an attempt at a natural fence, planted as if by a madman with a million seeds to waste, creating a nasty fight for air and space. There were no birds apart from the bald eagles that stooped and rose, moving their heads only fractionally in flight; they knew their world and we merited no more attention than a slight straightening of the neck.

After the rum we went to bed early and lay in our electric-blue tent shoulder to shoulder, sardines, but comfortable sardines. Sota mercifully outside. Ben fixed one of his candle lanterns from a convenient loop in the tent roof and it cast a good warming light. I scribbled in my notebook, Ben read about sandpipers and John lay on his back, motionless, with the beatific look some people have when their glasses are off. What was in it for my fellow voyageurs? I at least had the excuse of writing about the journey, which stood up to some examination but not much. In reality, the writing was the cart and the journey the horse. If writing books was one's main motive there were plenty of easier places to find material, in a library or even a war zone. My aim was different, to find a life that was compatible with writing but that also had some value in itself, voyageur not voyeur, working my ticket, a writing life not parasitic on its subject but part of a more satisfactory whole. Ben's motives and John's I could only guess at. I hoped they would be satisfied too. I'd got them up to this lark and no one wants to be the instigator of a boring or unpleasant time. Did that mean they were here just for a holiday? I could think of better destinations. Ben, I knew, wanted to see wildlife; John I was less certain about. He was keen to see if his canoe (still unnamed) was up to making a tough journey. And the way he talked about his work, the cabinetmaking rather than the canoe-building, made it clear that he valued time away from the mundane, valued it enough to sacrifice time and money to achieve it. But the more I tried to fathom their motives the more I began to see that behind such justifications and alibis lies a 'life motive', the mainspring of what we do, the decider that hurls us into things or makes us hold back. The life motive acted at the unconscious or barely conscious level. It was the default setting, the level of dreams and long and deeply held desires. Sometimes, I knew, it felt like that melodramatic and used-up word, destiny. At other times it was simply like an obsession.

V

The morning ritual was quickly established. First man up re-kindles the fire and makes the porridge. Second man up makes the tea. Third man up – Ben – who had also been the first man to bed, hangs around waiting for the tea and porridge to be handed to him. 'I just need more sleep than you guys, OK,' he said.

Smoke from the fire lay for a moment like mist on the river. The boat had switched direction in the night, caught in a back eddy along the bank. The high-sided bow had banged repeatedly against a protruding branch and the bark had cracked. It was a long serious-looking crack but John brushed it off: 'It's way above the waterline,' he said, but he did add, 'We should tie it up both ends next time.' My beautiful canoe no longer pristine. Before we left that morning John sewed up the crack using nylon thread rather than watape, spruce root.

We rounded a bend and saw a giant ancient factory building poking up through the trees. It was plated with rusted corrugated metal, an access door high up on one side. To get there we scrambled up a black, sticky dome of bitumen, as shiny as plastic, soft in the midday sun. Mackenzie wrote: '[Here] are some bitu-minous fountains, into which a pole twenty feet long may be inserted without the least resistance. The bitumen is in a fluid state, and when mixed with gum, or the resinous substance collected from the spruce fir, serves to gum the canoes.' Nearly a century earlier, in 1717, a Cree Indian had brought a sample of bitumen from the Athabasca to the Hudson's Bay Company fort at Churchill. This substance, which today has made Fort McMurray the richest town, per head of population, in Canada, was decreed worthless.

Inside the old bitumen factory, built in the 1930s, John popped his head in and out of giant cogs, chain buckets and corroded vats. We trod a half-rotten network of iron walkways high above the oily dark depths below. 'Great place for a shoot-out,' said Ben, 'or a ransom handover.' It gave me the creeps and I was glad to be back outside amongst the trees and brilliant sunshine.

We paddled on, always looking for reasons to stop. John found a moose skull and antlers, huge and heavy, the blades two inches thick. It was sitting on a bank of shingle high above the river. We lit a fire on the shingle bank and ate food.

Far over the river a bright orange speedboat careered over the water, hitting each wave with a dull thump and an altered engine whine, sweeping perceptibly from side to side out of the way of unseen obstacles. We waved and the two tiny figures waved back. It was the first boat we had seen. Then, as if caught on an invisible line, the speedboat dipped and turned in a wide circle, throwing its wash out wide until it came to quietly alongside our own canoe, powered up and rammed the beach. A wiry grey-haired man, dressed in light blue denim, eyes the same light blue, ran along the deck and jumped down, just clear of the water. He was holding a can of beer. Paying out a painter behind him was a large Indian woman with big tortoiseshell-rimmed glasses, dressed in natty Bermuda shorts and a blouse. She looked too well dressed to be messing about on the river.

'That your canoe?' asked the man, a trace of a foreign accent in his voice.

'Yes.'

'It real birchbark?'

'Yes. John here made it.'

The man grinned and showed a good set of teeth, his blue eyes and lined face full of amusement. He looked in his mid-fifties.

'She told me it was' – he pointed to the woman, who nodded – 'but I said no way, not on this river, but there it is. You want a beer? 'Fraid it's the last one.'

'I told you it was real,' said the woman.

'She told me but I said no. But something made me pull over for a look.'

I shook his friendly hand.

'Arnie Peterson,' said the man. 'Norwegian, long time ago.' He had a strong grip though he wasn't tall or big. 'I been here thirty years, never seen one of those boats, not the real birchbark. I seen a lot of changes.'

He looked downriver, following the sun's long rays. Then he nodded in the other direction. 'Going over to a buddy of mine to drink his homebrew. He's just finished a new batch.'

I wondered if we would be invited along but Arnie went back to talking about the changes he'd seen.

'This river is always changing. Yes, I been up the Peace a bit, far as the Boyer Rapids. It's a fast river. But it doesn't have the sandbars of the Athabasca. This river, you can't map it. No map lasts longer than five minutes. You have to know how it changes, the pattern. You'll be all right in your canoe, it's a kind river. Has been to me. I built a ratboat with an Indian pal when I came, but not a birchbark canoe. Indians all had ratboats in them days, canvas and wood thing, use a pole or a paddle. Damn Indians all got jetboats now.' His wife smiled benignly.

'I'd invite you along to my buddy's but I'm not good company when I drink. But stay at our cabin. It's just up that-a-ways. Been here so long they marked it on the map.'

Sure enough, 'Peterson's Place' was marked on the 1:250,000 topographical map.

'See, a man does nothing but stay in one place long enough and they think he's worth something. Name the place after you. Thirty years. Lotta changes.' He looked pensive, but only for a moment. 'Least I can say I saw a real birchbark canoe in my life.'

The can of beer soon warmed as we passed it between us on the beach.

'Stay at our place,' said his wife. There was a mosquito on her brown calf but she only moved her hand in that direction. The mosquito flew off and then returned.

'I'll be back tomorrow, probably cursing the homebrew,' said Arnie, already moving towards his boat. He had blue deck shoes on his feet and bare tanned feet underneath. His body was lithe, used to movement. 'One thing about the Peace – it ain't like this river, it ain't peaceful. I don't know …'

His voice trailed off as he coiled up his painter. What didn't he know? It was tantalizing, maybe important information, but Arnie and his wife already had their engine going. And then they were away, waving. Minutes later the bow wave returned as a glassy slow big ripple that lifted our boat up and against the beach.

'Time to go,' said Ben.

'Thirty years, on the Athabasca, what do you think he's been doing, apart from drinking homebrew?'

'Trapping, hunting, some logging, like he told us.'

'But what else?'

'Drinking homebrew?'

'I wouldn't have minded some of that homebrew,' said John. 'He can't be that bad company.'

We flattened and buried our single can, thinking of Arnie and his wife getting loaded.

And of the thing he didn't know. Arnie's cabin was large and white-painted and had a white picket fence. It even had a lawn. Other cabins we had seen were much less salubrious. Mostly they were one-room shacks with shutters to keep the bears out. Others had door-sized panels studded with nails like a fakir's bed, lying on the ground under each window to dissuade inquisitive bears from peering in.

We paddled and paddled and Sota drifted alongside in the water, quite content, the heat of the sun on his silky black fur making it hot to touch.

That night we camped on a flat sand island only four or five inches above the river. The island was devoid of anything except for a half-buried spruce log and odd pieces of driftwood, bone-grey, giving a faint riverine odour when burned.

The following night we lodged ourselves on a mud spit at one end of an island. There were wolf prints in the mud, and bear prints, which we were used to seeing everywhere. Before nightfall we heard the high-pitched sound of an outboard, ebbing and flowing as it rounded bends coming towards us. A grey-haired man with thick steel-rimmed glasses drove his aluminium powerboat on to the mud. He clambered down awkwardly but with vigour. Cecil had arrived.

'Got your note,' he said. 'Couldn't let you go by without saying hello.' He passed out high-strength Players cigarettes, wheezing as he inhaled. His skin was grey and thick-looking; mosquitoes kept away from it, as if comprehending its poor nutritional value. His hair he poked back under his Suncor cap, squinting at the last of the sun's evening rays.

Cecil was an oldtimer, the kind you have to be really interested in or else they shut up. You can't try to be their equal because you aren't. Cecil told us all about the shop he was building at his cabin. We had passed it earlier that day, when we left the note. We had already seen all the machines he had, the neat lawn, the locked sheds made of logs and the main log cabin itself. John said, 'I've got a shop back in Quebec,' but Cecil wasn't interested.

'Some bad uns came down from Chip and stole my kicker,' he said, changing the subject. A kicker was an outboard. 'I know who did it. I got a Mariner and they all got Mercs and Johnsons. There's a Mariner up there and I know it's mine. But they say it ain't. My word against theirs. And this is Indian country. I chain it all up now like you saw, when my partner and me aren't around.'

'Are you married?' asked John.

Cecil gave John a look of uncomprehending displeasure. He was rooted in the world of imperial measures and old words – gallons, miles, yards, mistress, girlfriend and wife. Partner meant pardner, the friend and fellow trapper, Jim, who Cecil shared his place with. But just in case we were so modern we misunderstood things Cecil said, 'No more marriage for me. I tried that once. I got a wonderful daughter who comes to see me. Her mother is always yapping. Never could stop that yapping.'

When Cecil heard our plans he gave us detailed instructions about how to get from the Athabasca River through the myriad channels of its delta to the land below Old Fort Point. This was the original site of Fort Chipewyan, which now stands nineteen miles across Lake Athabasca.

It had been news to me, rather lately gathered, that Fort Chipewyan had moved several times, and the place we had focused on for so long as the starting point was not, in fact, the place where Mackenzie set out from. It was a dilemma. In our minds the town (which had been built under orders of Mackenzie in 1803) was where we would set off, possibly cheered on by the townsfolk. Now it seemed we ought to start from a boggy, uninhabited spit of land on the other side of the lake. We decided to split the difference and make an 'official' start when we reached the lake, a place a few miles west of Old Fort Point, but near enough. Old Fort Point was now an Indian reserve, but of the original settlement nothing remains; even its exact position is long forgotten.

Cecil thought we'd be OK getting as far as the lake's edge, but he was dour about the rest of the journey. 'It can get dangerous,' he said about the lake, 'five-, six-foot swells. You don't want to get out too far from the beach. You want to hug the coastline.

'And no disrespect intended but you boys are going to need a kicker on the Peace. If mine hadn't been stolen I could have helped you out. Everyone I ever heard went down the Peace River. Never heard of anyone ever go against that current. No one.'

With a doleful look he handed out more cigarettes, our final smokes before certain execution.

We drifted through high cliffs or red sand past the spot where Mackenzie overwintered with Peter Pond. The river has shifted so much that the cabin remains have long been washed away. A change came over us as we passed this spot. It had been the first settlement in the area, and the place where Mackenzie hatched his plan to reach the Pacific. It began to feel as if we were at last on our way.

The country began to flatten out as we approached the delta. Spruce and hazel gave way to willows. Following the channels, I had to navigate, practically for the first time on the trip. You'd think you couldn't get lost on a river, but you can take wrong turns and then you start to doubt the information on the map a little, saying to yourself that the river must have changed, and then you can get lost.

The willows got lower and lower and it began to spit with rain. The channel spread out, anticipating the expanse of the lake. The current backed up to a lazy nothing. Round a last bend we saw something like the sea, studded as far as we could see with the great wrecks of trees. Spruce, poplar and cottonwood, all in attitudes of repose, huge trunks as big as beached whales, white from the sun and the constant immersion, branches sticking skyward mad and root-like. Beyond them the lake's horizon curved with the planet.

The only camping place was an oozing platform of mud, perhaps an inch or two above water level. Standing too long in one place left a blood-let of water around each boot print. To put up the tent we uprooted willows, water flooding each small hole left behind. The rain increased, angling against us.

'This is possibly the most unpleasant place I have ever camped,' said Ben, a statement he'd later have to take back.

'Apart from the amazing trees,' said John.

'Apart from the trees,' Ben grudgingly agreed.

That night the wind increased and drove the rain through the open vestibule. John's sleeping bag was soaked and Sota's muddy pawprints were over everything.

Then the dog stuck his paw through the mosquito netting – open sesame to the excluded swarm. I put up my sleeping-bag hood, sprayed repellent on my face and waited for dawn.

Four

AN IGNOBLE DEPARTURE

'I delivered my sentiments in such a manner as to convince them that I was determined to proceed.' Alexander Mackenzie on the Parsnip River

I

Two hundred and ten years ago Alexander Mackenzie departed, like us, to cross this lake with eight men: Alexander MacKay his twenty-two-year-old Scottish assistant, Joseph Landry and Charles Ducette, who had been with him to the Arctic, François Beaulieu, François Courtois, Jacques Beauchamp, Baptiste Bisson and two Beaver Indian guides. And a dog. They were on their way to the Pacific Ocean. Just as we were.

I re-checked the map. 'This is it,' I said, 'the official start.' Sota was squatting in the bushes and Ben was washing the mud out of our mess tins. There was very little sense of occasion. When Mackenzie departed he was piped out with fife and drum and a rattle of musket fire.

'Say, Raab,' said John. 'See that boat?' A low, sleek black boat was cutting up the channel right on the other side. A man, maybe Indian, we couldn't say, in a black shirt with a black cap and dark glasses was standing like a jockey at the controls. As if sensing our eyes on him he looked our way and grinned. He had a tan face and his teeth were very white. And then he did something inexplicable. He drew his finger across his throat and continued smiling and then the man in a black boat was gone.

'You see that?' I said to John.

'Kind of weird, eh?'

'What?' said Ben.

'We just got our final warning.'

Looking out over the lake, into the mist beyond the last of the sunken logs, we could see the waves, driven by an unvarying wind. It was, indeed, a bad day for a crossing.

We roped in all the gear and covered it with a nylon tarpaulin; camouflage-coloured, it gave a military earnestness to our prospective voyage. We formulated a plan. The waves were formidable and were pounding from east to west along the lake. We would, since the waves were so high, not risk cutting across them. Instead we'd paddle into them. Unless the weather dramatically improved we would give the modern settlement of Fort Chipewyan a miss. We had enough food to last a month, and though it felt as if we had been travelling for ever, we were only at the start of the real journey. It seemed wrong to be having a rest-break so soon. The only item we had run out of was liquor. High prices of the stuff meant we only ever carried a fraction of the two hogsheads (each one weighing ninety pounds) that Mackenzie carried.

Roland had given us some photocopied notes by a Swiss couple who had paddled down the Athabasca to Fort Chipewyan. They had cautioned against cutting across the bay behind Lobstick Island and High Island. The wind was so great on the far side of the islands they had been windbound and forced to stay on High for two days.

We were pumped up on coffee and anticipation and ready for the worst, holding the boat into the wind, mist and rain sweeping across the lake, not even the islands visible. I got in last, getting wet to the thighs from a wave, then we were off, riding up and banging down into the rollers, John at the back, me at the front and Ben with Sota down at his feet in the middle.

In a particularly dramatic and storm-tossed moment, when we were out of sight of any land at all, Ben stuck his paddle into the water. It touched the bottom at about four feet. Capsized, we could jump out and stand in the lake. We all felt safe again.

But not for long. We battled on through the spray and despite

Ben's lengthy arm plunging down into the water with his long paddle extended he touched nothing – we were now in deep water. Waves broke over the bow and I was glad of the upturned prow of the canoe, the typical design feature of all voyageur canoes. The prow sometimes caught the wind, which was awkward, but it made resting the boat on its side easier and it helped keep water out from the troughs we plunged into. The wind blew away the mist and even a few pale blue spots appeared overhead, but behind us. Ahead there was only dense low grey cloud and pouring rain stinging our faces. With the mist suddenly gone we could see the islands and the buildings of Fort Chip. Ever so close they looked. So close John was tempted.

'Say, Rob, shall I go straight there behind those islands?'

'No,' I said. 'That wasn't the plan we agreed.'

Ben joined in. 'It doesn't look far.'

This is how things go wrong, I thought.

'Look, guys, we made the plan, we should stick to it.'

Ben said in a stricken voice, 'Does that mean we're not going to stop at Fort Chip?' In his voice was all the pansy longing for a hot shower I felt so keenly myself. Hot shower, warm dry clothes, glass of beer in a bar. I looked into the grey firmament and saw ahead of us only rain and the unmistakable barren rocks of the Great Canadian Shield.

'All right, let's head for town, but not behind the islands.'

Two hours into a potential two-year voyage and we were already bunking off.

But there was no mistaking the renewed surge of energy in the paddling as we roller-coasted up and down the waves. I kept turning and looking over my shoulder to judge how far we would have to overshoot the rock-breakwater-enclosed harbour of Fort Chipewyan before our turn through the waves. There were several large cargo barges and small powerboats straining at their buoys even within the protective calm of the harbour wall.

As I waited for a suitable gap between waves I saw the absurdity of navigating from the bow. I should have been at the back, ready to turn without the necessary delay of passing a command

54

verbally. But I wasn't strong enough or skilled enough to be at the back: that much had been proved when we turned off the main Athabasca into the channels of the delta. We had only overshot the correct turn by two hundred metres, but fighting our way back against the current almost overwhelmed us. It was a monumental struggle, all of us shovelling at the water, eyes bulging, all technique lost, pounding and splashing our way back. I could feel the shuddering as each of the others drove us forward, but when I paddled it seemed to make little difference, despite the huge strain I felt, especially in my injured arm. As we clung to some roots streaming with the current at the entrance to the side channel John said, between gasps for breath, 'Your gonna have to paddle stronger than that, Rob.'

It was humiliating to be the weak link in an expedition one aspired to motivate. It seemed to emphasize the out-of-kilter wrong-footedness, or wrong-handedness, of the venture.

And now, again, I was reminded of this, shouting down the boat with the wind and rain to turn, turn, turn.

The last wave caught us on the quarter and then we were running for the harbour entrance. With the wind behind us we were flying along, going so fast we almost missed the entrance, just scraping our way in past the big rusty pilings.

We were watched by a motionless figure in dark green water-proofs standing at the dock. All through our long paddle to the back of the harbour he stood at the edge just watching.

We tied up to the jetty and with the briefest of mumbled greetings he started lifting our gear out of the boat and into the back of his pick-up. Despite my waterproof I was soaked to the skin and shivering.

The man, in what I now saw was thick industrial raingear, was young and fit-looking, with a quizzical smile. He ushered me to the pick-up cab and handed me a cigarette; the other two and the dog climbed on the back in the rain.

'How did you know we needed a lift?' I asked, water dripping from my hood, spotting the cigarette gripped in my cold claws.

'I saw you out in those waves and I thought, Is that a boat or a dead tree floating? There ain't no other boat out in this weather and then I saw that it was just you three and that crazy canoe. Then I knew you boys were gonna need all the help you could get.'

II

The young man, a metis Indian with bright blue eyes, was called Donovan. He drove us the five kilometres to the edge of town (there are only seven kilometres of road in total in Fort Chip) where the Cree band chief, Archie Wacquan, ran a bed and breakfast. It seemed a bit of a comedown for an Indian chief to be in the hospitality business, so we were all intrigued to meet him.

'You want to put your canoe up on my barge for safe keeping?' Donovan asked. 'People they come and look.' He grinned, 'Sometimes they look too hard.'

Sometimes they look too hard. I liked that construction. Maybe one could travel too hard, miss out the essential nourishment that travel provides by being too caught up in moving forwards, of making miles. At that moment I decided it was foolish to be racing the clock in such remote surroundings. And stocking up on rum was as good a reason as any for stopping at Fort Chip. Whatever miles we made, that would be good enough. But in thinking this I would soon be proved dead wrong.

III

'Mostly I get professionals here,' said Archie, looking disdainfully at the mess tin of water Sota had upset and lapped up, the mound of clothing, wet and stiff and stinking of woodsmoke, all with the texture of waxed paper, capable of holding any shape you cared to bend say your underpants or shirt into; should origami with filthy laundry be your thing. Then there was our arrival, as wet as drowned rats and demanding a discount. I was in 'abroad' or even 'third world' mode: bargain for everything; everything is negotiable. Archie was expensive, probably because he dealt with professionals, but we needed cheap. We got a room between all of us and the dog was reluctantly allowed too. Archie made a big deal of showing us the satellite TV and all the other amenities that professionals really appreciated – things we hadn't come 300 miles along rivers and lakes for, in fact, things we were hoping to avoid. His favourite clients were the white guys on salaries from the government and the oil companies – guys used to 'service', choppered in and out with an attaché case and a change of underwear, a sat phone and an expense account. Nice enough guys, people with money, not us.

We banged into town in the low-slung brown saloon Archie rented to professionals. Halfway along the wet, windy, well-tarmacked road we picked up an Indian boy with big glasses on his moon face, hitching. He said little except to echo our questions. 'Where you from?' 'Where you from?' 'Where you going?' 'Where you going?' 'Bad rain.' 'Bad rain.' When we dropped him off he nodded his thanks and walked away in his blue shellsuit.

Fort Chipewyan had grey one-storey unit housing for most of the people. There had been a land settlement with the band and the people had houses and pick-ups as a result. The town was full of Indians riding quad bikes, mostly camouflage-coloured green ones.

Chaddy, a bulky and friendly guy who looked like an Indian but was of Lebanese descent, had a liquor store made of steel. Steel walls, steel doors with crowbar marks, no windows. Inside the steel walls were unpainted with metal shelving which held bottles of liquor, all plastic. Chaddy sat behind a steel desk in front of the metal shelves full of liquor. Because we weren't drunk we were allowed to pick our booze ourselves rather than Chaddy getting it.

The hotel on the hill had a good view of the lake and served beer. Through my monocular, which I never used again because it was so fiddly and small, we looked for the channel that left the lake for the Peace River. Mackenzie had taken that channel and so would we. Pelicans flew up the lake and Ben excitedly checked them in the wildlife guide. A thin attractive Indian girl with the long legs and narrow hips of many Cree women brought us the beer in cans. I asked for glasses and got an odd look. After a lot of rummaging behind the bar the girl came back with two glasses and a plastic cup.

'Those the last two glasses in the whole place,' she said.

'Why's that?'

'Usually we don't give 'em because of the fighting on Friday nights. We got in the habit now of only plastic cups or in cans.'

In the toilet the mirror was stainless steel, less easy to smash.

'What's this place like on Friday night, then?' said John, sipping his beer.

'It's OK,' said the Indian girl. 'Now we got the plastic.'

Fort Chip has one thousand two hundred inhabitants and five full-time policemen, RCMP Mounties with stripes down the sides of their trousers. A lot of police for so few people, but then the RCMP have always been more than a police force in the far north. They are also there to deter too much foreign interest in uninhabited areas and to quell any signs of native rebellion.

The few Indian drunks we saw in Fort Chip all wore moccasins and moccasin rubbers and white socks. They sat on a bench outside the Northern store and wished us well. One of them, unshaven and unsteady, said we should watch the current on the Quatre Fourches, or 'Cat Fork', Channel. It would be against us, he said. I went to pat him jovially on the back and he gave me a look of considerable dignity, despite his evident inebriation. The look told me: I know what I'm talking about and what I said will be useful to you.

Back at the chief's B&B, Archie told us about the dam. He and his white wife were fighting the dam. Despite his preference for professionals, I liked Archie. Not only was he fighting the dam, he was fighting the road. 'We haven't had a road for two hundred years and we're fine. We don't need one now,' he said. Archie was right that a road would change many things.

We were treated as honoured guests, or at least hooted at by kids and drunks wherever we went. Everyone had seen us arrive and knew who we were. In a road town that wouldn't be possible. Cars come and go and you can't keep track of everyone. So you get used to strangers and ignoring strange faces. You get used to ignoring people. It was pretty obvious. But if you want more business, build a road. Accept you will lose these things. 'People want everything,' said Archie, 'but if we want one thing we have to say goodbye to another thing.'

He had long hair in a ponytail and was in his mid-fifties. Unlike many Indians in Fort Chip he had a Cree surname. The Cree made up nearly 45 per cent of the Fort Chip population, whereas the Chipewyans were only about 15 per cent. Mackenzie was fonder of the Chipewyan people: 'They do not affect that cold reserve at meeting, either among themselves or strangers, which is common with Knisteneaux [Cree], but communicate mutually, and at once, all the information of which they are possessed ... I do not hesitate to represent them, altogether, as the most peaceable tribe of Indians known in North America.' In Mackenzie's time there had also been Beaver Indians, a more nomadic woodland tribe, who were pushed further and further along the Peace River.

The dam. That was going to dominate our lives from now on. The river and the dam. They went together. The white man dammed the river and changed it. When Mackenzie went up the Peace there was no dam at the top. How had it changed things? That was one thing we would find out, going against the current; we would really learn the river and we would, after a thousand miles, learn the nature of what controlled the river, which was partly nature, but partly man, too, with his great hydrodam and lake feeding it. I never met an Indian who approved of the dam on our entire journey.

Once the dam had been built, for five years they restricted the flow of the Peace to fill the lake. That five-year drought destroyed much of the wetlands around Lake Athabasca. Archie showed us the original level of the lake from watermarks on the rock around Doghead Point. Even now the level of the lake was low. But it was that five-year drought that did the real damage. Now the flow of the river was controlled. It went up and down depending how much power they needed on the west coast, in British Columbia, Oregon and California.

IV

Chaddy also owned a restaurant, and we went there to meet Joe Vermilion. I liked the name already. The next big (*Big!* Say, twelve hundred people!) town we would go through was Fort Vermilion, just after the infamous Vermilion Falls, a mile-wide waterfall stretching across the Peace River. Joe was the first Indian who had shown much interest in our trip. By phone, through a helpful ex-ranger who also ran the museum, I had tried to recruit a native guide, but no one apart from the ageing George Wandering Spirit had come forward. But when I phoned George his wandering spirit had deserted him. 'My back's gone bad. My son's gotta take me to the hospital. Sorry I can't help you.'

Of Mackenzie's two Indian guides, one is never named and the other is only referred to by his childhood nickname 'Cancre', meaning duffer or dunce in French. These two spoke Cree and Chipewyan and were useful for making contact when guides were needed. Mackenzie's plan required guides as much to show the way as to ensure safe conduct through Indian territory. On the several occasions that they approached natives without a guide to smooth the way the usual reaction was either hostility or terror.

Chaddy's restaurant was a windowless shack, like a workers' canteen at a logging camp. Indians in plaid lumber-jackets and white men in bib overalls crouched over big plates of food, a dribbly red and yellow sauce bottle in the middle of each Formica-topped table. Some days Chaddy did Lebanese specialities with a Canadian twist: falafel with gravy, shish kebab on toast, stuffed vine leaves on a mixed bed of coleslaw and canned turkey slices. That day there was fish and chips with a fried egg on the side. 'That's a good one,' said Joe, so we all ordered it.

Joe looked about fifty or so, but it was hard to tell. He had a weatherbeaten, competent face, squarish; he wasn't smoking, unlike most of the men in the room, and perhaps because of this exuded a kind of independent steadfastness. We all shook hands with him, egregiously happy that we should have a real Indian giving us advice.

'The Peace is a fast river, but you'll be all right. There are many back routes. When I was young we all paddled up and down the Peace, but in canvas boats, not birchbark. My grandfather made birchbark canoes but I never knew him. Here, see this channel?'

He placed a thick brown finger on the map.

'The current is nothing in that channel. See here? Sometimes you even get a reverse current here; if the main current is strong it sucks the water back out.'

'Like the Quatre Fourches?'

He nodded. 'Many back routes. You have to be sly with the river. You'll be fine.'

Joe Vermilion was the first person who hadn't been pessimistic about our chances paddling against the current. He was also the first person we'd met who had any direct experience of doing what we wanted to do. The nearer you get to the challenge, the more real experience the people you talk to have, and the more likely they are to be optimistic and encouraging. It's people without real experience who try to scare you. I hoped we were getting better at telling the two apart.

'Do you have relatives in Fort Vermilion?' I asked Joe, thinking his name meant a connection to the place.

'No,' he replied. 'Only been there once, by snowmobile, along the Peace when it was frozen.'

'Do you still go trapping?'

'No more. Not worth it. Greenpeace killed the traplines. Used to get a thousand dollars for a lynx. Now you won't get fifty. But trapping was a hard life. Easier now.'

Joe reached for my pen and drew a wobbly line along the north side of the river. 'Keep this side.' Then he marked an X. 'That's my cabin. Stay there if you want. Here's Jackfish River – good fishing.' He gave a broad grin. 'You got a gun?' he asked.

'No. Do we need one for the bears?'

'I always take one.' Then he looked at Sota. 'But you got the dog. You'll be fine.'

V

Down at the dock Donovan was still there, watching over the canoe. He nodded his chin at a drunk Indian balancing his backside delicately on a discarded aviation-fuel drum. It was the same thin leathery Indian who had told us about the current direction of the Cat Fork Channel.

'They don't work,' Donovan grumbled. 'Got the treaty card. What's a metis got? Got nothing. No treaty. No handouts from the government. No tax-free tobacco. I like to smoke too, you know. Have to work forty hours a week. They collect the money for nothing. Know the difference between white man and the Indian? Time. Only time. White man came four hundred years ago. Indian come from Siberia twenty thousand years ago. Across the Bering. Only metis born in Canada. Only metis.' He looked at me with dark blue watery eyes trapped in the chinks of his brown face.

'You doing this for fun?' he asked. 'Me, I like getting drunk. Or hunting moose.'

'Did you ever hear about dream hunting?' I asked, wanting to get him away from the injustices he suffered. I had been reading about techniques of visualizing the location of prey used by natives along the Peace River. But Donovan had other ideas.

'I tell you the dream hunt. No Indian taking moose all year round. Metis only get their one moose in season. Indian take 'em all year round.' He laughed wryly. 'Lots of tricks for getting moose. You pour water from a jug on the floor. That's the sound of a cow pissing, brings out the bull. Or rub antlers together. Another thing, take a roll of bark like your canoe made of and make a trumpet. Don't sound like anything but it brings them running. You going upriver? Everyone else go downriver. Upriver! That's real work. What made you do this thing?

Smoking something when you thought this idea up? Me, I get drunk for fun!'

Three park officials had just arrived at the dock in their motor-boat. They'd been on the Cat Fork that morning. They looked out of place on the river in their uniform shirts and green fleeces. 'You're in luck,' said a bland, cookie-duster-moustached man with square metal-framed glasses, 'the current is with you. Peace must be down and the Cat Fork's flowing into it.'

Quite a crowd had gathered for our send-off. A refined, elderly but spry Indian woman looked carefully at our boat. She still made baskets and decorations from birchbark. When she saw Sota she said, 'Mackenzie had a dog. You know that story? He lost his dog at an Indian village. When he came back that way they gave it to him again.'

John and Ben wore their lifejackets as we paddled away, fearful that the park officials might otherwise intervene. In a show of bravado I didn't wear mine. I was already buoyant with the anticipation of leaving, humming with the excitement of heading off at last. That and the news that the Cat Fork would be easy going. Sota was the last to get into the canoe, running up and down the dock looking for the best place to jump down.

VI

The lake was calm and pelicans flew overhead. In groups of two or three, their gullets streamlined without fish. Their huge wingspans beat the hot, humid air, thumping some life into it. Our paddling became slower and slower as we entered one of the branches of the Quatre Fourches Channel. We had started vigorously but now the wind was building against us and John had just noticed something very unpleasant. 'See that stick?' he said; 'look which way it's bending.' There was no doubt. The current here was against us. 'But it might be flowing from some-where else, we won't know for sure until we're on the main channel itself.' Optimism reasserted itself. Park official said so. We paddled on, my arm aching and John again telling me to,

'Paddle harder, Raab, I haven't got enough power here.'

'At least there are pelicans,' said Ben. We'd seen even more of them flapping and converging with their great bills above the star-shaped confluence of the channel, the Quatre Fourches itself. They were American white pelicans, *Pelecanus erythrorynchos*, with black-edged wings and big orange bills. We saw only one whose bill bulged with sudden movement – he had a big live fish in there. With a huge wingspan of over two and a half metres, it was the largest bird on the lake.

There were dogs barking at the confluence of the channels. They belonged to George Wandering Spirit, but we didn't know that until later. Despite his bad back he'd gone to his dog camp in the bush. We heard a few human shouts from the camp but saw no one.

Sota started his jumping-out routine as soon as we were off the lake. I was now far less sentimental and pushed him back in the water if he tried to get into my section of the boat. I had things the way I wanted and I didn't want to be splashed every five minutes.

When we turned the corner into the main channel Sota jumped in yet again. I noticed he was falling behind much more quickly than before. It took a while for it to sink in – the current was taking him backwards; the Quatre Fourches was really against us. The old drunk Indian had been right and the park official wrong. The Cat Fork was against us. Suddenly we had a hundred hard kilometres before we got into the Peace River. It seemed as if we were having to fight for every little bit of the journey we made.

Five

THE LAST BARK

'We all felt the sensation of having found a lost friend at the sight of our dog; but he appeared, in a great degree, to have lost his former sagacity.' Alexander Mackenzie finds his lost dog

I

The wooden seats, held in place by leather strips, proved to be hard and painful. Indians would have knelt, though voyageurs used seats like ours combined with a roll of personal kit on which to rest the knees. I used my sausage-like Ortlieb kitbag as something to straddle, only resting the edge of my backside against the unforgiving seat. Ben, with his larger bulk and more pronounced movements (he liked to bounce on his seat as he sat down), had broken both his leather strips. John was apologetic. He saw it as a failure of his canoe-building expertise. 'They were the only ones I had around,' he explained. We replaced them with nylon paracord, which also snapped every few days. From then on, fixing the seats became part of the morning ritual.

Another ritual was emptying the boat. There was a leak, a small one and very hard to find. By the end of the day there would be water at our feet and any mud or gravel we had brought in with us. At day's end we would rock the boat and let it ship water, swill that around and then tip it out.

The current against us when we had expected otherwise was a depressing blow, and our first camp, just up from the dog camp but on the opposite side, on a narrow strip of damp greenery, was not a happy one. I was still mulling over John's criticism of my paddling.

I was learning the hard way. You have to paddle hard, really hard, to shift a big boat full of men and gear against a current. My old conception of paddling was of just dipping along in a light-hearted way. Whereas back-breaking toil was the real thing. And I didn't dare allow myself the thought – We're not even on the Peace yet, we're not even in a real current.

It was raining the next day as we slogged on. Sota managed to shake himself when I was distracted and the water added to the rain running down the back of my neck. Pesky mutt! What was the use of him? He was beaming through his wet whiskers and thought he now had a new game: jumping into my part of the boat when I wasn't looking. When the dog plunged in the water yet again and swam back after another beaver I hoped he'd be gone for a good long time. We rounded a huge curve and I saw Sota far behind, swimming valiantly against the current. Good, I hope he stays back there, I thought with malevolence.

Ben noticed it too. 'Er, John, do you think Sota's all right that far back?'

John was as relaxed as ever. 'If he can't keep up in the water he'll just run along the bank. On the Mississippi he once ran eleven kilometres along the bank, I'm not kidding.'

We paddled on. Soon it would be lunchtime. We had established a vague routine whereby we'd stop around midday, light a fire and cook lunch. Since all our food was pasta, rice or flour plus tins of fish, Spam and corned beef, we needed to cook it to have anything to eat. The gas stove was small and piddling, took far too long, and seemed sacrilegious to use when all that driftwood was around. I found it laughable that gas stoves are touted as more ecological than wood fires in a forest environment. The ecoconsumers never seem to factor in that even if they 'pack out' their waste gas canisters they still have to go somewhere – yet another giant landfill, far from their idyllic wilderness but still a part of the planet. Starting a fire in the rain would not be easy, despite all of us being rather proud of our fire-lighting ability. I'd even been on a course to learn how to start fires by using a traditional firedrill, a fact I wielded against Ben, who had only desert-dry Australian fire-lighting experience.

This friendly rivalry, which stemmed from our intense shared experiences of ten years earlier, seemed to grate now. Ben, to me, appeared less comfortable to play the put-upon neophyte, the man happy to learn from his dumb mistakes. He was, after all, of similar age to Mackenzie when he made the trip; perhaps he should be accorded respect for that fact alone. Was I, too, less flexible than before, more intent on getting my own way; indeed, like Ben, sporting ten years more experience in this field? And though we kidded along there began to become apparent, under the surface, a deep drifting apart that had occurred that made it impossible to impose my vision of the expedition and yet also clouded any attempt to arrive at a joint vision, which is what I had hoped for. I didn't know then that a vision is always a destination, and we didn't yet have one. In all our talk it was always 'as far as we could go this summer'.

It was still raining, and, as I dipped along at the bow, I turned from pondering – why we seemed to disagree so much about trivial things (getting-up times, packing stuff away routines, where to camp) – to mentally planning the next fire. It would be tricky in the rain. And even harder for a voyageur dependent on flint, steel, and German tinder or amadou. This was made from the fungus *Fomes fomentarius*, which grew mainly on birch trees. It has to be taken from a live not a dead tree. The fungus is grey and looks like a gnarled horse's hoof attached to the lower trunk. The corky underlayer, pale brown in colour, was either kneaded into a chamois-like layer or, if dry, soaked for a few days and then pounded flat. When it was dry it was either charred or soaked in saltpetre, a supply of which was always carried on board the canoe. Once the amadou is ground up as powder, or used as a flattened strip, even one spark from a flint and steel will catch and start the tinder smouldering. Once smoke is steadily arising from the tinder either a ball of dried fibre from the inside of pine bark is used, or more usually a sulphur match known as a spunk. These were made in the fort before a voyage by dipping pine slivers in molten sulphur.

We, of course, had waterproof matches. But even with waterproof matches, of which we had many, all carefully sealed in plastic bags within bags, lighting a fire in the rain is no easy matter. First you have to get dry wood, and if it's been raining long and hard there isn't any. And any you do get soon gets wet. The solution is to find twigs and prickles and little bits on the underside of a pine, the side shielded from the rain. If none is available, split a log and use the dry wood from within to make firesticks. These are miraculous – simple and always effective. Simply repeatedly bring the knife blade down the edge, shaving again and again to make a mass of curls. You need a sharp knife and to press *against* the wood rather than down, or else the slivers will be too thick. Three such firesticks will be enough to start a fire, which, once going, can be built up using the rest of the split dry wood.

In real hard rain, of course, everything is getting wet all the time. You need to put up a tarpaulin to protect yourself and the fuel and then build a cover over the fire to protect it in its delicate early stages. Four sticks pressed into the ground with a grill resting on top makes a good enough protective cover. You then pile wood on top to make it waterproof. As the fire burns it dries the wood, which can then be added to it.

All this twice a day. It made a quick stop for lunch impractical, and unlike the voyageurs we weren't prepared to go from breakfast to evening meal with only ten pipes of tobacco in between. I was still smoking mine, but I had, unbeknown to the others, secretly broken into our 'parley baccy', the Players-brand cigarettes we'd brought along to offer to Indians as a peace gesture. Meeting non-smoking Joe Vermilion had weakened my faith in its necessity.

Sota was still in the river, or on the bank, though I hadn't seen him for a while. Ben picked up my thoughts. 'We haven't seen Sota for a while, do you think he's OK?'

John had to agree this time. 'Let's paddle back to where we last heard him.'

This took about half an hour. The bank was deserted.

'Do you remember hearing him bark here?' said Ben, 'About twenty metres in?'

'Maybe,' I said, not really recognizing the exact spot.

'Yeah, he definitely barked here,' said John.

'Guess he must have carried on along the bank without us noticing. He may be ahead of us now.'

We now paddled at full steam round bend after bend, past our last 'furthest' position and on up the channel. All of us were scanning the bank for signs of the dog, but there were none. Even the ever-present beavers seemed to have disappeared. The rain didn't stop and it was now past lunchtime. 'We must have overtaken him by now,' said Ben. John said nothing. We coasted into the bank at a spot amongst some big logs and boulders. Using firesticks with the nylon tarpaulin for cover we soon got a blaze going. I warmed the fronts and backs of my 'quick-dry' trousers against the fire, waiting for the sudden burst of all-encompassing heat that signified they were dry. It was gratifying to watch the moist darkened patches turn light-coloured again in the heat. The quick-dry trousers were another essential piece of kit. I pitied the voyageurs in their deerskin leggings and breech-clout or *azion*, draughty, damp and open at a crucial spot to mosquitoes. The voyageurs did not dry themselves or their cargo out except at night, though they might take a day off to dry everything if the weather had been especially bad.

As we chewed silently on our pasta and sardines with garlic (Ben and John were great believers in adding garlic to everything), John kept turning and looking up the river. He was mostly silent, removing his spectacles from time to time to clean off the worst of the rain.

Lunch was over and no Sota. 'He should have found us by now,' said John. 'He should have sniffed us out.'

'Maybe he's hanging around on the bank somewhere. It can get pretty dense, the undergrowth. Perhaps he's waiting some-place for us?'

John brightened at the suggestion. He and Ben decided to go back along the river, checking the banks more carefully for Sota. I would stay with all the gear and keep the fire going.

They paddled off in the lightened canoe. I loaded more wood on the fire and kept the bearhorn handy. The dark dripping trees, the grey river channel, my damp clothes, the dog missing, the current slowing us down, I'd only need an over-inquisitive bear to add to my woes.

Hours went by. The rock I was sitting on became immensely uncomfortable. I started to mentally prepare an elaborate risotto in anticipation of the lads' return. On John's suggestion I put out a mess tin of dog food for Sota on the slim possibility he might be able to smell it downwind. The rain and the isolation and inactivity shrank my world in on itself till it was bordered by the dripping visor of my hood and my wet arms (my breathable jacket leaked along the seams). I shrank into the area of my hood, holding myself like an aged gnome perched on the knobbly rock. Every so often I imagined I heard Sota rustling in the bush behind me. I fired off the bearhorn a few times for good measure, and after each loud echoing report the silence would sink in on itself again, broken only by the endless dripping of the branches around me.

Stephen Herrero's book on bear attacks was under my sleeping bag with several other books. I pulled out as few things as I could and found it. On dogs and bears: 'It is only a well-trained dog, experienced around bears, that is an advantage to its owner. An untrained dog can trigger an attack.' Sota was well trained, but as a truck dog, a friendly river dog, a beaver dog – certainly not a bear dog.

The benefit of rain was that the mosquitoes were less prevalent, but even in a torrential downpour there would be a few cunning ones, somehow dodging the raindrops, loitering under the slight shelter of a bowed and hooded head, inside the double cuff of an anorak, in the high-up places of a pitched tarpaulin; here would lurk the constant bloodsucking companions of the river, hanging as if on a thread that could always jerk them to safety when you made a swipe at them.

In the Athabasca region there were supposed to be twenty-eight different species. There are only six native to Britain, and none is as large as the big, slow Canadian varieties. Slow, yes, but also everywhere. We had our nets and our repellent and we expected them.

It is always the female that bites and she is supposedly attracted, not by warmth, clothing colour or aftershave, but by the metabolic waste products in one's breath. The most successful bug spray I've found, N,N-diethyl-m-toluamide, or DEET, works by jamming the mosquito's CO_2 detectors. It is the higher levels of CO_2 in one's breath that attracts them in the first place. In theory. In practice mosquitoes are attracted to clean people smelling of soap, smelly feet, even in thick socks (they will prod and prod to break through the weave), fair-skinned people over olive-skinned and, most controversially in our case, clean people over those rank with woodsmoke and the grime of camp living. Ben and John favoured clean clothes every few days whereas I was a follower of the unclean school. I also stood as often as I could in the smoke of the fire. It seemed to work. Ben was the fairest and cleanest of us all and he was savaged on a regular basis. I had read up about the not-washing method in one of the handbooks we carried, the 1917 edition of *Camping and Woodcraft*, 'a handbook for vacation campers and for travelers in the Wilderness' by Horace Kephart, a former librarian who transformed himself into an expert hunter and mountain man in the Ozarks. I liked the sound of this, that a bookhead like me could turn into a dead-eye shot, skilled with axe and tumpline. But there was a cost to this transformation, as if the change had rendered his outward self too plastic for conventional living – it was reported of Kephart that he 'could alter his personality with a single drink'. But back to mosquitoes: Horace recalled, 'Last summer I carried a cake of soap and a towel in my knapsack through the North Woods for a seven weeks' tour, and never used either a single time. When I had established a good glaze on the skin, it was too valuable to be sacrificed for any weak whim connected with soap and water.'

But establishing a 'good glaze' had its own downside: my hands were becoming as grimy as a coalminer's, a deep grime that covered each palm. My fingers were drying out, what with the alternation of immersion in water with the heat and ash of the open fires. At each knuckle joint cracks opened, and on my thumb they had started to bleed. There was nothing in Horace's book about cracked hands so I suffered whilst dreaming of cold creams and unguents, of which I had none.

I continued in my rain-sodden trance, stirring from the stump only to nudge with my foot another log on to the fire. In truth the insects had not been, so far, nearly as bad as I had been led to believe. Horace Kephart again:

> Deer and moose are killed by mosquitoes, which settle upon them in such amazing swarms that the unfortunate beasts succumb from literally having the blood sucked out of their bodies. Bears are driven frantic, are totally blinded, mire in the mud, and starve to death. Animals that survive have their flesh discoloured all through, and even their marrow is reduced to the consistency of blood and water. The men who penetrate such regions are not the kind that would allow toil or privation to break their spirit, but they become so unstrung from days and nights of continuous torment inflicted by enemies insignificant in size but infinite in number, that they become savage, desperate, and sometimes even weep in sheer helpless anger.

I certainly didn't want that to happen, certainly not with Ben recording it on video.

I took out my small DEET dispenser and puffed at the mosquitoes. It might officially work in some clever way but it struck me that DEET was so noxious (it dissolves plastic like Airfix glue) that no organism with even one brain cell would want to hover in an atmosphere laden with its peculiar sweet, dull half-metallic tang, half-sweaty odour. Because I didn't want my watchstrap to dissolve I'd given up on 100 per cent DEET and stuck to 50 per cent solution.

I looked up. Hours had gone by and still no sign of Ben and John. I was now hungry so I gave up the risotto idea in favour of something simpler. So far John had done most of the cooking. He was a good cook and seemed keenest, so we let him get on with it. But he wasn't always keen and on those few occasions, because there was no routine, we'd go hungry until someone finally cracked and took up the frying pan. John's habit of spiking everything with garlic, even the bread he made, had been pleasant at first, a change from the usual bland fare of camping, but the garlic, being loose in a plastic barrel and subject to heat and rubbing against tins and open packets of spaghetti, managed to impart its odour to almost everything we ate, including the porridge and the coffee. It wasn't even a good-quality garlic, being part of my fifteen-minute cut-price shop in Regina, Saskatchewan: they were fleshy, cheap, probably GM heads of garlic with a flavour reminiscent of an unwashed plastic place-mat in an Indian restaurant. Coffee and porridge tasting of that is not a great start to the day; no wonder we were all losing weight.

I decided to do a one-pot special – rice, sardines, soup powder, a little garlic (I didn't like the stuff any more but I had convinced myself that even a few scrapings constituted our vegetable intake), salt and pepper and an Oxo cube for good measure. Just like a McDonald's burger, the key to one-pot cooking lies in the sauces and condiments rather than the main ingredients. I started the rice off and when it was bubbling gradually added everything else. When it was done I hooked it off the grill and set it close to the embers to keep warm.

It was nearly nightfall when they returned, drawn and tired-looking. They accepted the food without comment, and Sota was not with them.

'I was kind of hoping we'd round that bend and see Sota back here with you,' said John.

'We went back to where we last heard him bark,' said Ben. 'We went into the bush and looked about for what we thought was the exact spot – all we found was a pile of bear droppings.'

'He's not seen many bears before,' said John, 'and the ones he has seen have been used to humans and have always run away. Out here the bears probably think a yapping dog isn't too frightening.'

Somehow the pile of bear droppings became all that was left of Sota, as if he had been eaten, digested and excreted on one spot just as a reminder to everyone how dangerous bears could be. We were far from flippant in the damp, bug-infested camp that night. Without our usual requirement of consent, Ben swigged from the whisky bottle and passed it round. We all drank deeply and tried to cheer up John. He said nothing for a long time; finally he took another swig and said, 'Guess he's gone.'

'No, he'll turn up,' I said.

'He's not gone,' said Ben.

'Dog's can do incredible things,' I said. 'They can swim and walk for hundreds of miles just to get back to their owner.'

'That's a real dense bush back there,' said John. 'I certainly wouldn't want to hike through it.'

'But you're not a dog.'

'Guess not,' he said, defeated.

After another round of whisky John said, 'Guess what? I never told you guys, but Nat and I are getting married. We got engaged the day after you guys left.'

'Way to go, John!'

'Great stuff.'

'Fantastic girl.'

'Thank you.'

We clapped John on the back and he kind of turned into it as if expecting a much heavier blow. We swigged more whisky.

But John's impending marriage did not drive away the image of Sota, a husky by name only, really a rather pleasant and well-brought-up, fairly urban dog used to riding in trucks and sitting around in heated woodworking shops, a kind and intelligent dog, out there, if still alive, dripping, alone and very, very lost.

'He's got his name and our phone number on his collar,' said John. It was a bit like Bishop Berkeley's tree. Did a dog really have a readable collar in a place where there was no one to read it, at least for sixty or more miles?

It was a horrible feeling, and guilt began to gnaw at all of us. I distinctly remembered the elation I felt as I saw him failing to keep up with us, as the current towed him backwards, further and further away. I could have mentioned that much earlier, got him back on board before he was out of sight.

'We should have kept a better watch on him,' said Ben.

'He's just not really a wilderness dog,' said John. 'Maybe it was wrong to bring him here.'

'I'm sure we'll find him,' I said, because someone had to.

'Yeah,' said John.

'Congratulations on getting married!'

John nodded and shuffled over to the tent.

II

We hung around the camp until lunchtime the following day, waiting for Sota to turn up. We set out mess tins of dried dog food in a ring around the campsite, covering every possible entrance from the deep, tangled undergrowth of the bush. Nothing. Mackenzie had lost a dog and we had lost a dog. But there was no Indian village nearby for Sota to shelter in.

Mackenzie had gone much further than us when he lost his dog. He had been virtually at the Pacific, at the 'Great Village' of the Nuxalk Indians. He was so preoccupied with other things, treating an Indian with 'a violent ulcer in the small of his back' with Turlington's balsam and confronting the chief over a stolen axe, that he did not mention the dog. Only when it was re-covered was the story of the dog's loss told. Earlier he remarks on the dog barking and scaring away a wolf. Calling it simply 'our dog', Mackenzie is characteristically spare on description, not even mentioning the breed.

We could wait around no longer. With a final look back John pushed off the canoe and we continued our journey up the Quatre Fourches Channel. All our talk was of the lost dog and we determined to ask every boat we saw (we hadn't seen one yet) if they had seen the animal. We camped early at a cabin on top of a rock bluff. It was a good spot, almost free of mosquitoes. 'Must be an Indian cabin,' said Ben. It was true, the places where Indians put their cabins were very often low in insect numbers, perhaps due to increased windiness, whereas the worst place we'd been was an official park cabin on the Athabasca.

It took a while to get the fire and the food going, as if the loss of the dog had sapped our will, sucked some of the motive power out of the trip. A motorboat went zinging by, but though we waved he just waved and kept on going.

At the confluence of the Cat Fork Mackenzie would have taken another channel into Lake Claire. This led into the Pine River, which led into the Peace. We were forced to take the longer, main Cat Fork because the Pine, now called the Claire River, no longer flows. Lake Claire has become drier and more overgrown. A recent traveller, writer and canoeist Max Finkelstein, described the Claire River as 'a ditch with a trickle of water in it' which he hiked along rather than paddled. Mackenzie had been prescient: 'The lakes are now so shallow there is every reason to expect, that in a few years, they will have exchanged their character and become extensive forests.'

It was at this campsite that we lost the saw. It was a bow saw, not very useful, but now it was gone. I hate losing kit on trips and it added to the generally glum feeling.

III

'Have they seen us?'

'Seen us? They're going to shoot us! Wave!'

We waved madly. The motorboat with its small half-cabin powered in our direction. One man with his rifle resting on the cabin roof was aiming precisely in our direction. Though the boat rolled slightly on its wake his aim was spot-on. Then he fired and the report echoed all round the valley, five or six peals of thunder escaping. The boat shot past us towards the bank. The men, stocky Indians in waterproofs (it was still raining), jumped out and went a short way into the bush. They got back into their boat and came over to us laughing.

'It was a bear, just behind you – but this feller couldn't hit him!' said the older one, with thick glasses steamed up under his oilskin cap.

The shooter looked sheepish.

'We thought you were aiming at us,' said Ben.

'We would have hit you for sure, even him,' said their laughing leader.

John told them about the dog and they promised to look out for Sota. Something in John's manner dampened their levity. They didn't even joke about shooting dogs.

IV

It rained every day of the five days we took to meander up the Cat Fork Channel. My weak paddling was temporarily forgotten as everyone slipped into a slower, less ambitious routine. By a strange process the lunch and 'cabin exploration' breaks grew longer and longer, until the paddling seemed to be fitted around the rests and not the other way round. But even if you only paddle four or five hours in a day you make some distance. One day, wiping the raindrops away from the transparent map cover, I was able to point and say, 'Around that corner should be the Peace River.'

My navigation being somewhat approximate we needed to round two more curves instead of one. But it wouldn't go away – we had arrived at the big river, and when we saw it, it was overwhelming.

We clung to the bank of the channel deciding what to do, like toddlers at a swimming pool. A great grey turbulence of water swept across the entrance to our channel. A sea-like wideness after the narrow confines of the channel – this river was over a mile across. You could see the way the fast current of the river hit the slower current flowing into the channel, the line was a humpy ridge, waiting to rip us away.

'No good just sitting,' said John, and pushed us off. As soon as we nosed out into the current we were swept away. So strong was it that we couldn't turn and remain on the same side as the Cat Fork Channel. We were swept out and downriver into the waters around Rocky Point on the far side. John shouted at us to paddle harder. We were already paddling as hard as we could, harder even than the last time we had paddled as hard as we could. There was wind, too, whipping up the water into grey waves with white breakers, cold water. Head down for twenty strokes, look up, no progress, head down for fifty strokes, look up, no progress. We were doomed to remain midstream for ever, battling against wind and current until our strength ran out. I could hear Ben grunting as he dived his paddle in. Then came a shudder as he really drove forward, literally shivering the timbers of our boat. More looking down as I paddled, and more and more – not wanting to see if we were making progress. We were swept around Rocky Point, which dipped out into the Peace and was surmounted by a rocky cliff and under it the largest pile of driftwood I had yet seen. As tall as a house and spread in a long arc around the point, rammed up against a barrage of gigantic logs, the driftwood mountain became our steering point.

'On-on-on,' we chanted, drawing a last bit of strength from the rhythm. Not like the voyageurs, who had plenty of songs, who even in the most trying of times sang about girls called Lisette and Jeanneton in the springtime.

We made it, but with the immediate realization that we had no way of going further. Behind the logpile the wind was a mere whisper; stick your head above it and you got earache. Out on the river it was worse, a whipping breeze that sliced the tops off the waves which were already churning in the same direction as the current. Even without the wind it was hard to imagine making headway against that current.

It was far too rough to leave the boat in the water. We emptied it of all our goods and carried it ashore. Rocky Point, or Desolation Point, as Ben called it, was our new home for the foreseeable future.

Six

DESOLATION POINT

'It began to be muttered on all sides that there was no alternative but to return.' Alexander Mackenzie on the Peace River

I

'Do you think it would be possible to burn all this wood?' asked Ben.

'We could set fire to the whole thing. Make a hell of a bonfire.'

'I mean, do you think we'll be here so long that we'll burn it all and then run out?'

'There's always the forest.'

Up the smooth curve of rock, past several pools with yellowish water in them, past a small, neat cabin utterly locked up, was the edge of the forest. It extended upriver as an overhanging, earthy cliff. There looked to be a trail past the cabin and into the woods but none of us wanted to leave the cosy protection of the logpile, which was getting lower and lower as we fed our huge fire's greed. The pong was bad too, the muddy, fishy, cloying pong of driftwood too long in the water before it has dried out. Driftwood, especially poplar, burns too quickly too, and since beaver prefer gnawing on poplar and willow, that was the bulk of the wood. We had also lost the axe. Where, no one knew. We hadn't used it for a while and it had never had its own place, unlike the cooking pots and the grill. It had been a small cheap hatchet, bought at Canadian Tyre, but it had been useful in the rain for splitting logs. It wasn't raining now but without axe or saw we were reduced to beaver-cut wood, or simply feeding giant logs slowly into the fire as they burned up along their length. This is the so-called Indian fire, where a star shape of long pieces of wood is periodically shoved a little more into the flames. It is supremely efficient, but not good if you use a grill, and the long logs are easy to trip over.

No axe and no saw – getting careless, you just can't keep on losing gear in the wilderness. That's the way a chain of accidents can happen, one small mishap after another snowballing into a catastrophe. Who could I blame? Myself? Ben? John? Ben would do for the time being, though he was no more guilty than any of us. I stuck my head above the logpile and my eyes watered from the biting wind. I grabbed another good-sized log and threw it on the fire.

We were officially *dégradés*, as the voyageurs put it, or degraded as it entered the English language, wind-bound and current-bound and unable to move.

Fur trader Daniel Harmon wrote in the early nineteenth century, 'The Canadian Voyagers possess lively and fickle dispositions; and they are rarely subject to depression of spirits of long continuance even when in circumstances the most adverse.' I hoped the same would apply to us. We had reached a roadblock, or rather a riverblock. There was no way forward, not that I could see. The journey had come to an ignominious and early end beneath the shelter of the giant logpile.

Lethargy set in. Lunch was late and ill-conceived – Ben tried sardine bannocks, a subtle combination of sardines, flour, water and salt. The result would normally have been classed inedible, but we were too hungry and downcast to complain much.

We built the fire higher as night closed in. We still had some whisky left over from the bottles we bought at Chaddy's. The stars came out but the wind did not drop. The fire warmed our faces while our backs were chilled. I walked down to the river's edge before turning in. The width and power of the flow were palpable. What had I been thinking in my cosy rooms in Oxford planning this great voyage?

The wind was still blowing fiercely the next day, despite the sunshine. More importantly the current was just as strong and looked just as impossible. I was up first, fairly late; our rising time, which had started at a respectable 5 a.m. had started to slip, becoming later and later, the sun's heat through the tent roof signalling the day's start rather than the puritanical bleeping of the alarm on my wristwatch. My first task was to get the fire going from the embers. Driftwood, because it burns so quickly, often left no glowing embers at all, just a pile of cold ash. In the cooking-equipment bag was birchbark, the backwoodsman's petrol. On the logpile were several birch logs which had almost rotted inside but still had good bark around them. This I peeled off and stored as lighter fuel, using one piece to get the fire going. With just one match a piece of birchbark will crackle into flame with an oily smoke and a sweet tarry smell. Small twigs from the logpile kept the flame going and soon I had a decent fire.

For breakfast we always had porridge, easily made and easily burnt – the secret being to keep stirring during the crucial five-minute bubbling time, without which you simply have hot muesli. Breakfast over, we threw more logs on the fire and from time to time poked our heads over the pile, looking for some sort of sign – a break in the weather, a lessening of the waves, anything.

It was at Desolation Point that I realized I had packed the wrong books for the trip. I had mostly taken books of an edifying and instructive nature rather than books I wanted to read in order to escape my present surroundings. There is nothing less interesting when you are surrounded by wilderness than a book telling you how to make the most of the wilderness. A good pulp thriller, an Agatha Christie or a P. G. Wodehouse, was what I yearned for. The paperback *Brothers Karamazov*, its page corners bent and rounded from deep immersion in my kitbag, remained unread despite several exploratory attempts. Thoreau's account of a nine-day canoe journey up the Maine River seemed utterly obscure, as if he had deliberately chosen words that conveyed no meaning. Even Kephert's description of building a raft out of a horse bridle and an inflated buffalo intestine seemed unreal and of no interest.

I don't think it was simply a consuming philistinism that had taken hold, rather that, now we were on an adventure, albeit an adventure on hold, we wanted to read books that were also adventures, or at least had fast-moving plots where things happened, because that was what we wanted to happen on our journey. We now had the adventurous worldview rather than the literary or intellectual. Non-fiction, except that which was of direct use, ceased to be of interest.

I glanced briefly at the photocopy of Mackenzie's journal. The footnotes were worth reading: the editor had followed part of the same route himself and allowed himself the odd illuminating comment. Mackenzie did make one observation that caught my attention: 'I did not find the current so strong in this river as I had been induced to believe, though this, perhaps, was not the period to form a correct notion of that circumstance, as well as of the breadth, the water being very low; so that stream has not appeared to me to be in any part ... more than a quarter of a mile wide.'

Mackenzie had left Fort Chipewyan on 10 October, very late in the season. Before the dam maintained the river's level it must have been considerably lower in the autumn, and the voyageurs took advantage of that. Our experience in high summer was quite different.

When it came to making another cup of tea, foraging in the food barrel (a kind of homebrew keg with an aluminium ring clipping the lid on tightly) meant pushing one's way past Sota's dusty plastic bag of dried dog food. No one had suggested throwing it out. We all carried on talking as if he would be found quite soon. 'Probably having the time of his life roaming in the woods,' said Ben. 'Maybe,' said John. 'Might even catch up with us here,' I said. Everyone looked out across the river Sota would have to swim to catch up with us. No one said anything.

The Wilderness Paddler's Handbook suggested cards, Scrabble and cribbage, or reading aloud from an explorer's journal, as a way of whiling away a wind-bound day. I think our inability to follow even these simple diversionary pastimes was due to the fact that we were mainly current-bound, and this made it uncertain as to whether we would ever get going at all. An entire summer playing Scrabble on an empty foreshore is a different prospect from a day of it.

Voyageurs were well equipped with their songs, endless pipe-smoking and boasting which, I had read, they could keep up for hours at a time. Ben and I had both given up our pipes as a temporary affectation. They were not the great comfort I had imagined. Perhaps it was the presence of the parley cigarettes that spoiled me, or the fact that I had no pipe cleaners and the stem of the pipe was soon full of a gurgly mess of tobacco juice – how did voyageurs clean their pipes? It was a piece of research I had failed to do.

None of us was well practised in boasting; besides, as a method of entertaining others it seemed to have gone out of fashion. Our only boasts were concealed behind a deceitful charade of self-deprecation, though John did manage to admit that he thought he could make a million dollars, but only if he took on the kind of work he didn't like doing.

'Hey, you know something?' said Ben from inside his sleeping bag, which he had unrolled on his mat by the fire. 'We still haven't named the canoe.'

An orgy of name suggestions followed. *Dragonboat. Moosehead. Indian Queen. Bircher. Barker. Moorhen. Unjigah* (nearly selected, but no, didn't quite make it. It means 'peace' in the Cree language). *Mack's. The Big Mack. Myrtle. Maude. Dreamcatcher. Dreamboat.*

It was a game that could go on for ever. I decided to go up into the dark woods to find some spruce gum. The crack on the stern, though well sewn, was not sealed. I was searching for a white spruce, which was the preferred source of gum for a canoe, though in fact most kinds of resin can be used. Many traditional builders use commercially available rosin, the kind used for violin bows, others use tar or pitch substitutes such as Vulkem. I wanted to prove to myself one of the underlying ideas behind the voyage, that we were self-sufficient, that we could gather our repair material *en route* rather than at a hardware store.

White spruce differs from black spruce in as much as its lower branches tend to point outwards or droop a little, rather than point abruptly downwards. At the top, it looks more like a good Christmas tree than the raggedy black spruce, which is nevertheless a better source for roots than the white spruce. The white spruce also has longer, larger cones than the almost spherical cones of the black spruce.

Any cuts or holes in the bark of the spruce allow oleoresin to seep out; this is a volatile substance that evaporates over time and becomes the hardened yellow nodules of resin that sometimes look like dried wax dribbles on a candle.

Past the small locked cabin I followed a path into the woods and quickly found some white spruces. Each time I saw a good deposit of dried resin I scraped it into a small zip-lock bag I was carrying. I carried the bearhorn in the side pocket of my trousers and every so often stopped and listened to the noises of the forest, noises of scratching and rustling, distant tree-fall and sudden explosions of feather beating against branch as a bird broke free, in hiding for too long, as I walked past. The rapid hollow knock of a woodpecker I could hear but not see.

In a cut-down tin I mixed the resin with some margarine over the fire. I should have strained the resin to remove the impurities but it worked well enough without. The margarine worked as bear grease, or any other fat, simply to reduce the brittleness of the resin. The moment the mixture drips from wooden spatula to pot without breaking and forming into globules, but just about flows in a single stream, is when it can be applied. The canoe was out of the water and resting upside-down on the beach. I daubed it over the crack with a split stick and waited for it to dry.

Round the campfire Ben and John had given up thinking of a name for the canoe and had moved on to the strangely fascinating subject of roadkill.

'Found this deer that had just been hit,' said John, 'gutted it and bled it but didn't know where to go from there.'

'You kind of imagine the tyres are really dirty and have spoiled the meat in some way,' said Ben.

'Guess you just have to be hungrier than I was,' said John.

On the third day the wind was just as strong but John had an idea. Ben had been reinforcing our gloom by reading from a guidebook: 'It is felt nowadays very few travellers would paddle against the current of the Peace, which flows with a speed of 8–10km per hour, so for practical purposes this book follows the river downstream.' Ben slammed the book shut. 'You hear that? We are officially impractical.' John wasn't listening: 'You see that island over there? If you look very close to it I think the current doesn't look so strong.'

Briefly the sun was shining and it illuminated, five hundred yards away, the faintest line demarcating fast and slow water, or at least that was what it looked like.

'We can't stay here. We've got to try something,' I said, thinking that if we stayed another day we might as well pack up and go home.

We lifted the boat into the water. Despite John's constant reiteration that bark was tough enough to withstand almost anything you could do to it, we were cautious. The voyageurs never allowed their canoes to touch anything solid, always jumping out before they reached land, never mind getting wet. We did the same, or attempted to. Ever since we had grounded out on the sandbars of the Athabasca, which had worn away some of the pitch off the bottom and caused a small leak, I intended to be more cautious.

We set off paddling at a ferocious rate, one that we knew we couldn't keep up for long. Just as we were tiring we made the island. As John had suggested, the current was slacker here, and since we were a few feet below the bank, the effect of the wind was less too. How long would the protection of the island last? It didn't matter, we were moving at last. *You have to be sly with the river*: Joe Vermilion was right.

A short burst of hard paddling brought us to another low flat island sprouting with willows about five feet high. When this island ended we faced the full might of the wind again and came swiftly across to the right bank, the same side as

Rocky Point but now we were three kilometres further on.

But here we hit the wall again. Even close to the bank the current was too strong for us to paddle, not with the wind against us as well. We tried, but we didn't have the power and I suggested we stop before John let me know I wasn't up to it. We held on to the willows that bent into the water. There wasn't even a space to pull out, as there had been at Rocky Point.

'Shall we drift back to the log pile?' suggested Ben. 'At least we can get a fire going there.'

'Should take about five minutes in this current,' I said, but I knew if we turned back now that would be it.

At the log pile I had been reminded of the four main ways Mackenzie travelled: pole, paddle, sail and cordelle. The cordelle. This was the hundred-foot rope used by the voyageurs for towing, or lining as it is sometimes called, up sections of the river you cannot paddle. Ben and John were doubtful. They had always been doubtful about towing. But it was there, in Mackenzie's journal, every few pages – a reference to towing. And in other books I read, the cordelle was as much a part of the voyageur's life as the paddle, the pole and the sail. Since most recreational paddlers seek relaxation rather than work, and since downstream is mostly the way to go, the tools of canoeing have shrunk to simply the paddle. But before the age of the outboard and the jetboat poling and towing were common.

The cordelle was sometimes attached to a one-shoulder harness, the other end was fixed to either a kind of bridle that went around the bow or simply to the front thwart. With voyageur-style towing, as we were to practise, the steersman remains in position, as does the bowman, so there really is little need to have an elaborate method of fastening the rope to the canoe.

Sceptical Ben and John stayed in the boat as I leaped out, keen to try towing. We had a long heavy rope which absorbed water, but it would do. I took up the slack and heaved. With surprisingly little effort, despite the speed of the river against us, I was able to move forward.

'Even if we have to walk the whole way, we'll do it!' I shouted to the others.

All too soon the clear stretch of bank became overgrown with tree roots. Now I had to dodge up and down, untangling the cordelle as I went. We went slower and slower until we arrived at a fork. The left-hand channel was longer, but the current much reduced because of its longer path. Just when it looked as though we were beaten we were able to paddle again. Slowly we were doing it. *You have to travel the back ways on the river. You have to be sly.* Slowly we were doing it.

Seven

ANTHRAX WITH EVERYTHING

*'They did not, however, seem disposed to confide in
our declarations, and actually threatened that ...
they would discharge their arrows at us.'* Alexander
Mackenzie meets Indians on the Parsnip

I

We passed a white canvas prospector-style tent, off-white, well
used, with a battered stovepipe coming out of one end. On the
gravel beach next to it was an aluminium boat with a small
outboard. An old thin Indian came out of the tent and waved
to us. Then a woman, younger-looking, came out and got in the
boat. The man got in too, pushed off, started the motor and
puttered over to us.

As we talked to him we were drifting back fast, towards par-
tially submerged trees. Around the emerging trunk the current
piled up in a glassy welt. The Indian was called John Buck. On
the knuckles of his right hand he had badly tattooed JOHN. He
was smiling and friendly. He liked our canoe. 'I travel in a canoe
like that when I'm a little kid,' he said. He was sixty-four. 'I'm a
pensioner. Come and go as I like. Get three hundred fifty dollars
a month. How much do you think this boat cost me?'

'Five thousand dollars?'

'Nope.'

'One thousand?'

'Nope.'

'Three hundred and forty-six?'

He grinned. 'One hundred bucks is all. I fixed it up myself.
Got an old engine.'

In the bow he had a shotgun laid out on its case and a couple of dead geese. John, our John, told him about the dog. John Buck nodded gravely. 'I ask everyone I see. You'll get your dog.'

II

For the first time since we had been on the Peace, the wind was behind us. The success with towing had made us adventurous. 'Let's try sailing,' said Ben.

It isn't known if Indians sailed their canoes before contact with Europeans, though they certainly did afterwards, using a Witney blanket slung from a mast set forward. The voyageurs routinely used sails and Mackenzie mentions sailing on the Peace several times. The voyageur sail was made from the oiled-cloth tarpaulin they carried, which also served as a tent and a cover for the furs when it rained. Our equivalent was camouflage nylon. Never mind; we hoisted it, after experimentation, suspended in the V of two whippy willows joined at the base. I held these wedged into a forked stick bound to the front thwart. Ben held two ropes securing the bottom of the sail and John steered using the paddle. With a good wind behind us, a few whitecaps on the wide river, we were soon whipping along. Or so it seemed. Using the GPS to measure our speed, one of the best things it did, we found we were going 4 kmph, but against a current at least as fast that wasn't bad going.

The river looped north, putting the wind in the wrong quarter, and we were back to towing and paddling. I was always keen to tow, Ben and John less so. I had boots made of wetsuit material with a sole that had some grip, whereas John had Velcro-strap sandals and Ben had knackered trainers, neither of which were as good on the mud. The Peace River was famous for its mud. Grey, deep and sticky; we quickly became connoisseurs. Sometimes there were terraces of mud, cut by successive water levels. The edge of the terrace would be harder and support a walking man. Or else there would be a line of flotsam along the mud and for some reason the mud would be most solid here. If the mud was too deep it was back to the canoe to paddle, or, if very desperate, crossing the river to check the other bank. This meant nearly half an hour of paddling, so it wasn't a decision lightly taken.

I actually felt healthier towing, healthier and fitter than I had felt at any time on the voyage so far. There had been, since the very beginning, a suspicion that the water might harbour germs, especially the obnoxious and, on rare occasions, life-threatening giardia bacillus, known in the Canadian north, sometimes with appropriate hilarity, as beaver fever. Information was sketchy, and guidebooks quick to exaggerate the dangers. In most cases giardia results in wind, poor digestion, headaches, diarrhoea and a general increase in lassitude. The cure is a powerful antibiotic that can cause nausea and weakness for several days, as well as weakening the stomach by wiping out all the beneficial bacteria. If one is seriously affected long-term damage to the system can result, but apart from accounts of men whose 'health was broken' the details remain vague. Wind, poor digestion, headaches, diarrhoea and lassitude described our medical condition quite well. Had we contracted the dreaded beaver fever through inept and careless processing of our drinking water? On the second or third day the expensive syringe-type water filter unit I had brought along had become clogged with the fine silt of the Athabasca River. Since then we had survived on water drawn from clear cold creeks draining into the main stream. But these were less common on the Peace, which was far more silty than the Athabasca. The Peace was brown with sediment and your foot would be invisible if you were standing only ankle-deep in the water. As a back-up for the useless syringe I had brought an ex-army Millbank bag, a fabulously simple and hard-wearing piece of kit. I was already learning that kit which has to be used by everyone must be of a different order of strength to kit used by one person only. Almost without exception modern camping and outdoor kit is insufficiently strong for communal use over extended periods: pot handles buckle, stoves clog up, water bottles crack, tent zips spray apart like a set of false teeth set free. Even boots and clothing fall into this category, if, from time to time, they have to be bundled up or transported by anyone other than the owner. It is as if some mysterious lack of care enters all inter-actions with kit that isn't one's own. And I too was guilty: using John's Thermarest mattresss on rocky ground when he wasn't looking, knowing I probably wouldn't be so casual (they are notoriously easy to puncture) if it were my own. But it wasn't.

The Millbank bag was of a different order of durability. It was meant for communal use – a simple, strongly sewn canvas bag with eyelets for suspension above a pot or water bottle. Dirty water went in the top of the bag and clear water dripped ever so slowly out of the bottom. This was the problem. The bag could only filter a few litres at a time, and each one dripped through as slowly as the worst kind of Chinese water torture. Ben grew impatient and started slurping from the river, sediment and all. We started to brew up using untreated water, and cook with it too, despite knowing that boiling will not kill all bacteria if there is floating matter in the water used.

The strange thing is, you know all this, but day by day you take such information less and less seriously. We were in and out of the river all the time. What's more it was a big, big river containing lots of water. It must be clean, apart from the silt of course, which I could feel accumulating inside me with every bowl of pasta or rice we ate. Sediment strips out flavour. You need twice as much coffee, four times as much salt, to get any kind of taste from sedimented food and drink, and even then it is always there, the gritty sludge under one's tongue, the faintly aluminiumish taste that everything has. The way everything eaten and drunk tastes more the same than different. No wonder our food supply was lasting so well; we were all reluctant to eat except when starving.

But towing straightened me out. Sitting hunched over my paddle hour after hour I found to be unnatural. There was something of wheelchair athletics about exerting your upper body to exploding point whilst your legs and toes remained as immobile as the bound feet of a Chinese princess. I felt it was doing something to me internally, upsetting some kind of equi-librium of the organs, which walking, honest and upright and sanctioned by evolution, did not.

Ben and John did not agree. Towing brought out the worst in them. It was too obviously masochistic and too obviously not the sort of thing one did on holiday. For the first time Ben made comments: 'This isn't exactly what I had in mind.' Even John, who was usually so uncomplaining, said, 'I wouldn't normally choose such a river to make a trip.' But the more they slacked at the cordelle the more I felt driven forward. Every step was a step nearer our goal, which was becoming more and more modest as the days wore on. At first I had hoped to emulate Mackenzie and make it to Peace River town. Now I saw that was impossible, and that even making it to Fort Vermilion seemed unlikely. We started talking about a remote native settlement called Garden Creek.

It took a while to work out what system of towing worked best: tied to the thwart, or held by the bowman, who could then flip it up when bushes and trees threatened to snag the line. On shore it was the snags that caused most of the delays. Walking through willows I experimented with keeping the rope high using a forked stick, but inevitably there were times when the rope got stuck and the canoe was pulled back on itself. On paper towing looked faster than any kind of paddling. The bow wave one could raise was impressive. The towing man usually walked faster than average walking speed, so theoretically one could do five kilometres per hour. But all the setting up of a tow, all the snags and the delays going around tree stumps and beaver lodges, meant that towing was really very slow. John and Ben were always keen to point out the inefficiency of towing. I responded that it was all we had. They they would be silent and I wondered how long they would put up with the self-inflicted torture of slithering up and down mud- and root-infested banks.

III

Long ago there had been a grocery store at Carlson's Landing but now the place was deserted, just an old logging road connecting the high bluff to the nearest town, Fort Smith, 250 km away in the Northern Territories.

It was supposed to be deserted but high on the bluff above the river there were five spacemen holding an American football. They watched with incurious passivity as we manhandled the canoe on to the beach and scrambled up the steep muddy path, up the cliff, through wet mosquito-laden vegetation, to the top.

On a grassy expanse, just hidden from view from below, was an entire encampment of wall tents with sealed doors, big black four-wheel-drives with blacked-out windows, big official-looking trailers with pull-out sections, and the five spacemen, who did not take their helmets off, though they did stop their lackadaisical passing of the football. They were all in full white bug suits, of a kind I had never seen before, like fencing suits with a mesh strip down each side of the body and a mesh visor over the face. In a sawn-off oildrum they had a great fire going fed by huge split logs. Behind them was a thing that looked like a cross between a barbecue and an air compressor, and behind that was a temporary electric fence. All the tents were inside the fence. Two of the men held cans of Budweiser in their hands. They were not friendly, only grunting when we said hello.

Ben was persistent. Apart from John Buck, these were the first people we had seen for days. 'How ya doin'? What ya doin'? How long you been here?' He tried hard, but all he got was that they were 'studying the bison'. 'What kind of bison? The wood buffalo or the plains buffalo?' Ben had been doing his research. There were both kinds in the park. The men studying the bison didn't seem to know which.

Now it was John's turn to break the ice: 'What the hell is that?' he asked. It was their anti-mosquito machine. 'Just sucks 'em up and then we empty 'em out.' The machine had a see-through cylinder half full of blackness. 'That's about four days' worth,' said one of the besuited men from behind his mesh. He undid the cylinder, which was about the size of a large mineral-water bottle, and tipped the contents on the fire. 'Smell that, will 'ya?' The million roasting mosquitoes smelled just like burnt hair.

Then a new man, a young chap, smiling, slightly podgy with

an open face and no bug suit came over. He was Canadian, an academic, his name Bill. All the others were American military, doing research into anthrax. Anthrax was endemic in the bison population, but usually in very low concentrations, and only a few of the weaker bison were affected. The men stood by as this was explained, looking smug. The withholding of information had been pointless.

Then a big grey-moustached man came out of one of the trailers. 'What we got here?' he asked.

'Some recreationists,' said one of the men, with the kind of disdain one reserves for talking about sex offenders or people who vandalize fire extinguishers. The great divide between us, the one they wanted to enforce, came out in that single sneering reference: recreationists. People not on a mission. People not backed by the military or big business. We had grown used to the attention our home-made boat garnered, but now, despite our best salesmanship, all we got was a stiff step or two towards the cliff-edge to peer down on our upturned boat. Recreationists. I fumed at some perceived injustice. I wanted to say, 'We were here first,' except we weren't. Only our boat, as a generic, had been here first, and that I felt vouchsafed us. Perhaps I could turn the word around, make the sneer a badge of honour: a recreationist recreates something. We were recreating a voyage that took place hundreds of years ago. The men had turned away. They had no more beer, or steaks. Ran out yesterday. Another smug look. They were packing up, ready to leave after two weeks in the bush. Couldn't wait to get to Fort Smith and check out the pussy. 'Man, we're missing the women out here,' said one, a lardarse with a goatee beard.

We returned to the boat to get our tents and sleeping bags.

'Two weeks, all the beer and steak they can eat and still they're whining!' said Ben.

'Bunch of wusses,' said John.

'Do you know what I really hated?'

'I know – being called a recreationist.'

'Bastards. Do you think they'll let us camp inside their electric fence?'

'No. But let's ask.'

Bill asked for us but the captain with the grey moustache announced with full pomposity, 'I'm afraid not, we have a lot of sensitive equipment in here.'

'Can we at least put our food bag inside, so it doesn't attract the bears?'

I sensed a flicker of concern across the captain's well-padded granite jaw. 'That shouldn't be a problem.'

There were others in the area who were more welcoming. A park helicopter pilot who dropped in to keep them resupplied agreed to fly back up the river looking for Sota as he went. 'This bird'll go real low, I'll see that dog if he's out there.' He let John use his sat phone to call Nat, to let her know about Sota, but she wasn't in.

Bill, who was from Yellowknife and used to bugs and the outdoors, said the military guys had just come from Florida, testing all the letters in the recent anthrax scare. Yes, that was the source of the smugness – knowing they were part of some ongoing news story.

We shared some gritty stew with Bill and watched the sun set over the electric fence. The anthrax men turned in early, locking their tent doors behind them.

IV

We were making slow progress. What with the increasingly late starts, the long rest stops brewing silt-laden tea, hours spent preparing tasteless lunches, the early finishes because 'we may not see another campsite for a while', we were lucky to be making twelve kilometres in a day. All of us were suffering from vague stomach ailments, Ben more badly than John and me. We were losing our momentum.

It was raining again, but the wind was up, a very strong breeze from the east, a tailwind to take us on our way. We set the sail and were off. From being downcast we were all laughing and optimistic again, but it was a strong rough breeze, cutting up the opaque grey water, creating troughs and furrows and biting watery chunks out of the current and leaving spray over all of us, making Ben laugh the louder but plunging me unwittingly into the role of 'the one who is worried'. Just as there is the one who pays the bills, there is also the one who worries. It was my boat and my idea, even if it was our expedition. I was the one who worried. Now I was worried lest we should (a) capsize without any of the gear tied in or (b) fail to find a campsite, our usual excuse for packing up, but now, it seemed, a real concern. Strange though it may seem, the wilderness is not one great camping site. Mostly it is devoid of places clear enough to put up even the smallest tent. The more remote a place, the less space there seems to be for man and the more space for nature's excesses – dead trees, mudslides, blocked channels, undergrowth so dense it disguises the relief of the ground from which it springs.

The Peace River, in this section, was without any kind of beach. Mostly there was only the inverse of a beach, an undercut of dangling root ends and the gurgling rushing water beneath. At six-thirty we passed a mud island, about three feet above the stream. 'Let's camp there,' I said.

'We don't want to waste this wind,' said Ben.

'I have to agree with Ben,' said John, who by steering achieved the moral effect of leadership, even if he mostly disdained this role.

'OK,' I said.

In truth I was feeling cold to the bone, wet through and miserable, holding on to the damn mast with hands red and smarting from the cold wet upon them. Stopping for a campsite was an excuse, but it turned out to be a prescient one.

By seven-thirty we were all feeling the cold and not reluctant to admit it. Now every bit of bank was scanned for flat ground, however small, lumpy or wet-looking. It was all too clear to me that if we carried on much longer it would not only be windy and raining but also dark, and we'd still have nowhere to camp and no way of warming up.

The undercut beach for a moment looked promising. There

was only about three feet of beach before the wall of roots, but up above, just before the treeline, was a hummock of weeds. With gardening it would serve as a campsite.

All of us were shivering when we landed. There was no plan. We all started to make the fire at once. But it was raining and all the wood was wet. I rigged up the tarpaulin while Ben tried to split logs with his knife. Everything had that dank slimy wetness that wood achieves after hours and hours in the rain. We had no birchbark, except the roll we had in the boat for repairs, which of course we forgot about.

When I tried to do up my coat I couldn't grasp the zip. My finger and thumb just wouldn't work together – an early indicator of hypothermia. Our thinking was confused. We were all making mistakes. John crouched by the firesticks Ben had made striking match after match. Then Ben remembered his candle lanterns. He took out a candle and stood it under the damp firestick. John crouched down with his backside in the air protecting the fragile flame. But smoke begat smoke and at last the fire was burning. It seemed like a miracle. We all stood and just stared. Then we made tea and I was able to reflect – the worst part about losing your perspective is that you don't realize it at the time. At the time you think you're battling the odds and doing not too badly.

With the fire crackling we all stripped off our wet clothes, something we should have done earlier. I noticed for the first time that John had a tattoo, a maple leaf on his stomach with MADE IN CANADA underneath it. It was slightly off-centre and one sensed a lot of thought had gone into its exact position. I asked John about it but he wasn't very forthcoming: 'I'm more into the Palestinian side of my background right now,' he said.

In dry clothes, sitting around the fire, out of the rain and under my cunningly contrived tarpaulin, which leaked, but not on me, I thought the shared aversion of disaster would bring us closer together, but John seemed distracted. He said, 'I really think I was losing it back there.'

Ben and I tried to entertain John with funny stories about our time in Japan but he wasn't interested. He even moved back away from the circle of the fire as if indicating his lack of involvement. Out of politeness we started talking about things we had in common and he shuffled back in close again. He didn't want a last cup of tea before bed. He put his hand over the top of his mug and said, 'You know Rob, this isn't fun any more.'

After he'd gone to bed Ben said, 'He's missing Sota, that's what it is.'

V

Another day, another campsite: in front of a lake-like inlet, good for swimming but with little firewood and the fire keeps going out, never catches hold. John says again, contemplating the charred sardine bannock in his hand: 'It isn't fun.' Earlier that day Ben had let slip, 'I'm not into this slogging-up-a-jungle lark.' I crawled into the tent and scribbled in my diary: 'I know it isn't just the relentless toil, though that plays its part. It's the fact that as a threesome we're operating at sub-optimum. As a group our setting is to be carefree and relaxed, kind of talking and reading the papers over a fine brunch, leaving when we want to, but staying because we enjoy each other's company. Our setting is primarily urban and "adult", i.e. circumscribed and passionless. There is nothing mad about our best setting, and the situation we find ourselves in day after day is a little mad, certainly more than a little strange. My only solace is the medieval self-punishment of towing, putting the rope over my shoulder and twisting my body into the strain, getting the boat going, feeling the stretch of the nylon rope and then as the canoe moves I move. One foot after another, sometimes slurping through mud, sometimes picking my way finely through a root-field. "You're really enjoying this, aren't you?" says Ben as the boat coasts near the bank. I say nothing and grin to myself. When it's Ben's turn he tows with the careful savouring of each fall and scratch necessary to appear in a favourite role: put-upon martyr. John, too, by insisting on towing in bare feet ("I want to toughen them up this summer"), makes life hard for himself, and his distaste for the job is apparent in his hesitation before a big rooty stump to be surmounted, or a patch of skiddy bank to be raced up or risk losing his footing. I keenly do more than my fair share and finish today by doing a running tow; knowing that the tow will soon end I can really put everything into it.'

The following evening, by the light of my head-torch, I was back at my diary, the other two already asleep. 'We often discuss how we'll do things next year, what we've learned and what equipment we'll need. John shocks me tonight by saying, for the first time, "I'm not sure that I'll be coming next year. Nat and I plan to have a child pretty soon and I am not sure at all if I will have the time."

'Strangely, I knew he was going to say it. In fact, in retrospect I feel I kept bringing up the subject of "next year" as a kind of taunt, like a child continually misbehaving, wanting his father to finally crack and give him a well-deserved slap.'

And it felt like a slap. I wondered what I had done wrong, how I could have made it better? Ben, at the time, was deeply immersed in his bird-identification book, but I wondered if he thought the same way.

VI

Raining again. Rain making holes in the river's surface, each hole a dent and at the same time a splash upwards. We are paddling in waterproofs that are wet inside and out, perhaps from a leak, perhaps from condensation, it is hard to tell. No one has spoken for ages.

No one says anything as a small purple jetboat approaches. Despite the name, it looks just like an ordinary boat. It is the propulsion unit which is different, churning a jet of water out the back, allowing the boat entry to places that would rip the propeller off an ordinary boat. It was a homely-looking boat with a windscreen and a canvas cover with flexible plastic windows. Two windscreen wipers going furiously added to its domestic quality.

On a river a mile wide there's a point when it becomes obvious that a boat is heading your way. The small purple boat was heading our way. As it got nearer they cut the engine and drifted down towards us. You could tell there were a lot of people inside, moving about in the cramped space – the plastic windows were steamed up. A glass section in the middle of the windscreen became a door and was flung open. A head popped out, a dog's head, or so I thought, but it was too quick for me to be sure; who, or whatever it was, sensed the rain or didn't like what he saw and went back in, barging into the crowded interior of the boat.

Then Joe Vermilion appeared and climbed through the door-window. He grinned. 'They all think you're dead back in Fort Chip.' He turned, pulled Sota out by the collar. 'We been feeding him chocolate,' he said, 'make him want to stay. He's a fine dog – you sure you want him back?'

Joe had plenty of news. The dog had been found three days ago, wandering around, by George Wandering Spirit at his dog camp. Sota was so freaked he wouldn't approach. George had to lasso him. George couldn't read so he sent Sota back to Fort Chipewyan so that someone could read his tag. In town Joe Vermilion recognized the dog, but not before a message had been left for Nat, suggesting that the dog was the only survivor of some disaster in the wilderness that had killed the rest of us. Joe laughed when he told it, but when we got back from the trip we discovered that for a day or two we were missing presumed lost or dead. 'I'll let them know you're still alive,' joked Joe.

Sota was back again. Everyone was joyful. The rain did not matter. When we saw beavers Sota did not jump overboard. When he was running along the bank it only took an odd rustling to send him scurrying back to the canoe. He had had a nasty experience and lost his taste for adventure. And so it seemed, had we.

The thrill of getting Sota back quickly palled. He couldn't help with the towing. In fact he was more of a passenger now, especially with his newly acquired bear-fear. Our progress slowed to less than a walking pace as we zigzagged back and forth across the river looking for decent beaches to tow off and slow water for paddling.

Outside Peace Point, an Indian reserve with cabins and people and even a coin-operated phone attached to a radio mast, we held a council of war.

'I say we go on,' said John, surprising me.

'What do you think, Ben?'

'I think ...,' began Ben, who was balancing a flimsy water bottle under the dribbling Millbank bag. It fell over and the precious liquid made a puddle in the mud. He looked up with a pained expression. 'I think we went off half-cocked,' he said.

I grew defensive. 'What do you mean?'

'I mean we started too late, with the wrong food and no appreciation of the water problem.'

'Does that mean you want to pack it in?'

He shrugged. 'No it doesn't, actually. I think we should go as far as we can, the absolute furthest possible.'

'I agree,' said John, ruffling Sota's ears as he lapped at the spilt water.

'The only problem is: where do we stash the canoe until next year, when we—'

'When you,' said Ben.

'When I come back and carry on.'

If we could get a lift to Fort Smith, we could perhaps leave the canoe with someone in town.

I found it incredible when I remembered my first itinerary. In my naïvety I had thought I might make Mackenzie, a logging town on the Williston Lake. Because of general slow progress, of going down the Athabasca, spending time in Fort Chipewyan and on the Quatre Fourches, we were far behind even my most pessimistic projection, which was Fort Vermilion. So far the trip had, from the point of view of emulating the voyageurs' achievements, been a catastrophic failure. Mackenzie had zipped along to Peace Point in four days! We had taken three weeks. Sometimes he made forty or fifty kilometres in a day – we took a week to do that. Just as a clock without oil will eventually grind to a halt through sheer friction, so too were we. Slower and slower, losing impetus all the time. I had thought that my bad feeling came from losing the dog, but it remained even when Sota was back. Then I thought I was agitated because of the slow progress. But that wasn't it exactly. I just didn't know.

At that moment the thousand miles of river ahead was like a huge raincloud, black, impenetrable and impossible to ignore.

And sitting there, black to the knees with mud, swatting away mosquitoes with an automatic hand, I knew I had to make a decision, even if it was the wrong one.

'It's over, lads.'

Eight

THE FOURTH MAN

*'I stated to the Chief that, as the canoe was intended
for a voyage of such consequence, no women could
be permitted to embark in it.'* Alexander Mackenzie
turns down hitchhikers

I

It was something I couldn't explain. There was nothing logical
about it. The wilderness and the river and the trip had got to
me. I was freaking out, like Sota, spooked and, when the others
didn't react as I'd expected, when they'd bitten the bullet and
said they'd continue, something collapsed inside me. It was all
that unknown in front of me. The Boyer Rapids, supposedly 'not
a big problem', but how did I know? I was a married man, I had
responsibilities, I just didn't know. I hid this unknowing in
discussions about the boat, where we should leave it, talk about
the route and the food supply. I mean, we had to stop somewhere, right? Nothing was really wrong, except everything was.
We weren't doing it in the right way. I had a bad feeling about
going on. We'd been lucky with the dog; we shouldn't push our
luck. There were a thousand reasons and there were none. In
the dream, in the beginning, I had been on calm water, clear
water, at home, ready for anything. I needed to get that feeling
back, the feeling that you were ready for anything. And we had
to stop somewhere – winter was maybe a month away, so why
not now? I needed to feel ... Ah, the agonies I went through
when really it was quite simple. We had to stop somewhere, so
why not now? Come back with a clear objective, a goal, a name

103

on the map that was set from the start. That was it. That was the nub of it. That was the real problem, the mistake: I'd started without a real goal in mind. If you just say we'll go as far as we can then the reasons to stop, however trivial, just keep piling up. And pretty soon, out there in the wilderness with the smoke in your eyes and the bugs and the emptiness of it all, your will just starts dribbling away. I knew this much about myself and about Mackenzie – you needed to be obsessed to make this trip. Only obsession would carry you through. And obsession needs a goal, a finishing point, a place where you can open the bottle of champagne. And if I came back that's what I'd need.

II

At Peace Point, high on the bluff, we saw a white man with a ginger moustache looking down on our painstakingly slow arrival. We were all surprised, he and us. His truck was on the path leading down to the river. The beach was rocky, with old blue ropes caught between rocks and disappearing into the sand, a child's tricycle minus its front wheel, pieces of driftwood with damp undersides dusted with sand. The truck was a Ford 350, dual back axle, with a water tank fixed to the flatbed with nylon cargo straps. The water tank was as big as a section of six-foot pipe. It was plastic, the kind you can see the water level through, a very tough kind of plastic with a drain tap at the back. The man with the moustache had opened the drain tap and all the water was running away, pouring down the track. We could see the water like a stream feeding the river as we paddled the last lap, the last bit of the journey – we still had pride about being seen towing our boat like donkeys. The water was flowing down the track and the man, who had glasses, watched it, smoking. He watched as we pulled our boat up.

'You guys need any fresh water?' he asked.

His name was Charlie, he brought fresh water to the reserve, he had the contract to do it. He was married to a woman on the reserve and he was the only white guy living there. At day's end he always ran the unwanted water away. 'Otherwise it'll go bad inside the tank,' he explained.

We drank as much as we could. It was such a waste, after all our efforts to dribble water through the Millbank bag, to see all this fresh clean water just running away. Drinking the fresh water I thought of all that silt I'd ingested. I felt queasy just thinking about it. Hopefully I could flush it all out.

The people on the reserve didn't drink the river water. There were pulp mills further upstream, more than seven hundred kilometres upstream, and this made them nervous. They must have once drunk the water but not now. This was the first time we heard the river was polluted, or rather that government officials thought the river was polluted. The officials wanted people to live on the reserve. But then they told them the river wasn't safe to drink. I think this was different from making the river not safe to drink, which no one knew for sure anyway. Not for sure.

The fact that a thousand-mile-long, mile-wide river, with only two small towns, some farmland and a pulp factory on it, could be considered undrinkable was deeply strange. Made me want to attack the folly of the industrial world. The two sides of it: the crapping in one's own water and the fear of drinking something that has not been chlorinated. The officials paid Charlie good money to haul water to a place which bordered a mile-wide river, and then because there were fewer and fewer people living at the reserve there was always water left over, so this water was run off. We watched that water, gallons and gallons of it, just running away.

Is this a temporary situation? Will the river ever be clean again? Will people return to the river? They have left the river and one reason they have left must be because they have been told they are living next to something poisonous, instead of the water of life it used to be. Peace Point was a beautiful spot but all that water running away was just plain weird, and slightly creepy too in the way industrial wasteland can be creepy. Even an animal knows better than to spoil its own place. It seemed to me then that any anger the Indians had against the white man's way of doing things was legitimate anger.

Charlie was cautious at first. He offered around cigarettes. We were like the Indians, being placated, arriving in our war canoe. He invited us after a while up to his cabin, one amongst about ten at Peace Point. He served us coffee after a conversation of silences and wry comments where all of us were being cautious. I wanted to find out if we could get our canoe to Fort Smith, but I didn't want to sound desperate. Desperation would double the truck cost.

III

Mackenzie, after going wrong and taking the Mackenzie River to the Arctic rather than the Pacific as he'd hoped, returned home to England for a year to learn navigation. This was an act of penance, I'm sure. He must have gone out on a limb with promises and guarantees and when he arrived at the Arctic and didn't know exactly where he was – not that 'exactly' really mattered – that was the final straw. He sought to remedy it by a bold external action – go to England, prove how much you care about your exploring, prove that you're worthy of being given a second try. He could have gone to Nantucket or Newfoundland and learned more than enough about navigation from an old salt in a sailors' rest home. The books and the instruments he bought he could have ordered and waited for in Montreal. No, the visit was a penance, and when he returned he decorated himself with his instruments as a kind of juju against navigational disaster and as a warning to his men that he knew where he was going. I had already apprehended that the leader – not that we had a leader, not really – was the one who knew where the expedition was, and where it was going, and how it would get there. He needed good eyesight to be able to discern the obstacles ahead. He needed maps and instruments to find his way, but he also needed them, I now knew, to ward off others from wresting his command away from him.

Not that losing one's command to a better man is such a bad thing; it honestly seemed to me that John, with his greater experience and skill at canoeing, made better decisions about the way to proceed upriver. But not all his decisions were good, and it seems the main problem is that people can't agree to switch leaders whenever it seems appropriate. I began to think that maybe the naval tradition was correct – there can only ever be one leader, one captain, one man calling the shots. I suspected this, even though I resisted the implications, namely telling people what to do and saying, in effect, 'I know better than you.' I'd always hated other people using rank and credentials to cover up their lack of knowledge and yet, from time to time, I found myself doing exactly that. If I disagreed with John my instruments guaranteed me, my map and my pocket GPS, a lovely yellow thing about the size of an unfashionable mobile phone, with a nicely engineered ring-turn device for keeping the waterproof back on and squidgy buttons that operated through the rubber coating, the whole thing serviceable and kept on the end of a lanyard in my breast pocket ready for use at any time but also on display, the lanyard like the yellow pistol cord on a dress uniform, there for the same purpose. It didn't matter that it was Ben who actually read the manual and worked out how to use the thing; now I carried it everywhere, like Piggy's spectacles, and it conveyed my authority.

In fact, on a river a GPS has little function except to let you know how far you've come, and, when racing, how fast you're going. Its real function is to make you, the user, the final arbiter in any disputes about exactly where you are. This is what Mackenzie realized. He could never be subject to the opinions of others; he would know where he was.

I had other instruments of leadership too. The maps, of course, which I kept in a special waterproof case, a kind of supertough zip-lock which gave me great pleasure to smooth shut and airtight with a sweep of my finger and thumb. But compared to Mackenzie, who had sextant, telescope, chronometer, barometer and thermometer, I was poorly equipped. Next time I would carry more. Only dimly was I grasping the connections between our poor progress, leadership, the instruments and other things, things that would have to change. I would have to perform my own penance, return to England, learn from our mistakes; my mistakes.

IV

Charlie's wife was Cynthia. She was half Cree, half Eskimo. Until this time I had been extremely assiduous in calling all Eskimos Inuit. But Cynthia, who was so open and so full of an incredibly infectious energy that made everything fun, told me she had always referred to her father and his people as Eskimos and she didn't see why I shouldn't too. She and Charlie played cribbage in the mornings. She had two kids by a former marriage and so did Charlie. Only one of each was around and they got on well enough, Alison and Nelson, she slim and ultra-white, he a brown teddy bear with a slight Far Eastern fold to his eyes. Charlie swore in front of his kids and told dirty stories which I'm sure Nelson, with his laughter a few moments after ours, looking around and checking our faces, couldn't understand, but I could tell that was Charlie's way of not being a hypocrite. Alison was eighteen and tiny and had a cat tattooed on her lower back, visible since her midriff was bare. She had a Leatherman at her waist and showed us soapstone she had carved. There was lots of this angular hard/soft material on the beach, like half-melted mini-icebergs. It had long been valued by Indians for making lamps and cooking utensils. 'I love it out here,' said Alison. She liked to walk alone in the bush toting her Leatherman and a 4/10 shotgun loaded with a single slug. 'It'll stop a bear,' said Charlie laconically. He showed us his other guns, a .22 repeater and an army issue .303.

Charlie and Cynthia chain-smoked; his were from a green packet and hers from a red one. Cynthia busied herself reading the tiny print on one side, the front of the packet depicting the horrors of a pair of charred lungs after a lifetime of inhaling. 'Hey!' she shouted with glee, 'my cigarettes got more tar than yours!'

Peace Point was named after the historic peace treaty agreed there between the Beaver and the invading Cree Indians. The place gave the name Unjigah, 'peace', to the whole river. In Mackenzie's time it was considered to flow from the heart of the Rockies, though these higher arms are now thought of as tributaries. Any ambition to continue up river wilted at the strange beauty of the place. Opposite us an exposed stretch of sedimentary rock was buckled into a cathedral arch; further up, a few kilometres or so, an island sat midstream, giving the river perspective and interest. John said he'd always wanted to eat moose and never had. Charlie took an ordinary woodsaw and cut off some pieces of moosemeat that his neighbour Gabe stored in his freezer. We cooked it up with wild chive and it was delicious. The next day Cynthia told us she'd had a dream in which she and Charlie had collected three sheds' worth of logs. 'Maybe that means it's going to be a hard winter,' said Charlie. He'd gone native all right and why not? Better than wading through river water with a sick stomach. Let's eat moosemeat and hang out.

We made a day trip to the island. As we sat on the beach picking up soapstone a familiar boat pulled in – it was Joe Vermilion, just back from his cabin. Off the bow of his boat, jumping with skill and care, was sixty-four-year-old John Buck, along for the ride. He wore rubber spats over his moccasins and didn't get a drop of water on his feet as he leaped for the bank. Then he headed for the smoke of our fire. Despite a supreme ability to keep himself comfortable in the bush he did it with such ease, unnoticed unless you were concentrating, that it did not amount to anything like the prissiness of Western people concerned to keep warm and dry at a campsite. John Buck greeted us and said, 'Know what this place used to be called? Drum Island. Because there used to be ghosts here beating drums at night – many moons ago.' He grinned. 'That's Indian talk,' he said.

John Buck said he would love to come with us on our trip, but I doubted if he would want to be too far from home. He told us that just beyond Drum Island there was a good spot for catching young geese. You just grabbed them from the water before they could fly.

Joe was surprised we hadn't made it further than Peace Point. Was there even a hint of reproach in his voice? 'We'll be back next year,' I kept repeating, but no one seemed to really believe me. When Joe left, John Buck pushed the boat off and leaped again, the most agile pensioner I'd seen, and sat like a schoolboy on the bow, contented, his legs dangling down, an intent interest in everything, a kind of interest you see on the alert faces of people who have never been to school and never learned how to be 'serious'. They are the one true element in Rousseau's fantasy, knowing all they know from living out of doors, far from cities and the places where a man doesn't know his neighbour. I'd seen the same look on tribesmen from remote places in Indonesia and Burma. It may be unsustainable, or dying out, or sheer romanticism to see it this way, but I cleave to such people as beacons of vitality in a world which so successfully undermines them.

Cynthia agreed to take us to her uncle's old cabin across the river. We emptied the canoe and at that moment another canoe, a sixteen-foot plastic one, green, came alongside the beach. A tall blond young male in big boots and stocking-foot waders, which, in combination with the heavy calf-length hunting boots, looked positively sweltering-looking, called a cautious greeting in reply to our enthusiastic hellos. His name was Harvald and he was a Norwegian, in the merchant marine, just as Amundsen had been, a first mate on a tanker. He was paddling down the Peace from Fort Vermilion and then down the Slave to Fort Smith. The Peace had not been his first choice: he would have preferred the Nahani, with a friend, but the friend backed out so he was spending a solitary three weeks going with the current we had been against.

'Meet anyone interesting?' I asked.

'No. You are the first people I have talked to in two weeks.'

He had blue eyes, alive to irony, used to teasing others in a slow, straightforward fashion. When he saw my plastic-handled knife he laughed in a mocking way. His own was finely wrought from reindeer antler and Swedish high-carbon steel.

But he had seen no one?

'No,' he corrected me, 'I saw some people, at Garden Creek I think it is called. But I am on the other side of the river so I do not cross. One man waved.'

'Did you wave back?'

'There was no point, I was too far away.'

'But how did you know the man was waving?'

'I saw him through my binocular.'

'Oh.'

'How long had you been on the river before you saw the man at Garden Creek?'

'One week. I think it was just before Garden Creek, at Fifth Meridian.'

I found it hard to imagine not wanting to make contact with another human after a week alone. I had done solitary long-distance hiking and after three days I was always ready for company, however lacklustre. Tanker mates were made of sterner stuff. With an ironic grin Harvald flashed open his fisherman's-type waistcoat and showed us a cartridge belt, but instead of brass shells it contained red plastic cases of bear bangers, mini-thunderflashes you fired from a metal pen-like device. He also had a big can of mace on his belt and two bear bells, like the bell on a cat's collar, tied to his rucksack. He comprehended our bearhorn almost before we showed it him and, comprehending it, showed no more interest.

He agreed to come with us across the river in our empty canoe, in which he showed a sceptical enthusiasm. Four of us paddled, Cynthia, Alison and Nelson trailing their hands in the water and telling jokes. Even loaded with seven people the boat was more than high enough in the water. I remembered an old print I'd seen of thirteen Indians in a sixteen-foot canoe; canoes take people better than they take gear, it seems.

And we went fast, crossing in about fifteen minutes. On the way back we got it down to ten. The river was wide, over a kilometre, but we were flying, slicing through the big current midstream and holding our course. Mackenzie had six paddlers. That was the key, the secret weapon, it had to be. I stored the knowledge away for future use.

At the old cabin we poked around looking at musk-rat traps wrapped in old newspapers, watching out for the holes in the floor. Outside in the humid sunshine Cynthia picked everyone a handful of saskatoon berries. 'Bears love them,' she grinned.

It was late afternoon. I thought Harvald would at least want to camp with us. He was our first fellow 'recreationist', we were his first fellow humans.

'We've got some whisky,' I said.

'So do I,' came back the straightforward reply. It was as if we were in some sort of competition, but Harvald had it wrong, we wanted to share, not triumph over him.

'Well, I must make it to Sweetgrass Landing by this evening,' he said.

'You're kidding?' Sweetgrass Landing was an old deserted logging camp and two hours' paddling away even with the current. He preferred slog and loneliness to whisky and a campfire.

'It is my programme,' he said.

'Bye then.'

'Goodbye.'

He lumbered down to the beach in his hot waders and set off, sitting in the rear seat of his canoe, which lifted up like a drag racer and kept catching in the wind, which was against him. He must have felt our eyes on him from the bluff, where we watched him, because he didn't look back, just struggled on.

'Nasty going into that wind,' said John.

'His boat's too high at the front,' said Ben. 'It's catching the wind.'

'He should have reversed his canoe and sat on the front seat backwards, it's further towards the centre,' I said. It was something the puntmaster back in Oxford had taught me.

'Either that or kneel,' said John.

'Probably can't kneel in those whacking great boots,' said Ben.

But Harvald was in such a hurry we didn't have a chance to tell him.

Cynthia and Charlie wanted to turn Peace Point into an up-market holiday destination. We agreed to help them and spread the word. I wrote a couple of letters, which they assured me would assist their case. In return for this and money for petrol, Cynthia agreed to take the canoe and us the 120 kilometres up to Fort Smith.

We drove there along a dirt road crowded with bison. In Fort Smith, a small northern encampment of a town, a town built for winter not summer, we were interviewed for the radio and Don True, the husband of the interviewer, agreed to store our canoe over winter. He worked for the park's fire department and had a big shed full of concrete blocks and lumber with plenty of space to store the boat in. The canoe, still unnamed, seemed heavier than at the beginning and there was a coating of fine grey mud inside the bottom. It made her look old and used-up. I took a long time settling the boat in the metal shed. It was hard to say goodbye. Good old boat. Good old nameless canoe. 'We won't go in here till May,' said Don. So that was it. Goodbye old boat until next May.

We ate a quick snack at the Ha-Ha Sushi Express, 'No Credit Cards Used Here Yet', and went to celebrate. We passed through several bars, some full and some empty except for drunk Indians sitting in the light cast by the cigarette machine and the bulb over the pool table.

In one bar, a dark-haired metis woman of about fifty-five, whom we had seen earlier when unloading the canoe in the Pelican Inn car park, came over and told us her great-great-great-grandmother had a daughter by Mackenzie whom he wouldn't acknowledge.

Mackenzie probably had several such children. He certainly provided for an Indian wife and children after he left Canada for England in 1799. 'I requested of you at parting,' he wrote to his cousin Roderick, who remained in Canada, 'to send fifty pounds to Mrs Mackenzie of Three Rivers on my account ... to continue as long as Kitty remains single.' Kitty was also known as 'the Catt' and is recorded as dying in 1804 in the *Fort Chipewyan Journal*. Andrew Mackenzie of Fort Vermilion, the metis son of Alexander, died in 1809. When he settled in Scotland at forty-eight, Mackenzie's first official wife was just fourteen years old.

For some reason we got on to a discussion of smoking versus salting fish with Betty, Mackenzie's distant relative. In his time the Chipewyan had been great fish eaters. She said the further north you go the more you have to smoke fish because of the humidity. She said that even when you dry a fish in the sun you should keep a smudge fire going to keep the flies off and the 'air dry'.

When Betty left, two big Indians, one with thick glasses, one as huge as a heavyweight boxer, crammed into the small, ornamentally carved seats and tried to get beers off us. John politely enquired if they preferred to salt or smoke their fish. The hugest one blinked with incomprehension. 'Ain't you never seen fuckin' Indians before?' he asked. When they left he patted my head, as if to say, 'Don't worry, I won't hurt you.'

Two more men, perhaps metis, perhaps Indian, came over and warned us not to have anything to do with the two who had just left. And certainly not to buy them drinks. The one with thick glasses was the nephew of a man called Phil Norwegian, a very helpful elderly man who looked after all our gear while we were walking around. In a small community there's no room to separate the good and bad into us and them; good and bad crop up and you are connected to them, like it or not.

A blond-haired blue-eyed metis who was drunk sat down at our table and turned to John and apropos of nothing demanded, 'Why are you so bald?'

With admirable composure John replied, 'Because I'm a Palestinian.'

The drunk metis had a German dad, who had died last year. 'My best friend, my best fucking friend,' he said. 'I never go a day without thinking about him.' The drunk metis was called Alden and everyone knew him. 'I'm a flunky,' he said with pride, 'in my father's company. Selling real estate.' Then he crouched in his chair and looked conspiratorial. 'You want to meet some sluts? Fort Smith sluts?' He offered us one of his empty buildings to crash in. 'Stay for a party,' he said, then bought us a round of whiskies. When he heard about our journey against the current he said, 'You guys are fuckin' incredible. I been out, shot my moose et cetera, but nothing what you guys have done. Hey, Tiger! Show us your tits!' He waved a metis woman approaching sixty over to us. She was smiling and drunk and when she got to our table she lifted up her blouse and flashed her tits at us, then burst out giggling. 'Didn't think she'd do that, did you?' smirked Alden. 'Go on, Tiger, flash 'em again.' But Tiger simply grinned. 'Oh, there's sluts in this town,' said Alden, 'sluts aplenty. It's a dirty little town all right. Not her! I mean young sluts.'

But we had to leave early for an early bus so we passed on the offer of young sluts.

The campsite was well out of town and we got lost in the rain looking for it. The mosquitoes were by far the worst we had seen on the entire trip. When you shone the torch the beam seemed solid with them. Ben's beaver fever had gone critical and he was running to the bushes every fifteen minutes to relieve himself. At each dropping of his underwear we heard the low moans of a man beset around the balls by a thousand blood-sucking insects. When he finally retired to the tent I listened to his whimpering as he tried to manoeuvre his savaged undercarriage into a position of repose.

The next morning it was still raining. I woke to the un-appetizing sound and sight of Sota being sick on the end of my sleeping bag. It was time to leave.

A minibus took us to Hay River, but then we had a big problem. The Greyhound connection refused to take Sota. 'Ironic that a company called Greyhound won't take dogs,' said John, very philosophically considering the huge distance ahead of us. Ben, limping from the sustained attacks of the night before, was determined to hitch on alone. I had an insane faith that we would all be picked up, dog, unshaven men, kit and all. It was a kind of post-trip high, a supreme and unfaltering faith in the moment and what it might bring. And despite four kitbags, a barrel and a big half-husky we did get lifts, one that lasted seven hours and took us more than half the distance – we had 1,200 km to go to get back to Edmonton.

The last lift was with some tree planters heading back to town in a 1970s camper wagon that was older than the oldest of them. I knew nothing about the subculture of tree planting in Canada, which operates as a kind of neo-hippy alternative to redneck participation in logging and oil drilling. The tree planters are paid high wages by the big logging companies for difficult, dirty work. They are choppered into remote places and spend all day bending up and down, sticking infant spruce and pine into the soil. It is the law of the land that trees cut down must be replaced. Tree planters are skinny and wiry, loggers have big arms and beer guts. One of them was called Joe and was half English, half Canadian. A well-spoken waif with a beard and sideburns, he had spent all summer planting trees and taking photographs. The photographs were very good and he was full of the post-wilderness energy that is so infectious, the feeling that you know something that others don't. That only you are really able to enjoy the luxuries of a town because you have been without for so long. John had backed out of coming the following year and Ben was looking indecisive. Relying on nothing more than the sight of his hands, cracked and disfigured from shoving seven thousand trees a day into the soil of the Rocky Mountains, I asked Joe to come on the trip the following year. It was a decision that would change everything.

Part Two

SECOND ATTEMPT

One

DRAGONFLY

'Mr Mackay brought me a bunch of flowers of a pink colour, and a yellow button, encircled with six leaves of a light purple.' Alexander Mackenzie on a gift, celebrating the arrival of spring, from his 22-year-old second-in-command

I

I was in a vehicle, heading north again, twenty-four hours of driving ahead of me, or rather us – there were four of us, most of the driving falling on Dave, the vehicle's owner. The rest of us were sprawled in the velour-covered captain's chairs in the van's dark interior. I was in a vehicle heading north again, a year later, a year wiser, a year more overweight, though I had hardly really noticed the latter, though I would soon enough. I was turning over in my mind something Roland had said, Roland who had dropped us off the previous year and whom I had met again just before leaving Edmonton. He had been accepted by seminary school and was leaving soon for a college in Saskatoon. We met briefly and he gave me a plastic barrel to use in place of John's barrel from the year before. A barrel is a great place to keep food when there are bears about and we were glad to have it. He was pleased and surprised to see me: 'You know, after last year, I had a feeling you wouldn't be coming back. Thought that old Peace River had you beat.'

'Well, I'm back,' I said.

I had a new team and a new way of thinking, and though I was somewhat shy of the full implications, I was the unelected self-chosen leader of the expedition. I also had a name for the boat: *Dragonfly*. It had been suggested to me by something John Buck said: 'The dragonfly is your friend – she eat all the mosquitoes.'

The rest of my team were all new to the game. John and his girlfriend Nat had, indeed, got married, and had also had a child, not bad going, just as John said they would that rainy, tearful night we lost Sota on the Cat Fork Channel. So he was out. Ben, what with the misery of beaver fever (it wasn't giardia, just a stomach upset, probably the result of poor hygiene) and the multiple wounds he received to his testicles from the mandibles of airborne bloodsuckers, had, over the year, hardened into a man stubbornly against ever visiting the wilds again, especially with me. When I told him there were people who paid to have such experiences he just laughed, the laugh of a man utterly convinced he's talking to someone mightily self-deceived. Perhaps I was. This time, though, no one was paying me to come along; I at least had some keen volunteers who accepted, in theory, my new and fragile grasp of the reins of command.

Joe, twenty-six years old, tree planter and photographer, was asleep in the back of the van, his feet exceptionally smelly, but no one had said anything yet: we were all too new to each other. Dave was driving, Joe's friend; at least he had been introduced as such. They met this year tree planting in northern Alberta. Dave was short, of Russian ancestry though as Canadian as they come, but he did have the tragic skull and broad, bare forehead of a partisan too long in the marshes of Kiev. Dave was weird, with the knobby, knuckly, nail-bitten fingers of a tree planter; he had also worked as a computer salesman in Seoul and had a degree in journalism. He was also twenty-six. At twenty-five, another nail biter, in fact everyone except me bit their nails, Barney, the godson of my friend Chris, a big guy, a former professional rugby player, now studying law. He had forearms of a different order of magnitude to the rest of us. He had the disconcerting habit of never looking away when you caught his piercing, blue, unblinking eyes. But he looked strong and this was what the whole thing was about this year: making the miles.

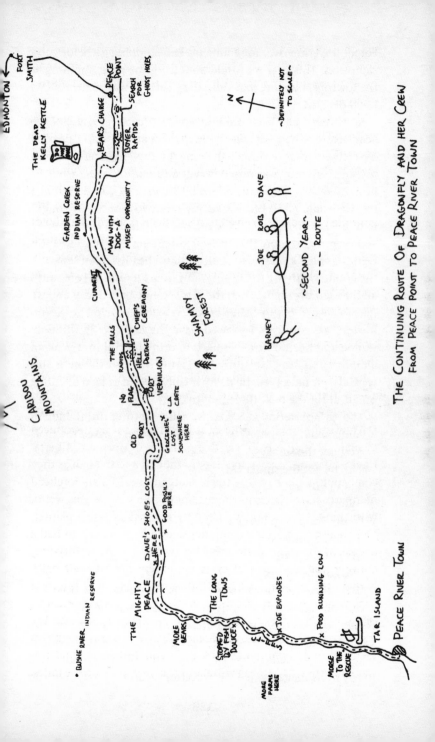

THE CONTINUING ROUTE OF DRAGONFLY AND HER CREW
FROM PEACE POINT TO PEACE RIVER TOWN

Forget lingering over long lunches and stopping early for good campsites. This year we would be forcing the pace, straining at the towrope, bursting to paddle, drag, sail our way to the Pacific. I had decided.

All winter I had been mulling over the feeble progress of the year before. I had got out the maps late at night and puzzled over them with a pencil, drawing in tiny numbers, forcing myself, very much against my will and nature, to be realistic, brutally realistic. I calculated that if we managed to do 15 km a day we would reach Peace River town in two months. We ought to be able to do more. Eight to ten hours of towing and paddling should bring in more than fifteen kilometres. My head was still running these kind of calculations as we headed relentlessly up the country, driving the twenty-four hours it took to Fort Smith all through the night. Then the van's engine boiled over and we had to take turns in being brave enough to undo the steam-blowing radiator cap. I showed Dave the Kelly kettle while we waited and he said he never liked to drink from things made of aluminium. Great! Not only the kettle, but also the mess tins were aluminium. Well, he'd either come round or he'd be eating off a leaf for the next three months.

At a service station at 3 a.m. we watched three drunk Indians arguing about cigarettes. 'Who got the smokes?' asked the first.

'You got the smokes.'

'No, he got the smokes.'

'I ain't got 'em.'

'Who got the smokes?'

Pause. Fumbling. Revelation.

'I got the smokes!'

'He got the smokes!'

'We got the smokes!'

'Hey, they got the smokes!' said Barney, who had been following the argument intently. Just as I had been the year before, Barney was keen on any manifestations of native culture. The van, with its tinted windows, was good for spying on others when we were parked, in fact it was rather like those vans used in spy films that are filled with electronics and two guys who do nothing but blink in the light when the side door is jammed open by the other side who have just discovered them. But this van, Dave's van, had cost $450, and was Dave's home when he was away from his parents' home. It was full of Dave's serviceable worn-out gear, his duct-taped rain jacket ('I sealed the tape with a hot iron and it's held for four years'), his crushed-up tent which was a 'top brand', his numerous thrift-shop woollies and hats, his angle-ground shortened spade for tree planting.

He and Joe were decidedly proud of their tree planting, the good times, the hard times, the wacky people, the days they'd made $700, the days they'd made none, the heroes, like Big Eric and Mark, who made $30,000 in three months planting and then did their own thing. Joe had brought along several special plastic bags containing spruce saplings. His aim was to symbolically plant them along the way. 'But you're not going to be able to bring that spade in the canoe,' I said. 'Oh,' said Joe, 'I thought I could.' Planting was connected to the iconic status of the spade, which each planter had finished to his own specification. Denied the spade, Joe agreed to plant most of the trees by the side of Highway 5 on the way to Fort Resolution. He kept back a few for Peace Point, our setting-off point on the big river.

'As long as she doesn't break down I just feed her as much gas and oil as she wants,' said Dave, sloping around the pumps, round-backed, round-shouldered, a hobbit in a woolly hat with a blond sprouting of beard on his chinny-chin-chin. He was an odd guy, I kept telling myself, but beggars can't be choosers. After Ben dropped out I'd found it hard to put a new team together. I'd been haunted by that final fast paddle across the Peace with Harvald the lonely Norwegian, how much faster four went than three. But getting four had been exponentially harder, it seemed, than three – well, two, since I was always in. When Joe mentioned Dave and his 'broadcast-standard' video camera I asked how much outdoor living he'd done. A lot; he was Canadian, after all. All Canadians in Joe's book were qualified by birth to be outdoorsmen.

Then there was the dope. Just as we were leaving Edmonton after a hellish food shop in which Dave and Joe insisted on an excessive amount of spices, seeds and small nuts, we made a detour past a single-storey suburban house in one of the too-tiny lots that characterize the Strathcona district. A sheepish guy looked over the fence. Joe went round and up the steps to the front door, appearing after too long a time – we were all raring to go, to leave the city – with a barely concealed shopping bag full of high-strength British Columbian weed. It cost them $200, which in western Canada, where even vicars and captains of industry smoke dope, buys you a lot of grass.

Things had taken a turn I hadn't foreseen. With two rabbity little dopeheads on board my voyage looked capable of derailment before it had really started. Barney, despite many incidents of extreme drunkenness and some of drug-related excess, had given up smoking cigarettes and anything else for the trip. I had joined him, aware the previous year how I had begun, like a voyageur, to measure my day out in pipes, or more usually roll-ups, which reduced the whole thing to a sort of soldiers-on-a-route-march experience. As for drugs, I wanted to have an open mind. I wasn't some old curmudgeon or squeaky-clean religionist, I was tolerant and easygoing, or part of me was. The other part was nervous, not because of the illegality (unlike the States, Canada is very easygoing about soft-drug use) but because it changed the focus, it brought a new master on board. Dope isn't like drink. You smoke to get high, get a hit. You don't smoke for the taste. There's alcohol-free beer but there isn't THC-free cannabis. The whole super-skunk-mega-strong-weed-genetically-modified-by-disaffected-hippies-on-the-islands-off-Vancouver thing was about strength, not taste. And dope reduces tension, makes goals seem less pressing, yet this year the goal loomed stronger than ever, it was the main thing, it had to be, we had to make Peace River town at the very least, or else I would have to abandon the whole enterprise. I could afford one more year after this and that was it.

I didn't want to be against the dope but I was. From the beginning I could not but see it as a rival. Surely the trip, my trip, should be enough – why should anyone need more? Of course, I could have banned it. It was my boat. But I wasn't yet able to think like that. My model of leadership for this section was not the draconian, rather it was the exemplary. A man who was followed not because he barked orders but because he set such a good example that others did the right thing naturally. A model of fairness. I would ask nothing of my men that I did not perform myself. I would be first up and last to bed and would never complain. It wouldn't be like the year before, where we did what we liked when we liked and as a result did not very much at all. No, this year the exemplar would do his best to be exemplary. Of course I'd sometimes fail, I told myself, but though I performed this ritual thought, I did not really believe it. In my mind I'd already done the trip and been exemplary, now all I had to do was continue being this new and excellent person.

Dave had a small glass pipe, psychedelically coloured; a gurgly micro-bong; a metal pipe for quick, harsh drags of smoke; papers and tobacco; and all the rest of the tedious paraphernalia of the doper. The kit always looks grimy, perhaps expensive, even well made, but grimy, cast in a minor key. As we drove north Joe and Dave sucked dementedly on the glass pipe, starting as early as 7.30 a.m. Apart from giving Dave bloodshot eyes and making him momentarily calm and detached, it appeared to have no effect. My own experience was long ago as a student, experimental, and too short-lived for me to realize that the purpose of drugs in the addicted is to return them to the normal, from which they have strayed. Drugs are not taken to get high but as a forlorn attempt at redemption, a homecoming to a childlike state of energy and enthusiasm and lack of worry.

What were Barney's vices? I thought as we ploughed ever on, along roads I remembered from the year before. We carried on over and down the hill through Peace River town. The river was majestic, brown and full, a river that revealed itself the better for one's being further away from it. Probably a view of it from the space shuttle would take my breath away. I remembered it close-up from the year before: muddy, cold, with a current powerful in the way things that have no concern or commerce with the ways of men are powerful. A natural force with some

125

nastiness to it. That was how I remembered the river. I looked at Barney sitting impassively next to me. He was big and strong and told me that 'the physical challenge was what attracted me'. Good. That made a difference from Ben's stated interest in bison and sightseeing and John's desire to kick back and hang loose. Dope or no dope, there'd be no hanging loose on this trip. Oh, I was full of good intentions after fitful sleep in the captain's chair, its brown velour impregnated with the pungent brown fried-sausage smell of marijuana. Barney's vices? I was sure, like my own, they would be on display all too soon.

II

We were interviewed by the local newspaper in Fort Smith and that cheered everyone up. It is hard not to be cheered when someone asks flattering questions and admires your courage. You have to have been interviewed a lot for that to wear off. The canoe was photographed. We poured water into it and found a few leaks, which I sealed with Vulkem, helped by Charlie, who had moved from Peace Point to Fort Smith and was living in housing provided for native people attending college, which is what Cynthia was doing. Alison was working at the Northern store as a checkout girl.

All the fine plans of the previous year had gone awry. Charlie looked older and less ebullient. His plan to turn Peace Point into a camping and outdoor centre with wigwams and an RV (recreational vehicle – the obese caravan trailers that Canadians prefer to tents) park had faltered. The water contract had been revoked because everyone had left Peace Point, even old Gabe, the man who had given us a piece of frozen moose the previous year. 'What? No one is living there?' 'Nope,' said Charlie forlornly. 'Except Alison whenever she gets time off.'

Charlie was waiting for a special grant to help him set up his business. My letter from the previous year had obviously not done the trick. There was no fire watching like last year either, only a bit of taxi driving around Smith, taking people home

126

who were too drunk to drive, fallen off their bar stools with their bags of shopping all around them. It didn't suit him. Charlie was a guy who thrived on hard work and the rewards that come, in Canada, for those who work hard in remote places. He still had his old truck 'Bark 'n' Bitch' but he kept it at Peace Point to keep his costs down. Charlie had worked the oil patch and made good money before he turned his back on all that. It was hard for him to draw welfare and be around the house while his womenfolk worked. Work had given him social opportunities and as he didn't go to bars he had fewer of those now. It didn't suit him.

Earlier, when we'd picked up the canoe from the store, all my fears about the bark cracking in the depths of winter proved unfounded. She looked dusty, as if sprinkled with concrete dust, but it was the remains of the mud we had been too hasty to brush out from the year before. And she felt heavier too, coming out of the windowless building, cold and clammy after a winter where temperatures had been below −40°C but not so cold as Cynthia's dream had predicted. Perhaps the hard winter was the times they were going through now.

III

After we'd patched the canoe, Charlie agreed to drive Dave's van, with the canoe loaded on top, down to the river at Peace Point. Here, 150 km from the town, Charlie lightened up. He cooked us pork on his barbecue and then we sat drinking coffee in his bug net on the lawn. But four strange men had an effect on him and I was reminded of when we first met by the river. He became laconic and unenthusiastic and the conversation lagged pitifully. Barney tried vainly to engage him but such questions as 'Just how big is the wingspan of a peregrine falcon?' failed to ignite Charlie's interest. It wasn't us really; life was getting him down. Then he sat forward and said, 'You guys want to shoot some firearms?' It was the perfect solution.

Charlie brought out his .22 repeater, his twelve-bore and

Alison's 4/10. Fey, trendy Joe was the best shot. He had been trained as a marksman by the RAF – he had been a cadet whilst at school, something he had never mentioned. Brawny Barney was the worst, or rather had the worst mishap. Just as he was raising the twelve-bore he pulled the trigger ('I just touched it, it's a hair trigger') and blew a hole in the dog kennel on Charlie's lawn. Dave was the worst marksman. We sort of forced him to have a go but I could tell he didn't want to. Guns were a novelty to us, less so to him. It was almost as if he was careless of aiming because that would cast him in a light he didn't want.

Charlie fired up his big truck and with the others clinging to the flatbed we roared up tracks looking for prairie chickens to shoot with the 4/10 which I cradled. Charlie took delight in revving with each gear change, deafening the lads behind as the barking exhaust pipes ran up the back of the cab.

We had more coffee in the cabin and talked guns. Now we had no dog as a protection against bears, most backwoodsmen thought us foolish to be travelling without a gun, either a twelve-bore with rifled slugs or a full-bore rifle. Not that having a dog had proved much about bears, or dogs, but somehow, perhaps because of a winter spent cogitating on so many pieces of advice from people who actually lived in these places, I had strongly felt the need to get a gun of some kind. I said to Charlie, 'Do you think if someone was in the outback they might meet someone who would lend them a shotgun as long as they got it back at the end of the trip?' He looked me in the eye and said, 'But that person would have to make a bus trip back with the gun, wouldn't they?' He wasn't saying no, but the ball was in my court and all I could think about was Barney blowing apart the dog kennel. Illegal drugs and firearms don't mix. I shut up about borrowing a shotgun.

IV

Charlie let us fire his sawn-off .303 rifle. He'd bent the barrel that winter whilst riding on a snowmobile and sawn it off to make it louder one New Year's Day. All the people on the reserve fired their guns off then to celebrate and Charlie's was loudest. It was accurate to about fifteen yards and so noisy the ringing in my ears didn't go for half an hour. Two hundred and ten years earlier, Mackenzie wrote in his journal, 'Thursday January 1st 1793. On the first day of January, in conformity to the usual custom, my people awoke me at the break of day by the discharge of their firearms, with which they congratulated the appearance of the new year.'

We loaded the canoe down on the beach of Peace Point, less littered now there was no one living there. Charlie mentioned four American tourists who'd come through and had a hard time at Garden Creek, the first Cree-speaking reserve we'd hit, after ten or so days. 'These boys told me they asked an elder for some water at the reserve and the guy just points at the river, says, "There's your water." They felt kind of intimidated and left in a hurry.'

'Why weren't they drinking from the river anyway?' I said.

'Guess they thought it was polluted.'

'Well, we'd better not ask for water,' said Barney, eager to get things moving.

The kit was stowed. We were ready to go. 'Make sure you catch a goldeneye at Jackfish River,' called Charlie. Goldeneye were a kind of fish, with large golden eyes, but our fish book was too scientific to contain any information about them. We were all looking forward to toasting goldeneye on willow sticks cut fresh from the bank. It was, Charlie said, the best fish dish in the world. The previous year we hadn't caught a thing using a conventional rod. This year we had gone native and had a gill net designed for 'survival' fishing.

So this was it – Peace River town or bust. I waded out boldly and was amused that the others were timid about getting wet. They'd learn. They climbed in, legs streaming with water. I pushed us away and jumped in the back and we were away. All four of us were paddling hard and I deliberately kept us mid-river in the strongest part of the current. I wanted to know how we would fare. The canoe felt wobbly and slacker than the year before, filled as it was with the gear and food for four, and though Joe and Dave were skinny it still felt overcrowded. But we were drawing ahead, beating the current, that was what mattered.

At Drum Island we towed along the beach. I received my first complaint. Joe said, 'Why didn't we tow earlier?'

'Because I wanted you to know what we are up against.'

This time we climbed the hill in the island's middle to find the limestone sinkholes that made the ghostly drumming sound. There were many, the whole area at the top riddled with vertical sinks half blocked with fallen rock and vegetation. We dropped a stone down one and listened for it to splash or hit in the darkness below. We dropped stone after stone but heard no noise. 'Must be full of soft leaves,' said Barney.

'Or bottomless,' said Dave.

OK, let 'em tow, I thought. Along the bank after Drum Island the mud was smooth, deep and sticky. The slip-on amphibious shoes we'd all bought at Wal-Mart for $10 ('Bargain,' said Joe, gleefully) were sucked off in an instant. Instead I wore my old, split, wet-sock boots from the year before. The others put on sandals and wore their slip-ons only on dry land.

Back in the canoe Joe said, 'Does everyone else feel on an emotional rollercoaster?' He said this after just one day of paddling. There is something about being forced to stare at a man's back hour after hour that gets to you. You start imagining he's thinking things. I usually supressed such imaginings. I was surprised that Joe voiced his. It was too near the knuckle too soon.

At the first campsite I did everthing. I was exemplary and, by nightfall, exhausted. I showed everyone how to rig up the water-filter bag – a much bigger and better version of the Millbank bag used the year before. They looked at it, *en masse*, as if it were something unnecessary that I'd invented just to make things more difficult. They'd learn. Dave piled wood on to the fire with confidence. Neophytes are often nervous of putting a fire out with too much wood and fuss around it blowing and fanning, or else they do put it out – he did neither, placing the load in the right place, where the fire had already gained a good hold. I ladled out the noodles into everyone's Chinese Army mess tins. Mess tins are infinitely better than plastic bowls or plates for several reasons: you can scour them free of grease with sand, you can heat things up in them, since they don't melt, and you can eat your porridge standing up holding one by the handle in the morning. I ladled noodles and sardines into each tin and no one complained. This is going to be easy, I thought, not like whingeing Ben and John. In an awkward movement Barney turned to pick up his tea. His foot caught the tin and spilled his noodles. 'Shit!' he said with real venom. Then he breathed heavily, getting himself under control. 'Never mind, there's more in the pot,' I said. He nodded, turned and kicked his tea over.

Two

THERE'S A HOLE IN MY BOAT

'Our canoe became so leaky it was the unremitting employment of one person to keep her clear of water.' Alexander Mackenzie

I

Barney asked to borrow my Leatherman. He used it to carve a monstrous ladle that owed more to the scoop devices used in *pelote* by the Basques than it did to any kitchen implement. 'Pretty crap, isn't it?' he said. Everyone thought so but uttered nothing but praise. We were all being polite and restrained and it was good. Letting it all hang-out, telling it how it is, giving it straight – that's all very well in the world of expense accounts and air conditioning, but out here, cooped up with three blokes on whom your life depends, a little politeness goes a long way. That was the theory; and so far, it seemed to be working.

There were four major obstacles on this section of the voyage: 1. Maintaining a good enough mileage each day against the current. I had read that the current increased in strength the further we went, so this would become harder, not easier, by the day. 2. Going up the Boyer Rapids. 3. Portaging or otherwise crossing the Vermilion Rapids and Falls. 4. Doing all of the above whilst keeping the team from imploding, giving up or breaking up.

It was only the second day but we were already upon one of the main obstacles, the Boyer Rapids. The year before, Joe Vermilion had drawn on both our 50,000 and 250,000 maps the correct way to take the rapids, but on each map he'd drawn a route on a different side of the river. We all looked at the maps and decided which map he would have found 'the most confusing' and therefore the most likely to sufficiently throw him off and make him draw the wrong route. 'Unless he was screwing with ya,' smirked Dave.

Mackenzie left little information in his own account, which we found, at crucial moments, often lacking in detail. In 1965, an adventurous scholar called T. H. Macdonald retraced Mackenzie's voyage to the Arctic. He wrote of Mackenzie's directions out of Lake Athabasca: 'had we tried to follow them we would have found ourselves carrying our canoe several miles through thickly forested land'. I sensed, that, along with his dodgy latitude and longitude readings, Mackenzie was actually a poor navigator. About as good as me, in fact.

The Boyer Rapids were named after Charles Boyer, a contemporary of Mackenzie who was trading on the Peace River before Mackenzie arrived there. In 1788 he founded one of the first fur-trading posts near Fort Vermilion. The Boyers are only graded class II on the scale used to describe river difficulties – 'rapids more frequent [than class I] but unobstructed, with regular waves and easy eddies. Scouting often not necessary.'

But the classification of rivers is aimed at those descending them, not going against the current. John had told me the previous year that a good way to learn how to handle a canoe was to walk it against the current through rapids, that is, past rocks that break the water. You learn how important it is to keep the nose into the stream; even a few inches off to one side and the current can whip the boat around and over. And a boat full of gear is a nasty, unforgiving prospect compared to the cockleshell lightness of the unladen craft. And I still couldn't understand why it seemed heavier than the year before. Was I getting weaker?

'It looks better on the other side,' said Joe.

'What do you think?' I said to Barney.

'I don't know,' he said.

Dave remained silent.

'Well, if we're going to give it a go we should cross now,' I said. It was the first of many such, rather unsatisfactory committee meetings. Up ahead, the white splashing of big boulders in the stream was apparent. We paddled across and avoided two big ones with whirlpools behind them, easy stuff, but at the other side things grew confusing.

We hit a mudbank about thirty yards from the edge. We all jumped out just as the boat hit. Then we started to walk in the shallows, upstream, hoping to make it across the gap to the bank. The water got deeper and deeper. Barney was up to his chest at the front and because the current was strong we all found it hard to keep our footing. The canoe lifted and swerved to one side and water came in over the gunwhale. It was only the second day and we were close to losing it. With everyone straining we got the canoe straight again. 'Let's try and swim it!' shouted Barney, enjoying it hugely, over the roar of the water, which was breaking around several rocks. I knew then that I would be doomed this time to be Mr Cautious, forever putting the boot into more interesting and dangerous plans. There were two options: swim it, as Barney suggested, from where we were, and hopefully avoid broadsiding on to the intervening rocks; or retrace our steps and walk downstream, getting closer to the bank that way. We retraced our steps.

No longer going against the stream we at last made it to the bank, all exhausted, several of the packs soaking wet. My own waterproof kitbag was half full of water. Somehow a hole had worn in the bottom, making it useless. The water poured out as if from a bucket when I upended it.

My notebook had been soaked, all the important addresses printing through in blue edged with yellow. The GPS was luckily dry inside its protective case. I put both back into my shirt pocket. In the next two years of river travel I never put either into my trouser pockets again.

Now all we had to do was hug the bank and walk against the current, hauling the boat past boulders spread with water, glabrous with it, sealed as if in moving ice or glass, separated from each other by a confusion of breaking water. The current

hammered on our unfit legs, sucking the trouser cloth around them, filling boots and socks with gritty silt, giving each leg such buoyancy that you had to force it down with each step. Going against the current's power made us almost weightless. Barney, who was already our benchmark of fitness, finally admitted, 'My legs are like jelly.' Everyone except Dave agreed.

Past the rapids we could paddle again, alongside a root-strewn bank. I saw the stick, protruding from a sunken log, but it was too late to more than flail at it ineffectually with the paddle. There was a noise like the 'pop' made when you open a new jar of instant coffee. 'We're holed!' I said.

This comment in itself created a certain atmosphere of panic, but it must have been rather like the *Titanic* when people just carried on dancing – nothing was happening immediately and since the hole was hidden under the waterline we all just stopped paddling and looked at each other.

There was still water in the boat from the rapids so it was hard to tell if the hole was significant or not. It was impossible to stop alongside the confused spikiness of the bank so we just carried on and forgot about it.

For about twenty minutes. Joe and I were then towing. Barney called to me, looking worried. 'Er, Rob, there seems to be rather a lot of water in the boat.' I walked back to look at the canoe. Barney was waist deep in water like a kid sitting in a paddling pool. We were sinking fast!

We were, at that point, on an island, a sand island with a light covering of tiny willows. If I can't repair this, I thought, we're going to be stuck here, marooned for good. We unloaded the boat and turned it over in the afternoon sun. The hole was a neat split just below the waterline. Feeling courageous I cut around the hole and plugged it with a thick piece of bark I'd found that morning. The bark had been around a rotten log but it had not rotted itself. The resin in birchbark that makes it inflammable also makes it superbly rot proof. I sealed the edges of the bark with some chewed pine resin and the remains of a tube of glue Charlie had given me. When we paddled off the repair held. No one seemed at all surprised. Except me.

The only campsite was again clinging to the river's edge on a sloping muddy terrace. Joe complained he hadn't had a good night's sleep for eight days and I felt the first stirrings of irritation. So what? I thought. This isn't a holiday camp. I knew from long experience of sleeping in terribly uncomfortable places – including a night spent resting my whole body on a rucksack wedged into a crack in a rockface in the Pyrenees – that even if you believe you haven't slept a wink you are able to keep going the next day as if you have. It's the physical rest that seems to be most important, not the psychological relief of believing you had a 'good sleep'. But more than the complaint was the tone – petulant, as if it were someone's fault. Probably just tired, I said to myself, not wanting at all to read it as a sign of future discord.

Three

MUD IN THE BLOOD

'To add to our distress we had no gun.' Alexander
Mackenzie on the Parsnip River

I

The canoe had within it a thick grey paste of silty mud. We pegged it with paddles close to the shore, but even the two steps to firm ground involved plunging deep into mud. It was worse mud than the previous year. It actually felt bottomless. If you didn't move it would take you down and down for ever. 'This mud sucks,' quipped Dave, and promptly lost one of his Wal-Mart shoes. We all gamely felt around in the hole left by his foot but the shoe was gone for ever.

Around the campfire Dave picked off the scabs of dry grey mud that had matted on to his leg hairs. 'I haven't showered in weeks,' he said proudly, 'I haven't any soap.' It turned out I had the only soap between the four of us, and the only watch.

II

As I had the only watch it dawned on me, literally, that I would have to get up first and wake everyone else up every day for the entire trip. I found it hard enough to get up when others were already up; to have to set the example as well went against a lifetime of morning indolence. But, cast against type or not, no one else would do it. Barney and Dave got up quickly at my gruff 'Tea's on the go, lads,' but Joe was still in his sleeping bag two hours later at 8 a.m. He arrived smiling at the camp-fire. 'That was a great sleep,' he said, preferring to be extra pleasant rather than apologize. He and Dave smoked a bong full of weed and we were ready to go, but both of them were careful to fit this into a gap in loading the boat rather than keep us waiting.

We had two tents. One large and comfortable with a big vestibule that zipped up – no more rainswept nights for me, I thought – and one tiny one that Dave brought along. He and Joe slept in that pongy little sock while Barney and I luxuriated in the bigger tent, which could comfortably have taken three. But for some reason, or perhaps no reason, they had one tent and we had the other and so it was fixed.

By lunchtime we had made it to Joe Vermilion's cabin, a year late. It was raining and the mosquitoes were bad and we had to scramble up a deeply muddy bank to get to the cabin. Later we came across an old patrol cabin from the early days of Wood Buffalo National Park before the war. Joe wrote on the rotting wood wall, 3 LIMEYS AND A CANADIAN – PEACE RIVER TO THE PACIFIC.

III

Towing had evolved from a voluntary activity to the highly regulated use of two teams, one hour on, one off, each man towing for half an hour before handing over to his partner, who would be just walking along. This was often one of the most pleasant tasks of the day – to be unencumbered by the towrope but able to walk along the bank, dawdling and looking at anything you pleased. The other two men stayed in the boat, the rear man steering, the bow man watching out for rope snags. Despite Joe's reluctance to get up early we had found ourselves a routine: up at 5.30 a.m., leave by 8, stop for lunch at 12, start again at 2 p.m., finish at 6. Eight hours of paddling and towing unless disrupted by bad weather. Most days, too, we found that we could do our target 20 km in that eight hours.

It was interesting to see how towing revealed one's mental

state. When Joe was in a bad mood he towed with all the jerky energy of an ill-tempered marionette. Dave too, when pissed off, towed with such fierce belligerence one was often nervous to inform him he'd just snagged the rope. Barney would lope along as if unconcerned but suddenly reveal his vicious side with great harsh pulls at the rope if it stuck under a beaver lodge or behind a waterlogged stump.

I, who had been looking forward to the towing, now found my attitude reversed. Now it was the paddling I enjoyed and the towing I found tiring and irksome. Had I lost some essential fitness since the year before? I had never in my life felt as tired as I did in those first few days after eight hours of towing and paddling. It was an unpleasant dog-tiredness, rather than the relaxing fatigue after a hard day's work. One felt burdened and dragged down by it, and I wondered if it had as much to do with emotional fatigue as physical exhaustion. Being exemplary is hard work, especially when you are knackered.

I was determined to beat the mud. With two pieces of drift-plywood I made a pair of mud-shoes, fixing my feet with rope to the boards. The suction was too great and they were a failure. I then realized the boards might work as portable duckboards, lifting one up and laying it down after the other, making movable stepping stones over the mud. This was slow but did work, just.

I messed with my mud-boards. I expected the others to laugh when they failed and I fell forwards into the mud. Instead they looked concerned. They, too, wanted a leader they could believe in. Barney started carving a spoon, which was an improvement on his ladle, though the handle did not protrude from the centre of the spoon bit but from slightly off-centre.

'Crap?' he asked.

'Nooo!' everyone lied.

Barney was kind to animals. We passed a lone duckling, deserted by its mother, or so it seemed. Barney cradled the grey fluffy ball inside his jacket. He wanted to save it and protect it. Everyone scanned the flat mile-wideness of the river looking for Mum. There was just silence and trees and grey water. 'The mother will come back,' I said. After a while Barney reluctantly returned the duckling to the water.

Jackfish River, when we got there, was flowing with clear water. You could see its clarity as the clearer water made a spike of current into the silty stream. The bank was muddy and after we'd tramped about setting up camp, water seeped through at every footprint. I set up the Kelly kettle to get a brew going. The Kelly kettle was a curious contraption made of two layers of aluminium. Water trapped between the two layers could be heated by a fire lit inside the kettle. A hole at the base and a through-chimney ensured almost anything would do as fuel. Again, there was general suspicion aimed at this odd piece of kit, and I made it worse by over-enthusing about its great qualities.

Barney struggled manfully with the water bag, a big intestine-like bag, heavy and hard to handle, much less string up whilst full from a branch, or better from a tripod made of the three paddles. His contraption of supporting branches fell over and the bag emptied with a splat on the sand. 'Oh fuck!' he shouted. He then had to strip off and got all muddly wading out far enough to get more water to fill the bag.

When the water has run through it is either boiled or stored in water bottles. Each bottle is dosed with eight drips of iodine to purify the contents.

Barney approached me, holding his fleece out in front of him. 'Is this a burn?'

'Yes, I burned my fleece too.' I didn't add it was nothing like the huge brown stain that covered the lower part of Barney's fleece.

'Mind you,' he added, as if guilty, 'I did spill a little iodine ...'

I looked more closely at the grotesque discoloration. 'You're right, that's iodine all right.'

Later Barney would outstrip us all in river competence, but at this stage he was unsure of himself. He approached me rather tentatively and said, 'Er, Rob, I just blew my nose and there was blood in it.'

'Really? Any further bleeding?'

'No.'

'Good.'

He hung about like a small boy seeing nurse.

'Actually I saved it – what do you think?' He proffered the bloody snot on a piece of old bark.

I examined the drying brownish bogey with professional objectivity. 'Doesn't look too bad to me,' I said after a while.

Being the leader automatically made you the doctor. Joe had a nasty crack between his toes that filled up with mud every day and took an age to clean. I doled out some cortisone cream to help it heal. Mackenzie had rather more dramatic ailments to cure: 'One of the young Indians had lost the use of his right hand by the bursting of a gun, and that the thumb had been maimed in such a manner as to hang by only a small strip of flesh. His wound was in such an offensive state, and emitted such a putrid smell, that it required all the resolution I possessed to examine it. I was determined to risk my surgical reputation and accordingly took him under my care. I formed a poultice of bark, stripped from the roots of the spruce fir, which I applied to the wound, having first washed it in the juice of the bark; this proved a very painful dressing: in a few days however, the wound was clean, and the proud flesh around it destroyed. I wished very much to have separated the thumb from the hand, but he would not consent to that operation, till, by the application of vitriol, the flesh by which the thumb was suspended, was shrivelled almost to a thread. When I had succeeded in this object, I perceived the wound was closing rather faster than I desired. The salve I applied on the occasion was made of Canadian balsam, wax and tallow, dropped from a burning candle into water. In short I was so successful that my patient [shortly] engaged in a hunting party and brought me the tongue of an elk.'

Would Joe bring me the tongue of an elk if I cured his foot? Probably not. With a plastic bag to protect his toe he hobbled about in the mud and made a delicate sculpture from woven willow branches. At every campsite he made some kind of sign using stones or wood, all of them mysterious and pleasing to the eye.

141

After our evening meal I suggested that we divide up all the chores. Each day there would be a fireman, a water-boy, a cook and someone doing the cleaning up. It was a huge leap forward in organization compared to the devil-may-care approach of the year before and I was, for some reason, expecting complaint. Instead they all nodded. 'Good idea,' said Barney. Dave started out by washing up and lost his mess tin. 'It just kind of slid away,' he explained. Joe dived in to attempt a heroic rescue but he was too late and the river too deep. As if to emphasize the treacherous nature of the place, Dave also lost one of his sandals. He had now lost two pieces of footwear, unfortunately not matching items. I was grumpy about the loss of the tin. 'Lose your equipment in the wilderness and you die,' I muttered theatrically. But it wouldn't do. We wouldn't be able to get a replacement before the trip ended. We put up the tents on the least muddy piece of ground. Ours was only ten yards or so from a berry-studded mound of bearshit, but we were too tired to move on and went to sleep promptly, forgetting all about it.

I was up at five, tending to the wounded Kelly kettle. Barney had mortally damaged it the night before. 'Er, sorry, Rob,' was becoming the regular prelude to his latest mishap. The Kelly kettle could not, UNDER ANY CIRCUMSTANCES, be used without water inside it. Without water inside the crimped aluminium seam at the base came apart and water added after this just dribbled out, as forlorn as a drooling pensioner who once wowed people with his suavity. The dribbles were hard to notice, since the heat of the kettle evaporated them immediately. Only the persistent failure of the fire within, and the damp sooty patch inside the kettle base, told one of the dire misfortune that had occurred. I tended to it with Leatherman pliers, trying to recrimp the base, but it appeared hopeless. The Kelly kettle had been a source of fire and hot drinks even when it was pelting with rain. Now that survival aid was gone.

I was sitting on a log, the muddy beach and Jackfish River in front of me, a thicket of tall spindly willows behind me. I heard within these willows, just as the kettle sputtered out for the fourth time, the distinct and unnerving sounds of a bear. I knew well enough, from the previous year, the *large* sound a bear makes. As befitting a large creature, only a clumsy human makes as much noise in the bush as a bear. Perhaps the moose can be as noisy, but I had no experience of moose apart from seeing them at a great distance or from a speeding truck. This was a bear all right, planting its great furry shoulders against the weak willows and tramping around. Stripping great pawfuls of verdure to feed an endlessly hungry maw, bears must spend most of their waking hours browsing food, and as the sun rose this one had begun his feasting. I scuttled back to the tent and retrieved the bearhorn. Barney was still fast asleep. Returning to the log, I fired off the horn and the scuffling and crunching of stems stopped, then receded.

Later, when I added together all my bear scares, one thing was common – bears will start sniffing around a campsite almost exactly around sunrise. If you are up before then you will be in a position to not be surprised. As for the fond belief that bears show less interest in tents than in men out in the open, I was soon to have some direct experience bearing upon this question.

Dave heard the bearhorn and got up. They must all have heard the bearhorn, but only Dave arose. He approached the campfire looking as if he had lost World War II and was about to spend five years in the gulag. To my cheery 'Morning' he gave me a baleful stare and held out his coffee mug like the Ghost of Christmas Future pointing his finger of doom. In short, Dave was crap in the morning. Adjusting myself to this, I regaled him with the noises I had heard. He was about to contradict me on some tedious point concerning the likely food requirements of bears when I saw an enormous cinnamon bear, that is, a brown black bear, lumber out of the willows some way up the beach, right past the bear turd, then lope around our tent and start sniffing under the flysheet. Earlier Barney had said with some heat, 'I really hope I see a bear on this trip.' He was about to get his wish fulfilled.

I just stared. Dave, however, acted. He started to shout and bellow at the bear. I fired off the horn. The bear skittered away as if stung on the behind.

Then, across Jackfish River I saw yet another bear, not quite so big and mercifully across fifty yards of water. This bear was pawing and stripping the leaves on the opposite bank. Dave went to get his video camera and started to film the bear, which only stared when I fired off the horn at him. Then Dave noticed that there was another bear further down the opposite bank. When I fired off the horn this bear obliged by swimming across the river to our side.

'What do you think?' I said to Dave. He motioned me to be quiet: he was too busy filming. Then we were charged.

There is nothing quite like being charged by a wild animal. It is different, for example, from standing in front of a car coming at you. With an animal there is always the wild card of psychology. Perhaps the bear/bull/lion will think I'm a bigger meaner predator than he. Or perhaps not.

The charge emanated from the willows behind the log. Dave filmed the trees shaking in the distance as the bear crashed towards us. Which of the four bears, I could not say. I fired off the bearhorn repeatedly. Alone and unarmed, Dave hiding behind his video camera, I wrestled a long stick with a burning end from the fire. The end glowed as the wind blew a faint blue line of smoke from the end. I planted the unfiery end in the ground next to me. If the bear attacked I would thrust the stick into its face like some Stone Age wanderer under threat. There was no space to be cowardly. Come and get it, I thought, and gave the horn a series of increasingly feeble blasts. Then it gave up the ghost and in one last asthmatic gasp delivered a spittle-like substance from its nozzle – just as the bear reached the edge of the willows nearest me. Perhaps it was the sudden silence that unnerved the bear. It stopped. Rustled around, turned, and went away. The sound of the willows breaking or being brushed aside grew quieter and quieter, which seemed a miracle in itself.

We woke Barney and Joe. Neither really comprehended what we were saying. Joe even wanted to hang around for a cup of coffee. For the first time we packed the whole camp up in ten minutes.

We sped across the Peace and made camp on a sand island

with no bear tracks and no willows high enough for a bear to hide behind. On the video I thought I might look rather resolute and brave. I didn't. I bore a closer resemblance to someone poking around in a bonfire after his lost baked potato.

IV

We nervously returned to Jackfish River to set the net. It was a long net, about twenty-five feet. Joe stuck a pole in the middle of the stream, climbing out of the empty canoe. It was a joy to handle the canoe, empty except for us four. The net stretched almost to the bank, where we shoved another pole in. Small empty water bottles served as floats and there seemed no need to weight the bottom of the net. We left it and paddled quickly back to our side of the river.

This was our first rest day. The previous year we had none, though we exerted ourselves correspondingly little. This year, every seventh day was to be a rest day. Dave read Haldor Laxness's *Independent People*, whilst I read a thriller by Ranulph Fiennes; true to my intentions of the year before I had only works of an escapist and unedifying nature, though the Fiennes book was very informative on open-boat travel in the Antarctic. Barney gave up carving to do a rather good sketch of the canoe on the river and Joe did a solo display of hacky sack. The hacky sack is the dope smoker's football. The sack, which is a bean bag, is shifted from foot to shoulder to back to knee like a lethargic game of keepy-uppy with a football. But it isn't easy. Dave, as a fellow smoker, tried hard, but I could see he was as talentless as I was. Barney, with the innate ball skills that had led him into professional rugby, was very quickly very good, keeping the sack up for twenty or thirty moves. But Joe was always the best. Joe the waif, the hacky-sack hero, happy as a sandboy in the middle of nowhere. It wouldn't last.

V

We checked the net the following day at dawn. Joe dived half-naked underwater to bring the net's haul aboard. Five goldeneye! We knew them at once by the solid yellow iris and the shape of the flesh on the bone, ideal for toasting on a spit.

We made a great fire alongside a driftwood tree and roasted the fish with a peeled willow twig stuck up through its fundament and out through its gaping mouth. Only Joe insisted on frying his, but all tasted as only fish-just-caught can, making you understand why people start fish restaurants and traipse down to the sea to cadge freshly caught mackerel from boats that have just come in.

A strange thing: we wrote a message in a whisky bottle for Charlie, tightened the cap, threw it in and it just went straight under, straight to the bottom without bobbing at all.

VI

That night Dave was agitated and muttering to himself as he built three huge fires in a triangle around our tents. He refused to say why he was upset. Finally he admitted, 'I've never been out in the bush without mace or bear bangers before, or someone with a gun.'

Barney looked up from the sketch he was drawing. 'You realize three fires in a triangle is the internationally accepted distress signal?'

'Yeah?' said Dave. 'And who's going to see it?'

He was right. In a week on the river we hadn't seen or heard a boat, a plane or another soul.

Four

A SOUND OF DRUMS

'Took up our nets,
caught but six fish.'
Alexander Mackenzie

I

You could see the blue plastic tarpaulins from the river, slung over hut-like frames made of long poles. Big Slough – Charlie had pronounced it 'slew' – was a deserted moose camp of drying racks and oddments: a broken snowshoe, a Pepsi can, a steak knife stuck in a wood-chopping block, a child's doll with one eye. The plastic-covered huts were half ruined and blackfly swarmed everywhere.

We fought our way through the brambles and undergrowth up a steep slippery bank to get there. The trees dripped rain and mosquitoes hummed under the sloping branches of black spruce. In dank places like this it seems there is no life in the forest except insects, and that the forest goes on for ever, dark and unyielding, with only vague animal trails as paths.

Joe morbidly photographed everything, including the half-rotten carcass of a dead fox. Big Slough had once been a permanent camp of four families, who now lived in Garden Creek. I was glad to leave the place.

We paddled heroically across windswept waters to get to Garden Creek. The waves had been high enough to give a scare, and we had pounded up and down them like comic-book Hawaiians bringing a boat through the surf. When we got into the reserve we were nervous, too, remembering that [story of Charlie's] about the four Americans who asked for water. Well, we didn't want water, so how would we be received?

At that moment a young lad of about fifteen came down on to the beach on a green quad-bike. 'You know where you are?' he asked with a shy smile. He looked and sounded unworldly, neither did English appear his first language. Cynthia had told us that from Garden Creek to Fox Lake they still spoke Cree as their main tongue. These reserves were so remote that Cree had never died out, and now the government encouraged it instead of trying to force everyone to use English.

'Garden Creek?' I said.

The boy smiled. 'Where you from?'

'England,' I said.

'In that canoe?' he asked.

The boy's name was Stephen. He took Joe and Barney up to the top of the bluff on the back of his quad. He lived in a modern log cabin with his parents. Stephen's father was a quiet, watchful, competent-looking man, who Stephen deferred to. He said he'd come down a little later to see our canoe.

There was a Northern store on the reserve, a supermarket chain that replaced the old Hudson's Bay Company stores in the north. We bought sweets and food because they were there. A man who could not speak English, a cheery, wide-awake Indian in a cowboy hat, a studded belt and jeans on his skinny legs, his face wrinkled and bent up with amusement, mimed paddling and looking out from the bluff, then nodded and gave us the thumbs-up. It was all very clear – he appreciated the effort we'd made to get here, he knew what it had taken. A fat Indian man in dark glasses, leather trousers and a leather jacket offered us crisps from his open pack. 'You come to the ceremony?'

'What ceremony?'

'In Little Red River they have a big ceremony for the new chief. First they have the pilgrimage but then they going to have the cermony. Everyone can come.'

Stephen's father came down to the beach. I was hoping he would let us stay on the reserve but he didn't offer. He said that the nearest camping was on an island just a bit along. He had come down to look at our canoe. I watched his feet with great interest. He agreed with our complaints about the new islands, the silting-up of channels, the decline in the white-fish catch, all the fault of the dam, but when I ventured to complain about the mud he said, poker-faced, 'The Peace has always been muddy like it is.' And shifted his feet. I was already glooped in. Lifting a foot caused a sucking sound, but both his feet were dry and only muddy on the sole. He wore Timberland-type boots rather than moccasins but this did not affect his ability to deal with the environment one bit. I felt an entire philosophy of living in harmony with the Peace was encapsulated in the way he was able to shift his footing just enough so that he did not sink, did not get bogged down, did not become wet and, what is most important, did it without even being apparently conscious of doing it, did it whilst talking all the while to us about the river and the people on it.

None of us wanted to get back into the rough water but we had no choice. As we were leaving Stephen's father said, 'Come to the ceremony at Little Red River. You will be welcome. That's where we are going now.'

I calculated we could be there in four days. If we managed that the ceremony would be the day after we arrived, though general festivities were starting in a day's time. 'It is the first new-chief's ceremony for twenty years,' he said.

We stood around for a while and he did his slow dance on the mud, his wife sitting on the quad, taking an interest but not talking. Everything about Indians out here was different to the white man: the way they shook hands, the way they talked, the things they didn't say, the way they moved. White people had been coming up and down past their villages for two hundred years and they had not changed – this resilience meant what? That they would never change? Like gypsies they would maintain their culture alongside one that seemed on the face of things the more dominant?

Nothing he'd said had been wasted information. His last comment was 'It would have been good for you to meet my uncle, but he's not here right now. In the summer he goes up to Fifth Meridian. If you pass him you should talk to him.'

That night we camped on another thin strip of beach. To get any privacy you had to pull yourself up a steep small cliff using the protruding roots of spruce trees. Barney came back from such an excursion smelling his hands and complaining, 'What's that smell? Smell's like shit or something.' His eyes followed mine as I looked at the yellow-brown spattering of his stay-dry trousers. 'Oh, it is shit,' he said.

III

We paddled past Fifth Meridian, where the river was a mile wide and split with long thin islands of sand – deceptive islands, it was hard to tell where one ended and another began and whether you were in the main channel or not. For a long time we paddled happily in the early morning light till Barney snapped, 'We haven't moved for ten minutes!' I looked at the bank, fixing on a particular tree. It was true, we were making no progress. We pulled in, unwound the towrope and began towing. Then the bank ran out and we were back to paddling. Though the crew were good for a burst of paddling none of them had the experience or inclination to be able to paddle hard for a sustained period. Like John the year before I was always having to chivvy – 'More gyp, lads!' 'Give it some welly!' 'More power, please!' They would gear up but soon wind down. If there was space to tow on the bank they all preferred that, if only perhaps because of the freedom of walking while your partner took his turn in the tow harness.

Paddling now with an eye on our progress, I would pick out a tree and see if, over a short time, we were gaining on it. Looking at the river was no use because the boat always appeared to be going forward, simply because of the current moving past. A far bank would show less progress than a near bank because of the effect of perspective, and if you chose a too-ordinary-looking tree, you could torment yourself with thinking you'd gone nowhere whereas in fact you'd just lost your landmark.

Way across the river, on the other side of a low sand spit, we heard barking. A wisp of blue smoke trailed its way up lazily between the trees in a clearing. A dog came down to the beach and a man – both so far away, over half a mile, that you could only register their general shape. The man and the dog sat down on the beach and looked out at us. We waved and he waved.

'That's his uncle,' said Barney. 'Shall we go and visit?'

I said, 'It'll be a bind to cross that sand spit.'

I was in a hurry to move on and we didn't cross the spit and visit the Indian on the beach. What a mistake. I regretted it almost immediately and for the rest of the trip. The man sat on the beach for a long time, as if expecting us, but then when it was obvious we weren't coming over he got up and left. Like Harvald, the lonely Norwegian, I'd let my city-bred stress dictate the journey. Always cross the river for a chat, what's half an hour? An hour?

The further we went on the more I felt I'd missed an opportunity, something vital for the trip, for me, for some inner journey. I really let it get to me. That man on the beach really got inside my head, as if he was a lesson for not hurrying past life in the future, as if he stood for all the encounters I've hidden from or hurried from in the name of efficiency and productivity.

As if to rub it in, as soon as we left the wide part of the river we wasted the rest of the day battling the wind, trapped in some tight powerful curves that we could not paddle against. It was a strange moment too when, landing against a muddy beach after nearly capsizing, no one would go any further. It was as if our collective will had dried up. My lassitude then turned into a furious temper and I ploughed on with the towrope, straining against wind and current, the mud sometimes up to my thighs.

And of course the beach did not go on for ever, better towing ground soon appeared. But it seemed then that if I had not taken us forward we would have given up, got back in our boat and drifted home. And compared to what came later, it really wasn't so bad, it just required a mental adjustment to the effort needed. I had an inkling then that by the end this trip would have demanded everything from us; we would find the limits of our own exertion, or they would be found for us. The wind continued hard and blew us back across the river. After making only ten kilometres we gave up and camped on a blustery point.

IV

It was morning, still dark, and the fire was blazing, Barney's ragged profile back-lit by the flames. He had taken to wearing his quick-dry blue towel as a kind of Bedouin headscarf and had grown a villainous beard. A new routine had emerged, with me waking first but Barney getting up first, to rake up the embers and get the fire blazing, and then make the porridge. Porridge had become an obsession with Barney. I think he sensed in its homely connotations some kind of return to lost innocence and control, the pre-adolescent world where drugs, drink and vice and family discord and nasty kids who beat up pensioners in the street do not exist. Powerful stuff, porridge.

Dave and Joe were forever experimenting, adding their potions and tiny bags of seeds and 'other sundry crap', as Barney put it, but only much later. At this stage he was as careful as all of us in not insulting each other's cooking. It was too easy to do, and also, with the circulation of the task, it would be your turn soon enough. But Dave's cinnamon porridge took some getting used to at five in the morning. Now Barney had wrested control of the porridge detail and since his tastes were orthodox (no bits of gritty chocolate or sunflower seeds for him) it was, to me, an improvement. It also meant I didn't have to be the one kick-starting the day. Only later did I realize the importance of Mackenzie's dictate that the leader must be the last to bed and the first up – always, even if it means sleeping in the boat during the day, which Mackenzie admits to doing several times. Simon Fraser, whose belligerent, portly visage contrasts with Mackenzie's rather fey but determined portrait, made fun of the great explorer, attributing any navigational error to the fact that he may have been asleep. It shows how much lack of cant there was in those times. In a major report, which Mackenzie had every opportunity to doctor to make himself look good, he chose to report himself as he was – a man who napped on the job. I imagine it was also received in proportionate measure since Fraser meant humour rather than serious disparagement by his comments.

The fire licked and flamed in the darkness. Soon we were all standing around it drinking our coffee, staring into the flames and warming ourselves. This was the fourth day since leaving Garden Creek. By leaving at three-thirty and paddling all day we might just get to Little Red River in time for the new chief's ceremony. Joe especially was moaning about the hour, but we had thirty kilometres ahead of us so there was no choice in the matter.

To be on the water before first light, with the moon and the mist your only companions, and then to see the tops of the pines yellowing in the first shafts of sunlight, this sort of experience confirms the overwhelming and subtle beauty of the wild. It was the same place the night before, but then I noticed nothing. In that warm, magical morning light, perspective seems altered. Everything is as marvellously crisp as a *National Geographic* photograph, which gives a clue – it is all in the head – that what you're seeing is just a series of light impulses, subtly different from the night before, and these convey beauty and a oneness of the scene and the observer. Is this, then, the reality underlying all of it? And if it is, why are we privileged only to see it in the odd hours, early morning or perhaps at sunset if we're lucky?

Joe started to take photographs. 'This is worth it,' I said warmly. He grunted assent and stood up in the canoe to catch the exact moment when the sun broke free from the horizon, as if from viscous liquid, spreading instantly everywhere.

Our paddles slipped smoothly through the still water and we paddled on, making easy miles against easy current, in silent appreciation of everything around us – banks of overgrown spruce, usually a mess to look at, achieved a strange dignity in the shafting sunlight, as if their confusion of exposed roots and tumbled tree boles were part of a wonderful and complex design.

We stopped for some early morning tea and out of the sun it was freezing cold. I banged the pots together and the echo came back from all sides like quadraphonic speakers in a car.

All through the wilderness we were flanked by extraordinary echoes. Long echoes that took ten seconds to come back – meaning the sound travelled nearly four kilometres there and back from whatever reflected it. Magnifying echoes, which took a shout and threw it back louder. Multiples – sometimes as many as ten, dying with a dying fall, as satisfying as getting ten bounces from a flat stone skimmed on water. There was no terrain that was better than another for echoes. Craggy cliffs and caves high up were no better than a featureless stretch of pines on either side of the wideness of the river. Sometimes a place that looked perfect for an echo was only average. The best echoes were discovered by chance, a splash or a voice coming back to you when you least expected it.

In the middle of all the serenity Dave had to start talking: 'Did you know that Canada is the only G8 country without an aircraft carrier?'

There was a pause as we sucked our thoughts from the mist on the river and our noiseless progress to the naval concerns of a great nation. No one could think of anything to say.

Later, while Dave was making lunch, he resisted my attempt to throw out some of the spilled seeds: 'I got big plans for those sesame seeds,' he said.

'What you going to do? Build an aircraft carrier out of them?' quipped Barney.

It was dusk when we heard the haunting double-reverb drumming from three or four kilometres away, over the hill. It was a zinging, humming background of drumming with knucklebone beat of bass, a soft thud central to all of it.

Drawn by the drums, we took the wrong channel, over some merciless shallows. We had to turn back and go the long way around an island that guarded the entrance to Little Red River. On a rock on the island perched two eagles, one with the white shoulders of a mature eagle and the other darker and younger. They sat on their rock and watched us go by, the first eagles we'd seen remain in one place and not fly off as we approached. Inexplicable as it may seem, I believe those birds had some purpose being there. Very Carlos Castaneda, but there you are.

All the drumming was variations of this same basic beat, a beat that fits extremely well to the archetypal and possibly made-up, certainly clichéd, image of the Indian doing his shuffling, jumping, hopping and crouching, whooping war dance.

The first sound of the drums had been discounted. 'That's not drums is it?' 'Can't be. We're still miles away.' But it was, the drumming encapsulating the hillside and surrounding terrain, holding it in its palm.

The drums had an echo within the beat and then echoed again off the hills and the islands as we approached. There was also a distinct smell of hamburgers, at least it seemed so to me. 'Bargain,' said Joe, who had perked up as soon as we heard the drums, 'I could murder a burger.'

It was almost dark now and we could just make out a few boats pulled up on the beach. A dirt road wound up steeply and away through woodland. The drums were booming but we could see no one. 'Remember, we were invited,' said Joe, the kind of mantra one repeats before gate-crashing a party where another guest rather than the host has invited you. The drums, though, countered any sense of desolation or loneliness; they united the land, just as the early-morning rays had. It was almost as if this place needed the drums to make us see it properly. The canoe nosed in through the small waves. At least we were arriving in the right kind of boat, no one could deny that.

Five

BECAUSE THE ELDERS SAY SO

'"What," demanded he, *"can be the reason that you
are so particular and anxious in your enquiries of
us respecting a knowledge of this country: do not you
whitemen know everything?"'* An Atnah Indian
perplexes Mackenzie

I

We lifted the canoe up the beach and stored all our gear under
it, very aware that anyone could steal it if they wanted to. But
at the same time knowing that we would have to trust these
people. We were on their turf and it would be bad to look too
suspicious. 'It's all right,' said Dave in a low voice, 'I'll stay with
the canoe until you've checked it out.' I was relieved. I certainly
didn't want to stay and yet it made sense to have someone guard
our stuff.

Halfway up the dirt road an Indian with a red maple-leaf
bandanna around his head sat on a quad-bike, staring out across
the dark water, his eyeline way over our heads. Barney, Joe and
I went up towards him, into the sound of the drums.

As we climbed, we saw more people. The man on the quad
was young and proud-looking. He didn't even look at us as we
approached. A young woman with a baby was climbing on the
back.

'Er, excuse me, is this the way to the ceremony?' I asked. The
Indian didn't answer. Great. Just the welcome I was dreading.
Then his wife spoke up in perfectly ordinary English. But not
over-friendly: 'It's just up the top of the hill.'

157

'Is it all right us coming?' asked Joe. 'We were told about it at Garden Creek.'

'It's OK,' said the woman. 'There's food up there.'

The Indian man said something in Cree and then roared off up the hill.

We trudged after them, the drums singing and booming; yes, definitely a musical note to the double beat. 'Definitely a musical note to that double beat,' I said.

'Yes,' said Barney, 'bloody loud too.'

Mostly white people are not welcome on reserves, that had been the subtext of most of my conversations with Canadians. Fear of bears and fear of Indians pretty much summed up the wilderness anxieties of the public. 'They do a lot of drinking on those reserves,' warned Jean-François the art-canoe builder I'd spoken to so long ago. Yet neither Charlie nor Cynthia drank and they lived on a reserve. You mentally prepare for the worst in such situations. 'If they tell us to fuck off, which I'm sure they won't, we'll just get in the canoe and paddle off,' I said.

'I was thinking that,' said Barney.

Joe was keyed up and excited, all hint of the tiredness he'd been complaining about since our dawn start driven out by the looming adventure. Curiosity and apprehension vied with each other, a good feeling. We wanted to be there after all. It felt like real exploration.

The success of Mackenzie's trip was totally bound up with the Indians he met. He often attempted to cure natives and win favour that way. 'A woman with a swelled breast which had been lacerated with flintstones for the cure of it, presented herself to my attention, and by cleanliness, poultices and healing salve I succeeded in producing a cure.' In another case, to cure blood poisoning he prepared 'a kind of volatile liniment of rum and soap with which I ordered [the patient's] arm to be rubbed'. When this failed to have an effect Mackenzie bled the man, but he was nervous: 'I ventured, from absolute necessity, to perform that operation for the first time, and [luckily] with an effect that justified the treatment ... in a short time the man regained his former health and activity.' Mackenzie was a trader and knew that even nominal enemies can co-operate if there is something in it for both of them. That canny ability, honed no doubt since his first days in a Montreal counting-house at fifteen, was one source of his confidence I am sure. The fact that he was a businessman not a soldier, though his group were armed, made him see potential collaboration rather than opposition wherever he went.

His method was to use his two native hunters to procure the first guides, and then for these guides to procure the next set before leaving them, and so on, thus ensuring a smooth passage. There were times when they were guideless and then had to be careful: 'My interpreters, who understood their language, informed me that they threatened us with instant death if we drew nigh the shore.' But Mackenzie was cunning. To win the confidence of frightened Indians he walked alone along the beach. He appeared defenceless but had one of his hunters sneak through the forest with his gun trained on the Indians in case they should release their loaded bows. Mackenzie also had two primed pistols stuck in his belt but out of sight. With the inducement of looking glasses, beads, and 'other alluring trinkets' Mackenzie succeeded in calming their fears and obtaining a new guide.

At the top of the hill we found the ceremony. A ring of battered pick-ups with their lights dipped surrounded a small campfire. There must have been over fifty vehicles in the ring and though the fire blazed it was no bonfire. No one sat around it. There was a big marquee-type tent fixed up out of huge blue tarpaulins. Indians milled about everywhere and a line snaked out from the big tent. There were people, children, the odd dog and roaring quad-bikes kicking up dust everywhere. Groups of men sat on the ground, always one or two of them drumming on big tambourine-like drums. The vibrato sound came from a cord stretched across the face of the drum, which was beaten with a double-ended stick. From time to time men would walk up to the fire and warm their drumskins against its flames.

A youngish guy in his thirties came up and said hello. I asked why the drummers were warming the drum skins. He explained that the drum went flat when it was cold. We told him our story and he said we should eat some of the food they were serving, a moose stew. People were friendly in the line and the women serving fished out good chunks of meat for us from the bottom of the huge aluminium cooking pots. The youngish man came over again and said we should meet his brother who was going to be the new chief. We hung around eating our moose stew and feeling a little guilty that Dave was sitting alone in the dark down by the river. Then a big fat man in his fifties came up. His name was Floyd. He welcomed us and told us we could camp up on the bluff if we wanted to. 'The canoe will be fine here,' he said. 'Everyone will keep an eye on it. These are good people.' Floyd was the new chief.

We went amongst the people and listened to the drumming and watched the hand games. This is what the men were doing, facing each other in two lines of eight, each with a blanket over his lap under which he hid his hands. Then the hands would come out and all manner of signs and gestures would be made. If you had a pebble in your hand then it meant something. There was also a stick that was used for pointing. All the time there would be drumming going on and the whole game was performed with the tempo set by the drummers. Some of the pointing men did a kind of sitting dance as they prepared to point. This was some kind of psych-out, or so it seemed. All the hand movements were as quick as wading birds dipping their beaks into water.

There was no gambling going on and no games of platter, which Mackenzie records as a favourite game when he passed through: 'Flat pieces of metal wood or stone whose surfaces are of different colours are put into the dish, and after being for some time shaken together, are thrown into the air, and received again into the dish with considerable dexterity; when, by the number that are turned up of the same colour, the game is regulated.'

The PA system broadcast all announcements in Cree. Every now and then there would be a burst of English we could recognize, like 'chief and council'. Then we heard our own

160

names, or rather, Barney's. 'Bar-ney!' boomed the PA. 'Bar-ney!' Children, excited by our presence, ran around calling, 'Bar-ney.' We were being summoned to a microphone under the big tent. Floyd made a short speech in English for our benefit and then in Cree. He said, 'They have come from England in a birchbark canoe. The last Englishmen came when they signed the treaty over a hundred years ago. This is a good sign. We have always had good feelings towards the Queen of England.'

I was then called upon to make a speech from the microphone, which I did, emphasizing birchbark and Mackenzie's dependence on the Cree people. After the speech Floyd gave all of us a tape of traditional drumming and singing. In the darkness his face loomed sweatily. 'Some of the elders think this is a good sign,' he said. 'You are very welcome.'

Was it being from England? Or was it appearing at night like ghosts riding in a birchbark canoe? All the Indians had come by pick-up or motorboat. We hadn't explained that Dave was a Canadian; I hoped that wouldn't spoil our reception. To assuage the guilt for having been away so long, Barney and I took some moose stew wrapped in bread down to him. He looked up nervously as we approached, his white face peering out from the darkness behind the canoe.

'It's amazing up there,' said Barney.

'They're good people,' I said. 'The canoe will be fine.'

'I'll take my camera though,' said Dave.

'Don't flash the dope about either,' I said.

'No worries,' said Dave.

Walking back up the track I could tell that Dave was not as entranced as Barney, Joe and me. He mumbled on about Indians he had been at school with, back in his home town in British Columbia. I got the impression that Dave didn't much like Indians, or rather, shared the common view that there was nothing magical, mystical or special about them.

Being new to it all made us more open. Being from another country meant the iniquitous welfare system that favoured 'treaty' Indians was of no interest to us. It was all academic. Our taxes weren't subsidizing their tobacco habit, the redneck view.

I wasn't even exactly sure what a redneck was – though Dave and Joe were. Tree planters on one side, rednecks on the other. Hippies and squares. Urban and rural. Good and bad. Their paranoia, especially Dave's, was always in danger of infecting us all.

II

The next day we were up early for the ceremony. Dave had asked to film it and the chief told him to attend a meeting at nine o'clock. The meeting didn't start until ten, when all the elders and the council could be there. The meeting was also in Cree. At the end Dave still didn't know if he could film or not and went off in a huff. He was full of the ire of a man who has never dealt with tribal people who hold all the power. Floyd had already said no to a CBC team who wanted to film, and a government health worker I spoke to said he had been waiting a week to find out if he could take photographs or not. Perhaps because this was Canada, and Dave was Canadian, he thought the Indians should behave like other folks. But there was no talking to him. Black with rage at all the stalling, he took to his small tent in high dudgeon to get high. Dave had a great Tupperware box full of anxiety-relieving grass and his flysheet was zipped tight against intrusion.

Later that day, an hour or two before the ceremony, we were told we could film everything apart from the ceremonial progress of the chief and elders into the area around the campfire. We went to find Dave, but he would not come out of his tent, such was his discontent. I didn't really mind. In the video of the trip I even looked forward to editing in a black section with a voiceover announcing that here there was no footage because the cameraman/director was too pissed off to shoot any. We could even have the drumming in the background. It would be fine.

162

I went down to the canoe to fix a leak in the bottom. The leak had been getting worse and worse and now we had to bale her out every night. The canoe was also getting heavier. It was a mystery as to why. I wondered if she was rotting away beneath the cedar sheathing. I poked around with my knife and the bottom seam opened up. It was all wet inside and there was silt forcing the two sheets of bark apart. Clayey silt had worked its way beneath the ribs and thin cedar sheathing and, when we shipped water, was absorbing it. I poked as much out as I could and plastered on more noxious Vulkem to seal it up.

'Looks like pretty hi-tech pine resin to me,' said a sarcastic voice. I looked up and saw a grey-haired man, maybe in his early fifties, in the fawn shirt favoured by government workers in the outback. It was Fred, a road engineer, who was here on a consulting job. He had earlier been keen to talk to us, but quickly we had all started to avoid him. He was a know-all, about bears and Indians, both of which he held in considerable contempt. When I told him about the two bald eagles we'd seen on the island he'd snapped back, 'Must be the only two for fifty miles. Guys round here shoot 'em for power feathers.' He snickered and lit up another green export cigarette. I didn't bother telling him we'd seen lots of bald eagles. It was his favourite tune, how Indians shot everything indiscriminately. 'No bears around here,' he said, 'they're too smart. Know what'll happen to them.

'I know these people. I've been around them all my life. They get a piece of technology, they use it until it breaks and then they dump it. Usually in a tree or on their lawn. There's no booze here, there never is at these ceremonies, but back on the reserve they make hooch out of everything from raisins to turpentine. Worst thing the government ever did was make the laws different for 'em. Why? I work. I pay my taxes.'

'But this work you're doing is paid for by the government. You're benefiting from taxes too.'

'Right,' he said, pointing his cigarette butt at me, his greying moustache thrust forward, 'but if this road happens it will be useful. I'm working for my wages, not sitting on my backside beating a drum.'

I had heard the elders were against an asphalt road to the reserve. I agreed. Why did every white person I talked to think that a road was necessary, inevitable and a 'safety issue'?

Fred thought the Indians had lost their backwoods skills. 'Hell, they'd be lost without a quad and a jetboat.'

I told him about an Indian boy who had walked from Uranium City on Lake Athabasca back to Fort Chipewyan when his snowmobile broke down. Fred waved the story away: 'Kid was probably a crackhead – needed to get home for his fix.'

Fred turned his attentions to our canoe. 'Prefer a cedar strip myself – stronger. Done some canoeing too – you know the Barrons Lake circuit?'

I did. It was a five-day jaunt on safe, still water. 'Ever paddled against the current?' I said.

'Yeah,' he said, but breezily, the way I'd have replied based solely on my experience on the Cherwell in Oxford. Real paddling against the current leaves permanent scars on the personality; even hearing the words 'against' and 'current' in close succession is likely to cause such a person to stare deeply into the distance or start giggling nervously. I looked at Fred's hard, confident face. There were no scars. Guy didn't know what he was talking about.

IV

After the ceremonial procession and the chanting and the speeches in Cree by the elders, everyone formed a long line to walk past and shake hands with the elders. Some people hugged and kissed the women elders (there were two out of a group of about ten), some did not. I decided just to shake hands, but one elder, in a cowboy hat and a grey mane of frizzy hair, gave me a hug with real warmth. Perhaps he was the man who had insisted we were a good omen.

The Little Red River site was dotted with old cabins. No one

164

lived there any more, they only gathered for ceremonies. All the Indians made little encampments in the trees and bushes; ours were the only tents that were exposed. I soon saw why Indians prefer camping under trees. The sun broiled us and the tent was uncomfortably hot. When it rained the trees also provided extra cover. The tents the Indians used were cheap camping tents or shelter tents made from blue plastic tarpaulins strung over a pole frame in the shape of a hut. A small number of wealthy Indians had caravan trailers, the ubiquitous RVs. In the little family encampments some offered food for sale. We bought bannock dogs – a sausage wrapped in an unleavened-bread bannock. Older kids roared about on quads and little kids played in the old cabins, but all were polite and friendly to us. Far more so than in any comparable gathering in the urban developed parts of the world. There was no drinking at all and not a single instance of rowdy, aggressive behaviour, which for a week-long festival is not bad going. This was a community in good shape.

I met Stephen and his father, who were watching the hand games. When I told Stephen we had seen his uncle but hadn't stopped he said, 'You missed a good chance. He is one of those outgoing-type Indians.' I felt again all the regret of missing my chance to make contact with the man. For a reason I couldn't fathom it felt more important than the bare facts suggested. Indians are not that outgoing and to find one who is is rare. But there was more to it than that. Like the mysterious two eagles and later a lucky charm we were given, I saw it as part of some kind of destiny, strange though that may sound. Messages from the river and its people. And who is to say the reality of a landscape isn't partly the work of those who have lived there for hundreds or thousands of years?

V

After failing to film the ceremony, Dave emerged from his tent red-eyed and mellow. 'It's fine, man, really, I'm fine.' Apologies didn't come naturally to Dave. He had a macho manner, gruff and rude to strangers, which contrasted oddly with his small, meek body. He had been around macho guys all his life and though he had their mannerisms and speech habits he also hated their insularity and ignorance. Of all of us, Dave was the best read, and on the trip he read literary novels rather than thrillers. Joe asked him once, 'How did you get so much time to read in your short life?' 'What makes you think I got a life?' said Dave. Like all serious readers, Dave had a book in his hand the moment we had any sort of break. At lunchtime he'd lie back on the sand and slowly turn the pages, his fierce brow relaxed, the veins, for once, not standing out quite so insanely. His habit was catching. Soon, all of us would be reading, lying in a line on the ground, lost in different worlds. I had finished Fiennes and was now on an inferior collection of short stories by Frederick Forsythe. Barney was steadfastly ploughing through a historical novel about Troy whilst Dave read Dostoevsky.

We spent three days at Little Red River. Dave grew less apprehensive. One day he was nervous again, though. 'Did you see that guy?' he said.

'Who?'

'The man with hardcore tatts. He wanted me to go down to the river with him.'

'To do what?'

'I don't know. Maybe he sensed I had dope on me.'

Dave painted a vivid and mysterious portrait of the man with hardcore tatts. The man had spoken only a few words of English and had simply made a sign towards the river, indicating Dave should follow. But Dave had stayed near his tent reading *Crime and Punishment*.

The night before we left, Floyd led a dance around the area of the campfire. All the pick-ups switched to full beam and flooded the area with light. Fred was still hanging around, demonstrating his superior knowledge. 'See that headdress he's wearing? Mail-order from Colorado. No woodland Cree ever wore feathers like that.' He smirked and fired up another cigarette. 'Even those hand games are a new thing. Thirty years ago they weren't doing it around here. All imported from other places.' Fred didn't understand that as long as the externals were Indian things it really didn't matter if they were adapted from other places or not. They merely filled the gap, kept people from becoming bored. The reality was all below the surface, but too much modernity damaged that reality, which was why they still needed Indian ways of doing things, even superficially, since they went better, fitted better with the occasion. Crucially the first language was still Cree and they still lived in their own place. All the quads and boats fitted with fish-finders didn't change that. Fred sneered at my ideas: 'They didn't even wear moccasins round here, used to be bare feet or birchbark shoes. Not too many in birchbark shoes out there dancing.'

But why shouldn't Indians borrow from each other? They always have – Mackenzie wrote of the Chipewyan, 'Their religion is of a very contracted nature, and I never witnessed any ceremony of devotion which they had not borrowed from the Knisteneaux [Cree], their feasts and fasts being in imitation of that people.' Fred's comments were as absurd as castigating the English for adopting the imported malignancy of the family barbecue.

An older Indian man who worked at Suncor in Fort McMurray had come back specially for the ceremony. He complained that the wildlife was disappearing, though this hadn't been our experience. 'Even the mosquitoes are getting less. Used to come out here in June and you couldn't walk without being eaten alive. You needed someone out front with a smudge pot to keep them away. Even the mosquitoes are getting weak.'

After the dancing, which went on for hours, we found Floyd, red and sweaty, swigging on mineral water by the edge of the fire. 'I never saw your boat,' he said, when Joe and I told him we would be leaving very early the next day. 'Whatever anyone else says,' he told us, 'I believe that we were honoured by your coming. I believe it was a special sign.'

It sounded as if Floyd had had to argue the toss about our spiritual significance. It didn't matter. Nor did it matter that any 'sign' was obviously of benefit to him in his role as new chief. Our journey had been long and hard and we had made it in a traditional boat, that was enough. At sunrise we loaded the canoe, ready to leave. The festivities had continued very late into the night and now everyone was asleep. A good time to slip away. The paddling wasn't easy but we didn't want to tow. After a mile or so Joe, who was sitting behind Dave, said, 'What's that hanging down at the front of the boat?'

Dave reached under and pulled out a metal hand studded with pieces of coloured glass. It was tied into our bow, under the curve, with a piece of blue woollen thread interwoven with the spruce root. Who put it there, or when it had been done, no one knew. We had been subdued leaving, but now we were happy. Now we had medicine on board, and *Dragonfly* and her crew were protected.

Six

PORTAGE FROM HELL

'At eleven we arrived at the rapids, and the foreman,
not forgetting the fright he suffered on coming down
it, proposed that the canoe and the lading should be
carried over the mountain.' Alexander Mackenzie

I

The Vermilion Falls were rather disappointing to look at. In fact, though we could hear the booming from two miles away, the kind of background noise that raises the pulse even though we were the safe side of the drop, I actually couldn't see them until Barney pointed out the white line across the river. We paddled closer and closer and we had to shout over the noise. Mist rose from the plunging foam. The boat wobbled and rocked from the disturbed water. Closer still, sheets of water plunged across exposed rock shelves that stretched the entire width of the river. Mackenzie estimated it to be four hundred yards, far short of the actual width which is 1.6 kilometres, or almost exactly a mile. I was always heartened by Mackenzie's errors, especially his massive ones.

We needed to go up them, or around them.

Though plenty of clever canoeists in boats made of plastic had manhandled their way down the side of the falls, hefting their boats from step to step, ours was too fragile; and besides, we wanted to go up, which looked impossible from my position in the foaming, ozone-loaded swirl-pool with dark quiet corners spiralled with river muck, like cream in coffee. Smell of pond everywhere, all of us shouting and pointing. The falls looked about twenty-five feet high. Not spectacularly high, unless you planned to ascend them, then they became impossibly high, like an easily climbed but locked gate must look to someone in a wheelchair.

We searched for Mackenzie's old portage trail – portage is the correct voyageur term for lugging your canoe and all your bits. We'd never done it before, not over a significant distance. The real sting in the tail with portaging is that you have to make several journeys. First the canoe. Then back for the packs. Then back for the cooking kit/water/food barrel/Dave's shoes/Joe's beaver skull and whatever other pieces of stuff we'd managed to accumulate. Canoes encourage hoarding – there's always a bit of space to stuff something nice: a fossil, a quartz crystal, the lower jaw of a wolf. Dave was the worst – his gigantic black plastic waterproof rucksack, as huge as a bodybag, was growing heavier by the day. It positively chinked with all the loose stones he'd collected.

Mackenzie wrote: 'The first carrying place is 800 paces in length, and the last, which is about a mile onwards, is something more than two thirds of that distance.' I loved that. Typical Mackenzie. He'd paced the first part and then probably lost count halfway through the second and thus delivered the masterful 'something more than two thirds of that distance', i.e. from six hundred yards to six miles.

Mackenzie was always underestimating distances; only very rarely does he overestimate. Part of this must be connected to his shaky navigational skills. After all, if you see something as four times shorter than it really is then you are hardly likely to be much good at finding your way in unfamiliar country. Mackenzie's errors and shortcomings – the fact that he dropped one compass in the river, the notebook he lost, the times he fell asleep when the canoe slid past some important topographical feature – all this endeared him to me, made him more human and fallible, and therefore meant that we too had a chance of completing the journey. When it came to the daily log of distance covered there was a good reason for Mackenzie's conservative guesses. He did, at the time, believe he was surveying a trade route to the Pacific. There was no value in it being a vast distance.

For potential investors the shorter it was the better. He was after fame, but only if it was profitable. There was no mileage in excess mileage. But Vermilion Falls only four hundred yards wide? No wonder Simon Fraser felt compelled to make fun of him.

We backtracked a thousand yards until we found a path leading up through the woods. Not Mackenzie's trail, but good enough.

I followed the path alone. It wound up and up through a dense woodland of hazel, spruce and poplar. It was late afternoon and the green light through the trees soothed my eyes, stung by so many days' squinting into the sun on the river. The woods smelled of damp moss and I longed to just lie down and stare up through the leaves to the blue sky. But I couldn't stop, not even for a contemplative break. Even twenty yards from the river the mosquitoes were bad. I thought about the Indian who missed the real swarms. He obviously hadn't been here. The hair on my forearms were soon matted with sweat, blood and the broken remains of twenty mosquitoes, two horseflies (always gratifyingly slow off the mark, too greedy by half), countless unimportant gnat-like biters and one blackfly – quite a coup, since blackfly look a little bit like ordinary harmless houseflies and you only know they've bitten you after they've flown.

I have to say to Mackenzie's credit he very rarely mentions being bitten by insects. When he was in deep trouble on the Bad River he allowed a single reference: 'To add to our perplexities and embarrassments, we were persecuted by musquitoes and sand-flies, through the whole of the day.'

The path began to curve to the right. Finally it met a bigger trail with quad tracks. This was a later 'big' portage trail from the Vermilion Rapids to Little Red River. The rapids are a couple of miles upstream of the falls and in the days when the Peace River was navigated by steam-powered sternwheelers the passengers would be driven in wagons pulled by horse teams the eight miles around the 'chutes' (a collective name often used for both the falls and the rapids but actually referring to a way through the rapids on the right side) and on to the then trading post at Little Red River. If we stuck to this track we'd eventually find it curving down to the river again. The track wasn't marked on our map, though later when I saw a smaller-scale map, four miles to the inch based on a 1903 survey, it had the falls clearly marked and the routes around them. The present maps have less information and, apart from contour lines, which aren't necessary for river work, are inferior in every sense to the old maps of a hundred years ago.

I went back and reported the news about the paths and insects to the others who were waiting by the river. The distance we needed to carry the canoe looked to be about eight kilometres. Which meant 16km if we did it in two loads. 'Er, no,' said Barney. 'It's there, back, and there again, so actually it's twenty-four kilometres.' Shit. The true horror of portaging began to sink in. There was no way we could do it in two loads. Even three might be pushing it. There, back, there, back, there = 40km. In thirty-degree heat. With insects. If it took four loads, it would be a staggering 56km. Portaging was like some horrific real-life verification of those maths teasers where you keep folding a piece of paper and after twenty folds it's thicker than the distance to the sun. We all stood round the canoe and stared at its full load, willing it to be less than four carries, the figure of fifty-six kilometres dampening enthusiasm to such a low point that no one could be even bothered to put on their headnet before shouldering the sopping bulk of the canoe with its lucky medicine charm chinking in the bow.

With a man under each corner with a lifejacket on his shoulder, we stumbled up the path into the mosquito-infested gloom. After a hundred yards my shoulder was killing me. I couldn't conceive of eight kilometres of this, never mind fifty-six. It was like Scott's final eleven miles to the fabled one-ton depot. Only eleven miles. Nothing. But in their situation as impossible as ... as eight kilometres carrying a sodden piece of stitched birchbark. I needed to get some perspective. We had to stop anyway. The former lassitude over headnets had vanished. Everyone was slapping and cursing at their blotchy noses and ears. The deeper we went into the forest the more intense the attacks, homing in with a blur of whining and diving, micro-Stukas of the insect world; we almost threw the canoe to the floor before pulling on headnets in a tormented rush. As the others rested and no doubt contemplated the impossible exertions ahead, I went into the bush to cut two poles to lash to the thwarts so that we could carry the boat more easily. It was even darker away from the path and I was in a hurry. I hacked with my saw at a thin tree, tormented by bugs making the most of just my wrists and the backs of my hands. With a hasty draw-stroke the saw blade of my folding Sandvik pruning saw, an otherwise excellent piece of kit, bounced out of the shallow groove and tore into the soft flesh between finger and thumb. The sudden upwelling of dark told me it was a deep cut, and like all saw cuts it was painful. White transparent flaps of skin immediately blobbed over with a fresh gout of blood after I sucked it dry – the best way to get a field cut clean since saliva contains its own antiseptic, and in my case, with a reduced ration of toothpaste, rather more antiseptic than usual. Joe was sympathetic – one of his most endearing characteristics – and found a bandage for me in the first-aid bag. It was now almost dark. The pole idea was quietly dropped as we trailed back to the river, wet sweaty shirts stretched tight, slapping and banging at our backs, across our shoulderblades, a favourite spot for horseflies to sink their teeth.

II

Was the boat lighter? After a night in the forest we convinced ourselves it was. Even so, it still felt as heavy as a bath full of concrete. From the brief inspection I made when repairing the leak at Little Red River I suspected there was mud everywhere inside the boat, in every crack and crevice beneath the sheathing; how much silt could you hide in that way? A lot, and it would all hold water, never drying out properly, hence, I now understood, the constant sogginess of the lower part of all the ribs. The full tragic dimensions of the situation glimmered: the boat was sucking up water like a sponge from the reservoir of moisture in the silt. The leaks constantly topped up the silt with water, which then bled slowly into the woodwork. No wonder the thing now weighed more than double its original 110 or so pounds.

From now on, I said to myself with great moment, we would pull the boat out of the water at every opportunity. Give it at least a little chance to dry out. The more radical solution of taking all the ribs and sheathing out did not really occur. I thought it would take too long and I was worried in case, like the electric yogurt maker I expertly disassembled as a child 'to see how it worked', it would never go back together again.

Now we had to shoulder that weight, despite talking up the drying effect of the night. It was quite cool in the shade by the river and by some kind of false consensus we all agreed the bugs were far fewer than the night before. To support this erroneous piece of group denial, no one wore their headnet as we hefted the boat. After just fifty metres we had to stop.

Everyone was being eaten alive. Worse than before. Not just mosquitoes and horseflies, but also blackfly. Barney was so incensed by the insects he put on his fleece, tucked his socks into his shoes, donned his headnet and wore his wetsuit-material paddling gloves. The sky was cloudless above the larches and poplars and it was heating up. Everyone 'netted up'. I doused myself with DEET, which worked a bit, as it always does, but never quite enough. 'How about cutting some more poles?' suggested Barney. 'The gunwhale's cutting into my shoulder.' All machismo had vanished. Anything that made things even slightly more comfortable was now an absolute necessity.

We took the boat five kilometres, returned, brought the first set of bags three kilometres, returned, and brought the second set of bags three kilometres. The returning part was joyously easy, like that trick where you stand in a doorway and push your arms hard against the frame. When you move forwards your arms rise miraculously. It was like that, especially after scrabbling like overloaded hunchbacks under the second set of bags. These were all the awkward things: the heavy grill that banged shins and carved out divots of flesh, the food barrel, the hundred-litre sausage-like Ortlieb backpack with shoulder straps so positioned they crushed the chest – walking with this on you drew rapid hot little breaths, like a baby rabbit trapped in some hideous medical experiment.

We soon separated out as each man bore his burden as best he could. I noticed the particular viciousness with which straps were released, bags flung, boxes dumped as soon as the agreed drop point had been reached. As each man arrived and saw the growing pile of bags he loosed his own further and further away. The bags spread out for yards along the track, like garbage strewn from a speeding vehicle. Sixteen kilometres down, twenty-four to go. It was lunchtime, a sad and silent lunch broken every so often by the sound of ferocious slapping. 'Hey,' said Barney, 'I can drink tea through my net.' Joe smoked inside his, radiating malignant gloom.

Lunch ended with everyone urinating on the fire. It was hot and dry so we wanted the embers properly doused. All of us pissing on the fire was like some collective sign of aggression against our surroundings, as if we were closing ranks against the evils of the forest. We hoisted bags to walk the remaining two kilometres to the canoe. These were dumped and the canoe lifted. Conversation was, at first, mere muffled grunts from beneath headnets. Then the trail narrowed and started to head downhill. Every hundred metres or so we had to traverse a blown-down tree. Sometimes by staggering almost on to our knees we could get under the trunk. Most of the time we had to lift the boat over. This involved sawing branches off and a delicate manoeuvring so that the stub-end of branch didn't puncture the skin of the boat. The path narrowed even more, so that one side or the other was constantly having their faces rammed into the oncoming spruce. Now the muffled grunts became clear expletives: 'Not this side. Go left!' 'Fuck. I'm in another bush.' Barney in his wetsuit gloves and fleece was purple-faced with heat. When we tottered on to the gravel beach at the end of the track he tore off his headnet and plunged his whole head in the river. The rest of us scratched at our bloody welts and thought about going back for the bags. Twice.

Then Joe, despite the sullen gloom that enveloped him, had a brilliant idea. He outlined the comparative ease of floating the boat back downstream to the head of the rapids. We had been forced to walk an extra two kilometres, because, at the end of the rapids, the track was a hundred metres above the river and took this distance to descend back to river level. Joe suggested we could slither down this steep hundred-metre slope with the bags in a way that wouldn't have been possible with the boat. This would save two kilometres. Times five. Ten kilometres. I was reluctant to accept the idea simply because it was Joe's. I preferred it when I had the great ideas and his were obviously stupid. But this was a great idea so with a show of reluctance I quickly agreed.

We walked joyously unburdened back to the bags and hoisted the rucksacks the short(ish) distance to the descending slope. This was made up of small cliffs and rotten trees lying uprooted and pointing downwards, ready to trundle off into the water below. With some difficulty we found a way down, but it was complicated and thorn ridden. We met an excited Joe as we ascended to get more bags. He had found an old portage trail nearby that dropped down to the river's edge just in front of the rapids. Even easier! It was well hidden, but very definitely a trail, overgrown, but cut into the hillside long ago. It was almost certainly the same trail Mackenzie used. Barney and I left them to finish lugging the gear and went back to get the canoe.

To be in an unladen birchbark canoe riding with the current, albeit towards the pounding roar of the Vermilion chutes, was a wonderful experience, the boat as light and easy to paddle as something filled with air. Barney and I enjoyed ourselves looking at the sights on the wide river, our fun not even marred by the slow bubbling of water in the bilge, one more leak I had yet to stymie. We had marked the place where we were due to land with our rucksacks, though we had told Joe to wait for us on the bank. The current was fast, and as the roar of the rapids and falls approached it became perceptibly faster. But this did not matter to Barney and me, in fact it was a source of pleasure since it meant our paddling could be easy and relaxed.

There was no sign of Joe or Dave anywhere on the bank. Then Barney glimpsed the colour of the dumped gear. I had almost reached the bank at the end of Joe's trail when I saw that the current was double its former speed. We shouted and Joe appeared at the bank looking indecisive as I zoomed the canoe in. He misjudged the power of the river and fumbled the grab and, quite slowly it seemed, the boat was torn from his grip. The current instantly whisked us away towards the rapids.

Which were suddenly very apparent. You could smell the coolness and river scent raised by the pounding water. You could see the giant boulders ready to smash us to bits if we couldn't get in to the bank. I looked at Barney and was about to ask his opinion as to what we should do, and just as I was opening my mouth the full absurdity of it struck me. Two things actually: 1. he would have no more idea than I what to do, and 2. by the time this civilized exchange was over we would be astride two bits of matchwood on our way to an even bigger pounding by the Vermilion Falls. It was a defining moment of the entire trip for me, the moment when some palpable change occurred, the need for action overwhelming the years of 'discussing' things before doing them. 'Head for the inside of that curve. Back-paddle!' I shouted. We spun the canoe, laboriously slowly it seemed, losing ground all the time. Joe looked on like a chastised child, lost and waiting instruction. Then he ran along the bank, keeping pace with us.

Barney and I paddled like madmen, men possessed of nothing except the need to make the bank in a quieter eddy, the last indentation of the bank before the rapids began. If we missed this time we would be sucked into the maelstrom of rocks and foaming water below.

And slowly, as if a good thing had finally come to us, the moment of decision was rewarded. We pulled ahead and into the slightly slower water of the curve. Joe waded out to grab us. Everyone was serious and grinning at the same time.

My paddle was inexplicably slippery with blood. I looked at my hand; the cut from the day before had opened up during the mad exertion, the fight of splashing water and heaving on the blade (all bad paddling practice, silent is more powerful, everyone will tell you). I had not even noticed, though now it stung and my mouth filled with the rusty taste of blood.

'That was quite hairy, that,' said Barney.

Seven

ROOM 101

> *'The Canadian missionaries should have been
> contented to improve the morals of their own
> countrymen, so that by meliorating their character
> and conduct, they would have given a striking
> example of the effect of religion.'* Alexander Mackenzie

I

It was appropriate that the missionary was fishing when we arrived at Fort Vermilion. He was at the dock and he hooked the four of us to be interviewed on his Christian radio station. 'I love to fish,' he said, laughing. 'Even if I catch nothing I love it. But today I am lucky,' and he held up a four-kilo Jackfish. The man, a Latvian, spoke almost unaccented English. He was blond, with a goatee and wore glasses and insisted on cracking awful jokes, which somehow made him likeable. We agreed to be interviewed the next day.

II

But the next day Dave had gone missing. The previous night he and Joe and Barney had carried on drinking in the bar of the hotel, the only hotel in town, where Tim, the enormously fat manager, had kindly given us a discount and allowed us to store the canoe in his garage, two miles away. Every day we stayed at the hotel in Fort Vermilion, I made a pilgrimage along the road to Tim's garage to apply more pitch to the bottom of the boat. I thought on that long, hot walk, past the Christian radio shack (more of that shortly), of great fat Tim who had an enormous, bulbous-bonneted pick-up, which he had kindly run us about in, but, that courtesy now outlived, I was reduced to walking. But why did Tim need a pick-up? With his huge whale-like bulk, sweating after the exertion of moving from his office to the restaurant, possibly to eat a 'Tim' burger, which was a 2lb burger with fries and all the trimmings, actually printed up in the menu in honour of Tim, surely just a little walking would have done him good? Just taking a stroll one way, say to work, and then hitching a ride back, would have made a serious inroad into his bulk, which was, frankly, worrying to contemplate. Tim was such a pleasant and helpful and friendly guy but his trousers had reached that point where trousers become inverted cones of cloth hiding elephant folds of flesh, and his face was a blur of chubbiness with great dark pouches, worryingly dark pouches, under each eye. Those dark patches spoke of monstrous ill-health, one felt, not helped either by his two-pack-a-day smoking habit. Tim had worked all his life in the north, but the lifestyle was killing him. Just walk, Tim! Perhaps it was too late. He looked ill at ease anywhere except on a large chair, preferably a bench, like the bench seat in his pick-up or the benches in the alcoves in the restaurant of the only hotel in town. There were other restaurants – a Chinese and a greasy-spoon-type café, but neither was as good as Tim's place with its menu boasting not a fresh vegetable in sight.

By lunchtime we were worried. Where was Dave? I poked around the windswept evergreens in the car park. Had Dave fallen asleep there? We asked Tim, who looked up balefully from his accounts and told us he would keep a look-out. By 4 p.m. we thought we ought to report Dave's disappearance to the police – last seen stumbling out of a bar, actually last seen sitting on a bar stool quite near a huge wide river, the town being only across the road and up a bank from the fast-flowing majestic Peace; he could conceivably have formed a foolish notion to take a piss in that great fluence, for old times' sake, or some other notion suited to advanced inebriation, have stumbled on the steep ladder of steps set into the high mud bank and fallen into the dark and silty waters. I'm not even sure he could swim. None of us was. He had rarely if ever stripped off, apart from his shirt, and his demeanour was not that of a confident swimmer. There was nothing of that sleek amphibiousness that good swimmers exude even when clothed and on dry land. Dave might well have drowned!

Joe fell asleep as we sat waiting for Dave so it was down to Barney and I to face the missionary DJ. On our way there we were already talking about Dave in the past tense. 'Remember what Dave said about Christianity?' said Barney. ' "I had enough of it in my childhood to last a lifetime." '

The missionary 'studio' had brand-new-looking equipment, a heavy microphone and expensive-looking mixing desk, in a trailer on skids in the town. After a bland interview and prayers the missionary DJ started in on us when he heard how impressed we were by the Indians of Fox Lake. 'They call it the dark reserve,' he said. 'It is a bad place, full of pain. Seventy-five per cent of children born there have foetal alcohol syndrome, there is gambling and illicit trade in alcohol . . . and murder. Yes, murder. Last week they murdered a man, a beautiful man, a Dene [Fox Lake people are Cree mainly], he was battered to death. The report said he fell, but I know.'

How did he know? He knew.

'I feel their pain. The pain of these poor people, these people who have nothing. They can beat their drums all day but nothing will change. I take their pain from them. They have such pain when I talk to them of their experiences in residential schools, when they were torn from their families, they cry. They break down and cry. Then I let them know that Jesus will take away their pain.'

How could he say they had nothing? He made it sound as if their whole lives were eaten up by regret, but that didn't square with our experience at all. We had heard about the residential schools, and, though they were blamed for a lot, these institutions, however misguided or cruel, were not the sole experience in the lives of Native Americans. He was going around finding people's vulnerabilities and stamping on them, enlarging and encouraging pain instead of moving towards something more positive. Then offering Jesus as a cure. His reward was not money, he got lots of money from subscriptions in Europe, no, his reward was the far more insidious one of knowing he was saving souls, bringing heathens to the Book. From feeling homely I now felt suffocated by his overweening confidence.

He said he would send a CD of the interview to us. He didn't.

III

Bamboozled by faith, Barney and I walked back to the hotel. Then Dave walked in, silent, hunched, hungover. 'I spent the night with some Indians,' was all he would say. After his uncouth behaviour at Little Red River, which had made us all, in our extreme love-of-all-things-Indian mode, rather uncomfortable, Dave had now been cultivating Indians all over the place. Well, in two places. In the bar Dave had shown a rather bossy drunken Indian called Dwayne his Haidar tattoo on his calf. It had settled an argument about something, settled it so well the bossy Indian shook Dave by the hand. I would love to be able to recount the argument but I had also drunk rather too much at this time. It went something like:

Bossy Indian: 'What do you care about Indian culture?'

Dave hoists leg on to table and exposes white calf with circular Haidar Indian tattoo.

Bossy Indian examines it and then shakes Dave's hand and smiles.

Before that Dwayne had bossily told me that the water of the Peace River was good for drinking. When I said, 'Really?' in the English idiom meaning, 'How interesting,' he had snarled over his beer, bought by Barney, 'I ain't lyin'.'

Shortly after that Dave disappeared, to the second place, where Indian fraternization occurred, now revealed as room 101. In a startling coincidence of particular interest to Dave, being an avid reader and a fan of George Orwell in particular, Dave had been hijacked by the two bulky, not to say fantastically massive, Indians we had glimpsed all the previous day glugging their way through cardboard boxes full of beer. 'I must have been out in the bushes for a while,' explained Dave, 'then I stumbled around in the car park but I couldn't find the entrance. Must have eventually, then I heard this music – Johnny Cash – really loud, you know that one about "going down down down". So I hammered on the door and these two massive Indian guys invited me in. And they were drinking. Those boxes are full of vodka empties, not beer. And they got beer too. I remember drinking three cans and the next thing I woke up next to this Indian who was snoring. Then the most gargantuan Indian I'd ever seen threw me a can. I lay there awhile, too ill to move, with these Indians drinking again! They're serious drinkers – it's a three-day holiday for them. Come here from some job in the bush, drink solidly for seventy-two hours and then go back.'

'So what happened with this one snoring next to you, then?' said Barney, voicing all our concerns about the night in room 101, but all Dave said was, 'Nothing. They were real gentlemen.'

IV

Louise Beth Kittler ran the local museum and knew an exceedingly large amount about Fort Vermilion and its position in the fur trade. She had that peculiar talent some experts have of focusing on all the information you don't want to know and leaving tantalizing holes where the information you do want to know should reside. Louise Beth was very friendly and helpful but for some reason we quickly developed a strong aversion to finding out more about Fort Vermilion's position in the fur trade.

We had met Louise Beth at the museum, where Joe pestered her for information regarding a stone he had found that he believed was an ancient arrowhead. It was evident to even the most poorly informed amateur archaeologist that the stone was merely a stone, but Joe had become obsessed. To Louise Beth's credit she did not laugh uproariously at Joe's suggestion – plea, almost – that his stone was prehistoric and valuable. Instead she did what all good museum people do in a tight situation: pronounce it 'not my field' and refer the enquirer to a greater expert, this one in Edmonton.

Whilst Joe was trying to gain backing for his prehistoric fantasies, I was buying up local books. I always do this wherever I go. Self-published, full of good photographs and the raw unedited text of locals reminiscing about their former lives. Fort Vermilion had a huge book full of such mini-biographies of people still alive and perhaps just dead but still remembered in 1988, the two-hundredth anniversary of the founding of the town. It didn't surprise me to see that Louise Beth had been on the committee overseeing the production of the book, and that her own entry was so long, but I skipped over it and delighted in all the other stories. Many people had fifteen or more children. Many lived into their nineties. It seemed that if you made it past twenty-five you would probably live until you were very old. Most entries contained the one heroic thing a man had done – getting some diphtheria serum though in the dead of winter, or rescuing horses from a hole in the ice, but the entry I really liked was this:

'Thomas Roberts. Thomas owned some big black dogs that looked almost like bears.'

That was it. But I could see Thomas so much more clearly without all the rigmarole contained in the other entries, lists of jobs, war service, births, marriages and deaths. Thomas had big black dogs that looked almost like bears. You could imagine everyone saying that about him: there goes old Thomas, you ever see those dogs of his? Indeed, what happened to those dogs? Were their offspring still around Fort Vermilion? Somehow Thomas Roberts took hold of my imagination. I investigated anything that looked like a big black dog, judging carefully its likeness to a bear. I asked the bespectacled man in the gun shop who sold me a catapult if he had seen these huge dogs. 'Indeed I have,' was all I could get out him. By the end of our stay I felt some creature like the Hound of the Baskervilles was lurking in Fort Vermilion, all because of Thomas Roberts, a man who provided such colour from such a brief biography. Thomas Roberts, I salute you!

Just as Joe was obsessed with his arrowhead, Dave had intensified his collecting of fossils and nice-looking pebbles. The bottom of his huge rucksack not only clanked but bulged with all the stones he was carrying, threatening our trip like the thirty pounds of rock samples Scott insisted on lugging back from the South Pole, or at least that was how I put to Dave. Barney and I had found a *few* nice rocks too, it was the inevitable result of the free walking time whilst your partner was towing. Just outside Fort Vermilion we had wandered through an area of gigantic ammonites. Dave looked longingly at one the size of a cartwheel. Walking the bank was a great way of finding out all its secrets; in fact, one of the reasons we tolerated Louise Beth's intrusion, apart from her car, was that she told us in some detail about an old trading post she had helped excavate the previous year. It was all a secret, she said, because they didn't want treasure hunters. At that point we were all interested. I looked at the academic paper covering the find and whilst pretending to write down something interesting about Fort Vermilion's position in the fur trade scribbled down the map co-ordinates. All kinds of booty might be there, just sitting on the beach waiting to be found. Everyone was keen on this idea, though of course we said nothing to Louise Beth about our grave-robbing instincts.

She saw us off from the dock with her quiet, pleasant-mannered husband, who let her do all the talking, and her quiet, perfectly all right daughter Dawleen. Their farm bordered the river some fifteen miles downstream. They welcomed us to visit. She would put a flag out to show where their place was. Then, just as we paddled off, she said, voicing, I felt, her real feelings towards us, the full hatred of the settled farmer for the nomad, 'But you be a bit careful coming up our lawn, might get your head blown off by a shotgun!' It was meant as a joke but even Dawleen saw it was in bad taste. 'Mum!' she said. We were all too stunned to say anything. All along had she had us taped? Known the score? Seen through our pathetic act of civility to the blatant disrespect beneath? Maybe we got what we deserved. Settlers 1 Nomads 0.

Not surprisingly, when we passed the farm there was no flag flying.

At Cook's Flat the river was changing. The willows had given way to spruce. If you climbed out of the deep valley carved by the Peace remote homesteads ate into the woodland. There were a couple of Indian families camped by the river in trailers with the wheels removed. I talked with an old guy who told me gleefully, 'Oh, we'll be here till the freeze-up in November. Best time of the year – no bugs and plenty of moose.'

'Where will you go after that?'

'Back to the Bushe River Reserve.'

It was hard talking to him but he was friendly. When we left, about six or seven kids, all under ten, followed us down to the rocky beach where we untied the canoe. Joe was avidly taking photographs of the kids when I saw one stoop down to pick up a rock. Joe instantly saw what was about to happen. As we bundled into the canoe he got them to line up and smile and say cheese. Then he splashed backwards, snapping away, keeping them distracted. As soon as he had one leg over the bow we were off, paddling like demons just as the first rocks began to fall. 'Bastards!' shouted Dave as the kids waded deeper to get more range. Rocks fell all around us with unnerving and increasing accuracy. Barney sent one back, neatly using his paddle as a cricket bat. It was a narrow escape. Not even Mackenzie got stoned by the natives.

V

One day the dwindling supply of dope, hemp, grass, ganja, bhang, weed, whatever, was lost, its dirty Tupperware box presumed blown off the back of the boat and floating downstream to Louise Beth's farm, ready for Dawleen to pick up and try. You can tell an addict by his reaction to losing his gear. Joe was frantic, Dave put-upon, defensive and disbelieving. He was

185

clearly in denial, whilst Joe was whining and hysterical. He didn't know how he would get to Peace River town.

I was quite pleased. I had seen the dope from the beginning as a secret second master, a surreptitious false prophet; it was beyond my control and I didn't like it. Also there was the morbidly interesting side, seeing how Joe and Dave would cope, the reality behind their dreamy bong-induced smiles, would they just suffer and wilt? When it was obvious it was gone Dave grew matter-of-fact and shrugged it off, turning instead to innovative ways of cooking pasta and other staples. Joe became withdrawn and bit his nails and smoked his roll-ups with a kind of fierce glare in his eye.

Dave had always been a keen cook, rivalled only by Barney, who had become a master at making bannock. Joe, too, always made an effort with the food, even when he was in a bad mood, which was increasingly often. Being obsessed by food is a good thing on an expedition, as long as you have plenty, and at that time we did.

But Dave was now pushing the envelope a little far. He managed to wrestle porridge duty back from Barney in order to subject us to his inventions: 'D'you guys want cinnamon in this,' he'd call out from behind his bubbling pot, already tipping the stuff in.

Dilemma: how to say yes but not in the quantities Dave used.

Later, Dave making noodles: 'D'you like the cinnamon on that?'

No answer, meaning definitely not.

Another day, this time rice: 'D'you like that jasmine rice?' Dave so eager we have to reply.

So everyone lies, 'Er, yeah, Dave, how did you make it?'

'Just tipped some jasmine tea into the rice as it was boiling.'

Another breakfast, this time Barney standing over Dave making porridge. 'Dave, you're not making jasmine porridge, are you?'

Dave, sounding hurt: 'I guess not if no one wants it.'

We were now in the vicinity of the old fort. Eager to find any artefacts that might have been left behind by the archaeologists, we scanned the beach for the remains of the fireplace. I used the GPS to get us bang on the co-ordinates given in the academic article Louise Beth had shown us, little realizing we were all grave robbers. In fact this struck me as one of the best uses of the GPS, since on the river it served little purpose except to give me authority. It's possible to get lost on a river, but only when it forks, and the Peace didn't fork.

But though we searched and searched we found nothing. Archaeologists leave less behind than tomb robbers or even zero-impact campers. At least a tomb robber leaves everything that isn't made of gold. We thought we'd find a few old clay pipes or broken hexagonal bottles. Nothing. It was a hot day and our enthusiasm diminished visibly as we tramped back and forth along the grey, clayey beach. Joe, already strung out, took it particularly badly.

'Why the hell did they choose here to make a fort?' asked Dave. 'Just down there would have been much better.' We all agreed that the non-existent fort had been badly sited.

Then the dope was found, in the boat under Barney's pack, the box wet but the grass tinder-dry. Everyone was happy, since the novelty of the dope-free experiment did not justify the full horror of addicts without their fix. Joe smiled for the first time in days and jasmine-flavoured porridge was off the menu at last.

Eight

THE BREAK-UP

*'It became a matter of real necessity that we should
begin to diminish the consumption of our provisions,
and to subsist upon two-thirds of our allowance; a
proposition which was as unwelcome to my people,
as it was necessary to be put into immediate
practice.'* Alexander Mackenzie

I

There was a brief period from the finding of the dope to the
losing of Dave's shoes when everything was perfect. It was
easy towing and it suddenly became obvious that we were
going to make it barring an accident or the canoe sinking. We
would reach Peace River town that year. It meant that the
four-man towing system had been vindicated. In those sunny,
long days, sometimes following a twenty-kilometre curve for
an entire day, we all started counting our chickens, making
plans. We went through a phase of having huge fires each night,
flames higher than a house, great crackling tongues leaping up
into the dark. Joe caught fish and we would grill them, everyone
perfectly content. I remember walking along the gravel curve of
the river's beach, tracking at the muddy edge the spoor of a wolf
and two cubs, watching ducks with ten ducklings swimming,
looking up at the looping lazy path from treetop to treetop of a
bald eagle, finding another fossil, thinking thoughts that were
untethered, free, thoughts that had nothing to interrupt them.
I remember many such days when you can't think why you'd
want to do anything else. The weather that year, compared to
the last, had also been exceptionally dry. I got used to seeing the

sun spangling into blinding fragments across the morning river, the warm breeze on our backs allowing us to sail, the sight of the Northern Lights, wavy white and green like a laser show, every night.

But it couldn't last. If life is perfect then things can only get worse. It was just a matter of time.

I think it started with Dave's shoes, his last pair, his nasty smelly pair of trainers which he left on the riverbank and only discovered were gone when we had been paddling for two hours. A brief recap: first pair sucked off his feet by mud. Second pair mysteriously slid down to river bottom with the mess tin. Now his last pair were gone and he blamed Joe, who had been the last getting in the boat and who, he said, he trusted to watch out for a fellow team member's shoes. But should Joe be responsible for Dave's footwear? Probably not. They squabbled in the early-morning cool, then I for some reason told Dave to shut up, at which he fumed, 'People should look after their own footwear from now on!' Which was pretty funny considering that Dave *had* no footwear from now on and would be condemned to walking barefoot or in socks.

As this antagonistic discussion hotted up, so did the speed of the river. We were aiming for the other side, where the water was even faster. The bank was coming in close. Everyone in the boat made the small preparatory manoeuvres we make when we think it is us, and only us, who will have to save the day, jump out, fend off, get wet. Dave, being barefoot, was in the best position to jump out but chose this moment to reassert his much-dwindled status as a man of the river. He spoke in his brook-no-dissent, supersure voice. 'You should turn now,' he stated.

For some reason this riled me. 'You look after your shoes and I'll look after the paddling,' I said.

'So there's only one expert in this boat, is there?' said Dave.

Now we were all paddling, with me directing which side to paddle on, in parentheses from the main conversation, which everyone was a part of, and shrunk from, to let Dave and me battle it out. 'Yes. And that's me. I'm the fuckin' expert, OK?'

Dave lifted his paddle from the water and swivelled round to look up at me, his eyes weasel-small and his shorn brow low; low in the boat too. Where was his body? It was like something wet hanging from a coat hanger, hardly noticeable, crowded out by his bullet head with Russian-prisoner skull and tender, vulnerable, pulsating temple veins. 'Just stop poking your nose into my private life, OK?'

It took me unawares. Where was he going with this one? 'I'm not poking my nose in,' I said.

Dave shot back, 'You are!'

There was a stormy silence. And a nasty crack as the canoe glanced off a rock. Maybe I should have turned earlier.

When we stopped and camped I spent a lot of time hunting for wood, filling a big backpack with it, making weaving scour marks in the sand dragging home small, heavy trees, long, dead roots wrestled from the sand. I had the feeling I was hiding and they at the campfire were plotting something. As I dropped the wood, Dave sort of burst forth and confronted me with the video camera, and in an unusually expansive voice asked for my reactions to the day. But there was eagerness too, a sign that he didn't want the bad feelings to fester. 'Just how do you feel the expedition went today?' All but saying 'skipper'.

I'd been turned on and bested! Good for him, I thought, ploughing out some Newspeak twaddle in reply. Then we all sat down and discussed how polite we should be. Barney kindly volunteered that I should tell him to shut up whenever he made a suggestion I thought was bollocks. Then Dave gave me a hug, which was very touching, though I couldn't help noticing how stiff his small body was, despite the supposedly relaxing effect of grass.

And now the dope really had run out. Joe had a few pills, horse tranquillizers* and oddments that he always travelled with. These tided him over for a while. One night he took out a melatonin pill a friend had given him. As we sat looking into the fire or lay back staring at the stars, he turned it over in his palm, examining it, his sole source of entertainment for the evening. Later he reported he 'slept very well'.

* 'I have never owned a horse tranquillizer' – Joe's note after he read the manuscript.

We stopped at the only place where the road joined the river for about two hundred miles. There were two fisheries policemen waiting for us, or so it seemed. One dark and stocky and friendly, the other lanky and nervous, it was he who picked a zip-lock, bag up triumphantly from our cooking barrel and said, 'Is that what I think it is?'

I couldn't resist this. 'What do you think it is?'

'Goosewing by the look of it.' Killing geese without a permit was illegal.

I opened the bag for him. 'Actually it's one of Barney's uncooked sultana bannocks.'

They had no interest in our birchbark canoe. But they wanted to get us. 'Mind if I look around?' asked the sly, nervous one. Probably I should have been annoyed and insisted on my rights but these people were the first we had seen for a long time and I still had my 'river head' on, which meant I trusted everyone's good intentions. They poked around and found nothing. Joe and Barney were angry. Still, it was pleasant to know we still had our illegal net, even if we weren't using it much.

Because we were near the only road that touched the river for miles and miles, word quickly spread about our appearance. In the end we had so many visitors they started to get in the way. In rapid succession we met:

two farmers in a pick-up fishing;

a man called Mark from Yellowknife who gave us some vodka;

a very fat woman conservation officer, armed;

an old man duck hunting;

the two farmers and Mark again;

the two ag & fish officers, also armed, who suspected Barney's bannock;

three women from farms out picking cranberries. Joe, short of cigarettes, begged six off them;

the old duck hunter again.

The old duck hunter gave us the most interesting information. He was a scrawny, tall man with a white military moustache, and he had also seen the ag & fish men from his shooting position high on the bluff.

'I take my ten ducks and go. That's how many they allow, and that's how many I take, though there's enough of 'em for me to take fifty or a hundred. Those sons of bitches love to make trouble. The quiet one is the worst, he'll sit all day waiting to see if a fisherman is using a gaff or barbed trebles, and then he'll be down with his hundred-dollar fines. You shoot a moose and you better leave the balls on the thing or he'll have you for good. Shoot a moose without proof of sex and they can jail you up here. Oh yes, they're sons of bitches all right – they come down here because they can. All this land and they pick this spot because it's easy to get to, that's why. You haul a moose out in a canoe like yours they'll never get you. But in a pick-up they'll be waiting for you at the gas station of the main highway.'

The old duck hunter had a pained expression as he wiped his brow, as if he had something personal against his own sweat. Then he smiled sweetly and shook out a tiny Tom Thumb cigar. Joe brought out one of his precious six begged ciggies and took a cupped light from the duck hunter, who, after a furious bout of coughing, continued his tale. 'Lived in the city till I was forty. Coffee-bean-importing company. I was a real bean counter. Then one day I quit. It was real easy. Thought it would be hard but it was real easy. I came here and it was the best thing I ever did. Guess I just about matched those first forty years,' he said. 'No longer regret leaving it as late as I did.'

First he had worked as trader's assistant. Then he became a trapper. Finally he lived alone for nine months of each year in a hut he built north of the Peace River. He had married a metis girl. 'Best people in the world for this kind of life,' he said. He had four children, 'all born in a sod hut,' he said, 'know what that is? Turf and mud.' Two still lived near by, one in America and one back east in Thunder Bay.

'I been lucky all my life, I just took my time, that's all,' said the old duck hunter. He relit his Tom Thumb. The sun was setting most beautifully. 'This part of Canada,' he said, picking up my thought, 'best sunsets in the world.'

Soon enough we got round to bears, grizzly bears.

'If you're going after a grizz, shoot him from cover, otherwise he'll try and come after you, even if he's nearly dead. Indian way of killing was to wait until he was right on you then stick a spear right down his mouth or under his chin.

'Grizz don't like smoke. Keep a fire going all the time.

'Grizzlies, you never know with them. It's a cliché to say they're unpredictable, but sometimes they're more than unpredictable. You can't even predict they're unpredictability. I was caught out once without a rifle – never again. You boys'll be all right. Maybe see one grizz around here in a decade. But once you get into those mountains you'll see a lot. If you stay in one place, have a routine, you need a gun. That's why trappers always have a gun. But travelling every day isn't the same. By the time the grizzly has sniffed you you've moved on. I'd still take a gun though.

'Only one thing can challenge a grizz – a wolverine. I've seen one rip the face off a bear and get away. Took his eye and his nose off. Even wolves wouldn't do that. Wolverine has a high-pitched scream. Worse than a cat or a baby. In the open a grizzly'll stand up and look at you. But if he comes after you, starts circling, then stands and starts clicking his teeth then you know you'll have to kill him.'

We told the old duck hunter about the bannock goosewing and he laughed. 'Those boys are so desperate to get someone they're seeing things,' he said.

III

Despite his six donated cigarettes, Joe was now running out, which, added to the dopeless situation, left him edgy and pacing the gravel shore in his tattered trousers and sandals, bending down every few seconds to look at a rock or a fossil or something dead. He set up a sweatlodge inside the tent flysheet, ten huge glowing rocks in a hole in the middle and all of us with sand sticking to the sweat pouring out of our skin. But even that didn't calm him. Nor did Dave's biscuit-tin bomb made from a firework or Barney's impression of himself spilling the tea. Joe spent a long time thoroughly washing his clothes, beating his shirt against a waterside rock. He wrung everything out with great gusto and made a wicker drying rack around the fire – it looked like Christmas with all his hanging socks. But then he burned a great smoky hole in his jersey, which he had draped over a log to dry. It was almost frightening to see his face as he picked up the log and threw it. The log flew a humorously short distance. He was consumed with anger, a practised anger that rose to defeat the possibility of anyone laughing. He kicked and kicked at the log like a soccer hooligan whaling on an opposing fan. Then he broke off abruptly and stamped off down the beach, even though it was dark. You could hear his feet kicking hard into the gravel. Later he half explained it by saying, of some time in his troubled recent past, 'My hands were all scarred from punching walls.'

IV

We spent a rest day on a high terraced riverbank, within sight of a ferry that carried logging trucks across the water. The thing had its own invariable routine, complete with horn and lights when it was dark. The ferry docked at a logging road. We could hitch to a town or even a gas station. Barney and I stood on the red earth of the dirtway that led up from the ferry. Trucks with six or seven logs bitten into by the side stakes roared past. Our frail petition was easily dismissed by the louvred bonnet, dusty chrome and tinted glass, the whole machine almost hysterically mounting its way through the gears and then it would be gone, the great sawn logs disappearing in a swirl of dust and our expletives. We tried hard to get a lift to La Crete, a Mennonite town *with shops*, but our *outré* beards and river-stained clothes were against us. We ate dust for two hours then packed it in. Joe and Dave polished up better; beardless and with a bounce in their step, they were gone a whole day.

Barney had given up carving spoons and now concentrated on a wooden knife. 'Good for making bannock,' I said.

'Or stabbing someone,' he said darkly.

It was a hot humid day and we lay on a bank above the river in amongst the cow parsley and low willow bushes. The smouldering fire gave up a single, lazy line of smoke. It was cooler in the woods where birch and spruce loomed in the darkness. I cut bark for repairs and collected resin, which was bubbling out of the spruce trees in such quantities I quickly had a fist-sized lump. All the time I was listening for any odd noises but the forest was dead quiet. In the far distance you could hear the shudder of the ferry as its engines backed off, then the muffled parp of its klaxon.

Joe and Dave came back in a foul mood, mainly with each other. La Crete had proved to be a dry town. Joe wanted to carry on hitching back to Fort Vermilion to get some beer. Dave disagreed strongly. Joe tried to persuade their 'lift', a Mennonite boy, to get them booze. 'You could have been born somewhere else then you'd think differently,' wheedled Joe. 'I never thought of it like that, I guess you're right.' But even this potential recruit to freethinking could not get them what Joe wanted, though he admitted there was 'a ton of homebrewing going on – always is in a dry town'. In Dave and Joe's anger with each other they had also left one bag of shopping in the back of the last pick-up. We mourned this lost bag greatly. It had contained, among other things, all the corned beef and the curry powder and twenty oranges. 'Could have really done with an orange,' muttered Barney, fire-hardening the tip of his new knife in the embers.

Mackenzie's journal covering the same section of river, from Fort Vermilion to Peace River town:

South-South East one mile and a half, South three quarters; East seven miles and an half, veering, gradually to the West four miles and an half. South-East by South three miles, South-East three miles and an half, East-South-East to Long Point three miles, South-West one mile and a quarter, East by North four miles and three quarters, West three miles and an half, West-South-West one mile, East by South five miles and an half . . .

Directions in a very similar vein then follow for an entire page, until:

South by East three miles. Here we arrived at the forks of the river; the Eastern branch appearing to be not more than half the size of the Western one. We pursued the latter, in a course South-West by West six miles, and landed on the first of November at the place which was designed to be my winter residence.

He had arrived at Fort Forks, a few miles upstream from Peace River town. Our destination.

Mackenzie's journals were a bestseller in 1801. They were even polished and improved by William Coombe, a ghost writer who finished the book in King's Bench debtors' prison. Even Coombe couldn't jazz up compass directions though – it is hard to see a modern editor countenancing page after page of such directions, and a third of the book is probably compass directions. It reminded me of a similar list I made of my 'explorations' aged eight, across the gull-spotted fields behind my parents' house. I assiduously read off and recorded compass directions in my notebook, because it looked pleasing and because I had recently learned about compasses. Nowhere does the autodidact in Mackenzie, supremely confident in other areas, come through as strongly as in this visible pride in his navigation. Yet, with only a basic grasp of the subject, he crossed an entire continent.

Our own journey to Peace River town was not to be as eventless or easy as that of the great Mackenzie. On the thirty-ninth day on the river things started badly when I tumbled waist-deep wading through some rapids. The summer sun had by now departed and suddenly it was cold each morning, sometimes with frost instead of dew on the tent. All the insects were gone – around 15 August they just decided to pack it in, overnight.

Instead of hiding under mosquito nets we now shivered in our sleeping bags each night. No one wanted to get wet any more, certainly not before lunchtime, since now our quick-dry trousers stayed wet and chilly.

We were towing a lot now, great five-kilometre-long tows around endless huge curves. The novelty of making easy kilometres had worn off and you'd be shivering after just an hour sitting in the boat. Things only became lively when we had to cross between islands. There was always a fast current between them and we couldn't always decide the best route. That day Joe was irritable and Barney belligerent; neither of them agreed with my route. Eventually we settled on a course but Joe wouldn't speak to me. This continued all day until we landed on a long sandy island. Joe's resentment boiled over into another series of recriminatory discussions masquerading as being about choosing a campsite.

I'd had enough. 'You know what, Joe? You're just a moody little git.'

If there was one thing Joe hated that was being called (a) moody, (b) little and (c) a git. OK, three things. I had blown being exemplary. I was for it.

His whole face changed. It became a shrunken contorted mask of rage. 'You, you, YOU CUNT!' he shrieked. 'You bastard, you wanker, cunt!'

We were teetering on the brink of nuclear war.

'Let's not get personal,' I said.

Joe spat back, 'You cunt, you started it, you git, you mouldy old git.'

Joe was the kind of guy who relished the last word. I strode manfully ahead with my back to the tirade.

'You fucker!' he called after me. 'You cunt! I left England because of people like you! You should be paying me in rum and gold for this trip. Wanker! Doing a Lance [an obscure allusion to Lance Armstrong the cyclist, who won a stage of the Tour de France after crapping in his pants whilst riding and not stopping – his team-mates wiped him down as he pelted for the finish line]! You bastard! Wanker! Lance!'

At this point he was standing up at the stern and steering at the same time. Barney was towing dutifully and silently, head down, an unwilling witness. Dave was in the front, ineffectually swiping at imaginary obstructions with his paddle. As Joe berated me at top volume I said nothing, realizing it would do no good. Hundreds of miles from any town, quite alone on a wide river, walking up the edge of a sandy island being shouted out in the vernacular of England after the pubs have shut. I even laughed to myself, but I felt bad inside.

When Joe began to tire he would pause a few minutes then start up again. 'Wanker! Cunt! Cunt! Wanker! You fuckin' cunt! I paddle twice as hard as you! Cunt!' But not once did he endanger the boat, deliberately steer it into a rock or the bank. If his moods affected our safety, or the boat's, he would have to go, but they never did, unless you allow mental stress as a factor in general safety. Increasingly I did.

We arrived at a good spot for camping, right at the end of the island. The ends of islands that faced upstream were always good for driftwood, and, since the prevailing winds were now easterly, often sheltered. We lifted the boat out, Joe now silent but still vibrating with emotion. The canoe was even heavier than I remembered. Was it psychological? I was glad there were four of us, it would have been a struggle with three, but then we might just have to struggle.

As Joe ranted and raved I had looked at the map slung in its transparent case and calculated how far we were from a road. It would mean a significant hike over the hills on the northerly side, but there were dirt tracks and farms up there and I was sure Joe would soon find people who would help. Still, abandoning a man in the wilderness just because he called you a wanker was pretty harsh discipline. What if he was eaten by a bear? It would be on my conscience for the rest of my life.

Barney and Dave, like kids in a troubled marriage, made a great effort to be helpful and quiet. Tea was quickly brewed. Joe was now sitting on the end of a long log sobbing. It was rather awful to see; he sucked in the air, and his face was now distorted in a different way, wet and shapeless, without hope. It was not good to see him crying like that so I carried over a mug of tea to him. I was still sufficiently annoyed with him to not feel bad myself at seeing such a sad display, but I felt no ill-will. Now he was punishing himself, it seemed. I even put my arm around his shoulders and briefly felt his stiff little body, still quivering with crying and spent rage. 'I'm sorry,' he whispered.

Joe went to bed early. Barney, Dave and I sat round the fire in silence. After a while Barney said, ' "You should be paying me in rum and gold" – where did that come from?'

We all tittered quietly, but the whole group was still smarting from the emotional ructions. Later as we got into our sleeping bags Barney did his best to make me feel better. 'It's not true you were the first to get personal, Dave called you an arsehole two days ago.' Er, thanks, Barney.

V

The next morning I knew we would not be saying goodbye to Joe, at least not until we got to Peace River town. He sat on a log rerolling his five remaining cigarettes into six, his hands shaking. A week's towing and paddling. We could stand another week of Joe, surely.

Mackenzie's technique for dealing with mutinous behaviour was simple: if passions are high . . . ignore them. When the men are calmer, possibly even with a dram in their hand, bring it up and demand that they voice, here and now, their commitment to their leader. Mackenzie was a master of the poker face. When Mackay comes running with the men's complaints Mackenzie listens, but in front of the men gives no indication that he has received the information. When the men load the boat to leave, without an order, Mackenzie ignores this action and simply remains on the bank waiting 'the issue of further circumstances'. On the Bad River when one man refuses to embark out of sheer fear Mackenzie makes a joke of it and ridicules him in front of the other men. The message was simple: if you meet opposition, pretend it's not there.

199

Then it was Barney's turn to go mad. It had started to hail, big painful hailstones before a real downpour. In an ecstasy of confusion Joe tried to light a fire on a rock ledge under the big tarpaulin which I was putting up at the same time. The fire caught, burned away its supporting timbers and slid off the rock into a puddle. Now we were cold and wet and fireless in a situation similar to the previous year when John and I became hypothermic. I brought the tarp lower and, after an age, Joe got another fire going and promptly burned a hole in it. Dave ran around gathering wood, but where was Barney?

For no known reason Barney had decided to light his own fire under the small tarpaulin. When I told him he'd be better served finding and splitting wood for the main fire, he said roughly, 'I came on this trip to enjoy myself, this is my holiday.'

'Look, Barney, if anyone came on this trip to enjoy themself they're nuts.'

But one look at Barney's icy blue eyes, tangled beard and sunburned face told me he probably was nuts. 'I know what I'm doing,' I said, cringing inwardly at having to be the 'expert'. 'We did it all last year.'

'Did it hail like that last year?' Barney snarled.

'Call that hail? That's nothing. We were pelted by ice the size of cricket balls!'

Barney just grunted and carried on with his solo effort.

The weather was definitely worsening. On a day when we made many miles sailing we found ourselves being chased by a storm, the mother of all storms it looked, great shoulders of black cloud pressing steadily up the river valley towards us; every time I turned to look they were a little closer. We needed to make camp before everything was soaked but things weren't quite so simple. Somewhere in the region was 'Tar Island', a hideaway retreat of eight huts and a restaurant on a small island somewhere in the Peace River. It wasn't marked on our map, only on an inaccurate sketch map we had. Tar Island supposedly served steaks and beer, and after forty-six days of rice and sardines we wanted to find it.

It was at this precise point that I made the decision that route-finding by committee is a bad idea. I'd tried to involve the lads, give them a go at being in the back of the canoe, steering and finding the way. But it hadn't really worked. In a canoe the man at the back has to make route-finding decisions. Not for nothing was the most experienced (and best-paid) voyageur the one at the stern. When difficult water approached, it was hard to shout instructions back down the canoe. Likewise, when it comes to navigation, only the man who has been reading the map and the land continuously has the right perspective to make route-finding decisions. The others can only go on what appears to be the case, which it may not be. I was also learning that intuition comes with continued route-finding, that I was getting an instinct for the way to go, but this instinct couldn't always be justified. If we discussed everything I might easily be swayed by a more conclusive argument, or lose my slender sense of intuition. It is because of this, and not some paranoid sense of losing control, that guides and navigators so resent intrusive suggestions from others. As we argued the toss the storm came down, belting us with gallons of water, cutting in seconds through all our waterproof clothing, leaving us drenched and gasping. I could feel myself swayed by Joe, and Barney who agreed with him. But my intuition said no. 'Let's just check out this last island,' was all I could manage. If I was wrong I knew I'd never hear the last of it. In fact I'd probably have to delegate all route-finding to the committee from then on.

But just as the place looked most unlikely, Joe, who had the sharpest eyes, saw a ladder running from the beach up the steep bank. We had reached Tar Island.

VI

'Go and wake him up,' said Barney. 'The porridge is ready.'

'I don't think he's gonna like being woken up,' said Dave.

'We've got to get moving,' I said.

'OK.' Dave trundled off from the purpose-built campfire circle on Tar Island where we were damply making breakfast. It had rained all night, but we hadn't noticed, snug as we were in our dog kennels, micro-Quonset huts that had been adapted into individual cabins on the island. There had been no steaks and no beers – the place had shut down for winter. But four cabins had been left unlocked, and we felt like Goldilocks lying down to sleep. And the mirrors! I spent ages examining my face, just familiarizing myself with myself again. When I walked past Barney's window he was doing the same. He saw me and said, 'Just checking how long my beard is.' A good cover story. The mystery we had become to ourselves. The new person we hoped to see revealed. The lines that signified some growth in knowledge from experience. The sad fact that the more you look at yourself the more you look the same as you always did.

The island, which had never been logged, was like something out of Arthur Ransome. There were huge birches and spruces and lovely little paths winding through them. The outdoor jakes was a nice change too: with the door open it had a commanding view of the ever-flowing wideness of the river. Even had toilet paper.

The cabins were either side of the locked restaurant building – we had missed their last day open by a week.

Since the loss of the groceries at La Crete we were all on reduced rations. The menu, shoved inside against the window, was tantalizing: steaks, chicken, fries, apple pie; Barney thought he saw beer cans in a box; but the door was well locked and no windows were open.

Dave came back from waking Joe. 'I told you,' was all he managed before a strutting, spitting, vituperative Joe, never at his best in the mornings, appeared. 'Why the FUCK do you have to bang so hard!' he shouted at Dave. 'I'm not deaf. Though I might be now. You could have knocked quietly!'

Dave turned wearily. 'If you don't like it, shut up, you whining bitch.' A bit strong but the sentiment was correct, one felt.

'You're here because of me, you owe me,' shouted Joe.

'Shut up, bitch,' said Dave in a low growl.

Barney and I waded in to placate. It would be just like insensitive Dave to bang like mad to wake Joe up, but then Joe was foolish to rise to the bait.

The upshot: Joe is banned from Dave's stinky little tent. A day of towing and paddling in silence broken only by cheery comments from Barney and the *toe-lee, ler-lee, ler-lee, ler-lee* of a bird we never saw, whose haunting notes we had heard almost every day since the beginning of the trip. At first we thought it was a whisky jack, the camp-robber bird, but when we saw one eyeing our unwashed pans, we were sure it was something different.

Like many folk names for animals, whisky jack covers more than one species, in this case Clark's nutcracker and the grey jay; the nutcracker has a harsher cawing voice and a longer bill, though both birds are similarly grey and white. 'Whisky jack' is supposedly a corruption of the Cree 'Weesakejac', a figure in native creation stories. I loved the strange noise of the bird, almost mournful, ever present. When I asked John Buck what the bird was he shrugged. 'It's your bird,' he said.

No one was talking much any more. At lunch on a deserted muddy beach I took my time in carefully filling a moose print with urine, piss wavering into the wind, taking care to fill the print to the brim.

By the evening Joe said to me, 'I'm feeling close to apologizing to Dave.' A little later I saw Dave praise Joe's cooking and fishing (Joe was an excellent fisherman with just an old line and a lure he found abandoned – that night he caught five fish in ten minutes; the secret is to fish along the eddy lines, he claimed). Dave then filmed Joe fishing and we did not, after all, have to make room for him in our tent.

In a mood of reconciliation we all walked along the darkened beach and found a natural-gas vent in the shallows of the river, bubbling up. Joe was fearful but Barney insisted on putting his lighter to the area – a flickering blue-yellow flame flopped over the water, blown back and forth by the wind, roiling over the water, lighting up the night river's darkness. 'Let's leave it burning for ever.' But by morning the early mist or the wind had put the river flame out.

Losing that extra bag of groceries in La Crete had caught up with us. We finally ran out of food. Fifty kilometres from the end. Two days if we pushed it. Further than Scott's eleven miles, but then I'd stopped bringing up Scott a while back. Joe hated to hear the comparison. 'I don't get off on this explorer shit,' he said. It was going to be a hungry last haul.

After our last meal, a parsimonious lunch of a Cup-a-soup divided four ways with one noodle strand each, we all lay out on the riverbank as if already victims of starvation, hardly moving, stomachs a little bloated from drinking several pints of weak tea, all resenting the need to start moving again.

'You know what I'd like?' said Barney.

'I don't want to hear,' moaned Dave.

'I'd like a big baked potato covered in cheese and baked beans.' No one said anything, too apathetic even to join in the fantasy. 'And curry sauce,' he added.

I'd noticed before that it only takes an hour or two of being hungry, but hungry with a difference, hungry without the possibility of eating again in the near future, for all kinds of atavistic survival behaviour to kick in. Starvation is a state of mind. You coddle your stomach as if it's nurturing a baby. Even wind, previously unwelcome, gives an illusion of a full belly. All clever, theoretical and emotional thoughts are switched off; the body is saving energy as ruthlessly as it can.

In this state of bemused calm, with Joe endlessly unrolling his last needle-thin three cigarettes into thinner and thinner versions – a smoker's paradox, aiming for salvation in an infinite number of cigarettes, infinitely thin; he'd light one, puff once and it would frazzle up to his nose like a cartoon stick of dynamite – in this torpid state of proto-starvation we saw, right across the river near a barn-like building (we were now, at long last, seeing the odd barn to complement trappers' cabins), a stocky, short man cross down to a flat-bottomed boat with an outboard he started and then put-putted over to us, it being a small, old outboard and not one of the newer, noisier kind.

Hunger made me suspicious. I was definitely not going to indulge in what Barney called 'great river conversations I have known'. In such a conversation the desire for human company outstrips the matter to communicate, and, still afflicted with urban cool, we felt a need to disdain this cosy ritual:

'It's a great river, this.'

'Oh, sure.'

'A grand, a grand river.'

'It is. It's a grand river.'

'It certainly is.'

'You've been travelling a long time on it?'

'Forty days. Quite a while.'

Pause.

'But it's a great river, isn't it? One of the best.'

'It sure is,' etc. etc.

Yes, this guy would get the thousand-yard stare of a starving prisoner of war. Maybe an eye-blink of recognition. No more.

But the man, who had a down-sloping white moustache and overalls, overweight and smiling with his eyes, simply called out to us from his flat-bottomed boat, 'I'll bet you boys are hungry, aren't you?'

Was it that obvious, or was this little man psychic? Or worse, was he taunting us?

'I got some potatoes here you want them' – he hefted up a big paper sack out of his scow – 'and some tomatoes. Corn, just picked that. Should be pretty good. Cucumbers too.'

What magnificent generosity! What insight! What a saviour! What a true man of the river! His name was Morse Christianson, and he arrived as if sent by the higher forces of life. Quite simply he saved us from starvation. Admittedly it was starvation in the future, and probably only two days without food at that – pretty pathetic on the Bobby Sands scale of things (sixty-six days without a morsel before dying) – but even going twenty-four hours without food is unpleasant for a gut that is regularly serviced every day of the year.

Morse had been born on a farm near the river and still lived there. He had land all along both sides. He spoke about the river, but not in adulatory clichéd terms. 'People say the dam is to blame for all the silting-up, but it isn't the dam, it's the run-off. Everyone who sees this river a little has an opinion, but not many of those people see it year-round. Maybe that time when they filled the reservoir affected the lake, but didn't hurt us. But that clear-cutting does. They clear-cut and turn it into farmland and all the run-off ends up in the Peace, all the fertilizers and what-have-you. That's your problem, if you want one.'

He asked us if we'd 'seen the body'. 'Guess you haven't heard,' when we looked bemused. 'Guy threw himself off the high bridge in Peace River town Thursday. Drove up to the IGA car park and left a note or something. Older guy. Figured he'd be about here by now.'

It was another dead thing for Joe to get excited about photographing, along with his growing collection of putrid foxes, rotting elk, bleached rabbit skulls and maggot-filled eagle wings. Food and news of a dead man floating towards us. On those last few days we looked and looked for any sign of the anonymous suicide.

VIII

We saw cows for the first time in seven hundred kilometres. And smelled the Kraft pulp factory ten kilometres from Peace River town, the smell apparent nearly twenty kilometres downstream. Suddenly no one wanted to drink the water. Pulp factories smell of molasses and cardboard with sulphurous undernotes, one of those insidious smells that isn't too bad at first, but the sickly smell penetrates everything. All pulp mills are ghastly. Put them somewhere else.

We went under our first bridge since Fort Vermilion, whose own bridge was only raised in 1974. In its entire length of 1,600 kilometres the Peace River is bridged only seven times, one sign of its great width and inaccessibility.

This bridge was huge. It dwarfed us. The steel protectors on the bridge supports were scored deeply by ice. The concrete above and the sudden change in sound quality as we went under, the shadow and the thick boil of water around each leg of the bridge, made it an underworld; we were entering another world and we'd better be prepared.

All towns start slowly, usually a bit of a mess; sometimes there are signs letting you know, golf clubs and camping sites a little upriver. With Peace River there were mountains of accumulated driftwood. The biggest quantity we'd seen since being trapped the year before on Rocky Point. These piles, were all big stuff, like playing jack straws with telegraph poles, and huge deep pools in between the outlying log-ends, presenting a real towing conundrum. Chest deep or deeper in the water, and ghastly cold when you were out, the best technique involved a delicate picking of your way over the log mountains, flicking and flicking the rope so that canoe didn't get snagged and hoping you didn't slip on a wet log and tumble in.

I was weak now, I could tell. This trip hadn't been like the last. It had taken something out of me that hadn't been replaced. I was fitter and lighter, but inside I felt weaker. Everything was an effort. Joints ached – perhaps we had been eating the wrong food or not enough of it. Or was it the emotional rollercoaster we had been forced to ride? I dreamed of quiet and rest and cleaning all the mud out of the boat, scrubbing it clean, paying for my ill-treatment and disregard of *Dragonfly* by making sure she was properly cared for before the winter lay-up. And though we casually talked about carrying on, perhaps to Dunvegan or further, we all knew Peace River town was the end of the line for this year. There had been one light fall of snow and more predicted.

Nine

DAVE'S ARREST

'He made his escape, a design which he had for some time meditated.' Alexander Mackenzie on an unwilling guide

I

The last beach was a mudflat, boggy, below the railway bridge crossing the mighty Peace. All of us were befuddled, sore, cold and tired. We had walked and paddled eight hundred kilometres to arrive at this spot, under a bridge with old car engines leaking oil from their sumps in the bushes, and a path up through those bushes to the riverside access road. Joe went off for cigarettes and was gone an age. Barney went off to look for him and was gone an age. Dave and I just sat doing nothing, looking at the cold river sweeping by, wrapped up in all our clothes and waterproofs. Barney came back with Cokes and chocolate. Soon I would have to find someone to haul the boat out, look after it for a year, do everything that seemed so irrelevant out on the river. The forward motion would stop. We'd be back to the circling and buzzing and Brownian motion more common to most members of the human race.

We'd taken part in a different human race for a while, set our own modest time up the great river. The winter was coming in now. This was the end of the line all right.

After two hours Joe came back. No one asked him where he had been.

'Sleeping is breaking the law. It's illegal. I'm calling the cops. Now.'

The attractive, curvaceous, utterly poisonous bargirl really was speed-dialling the cops from her safe position behind the long bar. She couldn't wait to report us. Fifty days on the river and we had wanted some action. Now we were getting it. Poor Dave, asleep, or rather simply nodding, at his table. We hadn't even been given time to wake him. She was calling the cops. We were in trouble in Norton's Drinks Lounge in Peace River town on the night of our arrival.

It had started with a Chinese meal. At that stage the conversation was still somewhat forced. After all the emotional abrasion we'd been through small-talk was all we had left, that and stories connected to great Chinese meals we had all eaten in the past. We then removed to McNamara's Hotel, where we discovered that Johnny Cash had died. Suddenly we were all great fans of Johnny. There was a video biography on the TV in the pool room of Mac's and we watched it avidly, sipping our beers, which soon had whisky chasers as a tribute to the erstwhile hard man of country rock. Later I would blame Johnny for everything that happened.

In Mac's, which has a long history of being the first port of call for bush-crazy prospectors and trappers (though the original building burned down in 1986), we had been given a new lease of life. The Indians in the lounge all kept to themselves, it wasn't like Fort Smith or Fort Vermilion. Nevertheless, an Indian and his slim-hipped girlfriend challenged Joe and Barney to pool and beat them. The guy was average but his girlfriend had an insouciant genius for the game, cigarette in mouth, slim butt on the edge of the table for the difficult shots. Everyone was pleased to be beaten by her.

So then it was to Reggie's pizza house for cocktails, followed by the Norton's Drinks Lounge, where the trouble started. An oil crew were there drinking with their cook, an ugly, unpleasant woman who tried to incite violence between me and another crew man. 'This man's insulting me,' she shrieked to the tubby goatee-wearing oilman I had been pleasantly chatting to until that moment. I had said something as a joke and she had chosen to take it the wrong way, and now she wanted a fight. But the oilman just smiled and said, 'He ain't said anything disrespectful to me.' Then Dave told the bargirl she wasn't much of a bargirl because she didn't know how to make a Dr Pepper's (amaretto in a shot glass dropped into a beer or maybe a Guinness – you see, I don't know either) and that was when, I now see, she decided to avenge herself. Just before she started dialling, and I knew we were in trouble, Barney said, 'You know who Joe is? Peter Pan on ecstasy.'

The police arrived, very quickly, presumably not having much to do that night in Peace River, that night or any night, nothing much ever happening apart from old men throwing themselves off the great high bridge. We'd found out more about him from the manager of the campsite where we had lodged ourselves and the canoe. Albert told us the man had been to his daughter's wedding the previous day. Then he had driven to the IGA (a supermarket on the edge of town, above the river) car park, parked his car, left a perfunctory note, walked to the bridge and jumped off. His name was Paul Gulak. He was seventy years old and had a Fu Manchu moustache, Albert told us. A resident of Peace River, a German former jetboat champion, had been dispatched to find the body, but had found nothing, and neither had we.

We had speculated all evening, along with musing on the significance of Johnny Cash's death, on what had been the psychological state of a man, in apparent good health, who waits until after his daughter's wedding to top himself. Was it the wedding that was the final straw, or had he been planning it for months and then waited until after the wedding out of sheer good manners? He had been enjoying himself at the wedding, it was reported, though this could have been simply because he had made up his mind: many suicides stage apparent 'recoveries' from depression once they've decided to end their lives it's the uncertainty that's hard to bear.

The police filled the bar but Dave was too darn quick for them; like a doubled-up wolverine he was out through the twin swinging doors just as the cops rolled up looking for drunks, asleep. But they got Barney, Joe and me. Being in a good mood with the world, we told them the whole story of our fifty days in the wild and they gave us a lift home in their squad car to the campsite, which was on the other side of town.

At the campsite Barney managed to drink a whole bottle of whisky and went howling like a wolf amongst the permanent residents in their huge trailers. I fell asleep in the collapsed (by Barney) remains of the tent. Two hours later I was woken by a police torch in my face. Barney's howling had been reported and he was in the back of a police car; the policewoman asked could I identify him before she took him away?

Barney was sleeping on the back seat. There was a great wet stain on his stay-dry trousers – he had failed to make it to the toilet block before collapsing. I agreed to look after him and took him back to the tent.

He giggled and escaped into the shop on the campsite, where the nightwatchman, called Kenny, was exceedingly surprised and worried. I chased Barney around the revolving postcard stands and the ice-cream chest, him giggling like a five-year-old at the fun of it all. Cajoling eventually worked.

Next day he lay in the tent and moaned and was very sick. Joe looked after him.

Barney got up after dark and ate a KitKat. 'I think that was the closest I came to dying on this trip,' he said.

Dave was released from jail the next afternoon. They'd caught him when he returned to the scene of the crime looking for us. Later he told us he'd been chased all over town by prowling cop cars. 'This town's a police state,' he said. He had a court date for the following month.

Dave hitched back to Fort Smith to get his trusty Chevy van with velour captain's chairs. Joe said a tense goodbye and left for Edmonton.

Barney and I took the canoe apart, right down to the bark. Mackenzie had done the same, one of the few instances where he does something requiring manual skill. 'The sixth man and myself took the canoe asunder, to cleanse her of the dirt, and expose her lining and timbers to the air, which would render her much lighter.' There was a layer of silty mud, dried hard, now nearly half an inch thick, over the bottom. The ribs were still wet. It took four days with brushes and spoons to remove every last drop of mud and to dry all the ribs and sheathing. When it was finished the canoe seemed as light as an old bird's nest. It was ready for the final stage of the journey. Through the town museum we contacted a very helpful local historian called Adèle Boucher. She agreed to let us store the canoe on her husband's bison farm over the winter.

Dave came back at last. Charlie and Cynthia had received the funding for their Peace Point holiday cabin project. Cynthia sent a lot of fish which we ate gratefully. The snow fell more deeply and we got back in Dave's truck, this time heading south.

Part Three

THIRD ATTEMPT

One

NEVER AGAIN

'I send you a couple of guineas, the rest I take to traffic with the Russians.' Alexander Mackenzie

I

Of one thing I was certain: I was never getting into a canoe ever again with Joe. Ever. Ever. Nightmare. No chance. Rather go alone. Barney had to go back to law school but Dave was coming. I just needed two more people to make up the team. More than ever I was convinced we needed four men, simply to manhandle the canoe, which had grown so heavy by the end it had stained my memory. It had overwritten the experience at the end of the trip when we cleaned and dried the boat out and found it light and easy for two men to handle. I thought it could not last. The boat would become heavy again, at least I had to assume it would. And this year would be the toughest by far. We had the potentially impassable Bad River to contend with, the place where Mackenzie lost his boat. Ben Ferrier, in an attempt in the 1950s to emulate him, wrote, 'This is not canoe country. We wonder if the struggle is worth it.' He abandoned his attempt with a knee injury and his team bruised black and blue from the hips down. I hoped that with four men we could lift the canoe over the '200 log jams' Ferrier reported.

I had new criteria. Any team member must have a good sense of humour. They must be cheerful in the morning, or at least capable of replying 'good morning' when it was said to them. Other resolutions: no more democracy in the boat. One captain, one leader, one expedition – me at the back, everyone else up front paddling like crazy, *because they enjoyed it*. No more wimps who thought you could go on a canoe trip and not paddle.

And most of all, no more Joe.

I thought about every quality Joe lacked and found them in Nigel, an old schoolfriend. Nigel was easygoing, humorous, good-natured and vaguely, but only vaguely, pissed off with his job as a sales manager. He had two kids and was happily married. He was well-off and didn't smoke, do drugs or ever have arguments. I'd only had one disagreement with him in twenty years and that was twenty years ago. Nigel was tall, completely blond, skinny as a rake and fit as a fiddle. He played squash twice a week and was an expert at ceroc, a kind of French jive dancing. He'd run a business and he'd run a marathon, done a lot of kayaking when he was younger and he was an expert on wildlife. Nigel was obviously the man. More than anything he had a calm, grown-up quality entirely lacking in me, Dave, Barney and especially Joe.

Then, around November, the phone rang. It was Joe. He had moved to Oxford, where his sister lived. Did I want to see the photographs? Meet up for a drink?

The photographs were excellent and Joe was charming and amusing. He asked me to let him come on the final leg, the big one, the make or break.

I said no. But I said no in the way people say no to someone they prefer saying yes to.

He phoned me a while later and said that he really was interested and he wanted to show me how he'd changed. We agreed to go hiking in the Brecon Beacons as a test of how much he had changed now that he had (a) given up dope and (b) given up cigarettes.

We had a great time in the Brecon Beacons.

I changed my mind.

As soon as I changed my mind Joe's manner didn't alter so much as become more inclusive. He let me into his life. Joe, it seemed, had turned over a new leaf. He had given up his old vices, got a job, and in the evenings worked at his photography. We went to a series of gyms together (utilizing to the full the

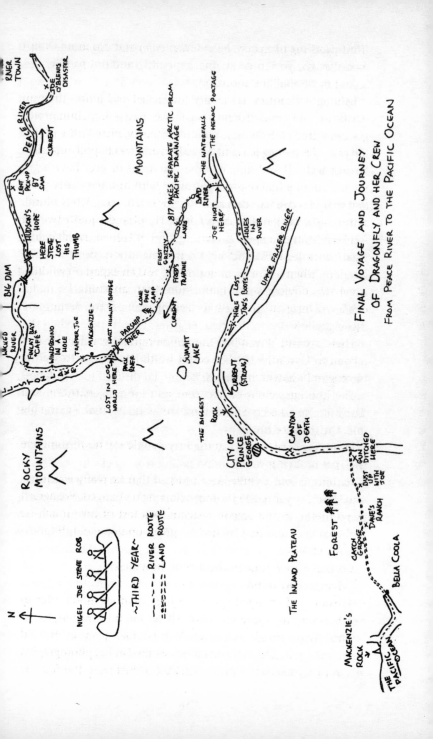

FINAL VOYAGE AND JOURNEY OF DRAGONFLY AND HER CREW
From Peace River to the Pacific Ocean

free offers for prospective new members) and encouraged each other at the bench press, the leg curl, the chin up. We were going to be tougher and stronger this year and we would do it together. Afterwards we sipped warm beer in quiet pubs and looked at the vast distances ahead of us on the map, undaunted. Joe was truly a reformed man, turning down a third pint in favour of a cup of tea and an early night. This year we'd be a great team.

And then, alone in the car home, fiddling with the radio to try to find some half-decent tune, I'd be thinking, Was he really listening? Was it just flattery? Is he humouring me? It was an odd sensation. I'd never been humoured before, though I'd done it a few times to old buffers I'd wanted to get round, women, people's friends you were supposed to like because you liked them. Humouring an old buffer. Me. Me? I banished the thought with the image of the new Joe, pumping iron and laughing at the eighties video in the gym. Eighties? He was three when that decade started. It was like me laughing along with someone about the seventies. Well, I could – after all, by the end of the seventies I was into my teens. Before, I'd disliked Joe's rudeness; now I was suspicious of his attempts at the opposite. I turned the radio's noise up and wound the window down to get the black night air rushing by.

A few months before leaving I received a message from Dave. He had broken his collarbone falling from rocks in the Queen Charlotte Islands off the west coast of Canada. He was backing out. Suddenly I needed a fourth man. At such short notice it wouldn't be easy. I asked everyone I knew. I even sent a fax to Sir Ranulph Fiennes. He and his office were very helpful. They suggested several people. They also told me that the Royal Geographical Society at Kensington Gore had a file full of people who wanted to go on expeditions. And that's how I found Steve Mann.

Steve was English but he had an American father. He spoke with an Essex accent, circumspect and diffident, though he had served in the US Navy – aircraft carriers, about as far as you can get from a birchbark canoe, but still, the navy was the navy.

Steve looked strong and worked as a painter and decorator, construction worker and stud-farm assistant, depending on demand. Next to the photocopy of his file I wrote, simply having read his CV, 'nice guy'.

Steve had been canoeing in northern Ontario and did a lot of hiking, though he didn't have a rucksack or a sleeping bag. I told him the best kind to get and he seemed grateful for the advice. Steve wanted to come. He was available. And he had been in the US Navy. I met Steve and there was something immediately likeable about his clean-cut face and keenness. I rehearsed my new role as dictator, asking Steve if he could take orders. He only smiled and said, 'I've had some pretty hard taskmasters in my time, Rob.' A man who could take orders was welcome any time. Any time.

Joe went to Canada early to do two weeks of tree planting before we set off from Peace River. We aimed to start as soon as the ice broke up. Sometimes this was in April, sometimes May. Mackenzie had left on 10 May, but the river was still blocked with ice on that date. We needed as long a season as we could get. I was allowing three months minimum for the journey, but if it took longer then we would stay longer. This year we had to make it to the Pacific. If we failed then I knew I would probably never come back, though I told everyone I would. Because Joe left early, he never had a chance to meet Steve.

Nigel, in his grown-up and entirely reasonable way, wanted to bring a sat phone. I was against it. We had done perfectly well without one until now, and a sat phone somehow trivialized being in the wilderness. I also knew that if rescue is too easily at hand then one doesn't take sufficient care. Nigel emphasized the utility of the phone in arranging pick-ups and rendezvous on the river, something we would have to do this year because the last 350 kilometres was a walk across the Inland Plateau without the boat, which we would have to arrange to leave.

I didn't want people, including me, phoning home each night. I wanted the wilderness to be wild and remote. What swayed me in the end was the experience of taking a cellphone whilst walking along the Pennine Way in England. It made no difference at all to the *experience* of walking. One knew, for example, that it didn't make a blind bit of difference to a fatal accident, say, falling off a rockface. It simply meant that one could be rescued more easily, probably. A sat phone is simply in the same line of business as matches and knowledge of rescue fires, heliographs, survival kits, rescue flares. There are many compartments of different kinds of worry in the brain (including possible ill-health), and the presence of a phone just calms one of them. A sat phone won't stop a grizzly charging you and it won't right a capsized canoe.

Also, as we found out, sat phones don't always work.

But we didn't want to be hampered by all the nonsense of charging so we agreed to restrict use of the phone to emergencies. Knowing we had a phone took away some of that theoretical anxiety you have at the beginning of a trip; the 'what ifs' you forget once you get moving. But in the Canadian wilderness a rifle makes more difference than a sat phone. Days before leaving I still wasn't entirely convinced about the phone. On principle I was suspicious of being congratulated for taking a sat phone by normal people I knew and liked. Too much good advice from normal people has the curious effect of making you stay home and watch television instead.

II

This year we faced the biggest challenge of the whole voyage: crossing the Rocky Mountains. There were five different sections to complete. 1) Travel to the beginning of the increasingly swift Peace River. 2) Paddle the length of the world's largest man-made lake. 3) Tow, pole and paddle our way to the headwaters of the Rockies up the Parsnip River. 4) Descend the notorious Bad River and the potentially wild Fraser River. 5) Walk 350km to the Pacific across the Inland Plateau of British Columbia.

Stated baldly like that, to passers-by, people at gas stations or the place where we rented the van we drove to Edmonton –

where we left our new paddles behind, a bad omen, nobody's fault – it sounded like a huge amount to do.

In Edmonton I had my ritual meeting with Roland, who had now finished a year of seminary. He seemed calmer and had lost the tiredness lines he'd had under his eyes. 'So you really got to the town of Peace River last year? Awesome.'

'The plan this year is to make it all the way to the Pacific.'

'You should be fine,' said Roland, but a little glibly for my taste. Then, after a pause, he continued, 'But if you don't mind I'm going to pray for you, Rob, 'cause I think you're going to need it.'

We might need prayers but the boat still had its Cree medicine charm from Little Red River. As long as the charm worked I kept quiet about my belief in it.

Safety meant a gun. I had been thinking about guns, either rifles or shotguns, ever since the bear charge of the previous year. I even applied for a UK shotgun licence but a postal strike delayed my application. Yet again, with the exquisite planning that characterized this venture, we would be facing the wilderness unarmed. I wanted something better than the bearhorn, which had worked sometimes but was by no means the infallible anti-bear device you get the impression it might be from Stephen Herrero's book *Bear Attacks*.

In Edmonton we bought at considerable expense two cans of bear mace, enough for a four-second blast – it would blind a mugger for four days, though there were accounts of it 'not working' on grizzlies. I guessed it depended on how close you were when you pulled the various pins and levers. As with all semi-explosive devices you didn't want to accidentally let it off, perhaps in your tent partner's face as you backed inelegantly into the tent, so we left the plastic tie and the orange clip in place on the top. This meant at least twenty seconds of scrabbling before the thing would be ready to fire, and, like the aeroplane safety drill, I ignored how it actually worked until halfway through the trip. The other device was the bear banger. A metal tube like a pen was used to fire exploding flares either over a bear's head or into its face. It was advisable not to fire over the head as the explosion would then come on the far side of the bear, actually driving him towards you. There were accounts of such flares actually precipitating an attack rather than ending one.

But we still had no gun. And this year we would be travelling through heavy grizzly country. Plenty of people in smaller groups than ours regularly walked through areas infested with bears without a gun. Ben Gadd recommends it in his Rocky Mountain guide. But no trapper or Indian we had ever met went out without a rifle or a twelve-gauge shotgun. Opinion was divided on whether it was better to use rifled slugs or birdshot for a devastating spread at only a few yards' range.

Were we eco-minded holidaymakers or professional woodsmen? The professional spends all his time in the wilderness. He is apt to get routine, and even careless, about safety. He may gut fish and leave the remains around a camp. Very often he is alone. The rifle is the safety net. The holidaymaker, the recreationist, even the hiker, is moving on. He may spend two or three weeks in the bush and he will be alert all the time. He goes to a new campsite every day and there is no chance for bears to get used to him. Accounts of bear hunting indicate it takes several days for bear bait to work; in fact, for people scared of bears, reading about bear hunting is a salutary and worthwhile inoculation – these creatures aren't that common, neither are they always intent on causing harm. Nor are they that easy to get a shot at.

But we were going to be out for months on end. And though moving on, we too might begin to get careless. A gun would be good security.

At this point I remembered Barney blowing away Charlie's dog kennel. None of us was an experienced marksman, except Joe, with his surprising background of rifle competition. Joe had been a square before he got hip, and he was a very good shot. Steve had been trained to use small arms when he was in the navy, but that was all. I had been trained by the Arizona police force (for a newspaper article) to fire a pistol and a combat shotgun. Apart from Charlie's sawn-off .303 I'd never fired a rifle in my life. Nigel had no experience, and unlike the rest of us no particular interest in guns. He had two boys, one in his early teens, and in many ways projected that particular adult vibe of being 'sensible', which comes no doubt from realizing that if you say stupid, irresponsible things your kids may end up doing them.

III

We pulled up at the IGA car park in Peace River at 5.30 a.m. I wondered exactly where the car had been parked, the one left behind by Paul Gulak. Had his body ever been found? By 7.30 we had done all the shopping necessary for the next twenty-five days. Since the first year, when everything had been hit or miss when it came down to provisions, we were now pretty fast and accurate. Each man consumes 1lb or 450g of carbohydrates a day, split three ways between oats for breakfast, rice and pasta for later. Four guys for twenty-five days will need roughly 100lb or 40kg of carbs. This is for a heavy-exertion programme of paddling and towing. Add to that tins of sardines, corned beef, curry powder and sauces, two Mars bars a day per man, nuts and raisins, and the food adds up 60 or 70kg for four men for twenty-five days. This gives a wide margin for safety. No one will go hungry on these quantities.

The cost, too, was reasonable. About $Can500. I was paying. It made things easier: Steve and Joe were both hard-up and it meant there were fewer arguments over food. All part of my plan for streamlining the leadership situation.

In the weeks before the trip I had been worried by Nigel. He knew me well. He was older than me, which at school had significance; twenty years on, would it still? He had run his own business, was used to giving orders. And when I'd suggested several pieces of kit he had done his own research and decided on different footwear and rainwear. Which was OK. There was a lot of latitude in kit. It was almost better that people thought their kit was 'best' than for it to be objectively good but disliked. A lot of the performance of equipment is how well it is looked after and if you like something you'll look after it, nurture it. But when he disagreed over the waders I had to draw the line. Waders were going to be our secret weapon. On Bad River everyone had complained of the glacier meltwater. If we were going to be in and out of that water we'd need protection. Nigel suggested wetsuits but I knew simple, cheap stocking-foot waders would be best. They packed up small and in icy water were warmer than a wetsuit. They were more dangerous – if you turned turtle the air trapped in the feet could keep you submerged – but we weren't solitary fishermen and each of us had a knife for such emergencies. Then Nigel wanted Gore-Tex breathable waders. These are more expensive and less flexible and less hardy than the non-breathable kind. In the first stirrings of the paranoia that goes with bossing others around I sent a lengthy email forcibly reiterating my position. As soon as I pressed 'send' I regretted it. I'm getting het up about waders, I thought. I'm going out on a limb with an old friend over rubberized footwear. I've lost my sense of proportion. But there was no turning back. On expeditions I'd learned you have to accept that some of the time you become a mockery of all you hold dear in the comfortable, sedentary life you leave behind. Nigel was unperturbed, bought what I demanded, and when I next met him, smiled and said, 'You just want me to be a "yes" man, don't you?'

'Just back me up when the going gets tough,' I replied.

Peace River town seemed less lively than I remembered, as if it were still recovering from the long winter. The mud from the recent melt had dried and turned into a grey dust which lay over everything. I had no urge to stay. We would slink off asap, towing not paddling, since the current was particularly vicious right near the muddy quagmire of the shore we had landed at the year before. I planned to take the first tow and we would slip quietly away. But news of our arrival soon leaked out. The new editor of the *Peace River Gazette* turned up. Originally from Mauritius, he was a tall thin bespectacled East Indian. He had emigrated to Ontario and ended up in Alberta. It seemed like a gigantic mistake to me. One look at his skinny Asian–Indian physique, his lofty ignorance of the great outdoors, his wrapped-upness though the sun was shining: surely he was in the wrong place? He had left behind a tropical island to become a news-paperman in a place that was under deep snow eight months of the year. He was polite and took a slight interest in the boat, but with careful thought he pronounced, 'I think this craft is too flimsy for the task ahead.' It was the way he said it, with a supreme detachment, as if he were not present with those he had just predicted would fail. He was detached from the con-sequences, as, I suppose, all good newspaper reporters should be, there to warn their readers and not the poor fools actually making the news. But I could tell that he believed it, he believed we were mad and would drown; he also couldn't see the point of it; he hadn't heard of Mackenzie (how many in Mauritius had?) and he had no idea that Native Americans and trappers used canoes like ours to explore and open the entire country that had become the epicentre of his own dreams. The dream of a new life he had achieved. I have seldom seen such incom-prehension as was in the eyes of that man.

The editor had arrived at the riverbank with another weirdo. At least that was how I initially thought of Herb, a white-haired, barrel-chested man with toothache. He had the inner preoccupation of a man in pain, but he surfaced from it to look over our boat and the huge pile of belongings all in colour-coded Ortlieb kitbags. This year we would be organized. Joe was in charge of food and supplies. He did a good job: no soggy oats and mud-laden sleeping bags. The Ortlieb is a vinyl kitbag with a roll-down top. This contains two strips of bendy plastic which, when linked together and rolled up, make a virtually waterproof bag. I say 'virtually' because if you squeeze the bag hard enough air will start to escape, but waterproof enough for our purposes. These bags would withstand any amount of rain and a dunking in the river.

Herb, who had a German accent, had arrived to put his car in for a service. He seemed to know Adèle, the local historian who had arranged to store our boat for the winter. I went off to buy a brush and some insect repellent – both of which we already had. You know it's time to leave when you start buying stuff you've already got. When I came back sensible Nigel whispered to me, 'That old guy over there offered to give us his rifle, but I said no.'

I looked at Herb with new respect. I went over and talked to him. He had my interest. Then he told me that he had been a member of the SS Mountain Division in World War II before emigrating to Canada in 1949. He said we ought to take his old Austrian service rifle, 8mm, great against bears. He didn't need it. We could throw it in the river after we'd finished with it.

'Is this guy for real?' I asked Adèle.

'Oh yes,' she said, 'he was also the world jetboat champion fifteen years ago.'

'Did you go looking for Paul Gulak?' I asked Herb.

'Oh sure, I went lookin', but I never found. Just like all the other times I agreed to go lookin', for dead bodies by this town. Never found one. This river doesn't give up its dead!'

Herb was semi-contrite about his SS background: 'I was fuckin' seventeen years old. I did what I was told. Everyone in my family supported the leader. It was the only way to get ahead. I had nothing against the Jews. They were just smarter than us. It was the Russians who were real bad.'

I still didn't know whether to believe him. I wondered if the SS thing had been a joke he made up in 1949 when he arrived penniless from Austria and had never been allowed to forget.

But he again brought up the subject of the gun. This time I said, 'OK, we'll take it,' not really believing he'd get it. He went and got his car, a Mercedes – what else? – and drove off. Then two policemen arrived, none I recognized from the year before, but like all outback towns Peace River had far too many police with not enough to do. These two were hassling a couple of Indians sitting on a bench drinking whisky out of Coke cans. Herb pulled up in his Merc but I could tell it wasn't propitious for an illegal arms transaction. He strolled down the bank and nodded his chin at the police. 'They got nothin' better to do. Those Indians aren't doing any harm.' I was surprised. 'I was married to an Indian for fifty years,' he said. 'They just like drinking, the same as everyone.'

But he hadn't got the 8mm service rifle. 'I think someone borrowed it from me. I need to ask my son. I'll come along tomorrow night with my son and bring it then.

He glanced back at the road, 'Too many friggin' cops around here.'

Nigel, Joe, Steve and I shouldered the canoe and carried it from the bank, where it had been lying on its side, to the water's edge. It was as light as something made of polystyrene, or felt it, all that cleaning out Barney and I did the year before.

Herb discovered I'd written books and had occasionally written for newspapers.

'You ever read the *Daily Mail*?' he asked.

'I even reviewed a book for them once.'

'Hey, noospaper man!' he guffawed.

'You know what noospaper man, they gave us the *Daily Mail* to read in the army. Had a few holes cut in it, but they liked us to read the *Daily Mail*.'

It sounded unlikely but then I did know national newspapers were exchanged daily throughout the war between the UK and Germany in neutral Sweden.

'All Nazis weren't bad,' he went on. 'We was just brainwashed.'

I laid out the tow rope, stowed the kitchen bag, grill and water bottles in their usual place at the front. It looked like we had way too much gear. As Mackenzie observed, 'An European, seeing one of these slender vessels thus laden, heaped up, and sunk with her gunwhale within six inches of the water, would think his fate inevitable in such a boat.'

'You ever in the army?' Herb asked me.

'No. Never was.'

'Too smart, eh?'

I wondered if it was a cunning way of discovering if I knew enough about rifles not to shoot someone. Just before we cast off, Herb got serious.

'This river can rise ten feet in a night, when they open the dam.'

227

'I better be careful then.'

'You don't have to be careful – just don't lose your canoe.' He gave me a look which echoed his comment. 'Being careful' was the wrong state of mind. It betokened worry, which was no good. Instead we would have to *do things* to stay safe rather than adopting a disabling mental posture.

We towed away from our bizarre sending-off party: a Mauritian Indian editor, a French Canadian historian, an ex-Nazi jetboat champion, the American photographer from the paper. The further you get from London–New York–Paris–Beverly Hills the more cosmopolitan the people. We towed away along the muddy beach, under the great metal railway bridge, Nigel and Steve waving back. Joe and I knew better, him at the stern of the boat and me towing on the rope, both of us face forwards, intent, knowing, in part, what was ahead and how no one could help us now.

IV

On that first day we saw two deer, a beaver, a wolf cub, two bald eagles and a Canadian mountain swallowtail butterfly. Nigel id'd them all. He had a prominent Adam's apple and excellent eyesight and craned forward, book on his lap, seeing and identifying wildlife everywhere.

When it was Steve's turn to tow he kept looking back at me as if I should have given him more orders. He had a strong build but he disguised it by standing in a way that made him seem smaller than he was. I noticed he was stumbling more than anyone else as he pulled on the long line. Then he fell up to his neck in the water. He laughed gamely along with us.

We had paddled across the river and made good progress but all too soon we hit fast current again. There was no getting around it, the current was speeding up. When Steve put his foot through the roof of a beaver lodge he complained, 'I'm just not as agile as Joe, OK.'

The river was just as I remembered it but faster. On either bank were poplar and spruce growing up the steep, gravelly slopes. Mackenzie described this country as teeming with buffalo, but even in his day the land had recently changed. He wrote: 'An Indian in some measure explained his age to me, by relating that he remembered the opposite hills and plains, now interspersed with groves of poplars, when they were covered with moss, and without any animal inhabitant but the reindeer. By degrees, he said, the face of the country changed to its present appearance, when the elk came from the East, and was followed by the buffalo.' The reindeer, or caribou, had then 'retired to the long range of high lands that run parallel to this river'. These mountains, even today, are known as the Caribou Hills.

Nigel had imbibed my fears of grounding out. He reacted by neurotically probing with his paddle every fifth stroke or so. 'What you doing, Nigel?' 'Just checking for depth,' he replied with the casual aplomb of a man used to selling things. Another tiny bacillus of paranoia eating at my brain: if Nigel stopped paddling every fifth stroke he was doing 20 per cent less work than everyone else. Was that right? Every time I looked up Nigel was 'just checking for depth'.

Even before we lost sight of the sad stripe of aluminium-clad buildings along the waterfront of Peace River town the clever felt-soled wet-sock boots I had bought were clogged with mud and useless. What a mistake! I'd assumed the river got less muddy but it didn't. I was also committing the cardinal sin of taking new gear on a trip without trying it first. On the final tow of the day I shouted back to the others that the mud was easing: 'I think it's pretty good here.' Then I fell over flat on my face.

The next day the towing got worse. Steve, who had donned a spotless white T-shirt, was up to his waist in mud. In the heat of midday we found two small garter snakes arranged like a yin-yang symbol on the drying crust of the mud. 'Are they poisonous?' asked Steve, as the snakes uncurled and shot away in different directions. (They aren't.)

The further we went from the town the more ice there was. The ice was opaque, like hardened snow, with a few clear spots like windows. It was mud-brown and at first we didn't realize the uneven lumpiness along the banks was the ice left over from winter. Towing over ice involved guessing how much weight a melting ice bridge could take and leaping from block to block. The surface was soft enough to enable one to grip, even with smooth wet-sock boots like mine. When the ice gave way to mud I looked with envy at Nigel's special amphibious training shoes I had breezily dismissed back in England.

V

Herb and his half-Indian son Gil turned up in the evening in their jetboat. Gil gave us some bear bangers in lieu of the gun and walked across the gravel beach to share a whisky around the campfire. Gil grew more confident as he talked to us, getting our measure. He helped run his dad's steel-fabricating business and collected German war memorabilia as a hobby. I thought they were going back on the deal but they said they'd come again with a .22 or a .410 shotgun. I asked Herb if he had ever been in a crash when he had been fighting his way up to the world jetboating title.

'I was in a crash once. A bad one.'

'Were you hurt?'

'I was fine. It was the spectators that was . . . in trouble. I always said they were standing way too close.'

VI

'You ain't got as far as I thought you would have,' said Herb when he turned up the next day at our two tents and fire on a sandy inlet.

He'd brought a gun this time with a .22, but with no ammo. He also had his family and lots of beer. Everyone was well oiled and soon a real beach party was in progress. Gil told us he always carried a 9mm pistol when he was in the wilderness with children, but he didn't have it on him, so I suppose we were not

230

yet in the wilderness. Then he said, 'You know there's no Cree word for "wilderness",' leaving it hanging in the air. Herb said he liked us boys and then added, 'But you have to be a real cunt for me not to like you.' Herb's granddaughter sang a jazz song, very well in fact, whilst her teenage boyfriend finished off a pint of vodka. Of a recent failed love affair of his own, Herb commented, 'It's only pussy!' and sprang open another can of Moosehead beer. He complained that he still hadn't got his teeth fixed. Coming to visit us was taking up all his time. He'd had a hip replaced recently and when he talked he shifted from side to side, skinny legs in his shorts like a small boy's.

Herb had started work in Peace River as a welder. Then he'd set up his own metal-fabricating company. He'd made a lot of money in his time. 'But I worked hard. Nothing comes from nothing. You have to work. Kids today don't know what they want to do. Not like you and me.

'How old are you?' he asked me.

'Thirty-nine.'

'Young man, half my age! I figured you were forty-five.'

As Herb left he said he'd bring someone the next day who had an old .270 rifle. 'You guys want to have fun. I don't want to spoil your fun. But just throw it in the river if you see a cop. Personally I think it's all bullshit – every fuckin' criminal got one, why not me too?'

And though I didn't believe it, Herb brought along his pal Edgar who gave us an old Winchester .270 rifle and thirty rounds of ammunition. Gil showed me how to load it and fired off a round into the sky. The incredible noise settled slowly, my ears ringing. 'Now you're ready!' said Herb, cackling with insane laughter.

VII

We cooked up the pemmican that night. We'd been given it by a historical re-enactment society. I had been grateful but the others didn't understand the incredible significance of pemmican, how it had been the fuel of the voyageurs, how mileage was measured out by the pounds of pemmican consumed. Pemmican was an Indian invention, like the canoe, that the white man took over and industrialized. Meat, usually buffalo, was dried in strips and pounded into granules, then mixed with sugar, tallow and cranberries to make a nourishing protein-rich staple. You could eat it raw or you could boil it up into a stew. The best thing about it was that it lasted for years without going off. Mackenzie wrote about burying pemmican under the fireplace in a campsite, ready to be retrieved months later on a return journey. The fireplace was the natural burying spot because the ashes masked scavenger-attracting odours. Voyageurs paddling the big canoes from Montreal used bacon fat but the northmen who went into the interior, like Mackenzie's men, used pemmican. (There were other differences between the two kinds of voyageur – northmen used tents and smaller canoes like ours, whereas, as Mackenzie wrote, 'the more frugal porkeater lodges beneath his canoe'.) Pemmican released voyageurs from having to hunt or fish each day. Until tinned food arrived it was the food choice of all serious explorers of the north.

I had longed to eat pemmican ever since I was a child. In Arthur Ransome stories they call corned beef pemmican. *The Young Fur Trader*, a book whose cover picture of a birchbark canoe had greatly influenced me, was full of references to pemmican. Now I was finally getting to eat it. But just as I took delivery of a four-kilogram lump of the stuff, the lady at the re-enactment society happened to mention that this particular piece of pemmican was two years old. Now that should have filled me with awe about the longevity of pemmican but the fact is I began to get nervous. What if we all got poisoned on day three? What if in making this modern-day pemmican some essential ingredient had been left out that meant we'd all get salmonella or botulism? I told the others and what little interest they had in pemmican evaporated immediately. We settled on cooking the stuff for hours in the frying pan. 'That should kill any bugs,' said Steve. We then mixed it with flour and water to make a historic dish known to voyageurs as rubbaboo. This reduced the pemmican to something with the consistency of burnt breakfast cereal, that one that tastes like grit. Everyone had a symbolic mouthful and then washed the greasy flavour away with a slug of whisky. 'I don't think I like rubberpooh,' said Steve. I forced myself to finish the pan off and lay down in my sleeping bag, expecting the worst.

The next morning I was still alive.

We kept the pemmican for weeks and weeks. 'After all, it's two years old already – what's a few more days? We'll eat it in an emergency,' we said.

VIII

'The team were getting to know each other. Nigel suggested to Joe he might make a good salesman, whilst Steve and Joe found common ground in talking about their careers as solvent abusers. In the navy Steve had sniffed an aircraft solvent called PD680, sprayed on to a rag you then stretched across your face. 'Only one beer every fifty days in the US Navy,' he explained. 'Everyone below the flight deck is sniffing PD680.' Joe countered with stories of sniffing butane lighter refills and being spun around until he blacked out. 'How old were you?' asked Nigel, perhaps thinking of his own son. 'About fourteen,' said Joe, 'maybe younger. You get mad dreams on butane.'

Great. From dopeheads to glueboys, it seemed I had a talent for selecting drug abusers.

Six days in and the first argument with Joe. Over the duration of the rest break and the quantity of nuts in the afternoon snack. Having Joe on board was like travelling with a 1970s-style union representative. It'll be all right, I told myself after I'd smoothed everything down. Joe's doing a great job. In fact, I had to reluctantly admit, he was better at steering the canoe than I was.

The rest of the talk in the canoe was all about celebrities, things on TV. I missed old Dave with his startling comments and questions: 'Is there Japanese existentialism?' 'You guys want boneless pork from a spineless pig?' 'Do you think a fire is a work of art?'

Good old Dave. Now I was a serious expedition leader, Japanese existentialism was right off the menu.

Two

A HERO OF OUR TIME

'At this time the water rose fast, and passed on with the rapidity of an arrow shot from a bow.' Alexander Mackenzie on the Bad River

I

The canoe coming towards us was the second we had seen in two summers on the Peace. Harvald the lonely Norwegian had been the first. But this paddler looked as if he had stolen the canoe, the hi-tech expensive canoe he was grinning from as he approached with his bent paddle – always a sign of either (a) considerable experience or (b) too much money. He coasted up, face sunburned to that state of rawness you see in down-and-outs and drunks who have fallen asleep on a hot day on a park bench. His hands were huge and so were his arms, but when he got out of the canoe his body was tiny, his backside non-existent. It was as if Joe O'Blenis had evolved solely for the purpose of long-distance canoeing.

'I was just saying to myself [this was a common Joe locution since, being alone and travelling fast, his only conversations were with himself], I bet on this trip the only other paddlers I meet will be doing some big trip like me.' He grinned again and revealed a big gap between his very white front teeth, which only added to the mountain-man look, a dental imperfection perfectly suited to the task of being outdoors all the time.

It was flattering to be included in Joe's self-designated group of top canoeists, though we were nothing like as experienced as he was. The previous year he had attempted the world record

235

for a single day's travel on a river. He had managed 270km going down the Peace in twenty-four hours before his shoulder gave out. 'I used a new paddle, untested, rookie error,' grinned Joe. Since starting this year he had already béen a month on the rivers and lakes of British Columbia and had another five ahead. He was aiming to be the first person to canoe across Canada in one season. A Russian, Ilya Klvana, had done it in a home-made wooden kayak in 1999, but a canoe, with its single-bladed paddle, would be harder. Klvana liked to travel light, he didn't have a stove and ate his food cold after soaking it for hours in water in the bottom of his kayak. Amazingly he did all his portages in one carry with his canoe perched on a little trolley. 'The key is travelling light,' he said. I thought about all the portages between the Pacific and the Atlantic and I had to agree: if you needed more than one trip it would really slow you up.

Joe O'Blenis's canoe had his name and the sponsor's name on it. He had a solar panel and a carbon-fibre paddle that weighed thirteen ounces. It cost $300. 'OK,' he looked sheepish, 'so I work in a gear shop.' He had given up his job to make the trip.

He explained that it took three weeks for his hands to harden up and lose their blisters and cracks. I had never been troubled with blisters but cracks were another thing. I thought I had finally solved it the year before with Udder Cream, originally made to soothe chafed cows' teats, but this year they were worse than ever. It was a combination of tending the hot fire, getting them covered in ash and not washing them enough, and once you had cracks they only seemed to get worse. Each finger joint split and bled, and then the fingertips started to open up. In desperation Steve taped all his fingers with duct tape. Nigel wore fingerless mitts. The result was the same: after a day or two the flesh went white and soft, as if it had been underwater too long or wearing a non-breathable plaster. Applying the cream at night to the softened skin meant the cracks at last began to heal. And, just as Joe said, after a month my hands were calloused but clean of dirt and cracks.

Joe asked politely if he could camp the night on 'your island', as he put it. It was a long wooded island with huge blocks of ice encircling it.

He pulled his boat up just clear of the water but did not tie it up. I thought it looked a little close to the river but said nothing. It was obvious Joe was a canoe master; one glance at his forearms, nut-brown and piped with veins, told you he was a serious paddler.

We offered Joe some whisky but he declined one of our mugs. Instead he brought out a huge pear-shaped Petzl mug with a cavernous base. 'Bet that never gets spilled,' said Steve, but what we were all thinking was: Now we know why you refused our tiny cup. Joe smirked as he brought out his folding backrest. It did look comfortable, but to me it was just one more piece of kit. When it was time to pitch his tent Joe lifted the biggest rucksack I've ever seen out of the canoe. It must have been 150 litres, double the size of a normal backpack, and with its great width and bulk it made the diminutive Joe look like a boy wearing something made for an adult.

Joe even had a laptop, which he typed into each night and then uploaded the copy to his website every time he went through a town. He had a digital camera for the photographs he put on his site. As we sweated over making a rice-and-corned-beef curry on the fire, he munched on a bagel sandwich for his supper.

The island camp was now dark. The last of the sunset made marmalade- and peach-coloured bars across the sky. Joe and I stayed up late talking and drinking the precious supply of whisky. Was Joe an incurable optimist or would he succeed in his epic cross-Canada canoe dash? He had the gear, too much to my mind, but he also had the fitness and the experience. He'd already ridden a mountain bike across Canada and competed in many canoe marathons. I wondered what other methods of crossing the continent he would try next. Swimming? Running? It would have to be something stripped-down and athletic enough to appeal to his sponsors. Joe was proud of his sponsorship, rightly in my view. Sponsors aren't easy to get and you often end up doing more for them than they do for you. One of

Joe's main sponsors was a sunglasses manufacturer. This seemed trivial until Joe explained how many pairs he had lost or broken, plus they gave him special fleeces and paddling shorts. His canoe was also a freebie, a carbon-fibre special that looked as sleek and new-fangled as a missile.

There was something in Joe's face, though – cheerful, toothy, off the wall in an indefinable way – that hinted he was approaching the whole enterprise with the emphasis just wrong, a fraction out of kilter. But who was I to pass judgement? We drank to the success of each other's enterprise. It was not hypocrisy. On one level I honestly admired him, his courage to go it alone (he'd already been trapped in a deserted cabin by a grizzly wanting to get in through a flimsy door) and his dedication to take six months off to do it. At the same time he understood exactly what we were doing. Even better than Herb. Herb sympathized, but to him an engine was just as good as a paddle. Joe knew. He knew why we were going against the current, why we were doing it in a boat that went out of use a hundred years ago, why we were suffering and yet enjoying it immensely despite and at the same time because of the suffering, all self-induced. Joe understood all that. Us against the world. People who seek challenges and people who do the sensible thing and avoid them. He knew it and appreciated it though our ventures were quite different. His would take longer and would always be under time pressure. Ours was through more difficult and remote terrain but covered less distance. But Joe's emphasis on laptops, sunglasses and backrests made me worry for him. He didn't need all that gear, and on a long, difficult trip everything lugged must be essential, otherwise it spits its uselessness in your face each day of travail and bleeds your will, bleeds you dry. Stripping down to the essentials isn't just about keeping things light and easy to transport, it's about maintaining focus. Because in the end it is the imagination and the will that carries you through; body and boat are only servants.

In the morning, the pre-sunrise time when mist was on the river like homeless smoke, I got up because the river woke me up. I pulled on my boots with the increased clumsiness that seems to come with exercising too long each day, my back pressed hard against the nylon of the vestibule, a clumsy over-dressed soul. I hardly noticed the river until I saw that the cook shelter was half submerged. The river had risen five or six feet. Nigel and Steve's rucksacks were underwater. I shouted to the others but it was Joe who waded into the river. Everything in Steve's pack was saturated. All the video films were ruined. Despite the excessive neatness of his packing, Steve's stuff wasn't watertight. In the lull after rescuing all the gear we noticed Joe's canoe had either been moved by him during the night or was gone. He had still not emerged from his tent. We looked around for the canoe, its huge absence immediately apparent – it was gone for sure. How were we going to tell him? His record attempt was over. He was stranded on an island fifteen miles from the nearest road with a pack weighing two tons. He was stuffed. What would his sponsors say? It looked like another rookie error.

'Er, are you going to tell Joe?' asked Steve, already meticulously laying out his wet and damaged gear on a folded groundsheet.

You can't knock on a tent door. 'Joe,' I called close to his flysheet, 'are you awake?'

'Er, yeah.'

'It seems your canoe has gone. The river rose a lot last night.'

He stuck his head out of the door and grinned. He pulled on his boots and after stamping around for a while said, still grinning, 'OK, guys, where is it?'

I shall never forget the transforming look of horror as we balefully returned his gaze without answering. The happy grin was now a stricken look, the look of a woman led away from a bombed house in the Blitz, her children buried under the rubble, a look predominantly elsewhere.

He lolloped off up the beach, his boots unlaced. There was nothing we could do except be glad that all we had lost was the whisky, a water bottle, Joe's bobble hat and the fishing rod. We could exult in our survival. But how do you comfort a man who has lost everything? His dream, his transport, his equipment, his *raison d'être* – all swept away by the merciless current running five miles an hour every hour? His boat would be long gone and lost among the myriad islands downstream by now.

'It'll turn up,' I said, when Joe returned empty handed.

'It's got to,' chipped in Nigel.

'It might even be on the other side of the island,' said Steve, a highly unlikely suggestion.

'I already looked,' said Joe, his voice emotionless. It is appalling but always interesting to see people when everything is stripped away and nothing is hidden. That was Joe *sans* canoe. *Sans* $4,000 canoe, solar panel, hi-tech stove and $300 bent paddle.

Joe walked again all round the island and found nothing except the wreckage of a big wooden motorboat, its great spars splintered out like a collapsed barrel, the engine a massive rusty block overgrown with stinging nettles and willows, and everywhere underfoot nails and bolts that had dropped from the rotting timbers. It looked as if the boat, or small ship, had been dropped from a great height right into the middle of the island, smashed up on the highest part, well above the water level; it must have been wrecked there years before the dam was built, when the great meltwaters of the spring were unregulated and carried the season's silt all the way down to the Athabasca Lake.

We discussed various options with Joe, who had meekly asked to be transported to the mainland to 'continue walking'. On the slippery sloping bank with his massive pack he would have found it tough going. Nigel had a better idea. He got out his satellite phone and called Adèle, who called Herb, who agreed to come and look for the lost boat. Meanwhile we loaded Joe's bag into our canoe and started walking upstream with him to Dunvegan.

It was at this spot that Mackenzie had written that 'the West side of the river displayed a succession of the most beautiful scenery I had ever beheld'. He must have been in a good mood, having overcome the chagrin of the previous day when he mentions, 'I had the misfortune to drop my pocket-compass into the water.' He must have had a spare because the interminable directions continued: 'West half a mile, West-South-West four miles, West half a mile.' There was something irritating about the man. How could he be so careless as to drop one of his instruments, his symbols of authority, into the water? Mackenzie described the river: 'Groves of poplar in every shape vary the scene; and their intervals are enlivened with vast herds of elks and buffaloes; the former chasing the steeps and uplands, and the latter preferring the plains.'

Without the vast herds, the scenery, though made up of lovely hills artfully moulded to suit the wide sweep of the river, seemed empty, waiting to be filled. Every now and then we would surprise a deer or two, who would pound up the steep hills, sending stones skittering down after them. We saw moose and a bear in the distance, but the vast herds of elk and buffalo had long gone.

In an admirably short time Joe had recovered his grin. We extolled the virtues of our reformed Nazi jetboat champion. How he was certain to find the lost boat. Joe asked if he could paddle the birchbark canoe for a while. With those arms, I thought, he could probably paddle his way to the dam without a tow.

Later, when I re-read Mackenzie's journal alongside my own diary, I found something odd: on 5 June 1793 Mackenzie wrote, 'This morning we found our canoe and baggage in the water, which had continued rising during the night.' I checked the date our baggage was submerged and Joe lost his canoe: 5 June. We'd been at a different place, but it was the same date, 211 years later to the very day.

II

Near Dunvegan Herb arrived with a roaring engine and bad news: 'First thing I gotta tell you, I didn't find your canoe. I was tellin' Grinder here,' he indicated the pleasant youngish guy in the front, tying spinners on to a line, 'that canoe has already been sold by some Indian for fifty bucks or a gallon of homebrew.'

Joe looked glum, but did well to more or less hide it.

'How much that boat of yours cost anyway?' said Herb. 'You got a rich daddy paying for you?'

'I got sponsorship,' said Joe.

'Me, I always paid my own way,' said Herb. What a bastard. He was handing round beers and Kentucky Fried Chicken and having fun making poor Joe O'Blenis squirm.

'Old Grinder here' ('Who's Grinder?' I asked. 'Mill operator,' said Herb, 'he's shacked up with my daughter') 'reckoned a fancy boat like the one you lost would last about three minutes on the reserve. You have much in it?'

'He's got a three-hundred-dollar paddle,' I said.

'Firewood,' said Herb.

'Solar panel.'

'That'll just get thrown in the drink. You might find the carcass of your canoe, the shell of it – that is if they can't sell it.'

'Or cut it in half and make a kiddy sled out of it,' added the artless Grinder.

'Yeah, or that,' agreed Herb, nodding seriously.

For a while the image of Joe's immaculate craft being hacksawed in half killed all conversation.

'How much you say it cost? $10,000?'

'$4,000.'

Herb sucked in air before returning to the many horrible deaths a canoe can expect if lost on the Peace River. Then he cracked a grin. 'Yeah, I found it. Left it round the corner, you can come back with me and pick it up.'

Reformed Nazis, they love a bit of *Schadenfreude*.

'Watch the crosswinds on the lake,' said Herb, 'they can make a six-foot swell in ten minutes. Watch from behind so they don't sneak up on ya. And there's rapids on the Parsnip. See, I been where you're going, and I know you got some serious water to cross. You make it down the Fraser and you're done. Send me a postcard.'

Herb had ridden his jetboat all the way to Arctic Lake at the top of the Parsnip, but he had never been down Bad River.

'Do you think we'll make it?' I asked.

'I haven't seen anything that suggests otherwise,' said Herb.

242

We drank more beer, which had a powerfully soporific effect in the heat. The Kentucky buckets were empty. Herb fiddled with the engine intake. There was a sad air of parting. Maybe he felt the same. 'I guess I'll never see you again. Pity there's forty years between us. Just send us a postcard when you get down that river.'

Then he perked up. 'Remember, that gun is the most dangerous thing you got. You could go to jail for that.'

And with a roar and high plume of water from the jet, Herb, Joe O'Blenis and Herb's crew were off.

'Kind of miss him,' said Nigel.

'Yep.'

'Joe O'Blenis fuckin' owes us,' said Steve.

'Herb'll make him pay.'

Three

GUN CRAZY

'They gave me a net made of nettles, the skin of a moose deer, dressed, and a white horn in the shape of a spoon. My young men also got a collar of white bear's claws of a great length.' Alexander Mackenzie
on gifts received in the Rocky Mountains

I

There were three deer, not far off. It had just stopped raining. The deer turned to look at us. I was reluctant to shoot but I took the gun out of its damp cover. The cover was cheap fake leather with a zip and a velour lining which sucked up moisture. I opened the box of shells. The .270 was a large cartridge necked down to a long slim bullet, the whole thing big, shiny and heavy. I pulled the cartridge clear of the plastic retainer and fumbled with the bolt. There were patches of discoloration on the bolt, a prelude to rust. The rifle was not well looked after. I pushed the cartridge down on to the ejector and it clicked into position in the magazine. I pushed another down on top of it and then another. Then I used the bolt to pump one into the breech. The safety catch was a sharp little thing you twisted at the back of the bolt. It wasn't like a switch, but it felt natural. I twisted it off and brought the gun up to my shoulder. The deer, one with antlers and two without, moved back and forth in front of a ten-foot grassy bank. They were thirty yards away, no more. There was a tree to one side, a big black poplar. I squinted through the metal sight, which was just a piece of sprung steel you could raise or lower with a furling nut. The deer were still there, looking at us. They must have been stupid.

'Hey, Joe,' I said, 'you shoot, you're the best shot.'

'No way,' he said.

I brought the gun up again to my eye.

I aimed and pulled the trigger. The noise blinded me for a second.

The deer ran back and forth then turned around. They were still there! I knew I hadn't hit one because I was aiming at the tree. At the last moment I decided we didn't need the meat. I decided to test the aim of the gun against the tree. But because the deer were still there it felt as if I should try again and really shoot one this time.

I thought about gutting the thing, gralloching it. That would take time. I wasn't even exactly sure how to gralloch a deer, though I had seen it done several times, admittedly very early in the morning when I wasn't really paying attention. I shot a second bullet at the tree. This time the deer ran off. I could feel the rain again on my cheeks.

'We don't need the meat,' I said.

II

Steve was towing along a straight stretch of the river. It was my turn to walk freely while the other two were in the canoe. When you weren't in the canoe and weren't towing, it was tempting to loiter and follow a zigzag path along the foreshore, reducing the constant pressure of walking on the slope.

I'd taken my time after a Mars bar break to replace my boots (any change welcome to already sore feet), poke around at some fossils, attempt to dig one out of the clay, when I realized that the canoe was not in sight. I climbed higher up the bank to get a better look. The river was empty, the canoe nowhere to be seen. The sudden magnitude of the place, the mile-wideness of the river, the gaping mouth of the horizon, caused a sudden and painful shrinkage of myself. From being the centre of things, feeling big and confident, I instantly now felt all alone in the Land of the Giants. The place was so big and I was alone. The canoe had gone! I started to run, painful foot and all. Had the boat sunk? It seemed impossible that in such a short time it had vanished. I ran on, over the top of a small headland to cut the corner off. The canoe I at last glimpsed within a shallow curve hidden in the main straight, like those dips on straight roads that conceal oncoming cars. The others were all unconcerned, engaged wholly in their task. I ran like someone going after a missed bus. No one said anything when I caught up, out of breath, chest heaving in the hot sun. They hadn't even noticed I was gone.

III

The best time for me was always the early morning. That was the time when the mist was still on the river. When the fire was lit sometimes the smoke from the fire would mix with the mist. You knew the smoke because it was usually a little blue in colour, but it wasn't always easy to tell. The mist lay on the river in lots of different ways. If you got up in the dark and the fire was leaping with flames and it was blackness all around, you could see the stars and there was no mist. Then, as it lightened, it would be like a cloud rolling up the river and mist would cover the water so that you could only see the edge of it lapping against the mud and small stones. Then the sun would appear like a silver coin through the mist and burn it off; that's really how it felt, the heat of the sun evaporating the mist. The last fingers of mist would be chased downriver by the sun and I was always sad to see them go.

The sun levelled the day. The higher it got in the sky, the more ordinary everything looked. The early-morning light made everything look alive. When Mackenzie wrote about the beauty of this river, I'm sure he was recording what he saw first thing in the morning. People say the same thing about the desert, how it is the morning and evening that reveal its true beauty. For some reason this idea almost troubles me. I want the beauty of

a place not to be solely dependent on the light. I want beauty to be more deep-rooted than that.

Steve and Nigel were always up quickly, Joe always last. There was no argument about this, everyone just accepted it. We had a routine with the tents. You shared with someone for a week and then swapped over. There were two tents, one bigger than the other. I planned it that way, that you were either enjoying the luxury of the bigger tent or looking forward to it. But the mathematics of swapping both partners and tents was tricky. Joe felt I was spending more time in the big tent than was fair, but by a quirk of arithmetic if I relinquished my turn in the big tent, as he thought fair, so would he. I could tell that situation bothered him. Was it worth the sacrifice? Lose his turn to punish me? He decided it wasn't worth it. This was a key to his character. Joe was not vindictive. He had no desire to punish. He just wanted his own way, now.

Joe and I were new tent sharers. I woke early and started to dress. It was difficult in the cramped space. The roof was low. My back pressed against it, straining the nylon. I pulled on my socks. I had to roll on my side to get my trousers on. Then I started to stuff my sleeping bag in its orange sack. Joe said in a clear, petulant voice, 'Do you think you could do that *after* I've got up?' Do I fight for my right to stuff my sack before breakfast and risk him being in a mood? Such are the politics of the tent. Now I knew why Mackenzie never shared his.

I left the sleeping bag half stuffed and went outside to brush my teeth in the river. I watched the last clouds of mist escaping over the water, almost as if they were shy of meeting human beings.

IV

We were pulling the canoe along under an overhanging bank, Nigel and I taking turns. Roots and rotting logs protruded from the deep and murky water. Often we missed our footing and went waist-deep. Hazels, willows and nettles crowded the bank.

A huge downed tree meant a decision – go under it hanging on to the fingers of the branches, risking the current's swirl, or mountaineer your way over it, scrambling on top of the root plate with the towrope snagging everywhere. Nigel and I preferred the edge of the trees, risking the water. You could hang on to the branches and swing over the deepest spots. Logs under water were slimy and sometimes your foot slipped and you went deep. It was then you had to be careful of wrenching an ankle in a submerged tangle of wood.

Beaver lodges had their own smell, a musty, sour, animal smell. As we stamped over them beavers zoomed out far under the water, leaving a few tiny bubbles. At a safe distance they would surface and watch with bristly snouts and black-bead eyes. Then they were gone with a great bellyflop sound as their pancake tails smacked the water. You get the distinct impression beavers enjoy making that noise a lot.

We found an old trap that day, a rusty old gin with a lead weight to keep it under water. The lead weight had been cast in a round tobacco tin and you could see the reverse imprint of writing. Joe wanted the beaver trap as a souvenir. It was a nasty, rusty thing. I could see there was even less romance in trapping than shooting. We put the trap in the canoe. I knew we would chuck it away in a few days. It was like the giant moosehead we carried for five days in the first year; after a while the inconvenience outweighs the novelty. But it's good to carry it for a while, turn the thing over and examine it at night around the fire.

One evening we were looking for a campsite, Joe and Steve towing. I had to take the boat wide to avoid a metal stake in the water under a bridge. Further out there were troughs and holes caused by the current, strongest under the bridge, knocking into itself. The canoe swerved from side to side on the end of the towline. Nigel had yet to gain an instinct for the right side to paddle, still too busy 'checking for depth'. We went round a slight spit and hit the current full-on. The nose swung out and Steve was pulled over. He held on. Water buffeted against the bow. I strained to get us straight. Nigel paddled crazily. Joe ran back and grabbed the rope to help Steve. The canoe straightened.

Joe and Steve were both hauling on the rope but it was slow going. I couldn't paddle. All my effort was needed to keep the boat from broaching again. When we made the quiet water Joe stood rubbing his sore hands, 'Remember what Dave said last year? "Now I know how a hooked marlin feels towing a fishing boat." '

We were halfway to the end of the Peace River and running through farmland with small towns here and there. Beyond the bridge we found a public campsite run by a straight-backed, bullet-headed oldster called Sam. It had low fences around close-mown lawns and a muddy inlet from the river where muddy kids played. Sam saw our boat and we got talking. He'd been a park ranger and loved the wilderness. He told us about some special pinewood he got in Florida. It was so saturated in resin it would burn even when wet. He gave us some of his precious sticks of fire pine and we all talked about lighting fires in the wet, a subject of great interest which we relished all the more because of its obscurity. Our rustic canoe looked odd lying on the mown grass of the campsite. Sam then said, 'You boys'll need something to get into town. It'll cost you seventy-five bucks to get a taxi. That's too much.' And he handed over the keys of his huge new pick-up.

Sam asked no questions about our driving history. He gave no advice except to tell us to keep down in the back of the pick-up when driving in town as it was illegal to ride in the back. I wrote in my diary, 'Men like Sam are rare in the world. Men who trust their judgement of others. Men who could trust others because they trust themselves. Herb is another. The further north and the further west you go the more you find them. Always away from the big cities.'

V

Taylor's Landing was the small settlement on the river next to the campsite. It was thirty miles from Fort St John, the fastest-growing oil town in Canada, and the place we needed to drive to for supplies. But we could walk to Taylor. Everyone spruced up. Steve demonstrated again his navy background: on a ground-sheet he unpacked his carefully folded clothes and put on a perfectly ironed T-shirt.

We crossed the road bridge to a strip of buildings along the highway. A fire station. Some wooden houses. A restaurant and a bar next door. The restaurant owner was a very fat Greek Canadian who gave us ouzo because of what we were doing. He warned us against the bikers in the bar next door. The chef had bought the place with his very fat wife and they did everything between them. The chef was also a volunteer firefighter, though I found it hard to imagine him scaling a ladder or running with a body over his shoulder, but he showed us his certificates proving he could do all that. I went outside to look at the bikers, up from Dawson's Creek on their chromed-up Harley-Davidsons. They were all old guys who enjoyed scaring ordinary folks. They gave off hostility but they too were all overweight. The fat chef joined me outside for a smoke. He tried to engage one of the bikers in a conversation about his paint job. It was unsuccessful. If things got hairy I could always run, I thought. Despite his fireman's certificates I didn't rate the fat chef's chances of legging it; maybe that was why he was nervous of the bikers. We went to the bar anyway. As we left his restaurant the fat chef asked, 'How long do you think I've been a chef?'

The steaks had been charred and the vegetables watery. 'Ten years,' I said.

'Nope,' he replied, pleased.

'Three months.'

'And guess what job I used to do,' he continued.

Out of politeness we all guessed wrongly: waiter, shopkeeper, accountant. He waved away our suggestions. It was a favourite game, you could tell. Finally he cracked.

'Welder.'

In the bar we met Kelly and Bill. Both had lived all their lives in Taylor's Landing. Bill was only twenty but Kelly was in his late thirties. Kelly did catering for a living. As a treat he dumped leftovers from a grand buffet on a bar table for everyone to eat. He bent over the leftovers and explained them, educating the bar regulars about this fortunate freebie of slightly exotic food. Kelly was square-jawed, lazily good-looking and wore a white sweatshirt and white jeans. He gave Steve a big bag of grass free. Steve went outside to smoke some of the grass with two girls he had met. Then the husband of one of the girls turned up, like an angry sailor on shore leave, I thought, with his cap facing back to front, and wanted to fight Steve. I was impressed at how cool Steve was. He made smartarse throwaway comments to answer the angry man as they sidled around the pool tables, all the regulars getting in between them.

Things cooled down. We talked to Bill, who was learning hieroglyphics, he told us. In front of him was a copy of *The Count of Monte Cristo*, the Penguin Classics edition. Bill was only young but he felt washed up in Taylor. He spent his time on the computer, reading classics and learning about ancient Egypt. He didn't want to work at the gas plant like everyone else, but he did. When he was younger he had been a local prize-winning knife thrower. His dad, whom Bill admired and quoted, had made the knives. His dad was one of those extremely competent handymen who can make anything. There are a lot of them in Canada. Suddenly the drunken sailor-type guy who'd threatened Steve (tattoos, T-shirt sleeves rolled up, shiny curly black hair) wanted to fight Bill. He was called Aldus and he menaced Bill with the black pool ball held in his hand like a stone. Bill crouched over his book and everyone got between them. Aldus's wife had been at school with Bill and their continued friendship was the problem. Aldus had a friend who seemed to be egging him on. His friend was dressed the same way, with a back-to-front baseball cap, but was only about five foot tall. When we left the bar these two stood across the extremely wide two-lane road and made threatening sounds which we ignored. In fact they were so far away we had to look quite hard to make them out.

Kelly wanted to show us something interesting. It was a replica of the birchbark canoe that Alexander Mackenzie had used on his epic voyage. The canoe was part of a monument to Mackenzie in Taylor, and was housed in a long open shed on the side of the main highway.

'I'm kind of attached to that old boat,' said Kelly. 'That was where I lost my virginity.'

We wanted the whole story.

'I was about seventeen. Been drinking all day in that bar with this girl I liked. We came out about five in the afternoon, but it was already dark. Climbed in that boat and made out. Cars driving past and everything. You could see the headlights.'

By now we had arrived at the boat. It was a long wooden replica of a bark canoe. Kelly showed us the exact place where he had made out with his girlfriend. Then he seemed to get shy, as if he'd said too much. I tried to liven him up again by climbing in the canoe and pretending I was him, but he just gave a sheepish grin and backed away.

Kelly had no plans to leave Taylor. He was living with a woman but not married, he said. I'd hoped the canoe showing would be a prelude to giving us a lift home. But now he was eager to leave. 'Sorry I can't give you a lift: I'm not insured to take so many of you,' he explained, as he walked a little faster to get ahead to his parked car.

Usually, after a drink, the walk home seems no distance at all. But one of my heels was killing me. I had worn my boots with wet feet when towing and I had a blister. This had become infected and now there was a penny-sized disc of rotting flesh on the back of my ankle. The plaster had come off and it was rubbing again. I limped over the bridge high above the Peace River, the fast stream far below. The bridge surface was made of a gridwork of metal, like a massive waffle iron. You could hear the flabby whine of car tyres going over this surface from a mile away.

We walked home with Bill, who told us how easy it was to jam police radar. He kept on about Aldus threatening him with the pool ball. 'D'you think I should have hit him?' he asked us earnestly, still holding his copy of *The Count of Monte Cristo*. 'My dad says sticks and stones, but I don't know.' We all agreed it wasn't worth it and slid on our backsides down the steep bank from the bridge to the campsite, the lights of Taylor strung out behind us along the highway.

Four

STEVE'S THUMB

'Our conductors informed us that the man we left in a dying state, and to whom I had administered Turlington's Balsam, was dead.' Alexander Mackenzie

I

The canoe was falling apart. The bottom was leaking so badly we had to bail her out every two hours. The root bindings were fraying and springing loose. The back thwart was held in place only by two pieces of quartered root, watape. I could move the gunwhales in and out a few inches, which was a bad sign.

We had four men and so much gear you always felt crowded for space. The canoe had been designed for three and it felt that way. With four paddling and all that gear you could feel an unhealthy wobble from time to time, as if the canoe was flexing too much, a sign that we were putting her under too much strain.

We had been going only twenty-three days. We still had the lake and the Rockies to cross. At this rate the canoe wouldn't make it.

Mackenzie had similar problems. Only a few days into the second leg of his journey he wrote, 'The canoe, being strained from its having been very heavily laden, became so leaky, that we were obliged to land, unload, and gum it.'

Every evening I set up shop to fix the leaks. The boat would be turned over to catch the evening sun. The birchbark dried instantly, it seemed, leaving wet patches around the leaks. The light brown and golden bark of the canoe in evening light was beautiful. It was marred only by the increasing number of bodged repairs. There were always new leaks and sometimes the old ones opened up again. This year the long thin 'eyes' in the bark were becoming loose and leaking. You knew because the centrepiece remained damp when the rest of the bark had dried. I prised out the thin line of bark in the 'eye' and filled it with pitch. Sometimes this was silicone pitch, sometimes roof tar, sometimes Vulkem and sometimes resin. I kept varying things because different wounds seemed to need different dressings.

I was less confident about fixing the root bindings. But if they gave way, the whole canoe would fall apart.

We stopped for the night and set our fire on a pasture above the riverbank. I went into the nearby woods to find spruce trees. There was a sandy bank with exposed roots. I pulled one out. It was knobbly and twisted, about a finger's width in diameter. I heard something snort behind me and turned round to see an elk coming towards me. It had a fine set of antlers. I was not concerned at first. But it seemed too interested in me. I threw a rock in its direction and it stopped for a second, then kept on coming. I fired off the bearhorn and it stopped again. Then it made a barking yelp. This animal is not acting right, I thought. I picked up a rotten log that would have made a useless weapon. The elk suddenly half turned and ran past me, keeping a bush between himself and me.

I was unnerved. Until now I had thought all deer and elk were frightened of men. I pulled out some more roots, stopping often to look around and sense any strange noises.

I was glad to be back with the others. Joe was cooking on the low hot fire. I sat down in front of it and prepared the watape. The others, in their ignorance, had faith in me. It took a while to peel off the bark. The root underneath was wet and white.

The magic of spruce root is that when it is fresh, or well wetted, it bends easily. When it dries it shrinks a fraction and sets tight in the shape of the binding. This means you don't need to tie knots in the root ends. The root is better than string in this sense. It is like a combination of strong cord and plaster of Paris. I threaded the quartered root through the holes in the thwart.

It went through easily. I bound up both sides and it looked almost as neat as the original binding. No one was as impressed as I was. They didn't know I hadn't believed I could do it.

The year before, I had repaired the bark. This year I had repaired the bindings. Now I felt we could go anywhere, and even if the canoe was wrecked, as Mackenzie's was, we would struggle on.

II

Now we were getting closer to the dam, the current was stronger each day. But sometimes it would slacken off, even sometimes to almost nothing. Then we would paddle and dare to think that things were at last getting easier. Then the next piece of current would be even stronger. It was hard now to cross between islands. As soon as you nosed out from slack water into the torrent you ran the risk of the canoe turning sideways and broaching. It would then fill with water or pull the towing man into the river. Often we all got out and waded alongside, walking the boat through the stronger current. But this was time-consuming. Usually we relied on the tow man and the stern man working together to keep the canoe nose into the stream. It was the changes that were the problem. Moving across eddy lines from weak to strong current. Once in the current we could hold it with the towrope. Though now we often needed two men towing to make any headway.

Nigel was towing the canoe past a spit of land and didn't tension himself ready for when the current hit. He was jerked backwards off his feet on to the rocks. From the ground he held on to the rope. He was tough and didn't like to complain but from the canoe I could see his hand was bleeding. We paddled in with the first-aid kit. We actually had three first-aid kits – two general-purpose ones and a sutures kit. I thought I might have to sew up Nigel's hand: it was a big, deep cut in the palm. He looked disbelievingly at the blood. There were big spots like red paint all over the rocks. It was bad but he could close it up and the bleeding stopped without stitches. The holiday stops here, I thought. Make a mistake and this river will hurt you. All rivers have personalities, and, despite its name, the Peace River had a mean streak.

Herb had told us to travel on the right side of the river. That was the north side. Whenever we crossed over we found it tougher-going with stronger currents. So we returned to the north side. This meant we were always walking on the same slant. My left shin began to hurt: all that walking on a slant was hurting a tendon. I had to place my feet carefully. Every time I made a mistake and put too much weight on the foot at an angle I winced inside with the pain. And every day it was worse. I made a bandage out of half a Karrimat sleeping roll. Closed-cell foam has this advantage over a Thermarest – it can be turned into something else. Joe made insoles for his shoes out of a piece of Karrimat and I made the bandage. The stiffness of the mat forced my knee and foot apart, giving me some support. I bound the whole thing up with duct tape each morning. With my trouser rolled up it looked like a yellow moon boot on one leg, but it worked and I was able to carry on.

I still had the putrefying blister on the other ankle but it was stable, getting neither worse nor better each day.

Joe however had a strange fungus all over his feet. It looked as though something had perforated his soles. He also still had a deep crack from the previous year between his little toe and the others. I used the same tube of healing cream as last year. He wanted to keep it but I wouldn't let him. I had a feeling we were going to need it a lot more.

Only Steve, despite his many falls, was still uninjured. His addiction to neatness was contagious. All of us now unpacked our kit on to a groundsheet and not the ground. In the first few days he wrote his duties on the back of his hand so that he wouldn't forget. Strangely, he hated putting up the tents. It made him nervous, he said. He really was no good at it, so the fear had some foundation. But to go on a trip that was a hundred per cent camping and yet to fear putting up tents? It took some moral courage. Joe or I would walk around the tent with Steve and show him how far to push in the pegs and what piece of the inner to clip to the outer. His fear was so great I could tell he wasn't really paying attention. When I looked at his pegs they weren't pushed in far enough. His fear had paralysed his ability to learn. 'Why are you so nervous of tents?' I asked. Steve looked cornered and sheepish. He was actually a big, strong man but he had a way of hiding behind himself like a small boy. 'I just don't like it. I had a bad experience with tents when I was in the Cubs.' He didn't want to elaborate so I didn't ask.

Steve had a tough childhood. He was brought up by his mother but they didn't have much money. He received a government grant to go to a public school but he hated it. He felt out of place. He didn't get good exam results and he left without going to university. 'Boarding school doesn't work for everyone,' he said. But Steve was an autodidact, far better read and better informed than the other two. He was also an original. Heard from the canoe, Steve to Joe: 'What's your favourite nursery rhyme?'

There was also something beady about Steve, as if he was watching me too closely. 'Noticed you were stumbling a bit at the end of the day,' he observed once. Hmm. Thanks for that observation, Steve. Mostly he had a very humble manner. He asked how to do the simplest things, especially if it was to do with the tents. He wanted to get it right. He was very endearing. Steve on his childhood: 'I used to live in Hendon. One day a man in a Rolls-Royce ran over my football and squashed it flat. I ran after him and he gave me a fiver!'

Steve on masturbation: 'Have any of you guys ever masturbated with Deep Heat?' A shocked silence. 'I did. It practically burned my knob off.'

He once spent a week eating only popcorn. 'My bowels inflated. It was awful. But I wanted hardship at that time. Actually it was more like five days than a week.'

When Steve towed he put his head down and wore the rope around his chest, pinioning his arms. He looked like our slave. We passed a young couple fishing just outside Taylor and they looked at Steve. 'Where did you catch him?' they asked. He wore his hat with the brim turned up like Popeye Doyle in *The French*

Connection, only for some reason it made Steve look like a teddy bear. One day after wading in mud once too often he hacked the bottoms of his trousers off. Instead of making careful cuts he made them all ragged like a desert-island castaway.

Steve wasn't greedy. Sometimes he gave away his afternoon Mars bar. 'You guys have this,' he'd say. Steve would certainly survive in a prison camp. He did just as much work as anyone else but needed less food.

He tended to get in to a rut, however. When he was towing, he was towing. He rarely looked back. Often the rope got snagged and he would pull the boat to shore. When we shouted, 'SNAG!' for the fifth time, he would look hunted and defensive. In his mind the job description didn't include watching out for snags.

Steve was always last to bed. You could see him in the moonlight, endlessly packing and repacking his rucksack, replacing his toothpaste at exactly the right stratum of buried kit, smoothing his shirts flat and refolding them. Steve was the only person who laid out his sleeping bag ready for going to bed. If he'd worn pyjamas I wouldn't have been surprised. A cut-away cross-section of Steve's pack would have made a perfect advertisement of how neat it's possible to be in utterly chaotic surroundings.

III

We reached a place Mackenzie called 'many islands', but the islands were more like land-masses cut through with vicious muscular stretches of water. The latticework of waterways provided no obvious way through. We clung to branches and paddled like madmen across nasty log-strewn rapids. At last we were almost through, but faced a choice: should we cut through a deep, fast section of about two hundred metres or go the long way round, following a wide, shallow section over a kilometre of gravel? I was getting more and more cautious by the day. The fragile skin of the boat demanded it. And being overloaded, a capsize would have been serious. We went the long way.

At the exit of the two-hundred-metre stretch I saw I had

been right to be cautious: its deepness and speed had actually increased rather than diminished. But pride (I wasted no time in pointing this out to the others) was immediately under assault as we had to now cross the river, and the increased flow confused things. 'That looks OK,' I said, pointing to a stretch of calmer water. But this time I was dead wrong. As we paddled madly to get across, the boat was sucked downstream like a lollipop stick in a rain-filled gutter. Then we hit a rock and the canoe grounded out on the bottom of the river, suddenly shallow. Broadside on to the current, we had seconds before losing the boat. 'Out!' I shouted. It was a superfluous command – the boat had already tipped and was busy swallowing great gouts of river. I saw Steve's head disappearing underwater. Water that was fast enough to be lifting me off my feet. Nigel and Joe threw themselves across the front of the swamped canoe and I grabbed on to it from behind. There was a trick in using the boat for stability yet also imparting movement to the thing. We heaved and turned with the kind of serious slowness associated with astronauts and deep-sea divers. At last we got the nose into the current, avoiding the danger of a side-on smashing from the waves. But where was Steve? Downstream, on the other side of the canoe, he emerged drenched from head to toe. 'I got my foot stuck,' he explained, 'and then the canoe went right over me.'

IV

It was about this time, with the constant pain of the blister on one foot and the constant ache of the swollen ankle on the other (alternating, in fact, as the marvellous thing about pain is that the greater always cancels the lesser), it was about this time that I fell to pondering, on the long sections of towing (or more likely the brief stretches of freedom limping along the bank whilst someone else towed), the precise significance of what we were doing. In my bleary-minded, rain-sodden, mosquito-bitten condition the significance was eluding me. I thought about Scott and about Mackenzie, our inspiration. There was definitely a

259

difference between these two explorers. Mackenzie belonged to the commercial age of exploration – he didn't want glory, particularly; he wanted money. Things were getting more heroic by the time of Stanley and Livingstone. The fact that Stanley was originally a journalist was significant. He wanted publicity, column inches, fame. Scott had always been seen as the last of the 'heroic' explorers, trading guts for glory. Then came the 'athletic' age: mountains were climbed by superior physical prowess, the poles conquered by super-fit men such as Ranulph Fiennes. This was a new development. In the heroic age, physical prowess was not emphasized. Richard Burton, who discovered Lake Tanganyika, spent most of his time in a litter slung over the shoulders of native carriers. Were we still in the athletic phase? I thought to myself. I began to think we were not. Now you can buy your way up Everest as a New York socialite recently did. You can pay £30,000 and slog your way to the South Pole. The old challenges of the athletic age have become the tourist routes of the present day. I considered the efforts of another type of modern 'explorer'. I thought of Thor Heyerdahl, Tim Severin and Redmond O'Hanlon. All of them embarked on expeditions with the slenderest of pretexts. It dawned on me that we had entered the age of ludicrous expeditions. It was a natural result of the times we lived in. Just as architecture had gone post-modern, so had explorers. Expeditions were now characterized by how ludicrous they were – and I was pleased to see that ours was pretty ludicrous. We were attempting to emulate an eighteenth-century explorer yet we wore nylon trousers and had a sat phone. Even without these aids we were travelling through country that had been mapped (albeit badly) and had, in places, roads and bridges. I knew what we were doing was still capable of giving huge insights into Mackenzie's achievement, just as, on a grander scale, Heyerdahl's *Kon Tiki* voyage, despite being into well-charted waters, was still closer to an ancient raft voyage than just sitting in a library thinking about it ever could be. I didn't want to deny the reason for an expedition by calling it ludicrous. On the contrary, I was happy that I had found a reason. An expedition that could be called ludicrous, or even faintly ludicrous, was fully justified in its existence. I strode stronger at the towrope, I paddled with new vim and vigour. I was a ludicrous explorer. It was simple. I had a label and I felt better about it.

Strangely, when I tried to explain this to the others they felt less sure about it. 'You mean, like, we're prats to be doing this?' queried Steve.

V

Steve and I were towing through a rocky canyon. At this point of the river, nearing the town of Hudson's Hope, Mackenzie wrote, 'The current was very strong and the coming up along some of the banks was rendered very dangerous, from the continual falling of large stones, from the upper parts of them.' Steve and I both had ropes attached to the boat. The current was too strong for just one towrope. Mackenzie continued: 'We were at every step in danger from the steepness of the ground, of falling into the river.' Steve followed about ten feet behind me. We towed in an expectant silence, like those gripping sequences in heist movies where no one speaks as they break into the strongroom. My eye was always straying upwards. Rocks fell for no apparent reason.

There were also small landslides. Dust and earth and small stones would avalanche down the slope. Some of the slopes were like icebergs of mud, carving away from the cliff. We climbed up the split between them. Then we flipped the towrope over the top.

VI

At Hudson's Hope, the last town on the Peace River, we camped on a beach below the houses. There was a dog turd somewhere in the bushes near the boat and you could smell it, but there was no other place to leave the canoe. I stayed with the boat most of the day and all evening. Young people came along the beach with cans of beer and fishing rods, amiable enough, but I didn't want anyone going for a joyride. I stayed with the canoe and the others went into the town and made friends with people.

In the morning my paranoia wore off and I visited the reconstruction of a fur-trading post. It was next to a suspended tractor tyre with HUDSONS HOPE written in white paint. Steve insisted I photograph him sitting in the tyre. He said it would complement the picture of him in Kelly's boat (as I thought of it) in Taylor.

Three people manned the fur-trade reconstruction: Holly, her mum, and a young lad who was introduced as 'of pioneering stock'. He had a blond skew of hair and a narrow head and looked like he was used to getting out of scrapes. There was something deeply cheerful about him. He showed me various traps. He carefully spring-loaded a mink trap on the floor. 'What are you doing?' asked Holly's mum, who ran the place. 'This is the most fun part of my job,' said the boy and threw a dollar coin at the trigger plate of the loaded trap. It sprang up from the floor in a clash of steel.

Holly told me how difficult beaver were to kill. She had been beaver trapping with an old trapper called Dan. The trapped beaver was shot and then dropped in the bottom of the boat, but it started to eat Holly's foot. 'Dan then snatched up this, like, monkey wrench and started beating the beaver's brains out. The blood splattered all over my jeans. But even then it didn't die. Not immediately.'

Holly's mum told us about an old trapper called Pen Powell who drove over a beaver on purpose while crossing a bridge. He got out of his truck with a tyre iron, ready to finish the beaver off. But he couldn't find the creature. He bent down by the front wheel and the injured beaver leaped up and bit through the femoral artery in his upper thigh, the biggest artery in the body. He almost bled to death driving himself to the hospital. The beaver bite also gave him giardia, beaver fever. It broke his health and he died not long afterwards.

Then she told another tale of a drunken Indian who went out to fight a beaver with a canoe paddle for a bet. The beaver bit him so many times and in so many places the Indian collapsed and bled to death.

I had been disdainful of beaver until now. Certainly not fearful of them. Holly's mum had only one reassuring piece of information. She told me there was no risk of giardia in the Peace River, or almost any running water. It was only still, almost stagnant beaver ponds where the concentration of the bacteria was significant. Unless, of course, you had the misfortune to be bitten in the crotch by one.

VII

Our second night on dogshit beach we got a good fire going and people came to visit us. Guy and Mary, two people who ran a honey business, brought a big four-pint pot of honey for us. We tasted it, knowing it would be delicious. Mary had been the reason we made friends. She worked part-time as a waitress at the Sportsman's Lounge. Nigel and I had had breakfast there and she was friendly. 'That's amazing!' she said. 'What an amazing experience you must be having!' She didn't hurry what she was saying. She didn't want to move on to the next person. She wasn't looking for someone else, someone more interesting. We were it. She managed to convey such a sincere eagerness of appreciation as she typed our bill into the cash register, my whole day was transformed. I went from being a bitter outcast on dogshit beach to being a bold adventurer. Mary said we could use her place to shower and make phone calls. But she really meant it.

Guy, her partner, had worked the oil patch as an administrator. He'd travelled the world and made big money. The way he spoke about it, you felt that life had taken something out of him and only now was he recovering. He looked like he'd survived something nasty. He'd quit and taken a course in beekeeping and found he enjoyed it. He loved everything about honey and his enthusiasm was infectious. He didn't charge high prices 'because for some people honey is a staple'. This was Guy and

Mary's way of doing their bit, of doing things differently from the oil business.

Guy warned us about freak waves on the lake beyond the second dam. Williston Lake, the world's largest unnatural lake, over four hundred kilometres long, was famous for sudden bad weather. Guy said freak waves were among the biggest killers of canoeists. His father had almost died after a freak wave upset his canoe.

The fire was leaping with the wind. Guy's glasses picked up and reflected the available light. We asked for the full freak-wave story. Told by Guy, it was resonant with meaning. There was something sinister about it and also transcendent.

'The way my father tells the story', said Guy, 'is that survival is not always for the best. Or that survival carries a cost, a cost you find too high to pay.

'He was with a friend, his best friend. This was in northern Ontario. They often went canoeing. The friend was a cheerful extrovert guy, very outgoing and adventurous. They were crossing a lake, not a very big lake, but they were more than a mile from the nearest island and further from the shore. It was summer and the bugs were bad. It wasn't windy and the lake was calm. But for no reason a freak wave turned their canoe over. All the gear was lost and the canoe turned over. Just like that. A freak wave. They couldn't right the canoe for fear of sinking it. My father was the better swimmer. The other guy held on to the canoe for ages. He got close to hypothermia. They had to swim. They kicked off most of their clothes to swim better. The lake was cold, but if they kept moving they were OK. Dad got to the island and saw his friend was in trouble. He went back in again and helped the guy. They were exhausted. They were on an island two miles or more from the shore. They didn't think they had the strength to swim any more. The blackfly were so bad they got back into the water and lay with just their faces out, breathing. The blackfly were murderous. If they got out of the water they thought they would be bitten so much they would die. They had no shoes and only vests and shorts on. My father knew they were miles from any sort of habitation and that even if they swam to the shore they would be eaten alive just walking through the bush. They had no way to make fire and no protection against the blackfly. They thought they would die. For eight hours they lay in the water, the warmer water at the lake's edge, their faces running with blood from the blackfly.

'Then some Boy Scouts came and rescued them.'

'Just like that?'

'Yeah, my father says it was like a miracle. The Scouts were miles from anywhere but they had spare food and clothes and room in their canoes for Dad and his friend. But the strange thing is the friend never really recovered. He stopped wanting to see my father; perhaps it brought back unpleasant memories. He became withdrawn and fearful of things. He was also bitter, felt his life wasn't going the way it should.'

'He should have been grateful to survive.'

'You'd think so, wouldn't you?' said Guy, poking at the fire. 'But the way my father tells the story, the experience was too much for the man. Whatever it released shouldn't have been. He couldn't take the experience, or what it showed him.'

By now it was dark. The fire was all there was. Square red coals glowing. I got my torch and it blinded everyone. Guy and Mary said it was about time to go. They disappeared into the darkness. We heard their pick-up doors bang shut. Then the rough, metallic roar and lights of the vehicle. It swung around in the tight space and drove off up the track from the beach.

VIII

Guy and Mary lived on a cliff high above the river, upstream from the town centre. We decided to visit them on the way.

We were all in a buoyant mood. Our hurts and injuries seemed less important. Everything had healed a fraction. I had sealed the main leak in the boat. And we were near the end of the mighty Peace. One thousand six hundred kilometres against the current. Now almost at an end. It was hard to conceive. I had lived with this river for three years. We were only six kilometres from the dam that meant the end of all that struggle.

It was easy towing. There were a few small rapids. These were caused by rock ledges extending across the river. Closer to the bank there were boulders and shallows, making it hard to get through. We found we could lift the boat over the worst rocks. The current, though, was very strong. The water was shallow, so it didn't matter too much, but I sensed the strength of the river's flow even knee-deep.

Guy had told us we could use their neighbour Al's ladder to scale the cliff they lived on. Because Al was ninety-two I had in mind something short and safe. But Al's ladder was 120 feet high. The cliff was sheer.

'Shit,' said Steve. 'It looks like it's about to fall down.'

Indeed, from below, Al's ladder, though a triumph of DIY engineering, looked precarious and wobbly. It was only embarrassment at being beaten by a man of Al's age that drove us upwards. The rungs were randomly nailed. A few at the bottom were missing. It was hard to see how it could stay fixed to the cliff, which was chalky and vertical, a loose mix of rock and shale. Al had driven stakes into the cliff as anchor points. He had built wooden stages between each ladder. There were three. At the third stage I looked down and gripped the ladder with extra care. The canoe looked miles below, perfectly surrounded by blue water. I had to admire Al doing this climb aged ninety-two. It gave me the willies and I wasn't even half his age. Slowly I made it up to the wooden housing at the top.

Al greeted me with the soft shark look of the aged and toothless. He had skinny, sinewy forearms. He showed me the electric pulley and cable he used to bring his dog up the cliff. I noticed he was missing one finger, on his right hand. He said he'd caught it in a cable when he worked in the logging business before the war. He smiled at our boat and said he'd seen birchbark canoes on the river when he was a boy. You could tell he didn't like talking too much. While the others climbed the ladder he examined a bush of red flowers. He opened the blade of his pocket knife carefully. He cut one red flower for Mary and one for the wife of a neighbour who came with her.

At Guy and Mary's, we drank fresh black coffee looking over the river. Guy's tall neighbour Maurice brought his niece and wife over. The niece, Kelly, looked too friendly and attractive to be working as a cop in Vancouver. Child pornography. No one could think of any questions to ask on that subject. 'I hear you have quite a drug problem in Vancouver,' I eventually said, but Kelly just smiled and said nothing. Maurice said he might take his jetboat out that day for a picnic – 'Maybe catch you later on the river.'

Guy showed us his honey store. It smelled as if the honey had seeped into the deepest grain of the beams and cross-ties. When the double doors were open the sun shone in over the big white plastic honeypots.

We could put off leaving no longer. At the ladder Al's wife, who looked to be in her mid-80s, was there, but not Al. 'Where's Al?' asked Steve. 'Down in his den doing his exercises,' said his wife, 'keeping fit.'

IX

More rapids. We had to unload the canoe completely and carry it over a big rock shelf. It was deep water in places, and fast. Everyone was slipping and sliding. There were tourists out too: a flotilla of identical white canoes shot past very quickly from out of a small bay. Going with the current. The water was rough but the canoes looked fun and stable. The people in them had sunglasses and T-shirts and shorts on. Our laden canoe was like a rag-and-bone man's cart by comparison.

We kept on, hugging the cliffs. Joe climbed a big rock to see which way to go. Two hundred and eleven years earlier Mr Mackay, Mackenzie's number two, had climbed the same rock. 'Mr Mackay and the Indians who observed our manoeuvres from the top of the rock were in continual alarm for our safety . . . the dangers that we encountered were very much augmented by the heavy loading of the canoe.'

We had the same problem. But now at last we could see the

dam, the first of two. This was the small one, narrow and high, a steep concrete curve joining two cliffs. We were almost there and in an unhealthy hurry to be done. Of the same spot, with an unnerving Nostradamus-like accuracy, Mackenzie wrote:

> One false step of those who were attached to the line, or the breaking of the line itself, would have at once consigned the canoe, and everything it contained, to instant destruction.

But we were hurrying now, intent on our goal; besides, there were recreationists on the river, neutering its apparent threat. The canoes we saw earlier, and two men in blue wetsuits and shades on purple jetskis. Then Maurice and family came hovering up in their jetboat with its high canvas sun cover, which gave the boat a fairground folksiness, belying the power of its engine needed to beat the current. There were people sunbathing on a small beach between two rocky headlands. A bald man was fishing in his trunks. There was also a slim boy in trunks and a girl and some people leaving the beach. By our standards it was a great crowd.

And we were in trouble. Nigel was paddling hard at the front. I was at the back. Joe was towing. Steve was the 'middleman'. Middleman was a new role, necessitated by the increased current. The middleman kept the rope tight and away from the bank. Without the middleman the tow-man might, when crossing a small headland, allow the rope to cut across the headland, dragging the boat to land. The middleman stood at the point and allowed the rope to bend around him, keeping the rope straight and the canoe clear of the bank.

But we were making no progress. The canoe wavered from side to side like a balloon in a high wind. This was the last headland before the dam. The last difficult water. As Joe passed the man fishing, the towrope snagged on the man's back. I could tell, even at a hundred feet away, that the man was irritated. Couldn't he see the urgency of our situation? Didn't he realize we needed help, not hindrance? Didn't he realize we'd come 1,600 kilometres to have him be the first pedestrian to get in our way? Out on the river it was big splashy drama. I was shouting and Nigel was shouting and slowly, very slowly, Joe pulled us while Steve held the rope clear of the headland. Joe was nearly face down on the ground pulling. Our paddling didn't seem to help. Out further on the river in the corner of my eye I could see Maurice and his damn jetboat, hanging there in the current as if in an official capacity to provide assistance. Damn him. The noise of his engine was off-putting. I disliked being on show, judged by people who had no knowledge of what we had been through.

We were almost past the flat-topped islands. We had seen them in the guidebook. You could camp on the top. They were like flat-topped mushrooms. There were rocky cliffs all around and the current continued to pound.

Slowly Joe and Steve pulled us in to land. It was here that Mackenzie had an accident: 'The agitation of the water was so great that a wave striking on the bow of the canoe broke our line, and filled us with inexpressible dismay, as it appeared impossible that the vessel could escape from being dashed to pieces, and those who were in her, from perishing. Another wave, however, more propitious than the former, drove her out of the tumbling water, so that the men were enabled to bring her ashore.'

From our safe place ashore, we could see yet another headland, a small one we hadn't noticed before. The current whipped around it in a powerful bulge. This really would be the last. Beyond it I could see the dam. We rushed our plan of action. I should have called a halt. I was in a rush. The water was rushing by. The jetboat was noisy. I should have been calm and collected but I wasn't. Steve had us on a short rope. We were ready to go. Nigel and I were pumped up from our last battle against the current. We thought we had this thing beaten. It was too noisy to hear properly. I told Steve to take in the slack so that we wouldn't shoot back into the rocks behind us once we hit current. I felt we were hurrying too much. The jetboat hung in the water, demonstrating Maurice's great ability to match the jet speed against the current. But what if we wanted to swing wide?

He was cramping our action. We were all in a hurry. We swung out and the current caught the nose. The line whipped tight. Steve screamed and was jerked off his feet. I saw something shoot in an arc from his hand. He screamed again. 'Let go of the rope!' I shouted. 'I lost my thumb!' he screamed. But he was still holding on to the rope like a hero. 'Let go, Steve!' I shouted. With some difficulty he loosed off some line. Nigel and I flailed with our paddles as the canoe smashed back against the rocks with a great shuddering thump. We're holed for sure, I thought. Joe came running. Nigel held us on to the rocks. We were now in quiet water. I grabbed the first-aid kit from its bag. Steve lay on his side, surrounded by rope. He held up his hand to me. His thumb was a red bubble. 'I lost my thumb,' he said. He was shaking. 'It's just cut,' I said, though I wasn't sure. I got out several dressings and kept pressing them on, each one getting red through straight away. I couldn't even see his thumb properly. 'It's fucking painful,' he said. Maurice and his wife Debbie and Kelly the policewoman were running towards us. Debbie was an infant teacher and had a first-aid qualification. She talked to Steve soothingly. He was shaking and his face was taut. 'Can I hold a rope or something?' asked Kelly. 'I hate the sight of blood.' Maurice said he would take Steve to hospital. Suddenly we were grateful for him being there. I gave Steve some paracetamol. He looked tense and pale. He kept apologizing to me for letting go of the rope, though it was me who had told him to.

Maurice took Steve and Debbie back to their car. Debbie drove off with Steve to the hospital, which was two hours away. Maurice returned. We needed to get the canoe around that point. There was a general feeling that we should pack it in for the day and return to the beach, possibly even get a truck lift to the lake. I knew this would be bad for everyone. It would be something we would later regret. We had to push on. Maurice was self-effacing and did not want to impose his ideas. He suggested we run a long line out across the corner of the bend, that way the canoe couldn't broach. We unloaded the canoe, which is what we should have done in the first place, though, as I reproached myself for the accident, I kept reminding myself, We travelled the whole river without a serious mistake, we used this technique many times before, we were unlucky, that's all.

Then Joe saw Steve's thumb. It was lying in a puddle quite some way from where it had been cut off. It looked like one of those toy rubber fingers you get in joke shops. It had the same pallid look. It was not the whole thumb, but because all the nail was still attached it looked like the whole thumb. You could see the white splinter of bone on the inside. No one wanted to pick it up out of the puddle. Everyone kept saying, 'Shit! His thumb!' Eventually Joe picked it up. We were all certain it might be possible to sew it back on. The son of the man Joe had tangled up with the towing line (years earlier it seemed) offered to run back along the riverbank to his truck and thence to Hudson's Hope. 'Don't put it on ice,' I said, 'cold water is fine.' A doctor once told me that putting severed body parts on ice can cause frost damage. The teenager ran off in his Bermuda trunks holding a zip-lock bag with Steve's thumb inside like a goldfish won at a fair.

Now the canoe was empty it was not hard to get around the point. We used poles to keep it off the rocks. It was all so calm and easy. Shit! Steve's thumb. He was out of it now, I thought. He was done for as far as the trip was concerned. He couldn't hold a paddle without a thumb. There was exposed bone in that stump. It would have to heal. I knew Steve didn't have insurance but I didn't think about it.

Soon we were again on easy water. Close to the dam was a hardly used track coming down to the water's edge. The ruts were overgrown with wildflowers. We lifted the canoe out and tied up to several trees for good measure. Then we stacked all the gear under the canoe and left it.

X

'It was Steve's fault.'
   'Why didn't he let go?'
   'He should've let go.'

271

'Why didn't he?'

'Steve's the kind of guy who would go over the top in World War One.'

'Steve would die obeying orders.'

'Steve's a hero.'

'I would have let go.'

'I wouldn't have coiled it up.'

'Why did he do that?'

'Because I told him to.'

'So it was your fault.'

'Why didn't he let go?'

And so the conversation wound on. We had returned to Hudson's Hope to wait for news of Steve. Troy and Christa, two friends Steve had made earlier, kindly let us stay on their lawn and invited us to a pig-roast party given by the local fire station. We knew Steve wouldn't want us to mope around so we went to the party.

The party was a good-natured, beer-fuelled gathering right next to a chain-link fence a hundred feet above the river. The town drunk tried to jump over the fire, but was restrained by his friends. He was a long-haired, skinny, sweat-faced mumbler ready to laugh crazily or take offence. After the fire he tried to climb the cyclone fence, but was talked down. A few years before he'd jumped off the bridge into the Peace River. A hundred and fifty feet into not very deep water. He hoisted his baggy shorts and showed me the scars where his legs had split open. He had his trailer parked at the edge of the campfire so he wouldn't be tempted to drive home.

Joe disappeared with a girl visiting from Peace River town called Shelley. She had taken four hours to get to Hudson's Hope, whereas we had taken a month. She was into the outdoors and loved Thermarest air mattresses. These are excellent and clever inflatable mattresses. You can even sleep on a glacier on a Thermarest. She inflamed Joe's desire for one. He only had a foam mat whereas Nigel and I had Thermarests. He started to plan how he could get one. He asked all round town but there were none. The Thermarest became Joe's main interest. Joe told us that Shelley had asked him, 'Shall we, like, make out?' Then they did, on her Thermarest. We wanted details, but there were none, or a few disappointing ones, nothing special, all over-shadowed by Joe's enthusiasm for the mattress. But Joe had pride: he didn't ask for Shelley's Thermarest; and she had priorities: she didn't offer it to him.

Steve arrived late at the party with a cartoon bandaged thumb. Debbie and Maurice had got him so quickly to hospital that the severed top part of his thumb had not caught up with them. Bizarrely, the teenage boy had left it at the grocery store, where it stayed for three days in the cold-food cabinet. Later, Steve recovered it and threw it back into the Peace River. 'Sort of sacrifice to the river-god,' he said. Steve came with Kelly to the party. When he later asked Maurice for her phone number Maurice growled, 'You already got her email, that'll do.'

Maurice had bad-mouthed our paddling ability, said Steve. We ran Maurice down and generally ascribed the root cause of the accident to his intrusive jetboating.

Steve said, guess what, Kelly worked undercover as a hooker in Vancouver. Everyone was intrigued but since Steve's thumb was the centre of attention no one remembered to grill her about her days as an undercover hooker.

Nigel said, 'Guess you won't be hitching home then, eh, Steve?' Steve gave a pained smile. He was very good-humoured and was on powerful painkillers. He told us that a visiting South African doctor had sawn part of the stump off. The exposed bone had to be lower than the flesh for it to heal. Anaesthetic? Only a local: Steve had refused a general because it cost $2,000. The local was only $50. The doctor had tightened Steve's hand in a padded vice and used a handsaw on the raw end of bone. 'The vibrations were horrendous,' said Steve.

Steve seemed almost more determined to continue now that he had been injured. I said we would talk about it in the morning, though I knew he would not be coming with us. He wanted to help carry the canoe over the dam, but even raising his thumb above chest height caused him pain. If his dressing got the slightest bit damp he ran the risk of infecting the exposed bone.

It would be impossible to keep it clean messing about with fires and water. Most people would have been booking the first flight home by now. Not Steve. He was heroic in his loyalty.

The next day, after spending the night at Guy and Mary's, Steve met Al, who had just finished his exercises and was now pruning his flowers. 'You're a southpaw now!' chirruped old Al, beaming his toothless smile and displaying his own stump.

Five

THE BACK DOOR

*'In order to lighten her, it was my intention to walk
with some of the people; but those in the boat with
great earnestness requested me to embark,
declaring, at the same time, that, if they perished, I
should perish with them.'* Alexander Mackenzie

I

At the end of the Peace, or rather, its beginning, the first dam
backed up the water some twenty kilometres to the big dam.
The stretch of water between the two dams was called Dinosaur
Lake because just as it had been flooded several large dinosaur
skeletons had been discovered. At the end of Dinosaur Lake
towered the big dam, the WAC Bennett Dam, the one everyone
along the river complained about – except the two hundred
employees of BC Hydro who earned their living from it.

Beyond the big dam was the big lake, Williston Lake. Herb
had given us a photograph of the lake and I often studied it,
along with the sketch-maps and diagrams, the hints and tips I'd
accumulated from others who had gone before. I kept them all
in my green army sponge bag, which seemed more use as an
important document case now that my grooming kit was
reduced to a bar of soap wrapped in a cloth in a soap dish, an
airline tube of toothpaste and a toothbrush.

Herb's photo had the matt finish and dull coloration of an
instant-camera picture probably taken in the 1970s. It showed
steep mountainsides plunging straight down into a lake laced
with white-capped waves. Herb said, 'Your most danger is on

that big lake. Forget this fuckin' river. You go over on that lake in a storm, that's your danger.'

But before that danger was faced we had to portage the small dam that blocked Peace River Canyon to form Dinosaur Lake. Peace River Canyon formed a vast curve around the southern base of Portage Mountain. Mackenzie gave up fighting the canyon rapids and spent three days cutting a nine-mile portage trail above the canyon along the southern side of the mountain. He had earlier ignored the Indian portage trail, which was twelve miles long and ran around the easier northern side, something he later regretted.

We started our portage by following a track that led us around the dam to Dinosaur Lake. Steve walked with us and even propped his shoulder under the boat from time to time to help share the weight. It was a hot day and we were soon sweating. We had to beg Steve to take it easy. He felt bad about getting injured and kept coming back to the boat, which we carried the right way up this time. We experimented and found the upside-down tortoiseshell style of the year before was not nearly as efficient as sitting the curved bottom of the canoe on your shoulder. The trick was to get it settled from the beginning. If the canoe felt right you could carry it for a long stretch without a rest. But if it sat wrongly on your shoulder from the beginning it was hard to go a hundred yards. Steve taught us some marine marching songs he'd heard in the navy. He needed our reassurance and everyone tried to show how much we appreciated him.

Dinosaur Lake was ice cold and the few speedboats stayed in close to the launch jetty. People from Hudson's Hope came to see us off. There were picnic tables, and Joe and Shelley were deep in conversation as we loaded the canoe.

Then they exchanged T-shirts in a ritual manner, though I noticed Joe somehow ended up in a rather nicer shirt than the one Shelley got. Steve waved us a sorry goodbye with his huge white thumb. Guy and Mary had asked him to stay with them until he was better. It seemed extraordinarily lucky that they had agreed to look after a complete stranger they had known for two days, but they were those kind of good people. Steve was already explaining to Guy how he could help move the beehives one-handed.

We made swift progress along the lake's anthracite dark waters, barely rippled by the wind, giving the impression of great depth beneath us. Mountains rose on either side, but not to a great height. It was odd to think we were hundreds of feet above the canyon floor, where Mackenzie paddled. It did not feel unnatural to be at this height, the lake seemed to suit the surroundings. Excess water, it seems, makes itself at home very quickly.

II

Now that Steve was gone, Joe was more noticeable. When I hesitated over the map for a while he said, 'I think it's straight on.' There are ways of conveying this piece of information that would be positively welcomed by any struggling navigator. Unfortunately Joe had mastered a different tone, goading, a mite sarcastic, asking to be ignored. 'Well I think it's left,' I responded. In fact it was neither: the lake cleverly snaked rightwards. An hour later as we searched for a specific camping spot Joe announced, 'We must have gone past it.' But in that mocking, challenging tone couldn't he see it was misplaced, unwanted, strictly *verboten*? That's why I had my binoculars, which no one else was allowed to use. That's why I had the GPS, which no one else knew how to use. Losing Steve had definitely upset the equilibrium. I would have to bite the bullet and put up with Joe undiluted.

Losing Steve also made the expedition lighter, quicker on its feet. No one was scared of the tents any more. Turns for cooking and getting wood and washing up came around too quickly. Three was more like two than four, which was an expedition, a team, something almost official. Three could have been mates, something unplanned. Oddly, three ate almost as much food as four.

Paddling on Dinosaur Lake was so easy after the murder of going against the current. We did twenty kilometres in three and a half hours. We also sailed, with the nylon tarpaulin strung from a pole, pot-bellied in the strong breeze. The beach we camped on was of level black sand opposite a smoking vent in the hillside. It looked like mist rising. Mackenzie wrote that his assistant Mr Mackay 'observed several smoking chasms in the earth that emitted heat and smoke, which diffused a strong sulphurous stench'. It was the same smouldering coal seams we observed.

We ceased talking as we approached the cauldron, the place where the big dam spewed the Peace River out. There was now a slight bubbling current against us. We dipped our blades silently past the last island midstream, a mushroom rock good for a picnic. Then straight ahead was the utter hugeness of the dam's shallow slope. Unlike the concrete lower dam with its sheer wall, this was more like the side of an earth pyramid, yet it was huge and rose and rose in front of us.

The big one. One of the world's biggest: 1.2 miles long, 670 feet high, half a mile thick at the base. The air was dead in the cauldron, around the exit cavern, a huge dark orifice cut into the rockface at the side of the dam, loaded with splashing water like something out of James Bond. Blofeld's back passage.

We were on a mission. Getting to the heart of the river. Its dead heart. I wanted to blame someone. Steve's thumb, I ruminated darkly, had been lopped off by the men who dammed the river, who changed the river and made it angry. The Peace was an angry river that wanted revenge on mankind for what we had done, for the buggering around with the flow and the islands and the freeze-up and the melt. The Peace had been genetically modified by the dam and it wanted revenge. We paddled closer, despite the current increase. We hoped the men who controlled the dam's outflow wouldn't get mad and let fly a billion gallons, causing us to ride a tsunami back to the source, for that is how we thought of Lake Athabasca, as the source, somehow, of the river that flowed into it. The dam was the end of the river for us, it couldn't be its beginning.

Way above us, at the level of the great lake, was the emergency slip channel, as huge as a tanker berth. A great concrete dry riverbed cut through rock at the side of the dam. If the Williston Lake ever threatened to overflow the top of the dam, they drained it using the slip channel. It had only been opened three times in thirty years. The force of the water rushing down it tore rock off the opposing river wall. The sluice gates had to be opened in the right sequence or the water would tear chunks out of the sides of the slipway. This was water as a terrifying force of destruction. As the amiable Max Finkelstein, author of *Canoeing a Continent*, put it, 'I'm distrustful of too much power in one place.' It was bad power too, a dark power that breathed the dead air of the restrained river. One day it would all have to go.

We were all fed up with the counter-arguments – it provided jobs and livelihoods and power for the cities – so what? Those arguments meant nothing to us. We had just made a 1,600-kilometre pilgrimage in honour of the river-god and to find it caged was, to put it mildly, annoying.

Either side of the cauldron were high, terrifying, shale-dropping cliffs. It had been a canyon before, a natural narrow point with thundering rapids, now all underwater. The dam itself was a technological marvel, as these things tend to be; amazing in its own right but just imagine blowing it up.

The dam is a fantastic idea, in every sense. It is power at the expense of almost nothing. Free electricity – what could be better? Everything bad about it is unmeasurable, insubstantial, invisible, and yet not a whit the less important for that.

Somehow the dam was the point of all our exploring. We were always moving towards it, until now, when we would start moving away from it. All our mileage was judged in relation to the dam, the vast stoppage of natural powers.

There were two ways around it. Either follow a five-kilometre maintenance road or climb straight up the face of the thing, like supplicants climbing a great pyramid at dawn. We could see steps, but earlier, when I'd called from Hudson's Hope, someone at the end of a telephone, a gruff-voiced female employee of BC Hydro, had said we were forbidden to climb it. Terrorist risk.

'In a birchbark canoe?' I asked.

'It's regulations. Since 9/11.'

'I've never heard of an exploding canoe before.'

She rang off.

We lifted the canoe out of the water in a rocky inlet, a safe backwater protected by a high bank from the outflow from the turbines. At the top of the slope was a dirt track and two good-old boys in a pick-up, general-purpose employees of BC Hydro. They'd seen us coming. 'That's bullshit,' said Murray. 'Just go up those steps. You take the road you got a five-kilometre walk.'

'But what about the terrorist threat?'

'If you boys are terrorists we got nothing to fear!'

Murray's mate chipped in, 'It's just the usual bullshit – the road over the dam is open so why not let people climb it? A hippy drove over it in his camper last year and discovered a fuckin' huge hole. Could've dropped his Semtex in it and turned the big tap on.'

'A hole?'

'Dam's made of earth. Time to time you get holes forming. Usually nothing serious.'

Steve's mate Tray arrived and lugged our bags while Joe, Nigel and I carried our home-made birchbark canoe up the face of the biggest earth dam in North America. At the time it felt like the defining image of our voyage; all else was mere inflow or outflow. Climbing, step by step, backs bent under the weight of our bark canoe, a tiny thing on three tiny men against the grey enormity of the power project, its hundred-million-ton weight, its buzzing pylons and underground transformers. Of course we had to climb the dam.

We took it in turns to be the man in the middle, bent double under the canoe, walking at a right-angle. The front and back men carried the boat diagonally across one shoulder. It was either painful or supremely comfortable, depending on its position on your shoulder, but the middle man always had backache. The middle man's job was a throwback to the Industrial Revolution, when jobs were unkind to the human form. Kids under looms or up chimneys, miners and quarrymen with dusty lungs and clicking knees. The middle man saw no light, only the ground beneath.

We dumped the canoe at the edge of the lake. Now we were level with the waves splashing the rocky beach it looked as if we were in a big bay at the seaside. And it felt as if we were going downstream at last.

Six

MR HODGES HAS A POINT

'With their usual regale of rum, they soon renewed that courage which disdained all obstacles that threatened our progress.' Alexander Mackenzie on
his crew

I

The lake meant a different regime, and we started with the best of intentions. We were up at three to take advantage of the early morning calm. Mackenzie wrote about getting up at two and two-thirty but this was before daylight-saving time added an hour. It was grey and cloudy and spitting with rain and no one wanted to be up except Nigel, tending the dancing flames of his wind-blown fire amongst the rocks at the edge of the water.

'Looks a bit windy,' said Nigel, handing me a cup of tea.

'You're right, let's give it another half an hour.'

We were all reluctant to start on this next leg of the journey, wary after all the warnings of sudden storms we had received. Because the lake was a flooded river valley, it was crossed at regular points by other valleys at right angles. These valleys funnelled wind on to the water, creating the storms the lake was famous for. And since the lake was not there in Mackenzie's time, we would be the first birchbark canoe to travel its 370-kilometre length.

Facing all that water at dawn we derived little encouragement from knowing other canoeists had been before us in plastic boats. Joe O'Blenis had braved the waves and so had Max Finkelstein. We had his book, torn into the sections of his journey that coincided with ours, and it was full of useful information, cheerfully written and, most importantly for us, exuding no sense of fear. But they were experts and we, most decidedly, were not.

'Another brew?' suggested Joe. 'One for the road?' Gruff nods of agreement. The pre-dawn gloom had given way to a band of bright cloud sitting below a dark load of thunderheads. After the confines of the river I wasn't used to so much sky. It was still spitting with rain and the drops hissed as they fell on the hot grill. The lake looked huge and grey and ready to eat us.

We wasted more time arranging the kit under a tarpaulin to keep it dry. Then a BC Hydro pick-up rumbled along the access road and drove down to the water's edge where we were huddled. A grizzled-looking dam worker called Mr Hodges climbed out. His face was brown and wrinkled into rubbery creases. Without saying a word to us he stood by his vehicle and looked for a full minute at the water. Then he turned and said, 'You boys got lifejackets?'

Mr Hodges was the first Canadian I'd met who didn't use his first name; it was so unusual it was as if the Mr served as a Christian name. We offered him tea.

'Got coffee in my cab. You boys got signal flares?'

'Er, no.'

He nodded a little sadly. 'Them storms can come from behind in fifteen seconds. How far can you paddle that boat in fifteen seconds?'

I looked at Nigel. He made a grimace. I casually began to handle my lifejacket.

'About twenty metres, I'd say.'

'Exactly,' said Mr Hodges, triumphant, 'you stay twenty metres from shore and you might be OK. Except for those open stretches where you can't. See, your problem is you got to cross Schooler Creek and Ne-Parle-Pas Point. That's easy a mile of open water.' He smiled out at the vast lake. 'Whitecaps are building.'

'We're actually quite fast when all three of us are paddling.' It sounded very lame.

'Fifteen seconds. That's all you got.' He snapped his fingers to emphasize our proximity to certain death. 'Then there's the tree rockets, gotta watch out for those.'

'Tree rockets?' said Joe, now fully strapped into his lifejacket.

'Million dead trees under that lake. Never logged it properly before it was flooded. The roots start to rot and pow! That big old tree comes right up your ass.'

'Ouch,' said Nigel.

'Exactly,' said Mr Hodges. 'Tree rockets.'

'How do you watch out for a tree rocket?' asked Joe.

'Can't. Don't give no warning. Just boom! Right up your ass. Say, what kind of canoe is that?'

'Birchbark.'

Mr Hodges nodded, taking in the true immensity of our folly.

The lake, though artificial, did not appear so. The effect of ice and weather and the rise and fall of the water level had created beaches all around the edge, miraculously it seemed. Only thirty years earlier the place had been a nightmare of dead wood and drifting logs, the result of a botched attempt to log the flooded area in too short a time. Charlie had told me that those who lost machinery when the valley was flooded received government compensation, 'unlike the Indians, who just got given some crap land someplace else'. The experts seriously miscalculated how fast the water would rise. Much of the valley floor went unlogged – hence the tree-rocket menace. But people took advantage of the compensation. Every old caterpillar or worn-out truck or skidder found its way into the valley just as the waters were closing in. The Williston Lake was a mechanical graveyard. Also buried here was the world's largest tree crusher, one of a pair; the other was permanently on display outside the logging town of Mackenzie, the only community on the lake.

Mr Hodges departed with a sorry wave. Instead of driving off he sat in his cab sipping coffee from a giant Thermos cup.

'That bastard is waiting for us to get swamped,' said Nigel, indignant.

'Or hit by a tree rocket.'

'Sod him.'

Under Mr Hodges' critical eye Nigel bravely waded thigh-deep to hold the canoe against the breaking waves, and we were off.

'Imagine if a tree rocketed right underneath us,' said Joe when we were about twenty metres from the shore.

On this great, wide lake between mountains a tree rocket seemed as implausible as being run over by a boat (we saw only one in three days – about two miles away). 'But imagine if it did happen,' Joe persisted. We needed our fears and dangers. Highly dangerous but very unlikely ones were better than the dull and common ones – burning yourself whilst lifting a pot, cutting yourself with the axe or falling into the fire whilst intoxicated – responsible for more deaths in the wilderness than any other single cause, including bear, wolverine and moose attacks, canoe capsizes, rock-falls, tree rockets and plain starvation.

I knew Joe still had a little comfort bundle of dope. He was keeping it secret but as long as he didn't smoke so much that he fell intoxicated into the fire, I didn't mind. We had a bottle of whisky but it was quickly drunk. It was nice to have but we didn't really miss it when it was gone. A new stimulant or treat just took its place – in my case coffee, made with exaggerated care and great strength. If we had run out of coffee I'm sure tea would have been the treat. No tea, and a single square of chocolate would have been the day's reward. The voyageurs with Mackenzie had three nine-gallon kegs of rum, the weight of one piece each, and these lasted them the whole voyage. Mackenzie used it carefully as an anaesthetic, a stem to mutiny, a reward and sometimes a last resort. One empty keg was set into the river at around the point we were now at. In it was a message about their situation and achievements. The keg was never recovered.

We made good progress through the waves. Taken on the quarter, or head-on, they looked worse than they were. At Schooler Creek we checked behind us for any sign of a storm. The sky was now blue and clear. In less than half an hour we crossed the mile-wide stretch of open water and were back to hugging the rocky shoreline.

In several places, in coves with small beaches there were vast holes in the sand, with huge logs sticking out in a fan-like spray. It looked like an elephant trap after the elephant had fallen in. We saw several. How did they form? One could imagine a storm creating a whirlpool in the rocky corner of a beach, where it abutted the cliffs. Perhaps the whirlpool dragged in the huge logs and cast them like spills about the place. The holes were often twelve or fifteen feet deep and damp at the bottom. Usually one log, longer than the rest, had fallen and crossed the entire width of the hole and it looked like fun to walk across it and jump down into the soft sand. Except there was something uninviting and too shady about such places. Too near the cliffs. They looked man-made, but couldn't have been. The logs were too huge, bigger and longer than telegraph poles. It felt like another artificial place.

By the second day on the lake we could see the snow-capped Rockies on either side of us. The water, warmer than Dinosaur Lake, was tolerable enough for a quick dip. We paddled all day for nine or ten hours, making good speed, but missed the variety of the river. We roasted in the sun and just paddled. All day we sat in the canoe looking at the back of the man in front and playing, with a sort of desperate lassitude, Twenty Questions and Botticelli and even I-Spy.

The good progress didn't last. On the third day the wind blew up into a real storm and when Joe emerged from his tent it blew away. He ran down the beach and dived on it. Then we loaded the edge of each flysheet with wet sand and stones. Six-foot waves pounded the lakeshore and the wind tore the tops off the whitecaps.

In the middle of the beach, which was higher than the level of the lake, was a deep hole, an empty one, not filled with logs. It was like a small, damp crater. It wasn't a good hole, but it would do. We roofed over one end with driftwood and it was almost cosy, no wind at all. We lit a fire at the other end. We spent all day in the hole, periodically climbing the edge to look out at the lake. The crater sides were soft sand and gave way underfoot. You had to run at them to get out of the hole. At the top the wind immediately caught your hair. The lake was all white foam and waves, bright white and bright blue under the hot sun. We were going nowhere, at least not for a while.

It rained and we sat under our tarpaulin shelter. The sun still shone and the air became dark and light at the same time. The clouds were oppressive, bulky and ink-dark, and the sun dazzled you when you stuck your head above the parapet of the hole. I saw a double rainbow between two mountains opposite. There was a hole in the cliff in the mountain and you could see the rainbow going into it. In the 1940s, this cliff was climbed by Swiss mountaineers who reported the cave tunnelled through the mountain to the other side. It made a whistling sound when the wind blew. Indians called it the 'Cave of Winds' and refused to travel past it.

We sat in the hole drinking coffee and talking about Chris McCandless, a source of endless fascination to those who venture into the northern wilderness. McCandless, a.k.a. Alexander Supertramp, travelled the States and Mexico living, at times, quite effectively off the land. It encouraged him to embark on a final adventure. Only twenty miles from a road in the Alaskan wilderness he was trapped by a river he couldn't cross and died of malnutrition and ptomaine poisoning from a variety of pea plant. He had been 105 days with only a five-kilo bag of rice and a .22 rifle. All of us had read Jon Krakauer's excellent but unsettling book about McCandless, *Into the Wild*. In the hole we had all the time in the world so we circled the key events in the story.

His decision not to take a map, which contributed to his death because the map showed the river that trapped him could be crossed: there was a logging wire only a mile or so downstream from the grotty dumped bus where his emaciated body was found. His fear of water – he was never a good swimmer and that made him nervous of crossing the river in full flood. His lack of bush skills – he tried to air-dry moose when at that latitude it needs to be smoke-dried; the moose went rotten. His inability to build a raft to escape across the river. But, despite all this, he almost made it. He comes over as rather extraordinary, principled and courageous. Yet also a blithering idiot. You have to accept he was both, which is discomforting. There's no easy answer to what we called the McCandless Dilemma. Do you ignore maps, sat phones, 4x4s and freeze-dried food and thereby really test yourself? Or do you ride into the wilderness on an all-terrain vehicle, your bulging waistline a sure sign of how unfit you are for that environment? Climbers easily solved the Mc-Candless Dilemma years ago when they first dispensed with guides, then Sherpas, pitons, little stepladders and bolts drilled into the rockface. Going into the wilderness armed with the equivalent of a bolt drill (a load of food and a sat phone) is considered, by very many, as the only sane way to proceed. Tipping the odds against yourself, as McCandless did, is seen not as a heroic 'freeing' of some wilderness experience but simply as foolish. If McCandless had deliberately scorned maps and modern gear and food then surely he should have been better prepared to live off the land? That was the moot point we reached, crouched around our stinky driftwood fire at the bottom of the sand hole.

I knew that the decision to take a birchbark canoe was part of my own solution of the McCandless Dilemma. I wouldn't want to do it in the latest plastic boat. We had to baby our craft, treat it like a blown egg nestling in cotton wool. This tempered any gung-ho tendency. This balance, between grit to continue and fussy care of the boat, was sometimes almost intolerable, but it seemed right in some way. Man in his bulldozer and tank-like 4x4 is living in a false dream. He is master of the universe, lord of all he surveys. Anyone who has been lost and alone in the wilderness knows the falseness of this state of mind. It's an arrogance that is only humbled by natural disasters. I could just see Chris McCandless rubbing his hands together when Mount St Helens blew its tope – 'Now they'll see how puny they are!'

We had compromised with our satellite telephone and ample supplies of food (fishing, thank goodness, a luxury – otherwise we would have been, at this point, very hungry) and yet we still had the boat, an emanation of the very woods we travelled through, a symbol. But also something very practical. You could bust it up and repair it without recourse to a plastics factory or an aluminium smelter. That was desirable, in a fashionable, ecological sense also. But deeper lay a groping towards authenticity.

Isn't that what McCandless was challenging, the inauthentic nature of what passes for a 'normal life'? Why is it inauthentic to use machines? It just seems so. Or rather, it is the overuse, the overkill. I once saw some tree surgeons pruning four-foot saplings with a chainsaw. They had it there and running so why not? But each branch was finger-width. A knife or pruning shears would have been better. It seems worse than just silliness. But is it?

It was the fact that McCandless spurned a map that made him so reviled. That was *so stoopid*. Yet the rejection of the map lies at the heart of what he was trying to do. He carried a gun, he used a sleeping bag. He didn't reject all technology. He rejected only that which gets between you and the landscape, the experience. That's why there's no better way of learning about a place than getting lost in it. Following a map, army-style, means the abstraction is greater than the real, or very often is. No map. That takes courage. And that was what really distinguished us from Mackenzie and all the other pioneers. They had their rudimentary maps, but they had to continually accept the map was a fiction, of very general use only. It was simply a vague idea. The reality was all around them. McCandless recreated this at a stroke. Then he paid for it with his life.

You get lost all the time, even with maps. But maps encourage a lack of real interaction with the landscape. You pay no attention to where the sun is, what the drainage pattern is, which side of the trees looks the most mossy and shaded. The map, and its companion the GPS, fix us most certainly in another world, since, to me at least, maps never look like the country they depict. They merely look like an X-ray of it, at best; at worst, something as abstract as a list of government statistics.

To get back to Mackenzie's and McCandless's experiences I have to go back to my childhood, when I used to 'explore' the surrounding fields and woods, making my own sketch-maps and naming everything 'Pigeon Poacher's Wood', 'Compass Island', 'Oak Hill'. Because I accepted that I was 'just playing' and therefore felt no need to conform to the OS map of the area.

Only without an accurate map can you see the landscape as a child does, or a Mackenzie, with his comments written alongside the river: 'River makes a hissing noise like a boiling water' or 'Stony current' or 'bright stony mountains'. It is instructive to see the differences between the original first journal of his trip to the Arctic (the Pacific one is lost) and the published account of the second voyage, after his education in navigation. Already the homeliness and originality are disappearing, replaced by an attempt at dull conformity.

McCandless was a kind of modern primitive. Perhaps rejecting maps is like the famous rejection of perspective, the return to a primitive authenticity.

We brewed some more coffee in the hole. Nigel climbed up the sliding slope to check the weather. It was now mid-afternoon. No one really wanted to move. 'Still blowing like mad,' he reported, with some relief. 'Tomorrow, though,' I said, 'we leave at the crack of dawn. Even if we only make a few miles we have to get out of this hole.'

Everyone nodded, glad that tomorrow was, indeed, tomorrow.

Seven

THE WORLD'S BIGGEST LOG CRUSHER

'Our way was through a forest of stately cedars, beneath a range of lofty hills.' Alexander Mackenzie

I

When we weren't pinned down by wind and waves we made rapid progress – forty or fifty kilometres a day. The lake still looked dead. We saw no wildlife on the banks. There were tracks of birds, wolves, moose and bear but we did not see them.

In good weather we paddled for hours each day. Hours and hours. Often the lake was rough and the waves, measured from top to trough, were four or five feet. If they started to break too often we pulled in. We stopped in unlikely places. Once on a series of rock ledges, pulling the canoe clear using a wave and lifting it on to a higher ledge. We made a fire and a shelter in this vertical world and waited for the wind to die down. Often it went calm at lunchtime. By the time we had packed up and finished eating it would be rough again. When the sun shone everything burned. My nose was as red as an alcoholic's and my eyes were sore looking at the glare. The hours went by slowly but we were making our way steadily to the old junction of the Peace and the Finlay rivers, the Finlay Forks, the place where Mackenzie's inclination was to go right, i.e. north. But an elderly Indian who had been on war parties in the region had told him 'on no account to follow it as it was lost in various branches among the mountains'. The correct way was left, south along the Rocky Mountain Trench to the Continental Divide.

The Finley Forks were now submerged, making the Williston Lake T-shaped. At the junction of the T, taking a bite out of its left-hand corner, was Finlay Bay. Herb had warned us about this spot, a bay next to the largest piece of open water in the Rocky Mountains, with winds blowing across it funnelled through valleys lying in four directions.

Finlay Bay was a mile deep and a mile or so across. In the back of the bay were buildings. Joe, who was good at spotting the unusual, said, 'There's something written on the roof of one of those buildings.' I looked through the binoculars, twiddled with the focus ring, and saw CAFÉ written in huge letters on the roof, just like a refreshment hut on the Serpentine or the River Thames.

'What if it's a joke?' said Nigel. 'That's a hell of a long paddle.'

'Nah,' said Joe. 'That's not the Canadian sense of humour.'

We were 150 kilometres from the nearest town. It was too good to miss. We paddled in, close to the shore, aware, even there, of the way the wind slammed the waves against the beach. As we got closer we made out other buildings: long low huts and a couple of brightly painted Alpine-chalet-type constructions. On the beach, we secured the canoe in front of three enormous, blackened piles of driftwood, still tangled with yellow rope. These were the escaped remains of the mile-long log pontoon barges pushed up and down the Williston Lake to and from the logging town of Mackenzie, the only town on the lake.

Next to one of the big logpiles was a forty-gallon drum of diesel, dented and empty. Further back was a giant yellow bull-dozer. The beach was churned up with crazy tracks, a frenzy of caterpillar activity, like an industrial-era version of the Nazca lines.

In a frenzy of anticipation for steaks and beer we ran past the three massive piles of blackened wood and up to the café. The windows were grimy but the door was open. Inside, on the bar, a coffee machine was spun with cobwebs. A cardboard box on a plastic-topped table contained paperbacks buckled with the damp; all the chairs were gathered in one corner in a circle, as if a hurried conference had just taken place.

The new-looking chalets turned out to be ornate toilets, abandoned and unfinished. The other huts were holiday cabins, all unlocked, doors flapping in the breeze. We wandered through and Joe found, and photographed as part of his ongoing dead-animal project, a dead swallow on the floor between two beds. 'This place is fucking creepy,' he said, motorwinding through the film. I went back to the beach and the apparent turmoil of the woodpiles became obvious. The owner, at his wits' end, overwhelmed by the project of maintaining or refurbishing his resort, decides to clear the beach of driftwood. In an increasing frenzy he drives back and forth with the skidder and makes three enormous piles. He douses them with the diesel, and, somehow in keeping with the doomed nature of the whole project, the fires soon go out. Hence the blackened wood. It's the final straw and he gives up, leaving the place open to the elements.

In Europe we always think of man encroaching, but this was a case of man being beaten back. Despite his machines the owner of the café was driven away.

One benefit of the lake – it had been loudly touted in the 1970s and 80s – would be the huge recreational opportunities it offered. But these were already stillborn. Natural mercury in the fish had supposedly accumulated to beyond an acceptable level. That was why the locals fished the Wicked River and other creeks but not the lake itself. The lake fish were considered inedible. That explained the lack of boats and the dead café. Maybe there wasn't supposed to be a lake here after all.

II

We didn't even manage to get out of Finlay Bay before we were wind-bound again. We paddled five hundred yards from the dead café and gave up our struggle against the increasing waves. Nigel got out his fishing rod. Mercury or no mercury, Nigel was going to catch a fish. Almost every night on the Peace he tried, and failed. We all gave him advice. He rarely followed it. He lost spinners and sections of line with considerable regularity. But he didn't give up.

There was a dirt road from Mackenzie town that ended at Finlay Bay. It was the weekend (though we had lost count of what day it was) and two adventurous groups of campers soon joined us. Three rough-looking men in their beaten-to-hell pick-ups pulled up near to us. They were towing a small boat with an outboard.

'That's quite the contraption you got there,' said the bespec-tacled, unshaven man, earning our undying hatred. Con-traption? His rubbish pick-up and knackered powerboat were contraptions. Our birchbark canoe was art. Couldn't the darn fool see that?

Both his mates were dark, unshaven and rat-like in demeanour. Neither said a word to us. They spoke in low voices between themselves like thieves on a job. They had beer but they didn't laugh. They were like men conveying the fact that they were on serious business. The contraption man was just a fat kid but the other two had mean faces. They had a gun too, but on show. Not like ours, well hidden in its waterproof bag.

Our new pal Warren knew them by name and chatted for a minute or two with them. Warren had also driven down the road from Mackenzie to do some fishing on the Wicked River.

Warren was full of enthusiasm for his new jetboat. He invited us to supper with his family and shared the last of his beer with us. Warren had a beautiful wife, a jetboat, a well-paid job at the mill. It seemed right that Warren had all the luck and the three desperadoes had little. Warren told us that one of them, in that very pick-up parked next to our tent, had deliberately tied a dog to the back bumper, knowing his girlfriend would drive off, which she did. They'd had an argument, and it was her dog. She drove a mile at sixty miles an hour before flashing lights told her something was very wrong. 'A mile at sixty mph, you can wear through a lot of skin and bone.' In that very pick-up. I gave it a closer look, rust-coloured, heavy-duty gas guzzler. I couldn't see any blood.

Warren started the fire with his chainsaw. His wife, Trish, who was pregnant, held the log down as he hovered the saw in a deep cut, spewing out sawdust. It was hard to get enough sawdust. The saw was noisy and having to start it just to make the sawdust made it excessive. Why not just use gas instead? Or walk up the beach and find some birchbark. There was a lot around, our constant companion, you could always find it if you looked. We kept a stock in the cooking-equipment bag, thick lino-like slabs of the stuff, just feather up one end and you can light any fire in any conditions with one match.

Warren was a good guy. When we met him again in his home town of Mackenzie he gave us a week's worth of meat – elk and moose – Trish lent us her car, he let us crash at his place for three days, we drank all his beer, he taught Nigel how to fish and his dad gave us a Swede saw and good advice about the Parsnip River. Warren was a real good guy. But like everyone he had his moments of madness that shed some light on everything he did. There was great determination on Warren's face as he revved the saw to produce the sawdust. Its loudness and petrol-fumed intensity were too much. Too much. But he was driven by some madness to continue. He had started and he was determined to succeed.

Earlier he had taken us on his jetboat to fish the Wicked River. He had advised bait *and* treble-point spinners and we were full of high hopes, since this combination was illegal and therefore promising.

It was my first time on a jetboat. They go fast and flat, hammering the wave-heads in a flurry of skim, the powerful engine roaring. Knocking the waves down and getting the spume in your face. Thud thud thud and everyone's faces covered with broad grins at the outstanding fun of it. Thirty mph seems fast in a jetboat. I thought of Herb doing a hundred in his – that would seem insane. A drain-like grille protects the jet from bits of flotsam. It gets blocked quite often and is cleared by a griddling action, like shaking the ashes through a fire. The jet sucks water up through the grille and spews it out the back. Warren's boat also had a half-inch-thick layer of Teflon covering the bottom.

The boat was only about fifteen feet long and the Teflon weighed 750kg. It allowed Warren to ram beaver dams and run right up a beach, hit logs and jump small spits. Though the Teflon cost an extra $4,000 it was what made the jetboat the bomb-proof river rocket that it was.

We fished the Wicked with bait and spinners but we had no luck. But back at camp Nigel caught his first fish of the trip in the lake. 'Squawfish!' hooted Warren in derision. Joe caught one too and we cooked them up and though full of bones I could not fault them.

Meanwhile Warren was still chainsawing away at the log, trying to produce enough punk to start a fire. We all looked on anxiously. We wanted him to succeed. We liked Warren and we didn't want him to lose face. It would be ignominious, after all that expenditure of raw power, to not get the fire going after all. And he did. He produced enough sawdust with his chainsaw to start a fire.

We wanted Warren to succeed even though it didn't seem the best way to light a fire. It struck me the friends and family of the good people who planned the dam, logged the valley and flooded it might have felt the same way. Once a bad idea gains momentum good people, as well as the mercenary, have a stake. Everyone then wants it to succeed for reasons other than any real need for the thing.

III

The weather calmed and we rounded the point of Finlay Bay. We were now on the old path of the Parsnip before the lake was made. Three more long days of paddling and we'd make Mackenzie, which was near to the end of the lake.

About a day from the town we saw someone. Trapper Joe on the other side of the lake in a beaten aluminium shell of a boat with a tiny held-together-by-string outboard on the back. His outboard was so tiny and apologetic-sounding it hardly even counted as an engine, it was more of a mechanical tick.

296

Trapper Joe smirked into view low in his boat, with a foxy face and a German accent and knowingly admired our canoe. 'That's a beauty,' he said. 'I gotta get word to the town,' he said, 'I gotta tell the noospaper.' He was excited and yet self-contained. He had lived the last twenty years in a cabin he built himself just set back from the side of the lake. Everyone in Mackenzie knew him. A man in a bar in Mackenzie later told me, 'We was in this logging camp a long ways from anywhere. Everything had been helicoptered in or come by boat. Suddenly there was this guy with a rifle riding a pushbike through the camp. Yikes! What was that? And he didn't even stop. Just rode right through. That was Trapper Joe. We'd set up camp on one of his trails. Only hunter I know who rides a pushbike.'

Joe now had a motorbike. 'That's how I get to town.' This was North America so I thought it would be a big Harley. 'Nah, an old 125 Honda,' he replied. Joe was my kind of trapper. He just didn't give a shit about appearances. He did the minimum. 'Just hunt, some fishing, take tourists out from time to time. Trapping is coming back. Good prices for marten right now.'

Joe loved the lake, despite its artificial origin. 'Oh, there's plenty game around, plenty. Just a ways back from the edge. No reason for it to come down and be noticed.'

He told us about all the Germans who had bought holiday cottages around the lake, most of them expensively fitted out. 'One guy even had European electric sockets fitted!' he chortled.

Given his enthusiasm for the canoe I thought Joe would want to meet up with us in Mackenzie, but it didn't coincide with his weekly run into town. He didn't want to change his fixed schedule. Later we found out he had a brother who lived in Mackenzie. They never spoke.

I asked Trapper Joe what he liked about the lake. 'No people,' he replied.

'What about the mercury in the fish?'

He shrugged. 'Helps keep the fishermen away.'

Outside Mackenzie a two-engined float plane buzzed us so close we could see the pilot waving. Warren's dad, Danny, had told a friend to keep a look out for us. Danny met us with Warren and Trish as we secured the canoe under a tarpaulin a few miles from the town centre. Danny approved our careful covering of the boat. Keep it away from prying eyes and drunken teenagers. 'This can be a rude little town sometimes,' he said.

At Warren's house we all got changed in the garden. We'd been outdoors for so long it didn't seem right to be inside. The jetboat sat on its purpose-built trailer, a recent acquisition. Warren already had an off-road Bronco, much altered and improved, a quad and a high-power snowmobile. His basement was used as a workshop. There were spare parts on shelves and pieces of equipment that looked as if they were mid-repair lying in oily puddles on the workbench. The floor was concrete, marked with paint and oil. Joe achieved his dream of a Therma-rest, buying Warren's for a bargain $50 – new they were over $100 – and slept comfortably on the basement floor.

The machines were fun, I could see that, but they needed maintaining. Warren and his dad were expert mechanics, but Warren admitted he might spend an hour in the shop for every eight hours spent snowmobiling. That sounded excessive to me. And add in the quad and the Bronco (actually awaiting repair) and now the jetboat and you see the magnitude of the task. It would get me down. I like machines that you can run and run until they disintegrate. I have the Indian approach to cars – a tendency to let them rot on my front lawn rather than sell or repair them. In fact I don't really mind, at all, being surrounded by dead machines, it's having to keep them alive that I don't like.

Stretching further Warren and Trish's generosity, Steve arrived with a new friend from Hudson's Hope, Bill. Now there were five of us crashed out on the basement floor. Steve brought the latest news about Guy and Mary and his thumb. He had been on a honey-selling trip with Guy and they'd stopped on the last proper road bridge over the Parsnip River to have a look. 'It's way faster than the Peace,' Steve gloomily reported. 'It's a fuckin' torrent.'

He was more cheerful about his thumb. It was healing well but it would be impossible for him to join us on the Parsnip. We arranged to meet again at Prince George on the Fraser River. Steve felt bad that his thumb hadn't healed any faster. He had brought along Bill as a replacement. Bill was only eighteen but he was amiable company. He was keen to join and looked fit enough, but I had decided we would continue as three. It meant we had less manpower to get the canoe over the Rockies, but it also meant carrying less weight, less gear and food. I looked at Bill and tried to gauge my instinctive reaction. He'd do, I thought, but so will we. The sense of adversity, of us up against it with little margin for safety or error, made me more determined. We'd do it as three. The canoe was designed for three and we'd do it as three.

Before they left, Steve and Bill came with us to see the tree crusher. We already knew the key fact that outside Mackenzie stood the world's largest. Alexander Mackenzie has many schools, a highway, a river and several lakes named after him, but this was the first and only town, a logging town built to coincide with the creation of the lake in the 1960s. The tree crusher was selected, rightly, many feel, as a symbol of the town and its main business. Warren and Trish and their family were not particularly proud of this fact. The machine, which had been designed to crush trees flat rather than laboriously require them to be sawn down, had not been a success. 'Darn thing kept getting stuck,' said Danny, 'apparently.'

'Ain't even the largest,' said Warren. 'They got one in New Zealand I heard was bigger.'

The tree crusher had a large diesel engine mounted with a generator on two long studded rollers, like giant rolling pins with vicious-dog-collar studs. Each roller was seven feet in diameter and weighed several tons. There was an electric motor at either end, driven by the central diesel and generator rig. This ensured smooth and powerful low-speed work. Sticking out of the front, to knock down the trees, was a great steel braced ram. It was built in 1960 in Texas by R. C. Letourneau Inc. and was officially designated the G175 Tree Crusher.

It looked perfectly up to the job as long as the ground was flat. But forest floors never are. It was a failure. And Williston Lake was created before a half of its timber could be reclaimed.

The idea was that the crushed trees could be hauled away quickly, but it hardly worked like that. Instead the tree crusher crushed its way aimlessly around the soon-to-be flooded forest getting snagged and snared at every turn. Even if it had worked there is something wasteful and barbaric about simply knocking trees down. Perhaps one should admire the DIY aspect of the tree crusher. It was a failed invention, granted, but the idea of using electric motors in the forest was quite intriguing. I bought ten postcards of the crusher. I couldn't get it out of my mind.

It seemed appropriate that the symbol of Mackenzie's town should be a vast and useless piece of super-machinery. This is, after all, the logical extension of the pioneer spirit – the tree crusher. If you admit the tool-using continuum from axe to saw to power saw to bulldozer then you end up with tree crushers. If you believe in tree spirits then you could call it a spirit crusher.

V

From a distance the first line of stumps had looked innocuous. But that line hid a denser line. And then a denser line. Until we were surrounded by the blackened remains of trees. The tree stumps extended on to the land. It made it hard to tell the land from the water. We were at the very end of the lake, looking for the Parsnip River.

The Pack River entrance was dead easy to spot. This had been the one Mackenzie supposedly missed. Simon Fraser made a jibe, insinuating that Mackenzie had been asleep at the time. Now the lake had raised the water level, the Pack was the obvious river. The Parsnip, however, was hidden somewhere in the field of stumps. And I hated to admit it but we were lost. All around us the blackened tree stumps threatened to hole the boat. There were thousands of them. It was like a mangrove swamp, except all the trees were sawn off. None was higher than four feet. Some were just below the surface. These were the most dangerous. Joe stood up at the bow, scouting a way. He tested the water's depth with a paddle. We nosed slowly through the stumps, looking for signs of the river entrance.

It was a warm day. There were horseflies in the canoe. They would ride along, sheltering from the wind, buzzing around your legs until they found some flesh. I took several GPS readings but they told me nothing. I knew where I was, it was simply that the river had gone. I twisted the map and orientated it with the compass. But it didn't look right. It was then I began to have doubts. At last I could contain myself no longer. I knew the answer, had used a compass a thousand times, but I could feel the pressure – you're leader, find the way, dammit! I twisted the map. It just didn't look right.

'Er, Nigel, the red end points north, right?'

'On every compass I've used,' said Nigel, but gently – he wasn't going to rub it in.

'You're lost, aren't you?' said Joe, his face scornful.

'No,' I said with great uncertainty.

I stared at the map and then the long line of trees at the end of the lake.

'I am relatively certain that, over there, lies the Parsnip River.' I indicated an area as vast as Hertfordshire.

We settled for paddling to the very very end of the lake, just to make sure it was the very end. It was. There were several windy little channels, winding between the stumps in a grassy field, but too small to be the mighty Parsnip. 'It can't be those,' said Nigel, 'Steve said it was a torrent.'

But if the Parsnip's so strong, where is it? Joe and Nigel and I got out of the canoe and started walking aimlessly through the stump-studded landscape.

If you've been lost a lot in various wilderness places, as I have, being lost is like being somewhere familiar, in that all the places you've been lost in seem part of the same world, which obeys its own strange laws. Lostworld. Because it doesn't fit the map, or fits it but with so many inconsistencies, Lostworld appears like unexplored territory. You keep trying different orientations and these instantly alter what is in front of your eyes. Valleys and hills are where they shouldn't be, surely unnamed virgin peaks that have never been mapped or even seen by another human? Rivers run backwards in Lostworld and the snow has melted on mountains that should be white. Paths peter out and go nowhere, or suddenly, with no warning or meaning, become well-made roads leading in the wrong direction. Fields become forests which can break out into a logged wilderness or the blackened remnants of a fire, or a lake from nowhere, so vast – could it be the sea? Out-of-place road signs, pieces of orange plastic ticking, paintmarks on trees, all would be clues anywhere except Lostworld. I've been here so many times I should be able to recognize where I am.

At this point, when Mackenzie was lost, in this very same place, he climbed a tall tree to 'ascertain the path' to the Parsnip.

'Er, Rob,' called Nigel from the great, flat-sawn bole he was standing on tiptoes on, 'is that it?' I clambered up to join him, aware that he was the taller and had better eyesight. All those eagles he'd spotted from afar that I only saw when they took wing.

I strained my eyes across the watery, stump-laden vista. It could have been World War I and we were looking for the enemy line. When tiny bush planes buzzed overhead it felt like war, or a memory of a child playing at war. We were too high up, heads way above the parapet, but at least we could see if there were any bears. I tried to follow the direction of Nigel's long, bony, chapped red finger. I thought of my son and how he pretends to see things I point out, just to be rid of my insistent enthusiasm. But I was in charge so I couldn't pretend. 'That water over there?' I said.

'No, behind it. I think it connects up.'

Ah, instant illumination! He was right! Or must be, because if that's the river's mouth then that must be the valley, that cliff the old edge of a meander, the Pack River in about the right place. It's just like Scrabble, when you hit the jackpot and you magically manage to add each letter to the small core word you first thought of, growing the thing amazingly until seven unpromising plastic letters link and click into a double word score and fifty extra points. Now all we had to do was paddle there. I wanted to congratulate Nigel, pour on the praise, but his lean back didn't need it. He knew he was right.

We had to go miles out of our way but the prodding and paddle-dipping at the looming roots in the peat-blackened water were tinged with hope rather than gnawing indecision now that we thought we knew for sure where we were going. It was nice to know Mackenzie had it no easier. After his tree climbing, when he was satisfied that the Parsnip ran along a deep valley (actually the Rocky Mountain Trench), he returned to the river. But the remaining voyageurs and the canoe were not there. In fact Mackenzie was not sure if he had returned to the right spot. 'Various very unpleasing conjectures at once perplexed and distressed us: the Indians with us, who are inclined to magnify evils of any and every kind, had at once consigned the canoe and everyone on board to the bottom; and were already settling a plan to return upon a raft ... as for myself, it will be easily believed, that my mind was in a state of extreme agitation.' After being lost for many hours, they heard a shot and found their people: 'It was almost dark when we reached the canoe, bare-footed, and drenched with rain.' Never get out of the boat.

'Stop moving,' said Nigel. We stopped paddling and prodding at logs. We had entered a wider stretch of water ringed with stumps. It was near to the open water we had seen from the tree. The canoe slowly drifted forwards under its own momentum, and then, very slowly, went into reverse.

'I never thought I'd say this, but I'm happy to be going backwards.'

We had found the entrance to the Parnsip River.

Eight

QUEENS OF ENGLAND

'To add to our distress we had no gun.' Alexander
Mackenzie on the Parsnip River

I

The Hart Highway bridge, carrying Route 97, is the only highway to cross the Parsnip. It's a few miles upstream from the stump field at the end of Williston Lake. But in that short distance we'd found the current increased from imperceptible drift to rip tide. We sheltered under the bridge, staring at the churning water. The bank had run out, making towing impossible, and we could certainly not paddle. Marooned. It started to rain and we all huddled next to the stained concrete support stanchion. Marooned. Route 97 carried on down to Prince George, an hour's drive, our destination, the last town before our walk across the Inland Plateau to the Pacific. Instead we had hoped to go up the Parsnip, almost to its source, then over the mountains and down the Fraser to Prince George. This journey might take a month or more. If we made it. Steve had been right: the Parsnip River was a torrent. Narrower than the Peace but a lot faster. We pulled the canoe out on the gravel bank. Mackenzie wrote of this exact spot, 'The whole of this distance we proceeded by hauling the canoe from branch to branch. The current was so strong it was impossible to stem it with paddles; the depth was too great for poles, and the bank of the river was so closely lined with willows and other trees, that it was impossible to employ the line.' The following day he wrote, 'the current became still stronger; and its velocity had already been so great as to justify our despair in getting up [the river], if we had not been so long accustomed to surmount it'.

'Do you think there's a phone up on the highway?' asked Joe.

'Bound to be. Warren said there was a gas station too.'

'Probably a restaurant. Maybe even a liquor store.'

It was decided. We tethered the boat under the bridge to the rusting engine block of a dumped V8 gas guzzler and went in search of places where money could solve your problems.

II

Back under the bridge I had two cans of Budweiser in me, and had smoked the last 'Tiny Tim' cigar, bought for fifty cents from the store adjoining the terrible Chinese restaurant on the Hart Highway where we had our last meal. 'New York steak?' said Nigel, laying down his knife and fork on the wiped-clean plate, 'I don't think so.' It was right, somehow, that the last meal should be crap; it told us we should be moving, back to the canoe, showing that we were not beaten by the river at a place where we could give up and call it a day, hitch a ride home.

We tentatively tried pulling ourselves along under the overhanging tree branches as Mackenzie did. It was slow work and our ears were soon cut and bleeding from all the branches whipping back when you let go of them. Nigel pointed below the bow: 'You know what? There are logs down there underwater. I think if you tied the towrope to me I could balance on them and pull myself along using the branches. That way the canoe will be clear of this shit.'

He was right, but it took towing to a new level of masochism. One slip off a slimy underwater log and you went right under. Lose your grip on a branch for an instant and you'd be dragged back into the current by the canoe. But it worked, and slowly he hauled us away from that miserable spot under the bridge.

We agreed that each man should tow for only forty-five minutes before a change. This made it less awful to contemplate. Only forty-five minutes, I could manage that, even with the attendant risk of FBI: full-body immersion. Maybe it was the beer, or the cigar, or perhaps all that meat we'd been eating, but when I took over the tow I felt a new energy, one I hadn't felt since the first year of the trip.

It was a gung-ho energy, safe to run at full power, knowing the pain would last only forty-five minutes. It wasn't like paddling, where you had to pace yourself; with short-duration towing you could blast on, and then recover for an hour and a half while the others took over.

And, strangely, I felt less tired at the end of the day than usual. It was just like running. Get the wrong rhythm and you're hurting after a mile; get it right and your lungs can sweetly click in and you know you can go for ever, or so it seems by contrast. To think I'd been going too slowly all this time! If only I'd given it more welly. Or was the real truth that only when you're in an impossible situation do you find your hidden strengths?

The next day was even better. Great long stretches wading chest-deep in water, punching my way through. The branches were there for hanging on to. Like a monkey, one could swing out over the deeper, swirly, faster parts and then come back in close to the bank. There were hazels, alders and willows hanging down, all ready to be grasped, but you had to keep up momentum, that was the secret. It was a kind of mental momentum too. You had to rush your mind to some extent: 'the next thing, the next thing, the next thing' was one mantra, but the thing with mantras is that you have to keep changing them; they work for only about a day and a half on average. The mind has to be moving forward and then the body follows, kicking through water, making a maximum splash (important, this: trying to keep dry lowers your momentum and is pointless anyway), always choosing the water route over the lengthier, drier way over the top of an upended root plate, like the splayed end of a giant cigar stubbed out with earth. I'd tread water round such obstructions, gripping the twisted cable of a root, and it always held my weight, the towrope around my waist in a loop.

It even got competitive. Every morning we did Scissors, Paper, Stone to decide who towed first. Steve had always, almost always, won in the past. Now he was gone it was random. An etiquette of machismo developed – the one who won always chose to tow first. Nigel, who had an impeccable record in this regard, balked once, the sight of the bank disappearing into the cold grey throbbing stream, certain dunking, an FBI at 7 a.m. assured, made him back off and let Joe take the lead. But this only happened once. As the going got tougher we rose to the challenge, we laughed in the face of the devil, that's how it felt, and at night we dined on Warren's elk burgers and Nigel's carefully crafted fried potatoes.

III

The Parsnip was a fast and furious river but it wasn't mean, like the Peace. It was an honest river, it let you know what was coming. There were none of the sudden bursts of killer current when you rounded a point. It was vigorous but friendly. The Parnsip didn't want us dead. We spent so much time in it, ingested so much of it, that anthropomorphizing a stretch of water seemed entirely natural.

At night we found tiny stretches of gravel to camp on or, better, an island of rounded pebbles. Sometimes we crept into the thick forest and hacked out enough space to pitch two tents. It was at one such spot that we realized we'd lost something. The run of heightened spirits, the explorer's kick, all drained to nothing when it became apparent, at dusk, with a meal ready in the pan, that one of the mess tins was missing.

'You're blaming me,' said Joe, aggrieved.

'I'm not blaming anyone.'

'You're not blaming yourself, though.'

A deep breath, oxygen on a cold night, cooled by a light shower earlier. There was something sad about the loss of the tin, one of the slightly smaller ones, Dutch army surplus, a definite improvement on the previous year's Chinese aluminium with bendy handles that melted in too hot a fire. Stainless steel, flexibly strong, easy to clean, one slipping inside another with the spoons criss-crossed inside, our companions of many days and nights, now down to two. 'I'll use the lid, then,' said Joe. But we all knew that we'd all be using the lid when it came to our turn. One virtue of democracy – it can't tolerate martyrs for too long. Where had the tin been lost? At lunch. Being pack-man, I should have checked, but then who left the tin, the billy tin, as Nigel always called them, behind that log? The little lost tin called to us from its impossible distance some five miles away. We'd never go back, too far, too far, and there was some-thing awful about retracing steps on a long voyage like this. Too much like giving in. Would we ever lose anything important? So far we'd dropped a bearhorn, a tarpaulin, a rope, and those things swept away when the river rose. One of the good bits in Ted Simon's *Jupiter's Travels*, about a five-year world cir-cumnavigation on a motorcycle, is when he talks about the desire to rush to your destination: 'First you lose a rope and then your pliers and pretty soon you're riding hell for leather with your trousers round your ankles.' Did the loss of the mess tin mean we would be crossing the Rockies in tattered trews? Or did it mean something symbolic, prefiguring the loss of our canoe, something serious like that? No one was happy about it, but I was the least happy. Our tents were pitched up a mossy bank and in the woods amongst rotten trunks that collapsed like a pie crust if you trod on them. It was darker there than on the bank by the fire and as I prodded the tent pegs through the papery nothing of leaf litter on moss I kept seeing the little mess tin, alone in that field behind the log where we had lunch. It wouldn't come back and now we had to use the pot lid, which would work, but dammit. Here the thought would loop uselessly back on itself. And unlike my life in the urban world there was no outlet, no night car ride round the ring road, no pub to visit, no pal to bitch to and make it better, just the moss, the silent tents and two lonesome shapes hulking by the campfire, talking in low voices about anything except the loss of the mess tin, I imagined. A night hike might have been calming but bear fear made that supremely uninviting.

Writing this it completely mystifies me why I took it so hard but I did. A clue comes from the unlikely world of high-altitude climbing. On his solo, oxygenless ascent of Everest, Reinhold Messner cried bitterly when he lost his rucksack. Admittedly he was suffering from altitude-induced delusions, but what are they except a magnification of what we feel at sea level? The mess tin was gone, gone, utterly gone. What made it even more frustrating was that I had thrown away two spare ones at the start of the trip on account of the extra weight. Thought loops in remote places.

I stomped back to the fire where Nigel and Joe were gloomily crouched, cradling tea mugs in their cupped palms. Nigel looked up, his long neck and Adam's apple bent back like a heron. 'All right?' he said. I nodded gruffly, pushing my bottom lip up to make a steadfast scowl, one up from a blank stare or looking away. 'I just think,' I started, sensing Joe's earnest, wayward eyes in the dark, 'I just think we should be more careful with our kit. There are no more towns for two hundred miles and we can't afford to get sloppy. This is a sign, a reminder, we mustn't get careless.' Nigel craned down to look at the fire, which could, perhaps, if interpreted generously, be a nod of agreement. Joe said nothing. It was like the silence after a family argument, a silence you can't get away from, except through sleep, so we did.

IV

A week of hard towing went by and we needed a rest. We tied up under a dirt-road bridge and went looking for a settlement marked on the map as Anzac Crossing. But all we found was the train. The dusty blue diesel train stood in the middle of nowhere, on tracks running through a replanted forest. Alongside it was a parked line of beaten pick-ups, bonnets open as if gaping for air; it was hot enough, with buzzing, biting insects keeping us moving along the dusty track, kicking up fine, fine dust and on our left the train, standing amidst small trees with too much space between them. In the middle of nowhere, a big diesel engine with coaches looks meaner and heavier than it does in a station. We had hoped without much hope that Anzac Crossing might be a real place, but all it was was a train.

The parked pick-ups were like the totems and spears outside a native encampment. They signalled redneck nation and I knew we looked, despite our voyaging, more urban and hippy than macho and rural. I had misgivings, but the desire for human contact was stronger. We walked along the dusty blue BC Rail train, the bumper slide arms shining out from all that sprayed-on mud and dark oily grime. Then we saw faces on the open back part of a carriage, the tread plate between one carriage and another, but way high up a ladder. Men with cans and sun-reddened faces. They were sozzled with booze and not over-friendly. We felt pretty fit but these were *big*, UGLY guys. 'What the fuck are you doing here?' called down the biggest, whose droopy moustache was like something out of Asterix. His eyes were hidden behind sunburned bulk, out of harm's way. His can described a slow and mysterious ellipse in the air way above us, something it would take a physicist ages to calculate but telling us immediately that he was completely pissed.

They all were. They'd been drinking since 2 p.m.; now it was 5.30. The blue cans lay bent in half and bleeding from stress punctures all over the tread plate. Restlessly men moved out and through this open area from one part of the air-conditioned train to another. They looked like hobos, migrants, remnants of the dustbowl days of the Depression, but fed up on beef, fit in the big, heavy, ill way of quarrymen and labourers. They were the steel gang, laying sixty metres a day to a new mine, far beyond the Caribou Mountains. It was to be their last job working for BC Rail. That day there had been a company announcement: they'd been bought by Canadian Pacific, itself owned by a US company. Everyone knew there'd be cutbacks. No wonder they didn't seem very cheerful, celebrating their own demise. The train, when this job ended, would no longer be their home for three weeks on, two off, a rolling dormitory on great sharp-edged wagon wheels.

We stood in the sun feeling exposed, under examination. I

noticed how thin Joe and Nigel looked. Urban thin rather than the broad-shouldered, wiry skinniness of the manual worker who smokes too much. And Nigel wearing that natty Helly Hansen undervest and nifty bike-courier shades, well, I wasn't too surprised when it came down from above: 'You fuckin' tree planters or what?'

'Fucked a few,' muttered Joe under his breath.

'No,' I corrected upwards the drunken navvies from my position near the weedy tracks, sun beating down hotly. 'We are paddling a birchbark canoe from Lake Athabasca to the Pacific Ocean.' I felt like I was making a speech to quell a riot.

I explained further, squinting into the sun, but it was like talking to a barrage balloon. Almost grudgingly we were invited up. But offered no beer. The one with the moustache shook my hand. His fist was like a hard boxing glove and his face radiated aggressive pride in the handshake: you may have a college education but I got working hands. In truth I was impressed, somewhat envious, since forty-five days of paddling hadn't turned mine into anything like his. He told us, unasked, that he was thirty-nine – my age! Yikes! His face was cracked and frost-damaged beyond its years.

Somehow it all went pear-shaped and nasty, as it can with drunks. One minute you're shooting the breeze, saying stuff that's frictionless, freighted with well-intended irony, a sort of parody of small-talk but still friendly, and then it gets translated by the paranoid as a patronizing piss-take, and the next minute Big Fist growls, 'So we ain't good enough for you guys, eh? Fuckin' queens of England.'

There was an instant silence, broken only by the sound of another can being crushed flat.

'It's that shirt, Nigel.'

'Did he say Queen or queens?'

'He's Canadian,' I said, pointing to Joe.

'Half Canadian,' said Joe bravely. We were surrounded. It was like being cornered in a field by inquisitive cattle. With horns.

'Well, nice meeting you guys, we really better be heading back to the river,' I said hurriedly, working out how to get through the knot of sullen men to the ladder.

'It's a long way to the Pacific,' quipped Nigel, dropping his shades back into place from their effete position on top of his head.

'Hold on, hold on. You guys want coffee? A meal? We got plenty of food. Too much. Ain't nothing else to do out here.' A man with a big face and a lopsided grin stepped forward. 'I was born in England. Some town I forgot the name of. My family came out here when I was three. Never felt the urge to go back, but someday I might.' He was loaded but not pissed, sunburned across the width of his face, a long thin moustache hacked back from his upper lip, watery grey eyes that did not blink. Again that feeling I often had in Canada of someone having just stepped from another era, perhaps the 1950s. Bill Wirtley, friendlier than the rest, took us to the mess carriage. 'Those guys are just pissed their company got bought,' he explained.

A young guy, the youngest by far we'd seen, who looked startlingly like Brad Pitt but with severe acne scars, muscled up to us at our Formica table in the mess carriage. 'You need a hired hand?' he asked. He had big arms, work plus weights, and you could tell he always said what he thought and that other guys, even older ones, didn't fuck with him.

'How much do you get here?' I asked.

'Twenty-five an hour,' he boasted.

'Can't afford that,' I said.

'Nah, it's twenty-two ninety,' said Bill, stirring his coffee with a coffee-ringed teaspoon.

'Yeah,' said the young drunk, in his free, wanton way, 'twenty-two ninety. Twenty-three and I'll come along!' Then he howled with laughter and blundered away. Bill said nothing.

A tubby woman, like a tough old nun, trundled out to serve us spaghetti bolognese. She told us in her bass voice to 'duke it out' for the larger portion on one of the plates. Her body was like a hedgehog's in her blue and white tiny-check nylon coat. Mrs Fezziwig amongst the trolls – was she chosen so that no one would want her for sex, or, if they did, so that she could look after herself? You felt a bit mean thinking and saying such things, especially as she kindly gave us apples and extra slices of cake.

In the early-evening sun Bill walked back to the bridge with us to catch a glimpse of the canoe. He seemed glad of the excuse to talk. His life story had swaths of unexplained time in it: some logging, repairing machinery, up and down the country in the middle of dark winters, but a lot of gaps. He was married but spent much time away from home. His son lived in Arkansas with a grandchild Bill had seen only once. In return for us showing him the canoe we spent a long time with Bill fruitlessly looking for the remains of an old steam locomotive dumped in the bush by the river. 'I saw it once,' Bill kept saying, 'but that was before these trees got so high.' In the end we had to take our leave. 'This country has been good to me, damned good. I love this country,' he said as we left him, his watery grey eyes squinting in the evening sun.

V

Two days later we had our rest day and I was up first, earlier than Nigel, who usually liked to be up first, getting his alone time; well, I was getting mine. I built a star fire on the gravel of the small island where we were camped. This is the best kind of fire for one person to operate. You just feed long logs into a central flame area, no chopping or sawing needed, and with the right pot hanger it is very efficient. I took a while whittling a double hook to hang the water pot from a crossbar resting on two tripods lashed with small lengths of parachute cord. We had brought hundreds of metres of the stuff but it's never enough. That and mosquito repellent, you always run out.

The gravelly island was joined to another island, where the tents were pitched, by a logjam of great complexity. Getting from the gravel bit across to the higher, overgrown campsite involved a route over several big, slimy logs, one floating free, so it shuddered down into the water and threatened to roll if

313

you weren't off it sharpish. At night, after a whisky or two, carrying my sleeping kit, Mini-Maglite slipping around my head in its headstrap, it was an unpleasant challenge. Joe was best at it, and revelled in our floundering. Being agile was part of his self-image. He'd berate himself if he fell down towing: 'Call yourself agile?' he'd say to himself, already up and on the hop, springy and wiggy, the hacky-sack hero.

The island with our tents, connected via the logjam to the campfire island, was small, with ten-foot-high banks. It was fully covered with thornbushes, nettles and shrubs with thick, soft, light green leaves. The only space for the tents was under the single tall pine growing out of its middle.

Early in the morning I crossed the logjam and the floating rolling log several times. I got better at it and began to enjoy the challenge. If you lived here you'd get the urge to make it easier to get to where you slept, but that would be wrong. The logjam was a constant test, keeping you fit. I remembered a magazine story I once read about a private investigator in LA (who had prosthetic hands after a childhood bomb accident) who instead of stairs in his home had stainless-steel ramps which he had to run up. It was all to keep him fit. It must have been impossible in socks and he can't have had elderly relatives visiting. But I agreed with the idea: build challenges into everyday life. Making it easy ends up making it more difficult: knees seize up, backs weaken, guts sag, feet splay. I hopped on and off the log and nearly took a tumble. Got to be quicker.

The lads waded across the river to cut poles. They tried the chest waders for the first time, moving as slowly as astronauts in the fast midstream current. The river had become shallower as we got closer to the Continental Divide. I hoped poling would replace the extreme effort required by towing. I knew from experiments in the previous year that the key to a good pole is smoothness. Even the tiniest irregularity will raise a sore flapping blister between finger and thumb, making it impossible to swing the pole up and down through the hands.

It was a good way to spend a rest day, gnawing at the poles with my sharp knife, smoothing them down with the blade and finally with sand from the beach. I didn't feel healthy, I was too beaten-up for that, but I did feel content. I fed the star fire, and revelled in the limits of my world, the tiny island with its lone pine, dark green against the bright blue of the sky.

VI

It was a week since our encounter at Anzac and the sound of voices was again enticing. There were two men near a kind of jetty. They looked our way but didn't call out. This was unnerving and made us shy. The jetty was more of a pontoon, with dark rusty drums lashed with yellow rope into a frame of grey nailed wood, something to rise and fall with the river level, with a flexible ladder connecting it to the bank. It had been a good day. We had perfected a manoeuvre where the force of water moving faster over a gravel slope could be used to shift us up its furthest side. These gravel slopes were a feature of the Parsnip, causing water from one part of the river to pour downhill into another, creating anomalous back currents and eddies. At last we were getting good enough to use them.

The poles had been a success, but at some cost. It was hard, awkward work and we often got the poles tangled. When it worked, which it did in bursts, we shot along faster than either paddling or towing, but these bursts were hard to maintain. And despite all the careful work they still were not smooth enough. Next time bring along an old leather glove, I thought.

The campsites had got worse and worse as the terrain got more and more swampy. One night we pitched our tent on a hummock of low willows, a couple of feet above the river but the highest clear ground around. The jetty and the men promised a better place for camping as well as company.

'They must have seen us.'

'They were looking this way.'

'Where've they gone then?'

'Shall we go up and look?'

'Definitely.'

We didn't need to get out of the canoe because the two men came cautiously back to the jetty where their flat-fronted motorboat was moored.

'Thought you were a moose. Heard the splashing but didn't see you,' said one man who was old and broad-faced with white hair showing from under his cap. He had a generous smile. The other was smaller and slimmer with square glasses, a younger man, but hard to say his age exactly. Their manner was almost shy. They were Rick and Fred, son and father. This was their trapline cabin. They'd been coming here since 1964. 'We got a bunkhouse you want to stay in it,' said Rick, 'kind of messy though.' Better than a hummock in a nasty bog. Fred, despite his years – he was eighty – scythed a path through the long grass down to a spot where we could pull out the canoe, to again try to fix the leaks. Those leaks! I was always hopeful, like a card player receiving a new hand, that at last this would be it. But at day's end it was always the same story: water sloshing around our ankles from a leak I could never identify. Later, Joe would take over the job and was far more successful than I. I was now using a silicone sealant, which was semi-transparent, like a rubbery white sauce, setting in tiny wave-tossed blobs along the fissures and opening seams of the boat's bottom. I thought about Mackenzie and how he complained about their boat getting heavier and heavier from accumulating repairs – I could see how. I needed to dry out the canoe, strip the old seams and simply redo them, but we hadn't the time to do it. Instead I just kept adding the silicone, blob by blob, disfiguring the purity of the bark covering.

'It's ugly,' I explained to Fred, who was watching me.

'Up here I guess you have to do what works,' he said.

Fred told me about the trapping. Prices had recovered recently, after the plunge of a few years ago when anti-fur sentiment spread around the world. Bearskins fetched $150; wolf $200; lynx $200, though there were no snowshoe hares around the upper Parsnip, which meant there'd be no lynx to catch; beaver, depending on the condition, perhaps $45. Best were marten, plentiful, easy to skin, and good prices at over $75. Fred had the little boxes on leaning poles used for trapping pine marten stored at the back of the cabin.

There was a cache raised up on fifteen-foot poles for storing food and meat. Tin sheathing nailed halfway up discouraged climbers. The cache had been built in 1935. Had Indians lived here then? Fred said, 'Maybe, but they would have been poor. This isn't easy country. You saw how wet it can get. Plenty of wolves, they eat the caribou, when they get caught in the snow. And there's lots of snow here in winter. No moose around here till 1915, I heard that from one old boy, they followed the logging further downriver, where you came from. They like the open country, but a hundred years ago there were none.'

In Mackenzie's time there were Sekani Indians, 'the People of the Rocks', living here, but by 1923 the total population of this nomadic tribe was down to sixty and most of them lived around lakes further north. Mackenzie encountered only one group on the Parsnip, very close to where we now were, though they saw houses and encampments all the way through to Bad River. The Sekani were hospitable and provided a guide who later disappeared when the going got tough on Bad River. Mackenzie wrote: '[The Sekani] most hospitably resigned their beds, and the partners of them, to the solicitations of my young men.' Fred and Rick were somewhat more reserved, but kindly gave us bacon, potatoes and coffee.

Mackenzie described the Sekani as 'low in stature, not exceeding five feet six or seven inches; and they are of that meagre appearance which might be expected in a people whose life is one succession of difficulties in procuring subsistence'. The Sekani hunted summer and winter and referred contemptuously to their neighbours, the Southern Carrier Indians, as 'fish eaters', making the best of their own impoverished situation. 'There's no salmon here, not like the other side, the Fraser side. Plenty salmon even in Bad River, they say, but I never been there,' said Fred.

Bad River. Fred was the first person I'd met who knew it by that name. The toughest challenge of the trip, the place where Mackenzie almost ended his life.

'Put it this way,' said Fred: 'they don't call it Bad River for nothing. But I know people who been down it. One old prospector came through here, he did it. He was the one who told me, "They don't call it Bad River for nothing." Some Boy Scouts even tried it. But they smashed up their boats pretty bad and had to be helicoptered out. That was some years ago. The only thing I know is that there's a waterfall in the middle that you gotta avoid, even though it looks passable. That's the only thing. You'll do it.'

He smiled his benign oldtimer's smile. He trusted what little he'd seen of us and that felt good. As an afterthought he told me bears had eaten the Boy Scouts' groceries in Arctic Lake; that was before they wrecked the canoe and had to be choppered out. 'Those Boy Scouts certainly had some bad luck out here,' he mused.

VII

We left early the next day. Fred and Rick had things to do and would be leaving later. As we loaded the canoe at the jetty I saw Rick's rifle in its functional plastic olive-green case lying across the thwart in their boat. Fred and Rick were the first people we'd told about our burdensome weapon and they understood its need without any explanation. A few days before, we'd sighted it in, Joe shooting across the river at a target 150 metres away and getting his shots into a six-inch cluster.

We were at some rapids when we heard Fred and Rick's powerboat. We were walking the canoe through. It isn't always easy to gauge the ferocity of rapids at first glance. These were noisy and the river forced itself through the rocks, rising in a shining cushion in the face of any obstruction. But again the Parsnip was kind to us and there was nothing of that vicious buffeting we'd had in the Peace. Earlier I had poled while the other two paddled. This worked well, but was tiring, and my hands were wet with the fluid from ruptured blisters.

Fred called out, 'You got further than I thought you would.'

Then he and Rick waved and attacked the rapids in their boat, Fred at the helm. It was good to see an eighty-year-old man doing something difficult and not a little dangerous. They leaned forward with concentration and then they were through, one wave and then gone, into the arched greenery of the narrowing river.

We saw our first grizzly that day, a shaggy, massive bag of fur, fifty metres away, its golden-brown hindquarters in a patch of sunlight on the bank. The grizzly turned and looked at us for a moment, turned with almost languorous disdain, full of the knowledge that it was the biggest and most dangerous beast in the forest. The heaviness and confidence was discernibly different from a black bear, I felt, the brown fur rippling with the muscle underneath and the lolloping gait different from a black bear's more hurried movements.

On and on we paddled, against the current but making good time, camping on more swampy mounds and long shingle beaches carved out from the curve of the river; you could scent the mountains now, and see them closing in. It was getting exciting, we talked about gold and all the prospectors who had searched this area. Fred said he'd guided a prospector through Arctic Lake and spent a week looking for Indian caves that were rumoured to be stacked with gold nuggets. Of course we'd look out for those caves. Fred said the best he'd found had been an elongated overhang of limestone, but he twinkled, 'You guys just might get lucky.'

The river narrowed and began to loop most irresponsibly, a lazy, double-jointed snake, not wanting to get to its destination. Then it would speed up as if responding to chastisement and then back to the endless looping and looping back on itself. At least the curves were short, now the river was a mere thirty yards or less wide, not like those days on the Peace, towing for eight hours and twenty kilometres and still on one curve. We kept checking the map – well, I kept checking, looking for a tributary, as narrow as the Cherwell in Oxford, signalled Arctic Creek, the way to Arctic Lake and the Continental Divide.

For the first time under the bow you could see fish swimming away: Dolly Varden, named after the character in *Barnaby Rudge*, as Gadd's identification guide told us, rainbow trout and squawfish. Then the river forked, and the pure clarity of Arctic Creek clouded into the brown stream of the Parsníp. We saw hundreds of trout, darting like black spears in the clear, shallow-seeming depths. Nigel just had to stop and catch several, which we cooked and ate on the spot.

Nine

TOP OF THE WORLD

'We saw this day two grisly and hideous bears.' Alexander Mackenzie in the Rocky Mountains

I

On this side everything flowed north into the Arctic Ocean. In a few kilometres, everything flowed south-west into the Pacific. It was a big deal, or would be, if we could only get through the beaver dams. Arctic Creek was dammed every few hundred yards. Some were below the surface, a submerged wickerwork in the brilliant clarity of the water, others were a few inches, perhaps a foot high at most. These we tore down with feverish haste, desperate to get to our goal. These beavers were never trapped. They had it easy. They were cheeky creatures, and I could never forget that old trapper, bitten in the crotch by an infected beaver; tearing their dams down was an act of pure revenge. Like the Vietcong, they'd build them up again all too soon. Tearing down beaver dams is one of the pleasures of life, but only once or twice. After the thirteenth time it becomes a little tedious. At one dam we were covered in hundreds of strange micro-leeches, the only ones we came across on the whole trip. Nigel and Joe were the worst affected and after wiping themselves clean their backs were covered in fine dots like the red spots Van Gogh put in all his later paintings.

The last few hundred metres the creek looped back on itself several times. We paddled on over submerged logs and then there was no current, only stillness. One more turn and we

321

emerged on to the long, cold, thin stretch of water called Arctic Lake.

The mountains on each side reared up straight out of the depths and immediately acquired a covering of steeply angled spruce trees. Looking along the V of the Rocky Mountain Trench was like peering through a gunsight. I stood up in the canoe on the calm, glass-clear water and looked at a snow-covered summit in the far distance, bang in the middle of the V. *The other side*.

II

Jetboats can shoot over beaver dams and the evidence of their presence was at the spot where Mackenzie camped on Arctic Lake. 'We advanced about a mile in the lake, and took up station for the night at an old Indian encampment. Here we expected to meet with natives, but were disappointed.' We were disappointed too, but by the recent presence of people not their absence. It was a lovely spot, on a rocky promontory, marred by a fireplace full of old beer cans and broken glass and .357 pistol shells, with a dead bear, rotting, for company. The bear was lying about twenty yards from the fire, its corpse melting into itself. It had been roped off with orange forest marker tape, and written along the tape was a warning and a date, about three weeks earlier. We carried on paddling and made camp at the far end of Arctic Lake. In front of us was a slight rise of wooded land before the next narrow lake. This was the Continental Divide. It was like being at a great moment in geography, the equivalent of a momentous occasion in history – the moon landing or the fall of the Berlin Wall – we felt a sudden significance and dignity had been granted our lowly strivings.

According to Mackenzie, only 817 paces separated us from the second, Portage or Divide Lake, which drained into the Pacific. A pace is an old navigational term equal to two steps, so you always count when your right foot touches the ground. Unless you walk very slowly there isn't enough time to count every step you make. Around 600 paces makes a kilometre. I loved this fact: that little more than a kilometre was needed to cross from one continental drainage system to another; from one major river-road to another.

You can cross Canada, hence North America, by water all the way and never need walk more than thirteen miles between waterways. It was as if the whole continent were floating on a lake of water, all land merely an island between the lakes, the country really an archipelago. Perhaps that was the way to look at it, to understand the essential character of the Canadians, a nation of inland sailors, island folk all, with the quiet, weather-obsessed moodiness of island folk, populated by islanders too, Orcadians and Hebrideans like Mackenzie, and Breton Islanders who became the voyageurs.

Eight hundred and seventeen paces. From the muddy beach on Arctic Lake, up the slight rise and through rough, dense woodland to Portage Lake. It felt further. Mainly because of the killing pressure grinding my neck vertebrae together from the tumpline, an ill-advised experiment that brought out the worst in Joe and me. Tumplines are part of the genius of native peoples the world over. Sherpas use them to carry immense loads high up the glaciers of the Himalayas, a single strap around the forehead connected to a load that sits like a toted sofa flat on the bent back. In theory the tumpline is the most efficient way to carry huge loads short to medium distances over even terrain. In theory the most hi-tech rucksack, like the bloated bag carried by Joe O'Blenis (What had happened to him? Had he made it? Was he still going? Or had he been eaten or sunk? We'd find out), is but a knapsack compared to those supported by the mighty tumpline. I'd taken care to discover how the voyageurs used their tumplines to carry the 90lb pieces. I had brought especially several old rucksack straps, to make the forehead bit more padded. This would be looped through a rope holding together several kitbags. It should have worked, but it didn't. The tumpline was a killer. There was a worn path but the ground was uneven and we were lashed by wet tree branches, and after five hundred metres (How far to go? How far?) I felt I was doing permanent damage to my spinal cord. I felt an inch shorter with a headache precisely located beneath the sweat-making tump pad around my head. Nigel, too, looked a bit ill. But in a show of true loyalty that would never be forgotten, he assumed the terrible burden of the tumpline without even a murmur of complaint, and you can't count 'Looks a little unstable to me' as a complaint.

But not Joe.

'That's a bloody stupid idea.'

'No, it isn't. A billion indigenous peoples can't be wrong.'

'Why not just carry them? It isn't far.'

'The path's too narrow,' I improvised. 'Besides, that's not the point.'

He stamped his foot into the mud, at least it seemed as petulant as that, but worse, he had a point. The tumplines were a fiasco, but without trying how would we know? He knew by just looking, but I needed to find out for sure. A billion indigenous peoples can't be wrong, can they? No, but the fault was in the loading, the hasty contrivance of straps and bags, not in the idea itself. I knew that, but Joe didn't. He hadn't read Mackenzie (on a page I hadn't photocopied and brought along): 'The voyageurs are frequently obliged to unload their canoes, and carry the goods upon their backs, or rather suspended in slings from their heads.' He hadn't seen that documentary on Nepal. And, of course, he'd never read *The New Way of the Wilderness* by Calvin Rutstrum: 'Your neck muscles are stronger than you realize and with continued tumpline packing they will develop greater strength. Special feats of 400- and 500-pound carries are known, but these are exceptional.'

Rutstrum recommended no more than two hundred pounds for a beginner. Nigel and I soldiered through the bush feeling shorter by the minute, with Joe glowering beside us, his arms full of loose bags. Then we were clear, at Portage Lake, a narrow mirror between mountain peaks, and his mood cleared like the sky clearing of cloud. Downhill all the way.

III

In amongst the logs floating in the next lake the water was stagnant and patterned with what looked like detergent froth. I would have put it down to some chemical spillage, perhaps from a float plane. One crashed in Portage Lake twenty years ago and as we paddled over the still, clear depths we looked down to see if we could catch a glimpse of its broken fuselage and mangled wings, imagining we saw a glimpse of something shining in amongst the bearded black-green of submerged boughs.

The rock side walls of the lake dived into the looking-glass water. The rock bent at an exact refractive angle as it went far, far down. Cemented into the rock was a bronze plaque. We paddled towards it, breaking the mirror surface with our paddle-strokes. The plaque had a jaunty propeller insignia engraved above the writing. It read:

FRED J. FENDELET 1933–83

PLANE CRASH JUNE 3 1983

The thin lake, alpine and deep, now also a watery grave, seemed to sum up a contest between man and the wilderness, and in this place the wilderness triumphed. You felt sorry for man and his pathetic contrivances. Nature was on top here and I felt it always would be. No need for our usual concern, for the wilderness and how we were going to muck it up with our machines.

But the froth was more ancient than the crash. Mackenzie wrote about Portage Lake: 'On the edge of the water we observed a large quantity of thick, yellow scum or froth, of an acrid taste and smell.' We didn't taste it, but it still smelled acrid two hundred years on.

IV

Rest break on Portage Lake. Bannock spread with honey from Guy and Mary. Joe can't resist. 'Don't dip,' I say.

We argue about dipping. He feels he has a 'right to dip'.

'Do you see me dipping?' I say. 'Or Nigel?' Where will it end? Dipping is the thin end of the wedge.

'There's loads of honey,' he says. 'Too much.'

'Then we'll glut out on it when we arrive.'

'What's the point of that?'

'Look, I'm the fucking leader and if I say dipping is banned, then dipping is banned.'

'It's a free country.'

'No, it's a wild country. That's why . . .'

Dipping honey. Dipping defiantly. Thin end of the wedge. Makes me mad though it shouldn't. And he knows it.

To enter Pacific Lake from Portage Lake, the third and last before 'the Bad', required a sustained lifting of the canoe, empty, over a barrage of logs. We got good at sawing off the nub end of branches to make a smooth place to slide the canoe over. I was glad we all had folding saws (we'd had one the year before, now we had three), essential for quick pruning of logs and, on the portage trail, of small bushes and branches. We also had the large Swede saw given to us by Danny, Warren's dad, but we had yet to use it. It sat, upturned, with a duct-tape guard over its wolf-like teeth, good back-up, a kind of insurance against the '200 logs across the river not counting the log jams' Ben Ferrier had written were on the Bad River.

Ten

BAD RIVER

'The Indians, when they saw our deplorable situation, instead of making the least effort to help us, sat down and gave vent to their tears.' Alexander Mackenzie on the Bad River

I

A family of otters barred our way, or was it the same otter showing its head three times, a rodent Cerberus guarding the entrance? For this was the entrance to the Bad River.

The otter, with its intelligent eyes, much more intelligent-looking than a beaver, popped up and chirruped, as loud and aggressive as those small kids on trikes with horns demanding passage on the pavement. Shouldn't it be afraid? We were, after the bears and maybe the moose, the alpha predators. Weren't we? Then another popped up – or was it the same one? Its head fur wet and streaked into ridges as if wearing hair gel. And then another. The eyes were all the same. Beady, cocky, defending their turf. We were all out of the canoe, swimming it through the barrier of submerged logs that guarded Bad River, hundreds of small silvery fish swimming around our legs. It was chest-deep water and even in waders you felt vulnerable. The otters were charming and threatening in equal measure. I mean wouldn't an otter nip be of the same order as a beaver bite? And who could forget old Pen Powell, lying on his back on the roadway bleeding almost to death from his incised underparts?

We'd crossed the divide. It was downhill all the way. 'It's downhill all the way, lads,' I said, far too often, and they looked at me with the bemused tolerance the insane must become used to, at least before they get locked up.

Downhill all the way. And it looked downhill. We scouted the first few hundred metres of the Bad and you could see the river floor dropping away, you could feel yourself walking downhill, it was a ramp, for goodness' sake, a stone-laden ramp running with water like a weir or one of those fancy water displays cooked up by architects. 'The Bad' dropped like a stone and tomorrow we would too.

II

At first the river spread out into many small streams that ran under overhanging bushes, some of the streams no wider than a metre. It was shallow and we hit bottom as we manhandled the boat around corners of golden shingle. Meltwater, cascading down both sides of the valley, quickly swelled the river. We walked the boat through the deepening fast water, siwashing from time to time, a risky technique where you hang on to the boat and float along with it, touching ground when you can, fending off as you go. We all wore our Neoprene waders with knives strapped to our bib braces, ready to cut a hole and release the trapped air if we'd flipped upside down. The Bad River was a different world, a narrow canyon of limestone cliffs with waterfalls plastered to the sides so big and high up the water looked like something white merely adhering to the rock, a kind of huge quartz vein. The air was damp through and the vegetation thick on each bank. We were in a long dark stretch when I looked up from the constant preoccupation of the river's run, the polished pebbles and which was the least shallow part, to see a grizzly. 'Bear!' I shouted and reached for the horn. It went up the bank like a teenage criminal surprised and outwitted, but when I fired the horn it stopped and took another look. I doubt if it had ever heard a marine alarm horn before and it was intrigued. The wrong reaction. I remembered something Gil, Herb's son, said: 'Bang pots and pans together. They know the sound and know it means trouble. That air horn might be just too interesting to scare them.'

This grizzly really reminded me of a young offender. It knew we were trouble but it didn't want to show it was scared. It gave us a long stare after the surprised leap up the bank of dry earth, like a heavyweight boxer doing something fast – it was surprising, the power under the loose fur, like something dangerous and out of place, like a riot or a natural disaster. Bears were too damn big and dangerous for the modern world. They didn't fit in. The modern world is supposed to be neutered and rendered safe for modern man. You get to thinking: How come bears are allowed?

As the juvenile-delinquent bear eyeballed us, Joe rattled away at the bolt of the rifle. We were ready all right, or so it seemed. The bear stayed long enough for the insolence to be apparent and then loped off. We were all of a twitter then, extra careful watching the steep greenery-covered banks, scanning the meltwater shadows of the stream ahead, on the lookout for the next one.

Also, how can a bear get so big just eating berries and leaves? Admittedly they rip off whole branches and stuff them into their mouths, rather than delicate single-berry exploitation, which is the human preference. Still, it just doesn't seem there's enough food out there for something so huge. Bears eat meat too: careless moose calves, carrion, wounded wolves and deer. But they're not like lions and tigers, whose bulk seems justified by their carnivorous diet. Elephants, I suppose, are vegetarian, but they are tameable and certainly not feared. The bear is different. There is something perplexing about his presence in the woods, yet his being there is what gives the northern forests their edge, the wildness you don't get in Europe. Being in bear country is like constantly patrolling through a bad neighbourhood. You're alert and not entirely relaxed. You don't want to wander around losing yourself. It's not Wordsworth country. In such circumstances you are always glad to have others around, especially if they are armed. And when you come out of bear country you feel you've been somewhere special and worth visiting.

III

We managed about three hundred metres of paddling, in a dark deep stretch of the Bad, before it became knee-deep and shallow again. Often there were deeper runnels under the alder branches at the side. We would run the canoe under these, all of us along one side, keeping hold against the rush of water going down, always down. It was incredible the way the river fell away in front of us. To find the best water-path was an art. The key was not thinking too much. Go on instinct. Big standing waves didn't always mean big boulders; sometimes riding the bubble of a wave was the best way through, as long as the gap was wide enough. When the going got too shallow we all hefted a pack and waddled uncertainly like decrepit, overweight Ninja Turtles, minding the lightened canoe, riding high and empty. One rucksack was the most loathed. It had the barest of internal stiffening and, because of that, all the weight was on the shoulders rather than the waist. It didn't help that it had over a hundred pounds of gear and food in it. When we came to an extra-shallow part there was a subtle jockeying for position to make sure you weren't standing next to the killer pack.

Some logs were just high enough above the water for us to be able to duck the canoe down, whale on its natural buoyancy and get first the raised prow and then the stern under the log barrier. But some logs blocked all passage. Again and again we unloaded, emptied the canoe of water – more leaks now we were taking hits all the time in the shallow water – and lifted the big boat up and over the log. We became fetishistic about trimming away all conceivable branches and nub ends that might puncture the bark as we humped it over.

And then it would be back to the gist of the thing, spotting the best route and going for it, taking the inside curve, since the brutal outside edge was always a deep, driftwood-infested sharp turn, with the current pounding into the stuck wood. Lose it on a corner and the canoe would be firewood, pressed side-on to the evil prongs of stuck lumber and a pounding current. That was why we preferred to walk, in the end; there were just too many nasty surprises to want to take any corner blindly.

IV

We camped halfway, maybe nine kilometres along the Bad, at Round Lake, unnamed on the map but referred to by Mackenzie. This lake had a marvellous serenity. Round Lake, protected by innumerable logjams and shallow rapids, was impregnable. No motorboat of any kind has ever visited Round Lake. I had the lovely, comforting feeling that it had not changed in two hundred years, nor would it in the next two hundred. The valley sides were too steep for logging and the river would never be accessible to motorized craft. Anywhere that is too difficult for powered craft is safe – mountains, swampy jungle, remote islands beyond the reach of a Sunseeker's fuel tank, these are the truly protected places.

Just after Round Lake the Bad got bad very quickly. Bad and deep and fast. You could see how Mackenzie got into trouble:

Notwithstanding all our exertions, the violence of the current was so great as to drive her sideways down the river, and break her by the first bar, when I instantly jumped into the water ... at this moment the foreman seized on some branches of a small tree in the hope of bringing up the canoe but such was their elasticity that, in a manner not easily described, he was jerked on shore in an instant and with a degree of violence that threatened his destruction. But we had no time to turn from our own situation to inquire what had befallen him; for, in a few moments, we came across a cascade which broke several large holes in the bottom of the canoe ... In this condition we were forced several hundred yards and every yard on the verge of destruction, but at length we most fortunately arrived in shallow water and a small eddy ... I was in a state of great pain from the extreme cold of the water, [and] it was

331

with difficulty I could stand from the benumbed state of my limbs.

The river was too wild and too narrow for a big canoe; catch the current side-on and you'd be whipping along as vulnerable as a fluorescent light tube in a sword fight. Often one of us would lose his footing and be hanging on to the gunwhales by his fingertips, clinging on like a tadpole until shallower water was reached. Then it would get ankle-deep almost immediately and you'd feel the sudden pull of gravity as you surged up from the water. The canoe would be bumped increasing callously across shallows and then back into deep, fast, thick current again. In one tumbling area of rock corners and boulders, I lost my footing and so did Nigel. Only Joe still had a handhold on the porous limestone cliff. He wasn't an over-strong guy but he held on, his face creased in concentration, whilst Nigel and I struggled to find anything to stand on. In front was a boulder as big as a house, impossible to miss if we lost control, dry grass and drift-wood broken across its front, a big wave rising in front of it like a swollen lip. But Joe held on.

Mackenzie's canoe was a wreck. 'A rock shattered the stern of the canoe in such a manner that it held only by the gunwhales,' he wrote. He gave the men a pep talk. 'I then addressed them, by recommending them all to be thankful for their late very narrow escape ... Nor did I fail to mention the courage and resolution that was the peculiar boast of the North men ... I confided their skill and exertion could put the canoe in such a state that would carry us on to where we might procure bark and build a new one.' It took some doing but he persuaded the men and they set about repairing the canoe. It took three days. They had dried out all their trade goods, those that had not been swept away, even laying out the gunpowder in the sun. That almost caused another disaster when one chain-smoking voyageur emptied his pipe on the distributed powder, but it didn't explode.

The river was getting deeper and rougher and the rocks were slippery with green algae. The water was cold, but because of the secret weapon of the waders it was bearable. The sun shone, though much of the river was in shade. On a sketch-map we had been given long ago by Adèle Boucher, the historian, there was supposed to be a 'boulder garden' somewhere in this stretch of the river. 'Let's scout ahead,' I said. Nigel looked at me and, unusually for him, ventured a contrary opinion: 'Shall we just give it a go?'

I knew what he meant. We'd been taking the river by storm. Dealing with everything it had thrown at us. We had our momentum. Pity to lose it. But I remembered Fred's warning. I guessed how far we had come and thought about that waterfall, the one the Boy Scouts wrecked themselves upon, and I calculated from Mackenzie's journal that he had portaged at about this point.

Nigel stood waist-deep in the stream, holding the nose of the canoe while Joe and I went on ahead, scrambling over the giant blocks of rock that littered the downstream banks. The valley was steep-sided. There was no way to sneak the boat along the bank, close in, away from the pounding current. Joe and I climbed up the tree-covered slope and found a path. It was an old path, well worn. It went into the woods leaving the river on one side. Then the path curved back and we were standing forty feet above the water, looking down a cliff at the river still agitated and swirling after its passage through the falls. For this is what they were. We skidded down the bank and went across the massive boulders to see just how much of a garden the boulder garden was. Our boat would have been wrecked for sure. It was a narrow canyon with a series of twelve-foot drops, water in white, gushing spumes between black water-hollowed boulders. If Fred had not warned me about the falls our trip would have ended here.

The portage trail was almost certainly the same one used by Mackenzie. But the trail was still clear because of animals, not men. A couple of trees had fallen, but a way had been found around them. Moose and bear were the original makers of portage trails: they are as unwilling and unable as men to scramble down a canyon pounding with water. The perfect system of waterways and portage trails across Canada existed before man arrived, and is maintained even though man has given up, in many places, using the river for long-distance travel. This was the proof. The forest here grew like jungle. Perhaps five or six people had been through in the last ten years, perhaps fewer. But the path was clear, well worn, easy to follow. It was animals, skirting the falls and the boulders below, that kept it this way. It was a comforting discovery. It meant that, however bad the river got, there would always be an escape. Later we'd discover the exception to this rule, but at the time it was immensely heartening.

Now all we had to do was haul the canoe up the slope, along the trail and somehow lower it down the cliff.

We flattened bushes, sawed off the projections from fallen logs, pulled up sprouting alders and speared ourselves on devil's club, fleshy prickly leaves that sprang forward like some trap perfected by the Vietcong. It was fifty feet up a steep slope to the path. After we had made the trail we unloaded the boat and carried everything to the top. Then we hauled the boat, all three of us lifting, one running forward while the other two held it, sliding lifejackets on to logs as protection, sliding back, but slowly, slowly, getting up that hill. The boat was wet and heavy and it was hard work. The sun was hot and the mosquitoes hung over the path in whining invisibility, coming out of the shade in squadrons, aiming for any pale exposed piece of flesh. It was enough work for one day.

V

I had no idea how we would get the canoe down the collapsing cliff at the other end. We slept at the top, almost on the path, which is never an advisable thing to do when you know it is used by bear and moose. I caught Joe pissing on the path just before we turned in. I had been about to do the same thing. Let the creatures know we were there. By morning we had a plan: we clothed the cliff with three tarpaulins to protect the bottom of the canoe. I tied myself to a tree and used the other end of the rope to lower the canoe over the cliff-edge. Halfway down, where the cliff had some hand- and footholds, Joe and Nigel helped guide it down.

Now it was rougher and deeper than before, but we had more confidence. We had passed the spot where Mackenzie's boat had been smashed up, and we had passed the waterfall, but we were still careful. The Bad River wasn't sneaky with its strength, like the Peace; it was just all coiled up and nasty like a naughty kid with too much energy. There was no malice in it, as long as you didn't trust it an inch. One of the main problems was the size of the boat and its fragility. A short plastic boat could have been humped over stones and logs much more easily and, being shorter, could have made the hairpin turns without so much risk of being caught side-on to the pounding water.

Swimming, bumping, dragging. Almost smashing her going over scooped-out boulders running with water. Some logs we could squeeze under. But then some logs were exposed when they would have been underwater if the river had been higher. In many places there was only just enough water to float the canoe. And I knew that less water didn't always mean less force in the current. Sometimes the more water there is the slower it goes. And it's the bottom of a river that's dangerous, not the top.

We had our lunch on a curve of sand, perhaps two kilometres, I guessed, from where the Bad River joined the Herrick, Mackenzie's 'Great River'. The Bad now divided into two or three streams, each blocked solid with fallen wood. Solid. This was the point where tired and injured Ben Ferrier gave up. I didn't blame him at all. The last two kilometres of the Bad were as choked as a beaver dam. And the logs were big. We couldn't cut our way through. It would have to be lifting up and ducking under all the way with a whipping current to further hinder us. There had to be a simpler solution.

Nigel contemplated the deep pools of water under the tangle of logs. Unfished pools, you could see the fish, big and nosing about in the shadows. He caught three big trout for lunch, then

Joe caught one and so did I. The river might have been blocked but we wouldn't starve.

Opposite us, on the other side of the river, it looked as if a path went up the bank. It looked inviting, perhaps it was an animal trail that skirted the worst of Bad River. If so, Mackenzie had missed it in 1793.

Bad River had been blocked for the last 210 years. Mackenzie's solution had been to cut a laborious trail to the Herrick a little lower down. 'We could proceed no further, from the various small unnavigable channels into which the river branched in every direction; and no other mode of getting forward now remained for us but by cutting a road across a neck of land.' I knew that Mackenzie's road would not remain. Not unless animals kept it open. But that was what we were looking at on the opposite bank. Full of optimism we decided the path opposite was a natural portage trail that Mackenzie had missed.

On the map it was a little less than a mile, 1,000 paces at most, it sounded so simple. Nigel and I were so confident we gave Joe, who stayed behind, the distinct impression we'd be back in about half an hour. We didn't say so exactly, it was more what we didn't say, the casualness of our leaving, and it was only through force of habit that I had the compass and the GPS with me. Joe said he'd bake us some biscuits for when we got back.

Once in the forest, the path climbed steeply then plunged into a bog full of giant fallen trees, a damp, dark world where a man is dwarfed by the root plate of a giant tree, where even jumping down from a log is quite hazardous because you are so high up, where the logs are so long they bridge whole gulleys, even small valleys, and you find you are fifty feet from the ground, surrounded by the half-light of the jungle and the noises of animals departing. The path disappeared completely. We started to walk on a compass bearing, but a lazy bearing, checked from time to time without any real steeliness of purpose. It was almost due east we had to head – what could be easier? Soon, however, we were absolutely lost. We blundered on, bolstered by a sense of the impossibility of really being lost. We crossed several marshy streams. At last I had to admit we really were lost and tried to take a GPS reading. But the thing wouldn't work, the tree cover was too dense. On we blundered. We had been going now for an hour, far too long for a walk of a mile, less than a mile. And of course there was no sign of any trail.

Another hour and we came upon a loggy twisting stream that looked like the Bad River. We knew nothing better than to follow it downstream. After fifteen minutes we arrived at the glorious sight of 'Great River', which, compared to the piddling, noisy, little Bad River, it really is. The Herrick must be a quarter of a kilometre wide at that point with not an obstruction in sight. It offers a sudden wide openness we hadn't seen since the Peace. You could see mountains in three directions, snow on the upper slopes, caught in the afternoon light. We walked up the side of the Herrick looking for the exit point of any portage trail. There was none.

'Well, it's simple enough,' I said. 'We'll walk back. This time let's count our paces. You count and I'll watch the compass.'

After what seemed like an hour of stumbling over roots, being hit in the face by devil's clubs, wading through bogs, I asked Nigel how many paces. He turned, his face smeared with mud, the whites of his eyes accentuating the sense of concern we both felt.

'Three hundred and fifty-seven.'

'Is that all?'

We increased our pace. We wanted to get home now, no mucking about. No mucking about. We wanted Joe's biscuits and a nice cup of tea. At such times, you think that upping your own sense of purpose will mysteriously be communicated to the natural world, as if it will now say, 'OK, enough pissing these boys about, let them get home. To their nice cup of tea and home-made oatmeal and honey biscuits.' You actually think that, for the next six hundred paces or so.

'We should be there by now. How many paces?'

'About two thousand.'

'Did you lose count?'

'A bit. In that marsh.'

The marsh. Mackenzie recorded going thigh-deep in the very

same piece of bog, at least I was fairly sure it was the same bog. In fact I wasn't sure at all. We were really lost, a state of mind that seemed unjustly forced on us; after all we knew where we were, didn't we? In the boggy bit, which was a meadow, long and thin, cut through with a sluggish stream (unmarked), I took a GPS reading and found we were way off to the east. That explained it. Half an hour later we found ourselves at the top of a hill. We hadn't really wanted to climb it, but there had been a path, a slight apology of a path, which looked promising and then turned up and up. It was a relief at least not to be scrambling up and over the downed monster spruces and cottonwoods, but where had this hill come from?

Then it began. I saw a stump, huge and rotten, spilling its soft white wood, like a stump of a giant's tooth. 'I know that stump,' I said to Nigel, who looked half convinced. But knowing the stump was little use because we were soon again in unfamiliar country, riven with gulleys and pools of dank water. I noticed several tears in my trousers, inflicted by thorns, and thought of Mackenzie's comment after he was lost at the other end of the Parsnip: 'our clothes in tatters'. I knew what he meant, ours were going the same way.

'Did I ever tell you that story, about the sister of my cousin's wife who got lost trying to sneak across the border from Canada to America?'

'Yes,' said Nigel.

'They let her out on the Canadian side and all she had to do was cross a loop of land, two hundred metres across, to get to the American side. She never arrived. They waited and waited and eventually went to the border guards and admitted what they were trying to do.'

'I remember, you said,' said Nigel, but with a nod, wanting me to continue this ritual retelling.

'They sent out a search party and found nothing. Three weeks later a hunter out in the woods found her body in a ravine, miles from the road, her leg broken. Two hundred metres. That's all it takes.'

We'd been gone three hours. It would be dark in another two.

'Wonder what Joe's doing?' said Nigel, reading my mind.

'I just hope he doesn't panic,' I said. 'If he makes a call to the ... the police or whatever, then we'll really be stuffed.'

Suddenly the sat phone became a liability rather than a benefit. If Joe got 'sketched out' he might just panic and make an ill-advised call, maybe to Warren or Guy and Mary. That's how things get out of hand. I thought of the rumours of our demise in the first year when they found Sota wandering in the bush. If they called out a chopper we'd be stuck for the bill – what was it? $850 an hour plus fuel, and those things just drink fuel. Please don't panic, Joe. Please don't make an ill-advised phone call, even to your mother.

OK, I thought, we may have to spend the night out here. Find our way back in the morning. As long as he doesn't panic, we'll be all right.

I told Nigel we might have to spend the night out. Without prompting, he said, 'I hope Joe doesn't panic and phone anyone.'

By now there was little semblance of defined roles, navigator and navigated. Nigel and I conferred over everything, over the instruments and over the tiny segment of the map pinpricked with GPS readings. We spent an age trying to work out if we should add or subtract the compass deviation. It seemed immensely hard, like trying to do sums at high altitude, like those experiments in decompression chambers where the subjects in white T-shirts just get slower and slower and slower and laugh maniacally at the obvious mistakes. Getting lost in the real wilderness is like having hypothermia: you just can't think straight, however hard you try; indeed, the harder you try, the harder it is.

Nigel said, 'In situations like this my dad always says, "Let's go back to basics. What are we absolutely certain of?"'

Thank God for Nigel's dad. I thought of him, a former businessman, stalwart and sturdy, just what we needed. Back to basics.

'We know we're in this area.' I drew a circle around all the GPS readings I'd managed to make.

'And we know that wherever we are in this area, if we go west we will hit Bad River.'

'We also know that, for some reason, we keep straying off a compass bearing.'

I had already doubted the compass's accuracy, the fact that we might be on a hill of iron ore, the fact that global warming might have inadvertently caused a polar reversal without us noticing. And then there was the deviation. Add or subtract? It seemed so hard.

'OK, forget the compass. Water runs downhill. Let's follow this stream until it runs into Bad River.'

We followed the stream through thick and thin until it disappeared down a dark, mossy hole and was gone.

'I've just thought,' I said: 'if we've got ourselves into another valley then following a stream won't be any use. It will just take us further away.'

We digested this fact. Then I blew the bearhorn. Several times. The immense noise faded into nothing, leaving the vegetation greener, more overwhelming and darker. It was getting darker, the sun low in the trees.

Suddenly there was a scream. Right in front of us, coming from a wall of shrubs and bushes and thin trees. A scream like a baby, no worse, like a high-pitched bird being strangled.

'What the fuck is that?' said Nigel, grinning with apprehension.

'Is it a bird?'

'Or a wolverine?'

'Wolverines can tear the face off a grizzly.'

We both grinned, keeping fear at bay with an even greater fear of appearing fearful. We approached the scream and the bush it came from but it stopped. There was a rustling sound. We walked on and through the bushes but there was nothing.

'Probably a bird.'

'Or a wolverine.'

'Or a baby wolverine.'

'Or Joe.'

'Do you think he's made those biscuits?'

'He'll have eaten the lot by now.'

340

'For sure.'

'JOE!' I shouted at the top of my voice. You've reached a certain stage of being lost when you resort to yelling. It takes quite a lot for a man to admit he's so lost he needs help.

We passed the stump again. 'Is that that stump again?'

'I'm not sure.'

'I'm sure it is.'

But just like before we were soon in alien territory, this time characterized by logfall over logfall, encouraging us to climb higher and higher, way off the ground, tempted by one tree trunk leading to another. Finally, almost at the canopy, I heard a sound. Running water. Real running water. Gallons of running water, not a feeble stream. Bad River.

'You hear that?'

'Yeah. Water.'

'Let's go towards it.'

But even that wasn't easy. Noise is deflected and messed about in the woods. You take a fix on the sound and then you lose it.

'That is definitely that stump again.'

'You're right.'

This time we were going downhill, down and down.

'JOE!' I shouted. 'JOE! JOE!'

And then the most wonderful sound in the world. Piping and small and far away. 'Over here! I'm over here!'

We were about thirty yards from Bad River.

VI

'I did think about phoning,' admitted Joe. 'But who? I finished making the biscuits and then I went into the woods looking for you. I went for ages. I even fired the gun twice.'

'Never heard it. Did you hear the horn?'

'No.'

It was time to make a plan. The forest seemed impassable. We would attempt to follow the river through the logjams to the Herrick. At least you can't get lost following a river.

Actually, you can, if it divides into separate channels. We used red marker tape every time it wasn't a hundred per cent obvious which way to go. It looked like vandalism, all that plastic hanging from tree trunks, but it was better than being lost.

If we unloaded the canoe and carried all the gear to the big river we might just be able to get the canoe over all the logjams. This idea lasted for about fifty metres. With Steve it might just have been possible. Even then, there were stretches of water that were viciously fast and too deep to wade. You'd really have to watch the boat in that stuff. Another fifty metres convinced me that the river route was impassable. We carried on, hoping things would get better, but they got worse. We chopped and waded and climbed and hacked our way the last two kilometres to the Herrick, not believing the big river would be there. But it was, huge, fast-flowing, wide, log-free. Waiting to whisk us away. Downriver, no problem. Except getting there.

We struggled back to the camp. It was becoming a familiar place, that curve of sand faced by a steep bank and the forest. It was time for another plan.

'Let's scout a way through the woods, but lower down,' I suggested. 'Nearer to where Mackenzie did it.'

'What, through that marsh?' said Nigel.

'I had a poke around while you were gone,' said Joe. 'It's like the Lost World in there.'

'Let's just see. Mackenzie cut a trail through there. We ought to be able to.'

No one was convinced, but no one wanted to attempt the logjammed river either. We set off after lunch, feeling down. I can remember how depressed and hopeless I felt. Balancing along a log, I thought, I don't care if I fall off, and then started to tumble. Joe grabbed my arm. That was lucky, nearly ten feet into a murky mess of logs and water. The log came to an end and instead of climbing down Joe jumped. I didn't see what happened but I heard the cry of pain.

His face was shut into itself, into the front of his chest, he was crying from the pain, screwing his face up, his foot half in and half out of a clear gravel pool of water. We got his boot off but no matter how gentle we were it was agony for him. When we got down to the sock his ankle was already as big as a melon. I really didn't want to see what was under the sock, but when we looked it was just swollen, with a great black bruise under the ankle-bone. Higher up his leg the swelling was white and bulbous with red marks where the top of the sock had bitten in. He could move it, a little, though there was pain. It was impossible to even imagine putting weight on it.

'I'm out of the trip,' said Joe simply, with tears in his eyes.

'It's not broken,' I said, though I wasn't sure.

'I'm out of the trip,' he repeated.

All hostility was gone. Nigel and I carried Joe back to the camp. Joe was thinking ahead when he said he was out of the trip. He was thinking ahead to the walk, 350km across the inland Plateau of British Columbia. But I was thinking about now. We would have to carry him to the Herrick. And there was no way he could be carried over all those logjams. And there was no way two of us could get the boat through the last two kilometres of Bad River. Loaded or unloaded. We were stuck. In the remotest spot. Bad River. Good name, that.

It was at this point that the Sekani guide ran away while Mr Mackay was supposed to be watching. Mackenzie noted severely, 'Mr Mackay, with whom I was displeased on this occasion, went in search of him but he had made his escape.' There had been a suggestion that they dump the canoe and simply find their way to the 'Great River', i.e., the Fraser, but Mackenzie, rarely for him, provides an insight into his cautious, canny approach: 'It was rather a general wish that the wreck should be abandoned, and all the lading carried to the river ... This project seemed not to promise the certainty to which I looked in my present operations ...' Mackenzie never chose a dramatic solution to a problem if a more cautious solution was possible.

Without a guide they scouted their way to the end of the Bad then hacked their way and portaged the canoe through the bush to the 'Great River'. I re-read the relevant section in his journal:

This journey was three quarters of a mile East-North-East, through a continued swamp, where, in many places, we waded up to the middle of our thighs ... At length we enjoyed, after all our toil and anxiety, the inexpressible satisfaction of finding ourselves on the bank of a navigable river, on the West side of the first great range of mountains.

There had to be a way.

VII

Nigel and I left Joe with his foot up on a roll of birchbark, his face still screwed up with pain. In camp all the confusion over the compass had been easy to sort out. We would march on a bearing of east-north-east through the continual swamp. So that there was not the slightest chance of getting lost again, we took a roll of marking tape.

Nigel walked ten yards into the bush and disappeared. 'Move left a bit,' I called. 'OK, that's fine.' He was exactly where the bearing said he should be. I walked up to him and then he walked another ten yards and tied a marker to a tree branch. I checked his position and again caught up with him. Joe was right. It was like the Lost World – a mass of downed trees and deep rivulets – but only at the beginning. Quite soon the terrain evened out. And so we continued.

I saw why we got lost. You go round a tree because it's in the way. You think you can remember the direction you were formerly going in and so you don't check. You can be off by thirty degrees and not even notice, especially if the sun isn't shining and the land is flat. And anyway, when you're lost you don't notice the more subtle direction markers anyway. Thirty degrees for every tree or log or marsh you skirt, very soon you can be heading in exactly the wrong direction and it still feels fine.

Nigel walked on, ten or fifteen yards at a time, and this time we knew we were on the right bearing. Sometimes I felt we *must* be going off course – we seemed to have completely changed direction – but I trusted the compass and returned us to the path it showed. And though it surprised both of us we arrived at the Great River. The way had been swampy, but only in parts. We'd waded across two streams, but they had not been very deep. There had been no more than eight or nine fallen trees to cross. If we could cut a path we could do it. So, with axe, knife and saw we retraced our steps, taking great pleasure in hacking at everything in our way. We cut and slashed and hammered and heaved logs, taking out our frustrations on the ever-encroaching green of the forest. Anyone who doesn't like cutting trees down in the bush just hasn't spent long enough there. And quite by chance we found a dry streambed that made a short cut past all the fallen trees at the start.

By nightfall we were back at the camp. 'It's a pretty damn good path,' I said, trying to cheer up Joe. He made a downturned smile. It was decided that Nigel and I would carry the canoe and all the gear the next day and then carry Joe. He was trying to be optimistic. 'If we make it to the Herrick I've got at least ten days before we have to start walking, it will have healed by then.'

'I've seen injuries worse than that heal in a week. If you have to walk on it you will.' I meant what I said but I was referring to injuries I'd seen in martial arts in Japan; I never mentioned the pain that had to be endured, nor the permanent immobility and swelling that often resulted. We still didn't know if any of his small foot bones were broken or if it was simply the ligaments and tendons that had been damaged.

VIII

The day of the big portage, we carried all the bags through first. No tumplines, just back and forth with monstrously heavy packs. Joe put on his waders and some Neoprene gloves and heroically started dragging himself along the path on his hands and knees. On a return trip I saw his grimacing face appearing at knee height from a bog. 'I'm returning to my primeval state,' he whispered, and slithered past me like one of the limbless beggars you see in India. We left the canoe until last. We had never carried it so far with just two of us, but we were stronger now, and the canoe had been drying for a day and a half.

And slowly, pace by faltering pace, we lugged that canoe over bogs and fallen logs and up muddy slopes and across stony streams until we got it to the big river.

It seemed incredible that the hardest part of the journey was over. Then I remembered what I'd been thinking the day Steve lost his thumb – exactly the same thought: Incredible that we've beaten the Peace River. Never, ever count your chickens.

We drank coffee and looked at the light green water spread out in front of us and into the far distance.

'It was a bad river,' mused Nigel, 'but it wasn't the *worst* river.'

Joe looked as if he was going to say something, but he just poured himself more coffee from his stretched-out seated position by the fire. The water in front looked like freedom. Downhill all the way. Really, this time. Downhill all the way.

Mackenzie doesn't always hit the right sentiment, but here he did: 'the inexpressible satisfaction of finding ourselves on the bank of a navigable river, on the West side of the first great range of mountains'.

Eleven

DOWN THE FRASER
WITHOUT A PADDLE

*'They believe, that immediately after their death,
they pass into another world, where they arrive at
a large river, on wich they embark in a stone canoe,
and a gentle current bears them to an extensive
lake.'* Alexander Mackenzie on Chipewyan beliefs about the
afterlife

I

We'd been on the big river about an hour, enjoying the effortless
sensation of descending with a fast current. But then it got a
little too fast. Joe put his paddle down and fought his way into
a lifejacket. He was muttering to himself, 'Sketchy, way too
sketchy.' I could see what he meant. The standing waves in the
MacGregor Canyon looked horrific, like the slavering teeth of
something alive – and they were coming towards us! One of the
things about going downstream, which was new to us, as
opposed to upstream, our familiar mode, was that even doing
nothing you were doing something, and with a seven- or eight-
mile-an-hour current you were doing something fast. It confused
any notion of direction finding. Going upstream, if you're
approaching danger you stop paddling and the danger recedes.
To move past it you have to paddle. Paddling hard becomes the
instinctive get-out-of-trouble-now response. But going downstream, paddling hard is blunted by the fact that the current is
still sweeping you along. You feel that moving sideways is harder,
an illusion caused by the onward sweep of the boat. Instead you

have to learn how to *not paddle*, to use the entire boat as a rudder-blade to re-direct the current's force to move it across the stream and out of trouble. Going upstream, any wavering of the bow is punished, the current pulling you broadside, as happened when we broached at the end of the Peace. Going downstream the boat tends to stay straight, kept that way by the current. What this all means is that when you're approaching pounding surf, permanent waves bouncing off sheer canyon walls, you suddenly find yourself in the middle of it without really aiming to be. You find yourself thinking, Shit, those waves are BIG and WET.

It didn't help my confidence, seeing Joe preparing to abandon ship, but there was little time for reflection: we were in the foam and going for it, yelling above the noise and paddling like hell and finding that the waves, though they looked ferocious, an interference pattern caused by the volume of water smashing and rebounding off the cliffs, were in fact deceptively kind. There was more danger in the deep swell of the lake than in those big flimsy waves, splashing us, yes, but having little effect on the canoe.

Then we saw the hole. Fifteen or so feet across and a good two feet lower than the rest of the river, swirling like a whirlpool because it was a whirlpool; we were heading straight for it.

I had read about such holes but never seen one before. There were no holes on the Peace – I guessed it was too wide and slow, in the main, for such turbulence. A hole is caused by some underwater obstruction, in this case a huge rock deep down creating the drop. The river rushing past sucks the water down, sometimes into a smiling hole, where the water escapes each side and on downstream, and sometimes frowners, which are worse, when the water gets thrown back into the hole. This was a giant frowner.

We shot at full speed into the edge of the hole and instead of being sucked into the vortex were flung out the other side with enough momentum to keep going. Then we hit more waves, big but benign. There were no, or very few, rocks breaking the surface. All the danger was in the turbulence upsetting our heavily laden craft. But so far we were doing all right, shouting, getting soaked to the skin and skirting those holes.

Now we were on a big river going fast, our daily average distance went from 25 to 75km. This was the experience of most canoe trippers, whipping along even when you were taking rests. In a couple of days we joined the Fraser, our last river to paddle.

It was fast and the curves could be mean. We shot through the Giscombe Rapids, which Mackenzie mentioned were five miles long. 'How come they're over so soon?' I shouted.

Nigel and Joe both shouted instantly, 'They're not. Go left, port, left!' I didn't react quickly enough as Joe then shouted, 'Watch out, there's a rock the size of a—'

BANG. We hit it. Very hard. About a quarter of the way along the canoe. That's it, I thought. Time to swim. But the incredible thing was, the canoe seemed to absorb the impact, you could see the ribs flex inwards and then expand again, bouncing off the rock the size of a . . .

'Mini, I was going to say, as in car,' said Joe.

'Shit, that's got to have made a hole. Is any water coming in?'

'Doesn't look like it. Hard to say. There's a lot in already,' said Nigel. 'And I broke my paddle.'

Nigel and I had broken a paddle each already. They just weren't tough enough, or we were getting stronger. The first year we never broke any.

We pulled over to the bank and I examined the side. There was only the smallest scrape. We'd received much worse damage dragging it over stones in the Bad River. The great flexibility of the bark-and-cedar-rib combination had saved us from any hurt. We were fully laden with three men on board travelling ten miles an hour. An aluminium boat would have turned into a sculptured ashcan and a fibreglass boat would have shattered, I'm sure, under such a powerful impact, but we'd just bounced off. It was a bizarre paradox that you had to be so careful with birchbark over little things such as sticks and small sharp rocks, things which modern canoes could easily ignore, and yet be so secure in the really heavy stuff, smashing into rocks at high speed. I suddenly revised my opinion of how the Indians must have travelled – I bet they shot all the rapids, however hairy, knowing their boats could take it. Only with the coming of wood and canvas canoes did excessive caution prevail.

II

OK, the lad had hurt himself, maybe even broken something in his foot, so why couldn't I feel a little more charitable towards him? Now it was his whining about safety, 'sketch factors' and wearing his lifejacket that were getting me down. Most sensible canoeists wear lifejackets all the time; a few, foolish, or enamoured of the past, like us, never wear them. But to insist on putting your lifejacket on seconds before an obstacle appeared, thus endangering the whole canoe's preparedness, as much in protest against the whole management of the trip as in fear, struck me as ... typically Joe. Deep down, I felt, at some level where such decisions are made, he had little faith in me or the boat.* It had little to do with the evidence, I knew that. We'd gone thousands of kilometres and done it safely, and cautiously. But faith for Joe was not something that grew with rationally processed experience. He lived in the present (one of his many charms I had to remind myself) reacting to what appeared at the end of his nose. If today it looked rainy he'd be depressed, never mind that the sun would soon follow. He had no capacity for looking ahead and burying his immediate response. He couldn't keep quiet with his deep reservations about safety, and when everyone is a little apprehensive the last thing you want is a screamer on board. Or a man pulling on his lifejacket as if it were the last three minutes on the *Titanic*.

And then I had to lose his boots. Or did I? The mystery remains to this day. By the evidence presented I was the guilty one. I was throwing boots into the boot bag (which also carried our concealed rifle) and yet, when the boot bag was next opened, Joe's boots were not there. I had no memory of ever seeing his

---

* 'Boat, yes. You, no' – Joe, on having read the manuscript.

boots on that memorable day when we set out, no more grumpily than usual, from the confluence of the MacGregor and the Fraser, where, as Mackenzie remarks, the Fraser is as still as a lake. We camped on the promontory of land on the corner of the two rivers, an area of close-cropped turf laden with duckshit ... and Joe's boots.

The boots were one. There was no going back. And surely, I reasoned, shouldn't the wearer be the man ultimately responsible for the boots? When Dave lost his smelly trainers it was universally decided, as a legal precedent of the trip I rather felt, that it was his fault. Now why should Joe's boots, which he had been complaining about for the last two months as being not waterproof enough, be subject to a different law, in which, I, the man merely responsible for the receptacle that held the boots, be suddenly held responsible for the boots themselves? And, what is more, I was loading the boot bag out of purely charitable motives since it did not exist as a set chore for anyone. Ah, the pettiness of such things, and yet the stubborn ill-will that they generate.

We paddled on in silence, mostly, the boots hanging over us like a black cloud dumping its own load of rain on us and us alone. Nigel, as he always did in such situations, became excessively jovial and good-natured. We were approaching a town, the biggest of the trip, Prince George, and that knowledge began to overshadow everything. Steve would join us again and we would prepare for the long walk. After Prince George, there would be perhaps two days' paddling before we ditched the canoe. I did not know whether we would cache it in the forest, as Mackenzie did, or whether someone could be inveigled into helping us; such details now began to loom. Earlier it had seemed like hubris to even think about them, now I wished I had.

The river grew wider and the air smellier, the ripe, sweet, beery smell of a pulp plant and at first, as before, almost a pleasant smell. But unlike most smells, most obnoxious smells, you don't grow to ignoring it. It just hangs there in front of your nostrils, getting more and more sickening, you can't seem to ignore it in the way you ignore cowshit and country smells; it must have something to do with what the smell means. It means the river is polluted. It means shit and chemicals from the plant are being pumped into your friend, the river. Because it doesn't just smell; rather the smell stinks of something worse, and that keeps bugging you, it won't go away.

The inflow pipes were sinister and clever, on little jetties mid-stream, freshwater sucked up by the tankerload for making paper. The outflow from one plant was just a dirty stream (all right, from a distance it looked perfectly clean, but you never can tell, you never can) plunging down the riverbank and into the Fraser.

And not to mention all the trees you need to cut down. Paper, up close, is just about one of the most pernicious things being manufactured, at least that's how it felt, floating past the little bungalows on the bank, the whiteboard churches and then suddenly the tubular steel chimneys with whirly thermal protectors, the pipes, and the windowless metal enormity of a plant, all hissing steam, external plumbing and that smell, sickly, sweet, meaning civilization at last.

III

In Prince George we checked Joe O'Blenis's website and found bad news – he'd given up his heroic, record-breaking attempt to be the first to cross Canada in a single season. Robbed on a reserve in northern Manitoba, he'd become sick with a stomach complaint, possibly giardia. On the website – which documented his rescue by Herb – he painfully went into the reasons why he felt he had to give up his attempt. It was sad and yet somehow familiar: he had simply reached that stage when you ask yourself, What's the point? One reason for not going alone is that the presence of others keeps you from asking that question.

Our Joe visited a physiotherapist who took an X-ray and told him it was torn ligaments in his foot but that nothing was broken. 'Just rest it for a month or six weeks.'

'But I'm walking three hundred and fifty kilometres a week,' Joe told him.

The physiotherapist paused and replied: 'If I were you, I wouldn't.'

Joe then went out and bought at considerable expense a kind of foot corset. It was black and laced up and though it dug into the swelling he said it made it easier to walk.

There was still the possibility that he might give up completely and not do the walk. I told him it was up to him. I certainly wasn't going to beg him to come along.

The others, including Joe, went out, got roasted, went to several strip joints where the girls stripped on to little quilts they brought with them and laid out on the beer-slopped and otherwise unappealing stage and as a signature gesture turned and pointed their behinds at the eager and noisy male crowd and slapped their own buttocks as if urging a mule ever onward, the stubborn mulishness of themselves, slap, slap; the lads next morning demonstrated this manoeuvre for my benefit in the Ramada Inn hotel room we had obtained at a slight discount but not if they knew there were five of us in the room, Steve and his new mate, Bill, having motored up from Hudson's Hope in Guy's pick-up. We had, the night before, in fact the afternoon before, all drunk champagne, insisted on by Nigel, who as a manager who travelled to sales conferences seemed most at home in the corporate mauve and grey interior of the Ramada; we drank the champagne but it was not real champagne and though it sounds churlish I could already feel the magical currency of the river slipping away from me. There I had been rich, in my tattered shirt and torn trousers I had been the wealthiest of men, but here, with a hobo's suntan and the accumulated grime, I could feel my defences being assaulted. How long could I last in such a place? We had three days to sort everything out, find a home for the canoe, buy supplies and settle our route through the Interior Plateau. We also needed information about the only really tricky whitewater on the trip – Fort George Canyon. It was thinking about all these things that kept me from late-nighting with the boys and going to strip clubs, all of which, I'm sure, would have provided excellent local colour. I also knew that it is hard to tell people what to do when you've fallen on your face and thrown up the night before.

The strip clubs had been safe enough, but after that they had visited a bar where people danced, though drinking not dancing was its primary activity. There Joe had foolishly danced and so had Nigel and then, in an interlude when all the others were not there, Joe had managed to get himself punched. His face the next morning bore the scars: black eye, scratches, odd bruises – it would heal quickly enough. Why had he been punched? He had tried to dance with the wrong girl. Joe explained, 'Usually I would have just slunk away, but this trip has changed me. I went outside and thought, I've just been punched and I'm going back in, I went back in to get the guy who punched me even though he was bigger than me.' He said this without any boasting, it was one of Joe's characteristics that he never boasted. 'But the guy had gone and I carried on dancing with the girl anyway – and get this.'

'What?'

'She didn't even know him.'

'But what about your foot,' I said, 'all that dancing?'

'Yeah, it's killing me now I'm sober.'

His foot was more painful than before and he could hardly walk a block without resting. Then he tried to inveigle me into buying him some new boots. Those boots, they kept coming back to haunt me.

When they sited the Ramada in the downtown area it must have been a good business decision; it must have been the happening place in town. Now it was crowded with drunks, drunk Indians, and a woman Indian beggar, who sloped along slowly, asking in the weakest of voices for 'any change'. Dead opposite the Ramada was a rough old bar full of drunks at 11 a.m.; we went in for a few drinks and then went somewhere else. At least we now looked the part: we had that deep and permanent reddish tan that only vagrants and street drinkers acquire, we also slipped easily into a habit of moving all day from bar to bar, fitting our chores into a rigmarole of beers and small cigars. We knew we'd be leaving soon so we wanted to make the most of it. It gave me a headache but it was preferable to worrying about the canyon.

The canyon of doom. The Fort George Canyon. The last rapids we would ever have to shoot, or portage. Ever.

Mackenzie wrote of the Fort George Canyon: 'The rapids were of considerable length and impassable for a light canoe.' In order to go around the canyon everything had to be carried. 'The labour and fatigue of this undertaking, from eight until twelve, beggars all description.' And he had eight men to help him. Steve's thumb was mottled red, yellow and green, still bubbling with pus and blood, and the dressing had to be changed every day. Despite his loyal protests, he could hardly paddle one-handed. So that left three. But Joe was 'totally sketched out'. Descending the Fraser had given him the willies. He also had his bad ankle to consider. It was still black and yellow and so swollen the skin looked fit to burst. If we capsized he would have a hard time swimming and fighting his way out of the turbid current. I did not begrudge him his decision to stay on in Prince George until Nigel and I had finished on the Fraser.

Steve out. Joe out. Though they would both rejoin us for the final walk to the ocean they couldn't help us now, on the last, most difficult hurdle. We could not portage the canyon with only two. We would have to go where even Mackenzie feared to go – we would have to shoot the rapids of Fort George Canyon. In the early twentieth century six miners died trying to shoot the canyon rapids. It had a fearsome reputation. As Mackenzie wrote: 'The great body of water, at the same time tumbling in successive cascades rolls through the narrow passage in a very turbid current, and full of whirlpools.'

Just Nigel and me. We had no choice; we had to give it a go. We called up every contact we'd been given to find anyone with knowledge of how to paddle the canyon. That's how we met Lyle.

Lyle agreed to meet and talk. But when he turned up, a beefy, big-chested guy in wraparound shades, he went one better and drove Nigel and me to look at the canyon. The others were all sleeping off the excesses of the night before. Lyle had on a T-shirt that advertised the Canadian national canoe rodeo team. In our innocence we did not realize that Lyle was the kind of guy who would never wear such a thing unless he'd earned it. Slowly we began to understand that Lyle was a top canoeist – he'd come third in the canoe rodeo world championships only a few years before. Third in the world at anything is pretty impressive, but in the competitive world of canoe rodeo (doing impossible-looking tricks in an open canoe) it made us feel, well, out-paddled, for one thing, but also rather honoured. But we should have been careful. When we skidded down the side of the canyon, along the track Mackenzie took great care to portage, still growing the wild onions he remarked about in his journal, we saw what the explorer so feared. But Lyle, who I now, for some reason, perhaps his combination of strength and diffidence and heroic past, began to think of as a King Arthur figure, looked down at the roiling cascades and simply said, 'You should be OK if you stay this side of that rocky island.'

Two rules about rapids: (1) Their apparent danger varies inversely with the square of the distance you are above them. Two metres above them = four times less dangerous than only one metre above. Four metres above = sixteen times less dangerous. We were perched on a rock about four metres, I'd say, above the mêlée. Even then it was hard to pick a route. (2) Never look at rapids with an expert. You see with his eyes, not your own. What was a 'fun hole' to Lyle was a death trap akin to an unexploded bomb on a building site where kids play. When you look with the eyes of the third best canoeist in the world, whitewater looks like it does on television, kind of interesting, but not wet, cold, laced with rocks and hydraulics, ready to suck you down and keep you down. We actually laughed.

There was one hard bit, said Lyle, and we were looking at it. The river narrowed and sped through a tight gorge. In the middle was a rocky island. If we kept left we had two choices: ride it through the middle, which was pretty splashy (i.e. horrendous mountains of surf), or sneak along the edge, which looked the better of the two options, from above, though the 'calm' water next to the rocks was moving awful fast and looked mighty slim. 'You want to watch those rocks, I guess,' said Lyle. Yes, those too.

Lyle was married to Marion. They had a marvellous log home and thirteen canoes and Nigel and I stayed there while the boys camped out on a nasty piece of ground next to the railway tracks in town. We'd run out of money to pay for extra nights at the motel. There was a very logical reason why Nigel and I were the only two to taste the fullness of Lyle's hospitality – it was to do with maps, routes, asking him to look after the canoe etc. And to tell the truth we felt a little guilty drinking beers cold from the fridge and eating freshly made blueberry pie and cream while the lads ate sardines and pasta in an industrial wasteground. But the guilt didn't last – it was us going to our death down that canyon and we deserved a little blueberry pie first.

Steve and Joe were going to meet us in two days at the start of the walk, assuming we made it. Good old Lyle had agreed to take them and then return with the canoe. Good old Lyle, it was a two-hundred-mile drive on his day off but he agreed. He would keep the canoe until it could be shipped to Peace River Museum, which had agreed to put it on permanent display, assuming it survived the canyon.

IV

Joe was standing on the bank reading Lyle's local paper as we arranged our kit in the canoe before setting off. 'Hey, a guy drowned here yesterday. Trying to save his son. The son survived but he got swept away. It says in the paper just by that bridge over there.'

We stared at the current piling up against the two bridge supports, like a pair of huge wet shoulders trying to knock them down.

'They haven't found the body either,' added Joe.

Now we were on our own, the very idea that we had somehow cheated the others by eating blueberry pie seemed even more laughable. Lyle's hospitality was like the party they threw for kamikaze pilots before they saddled up astride a flying bomb. We were going to die! We paddled away from the others feeling rightly apprehensive. The good thing was we had far less kit. It meant we'd lose less when the boat capsized.

Several hours later and the canyon was still ten kilometres away. Despite, or perhaps because of, the gnawing sense of anticipation I felt hungry.

'Er, Nigel, where's the lunch?'

'In that bag, isn't it?'

'No.'

We'd been so keen to get moving, enter the jaws of death, that we'd left behind our food.

Great. No lunch. And speeding towards our destiny with potential death by drowning. Now we were two it was weird, different, vaguely unsettling. Two can't be enemies, that's for sure. You can't get annoyed with someone just because they forgot the lunch. You have to make light of it. A light lunch in fact. We passed a commercial campsite, the first we'd seen since Taylor's Landing, way back on the Peace. Maybe we could buy lunch.

Now we were two, decisions were quick and easy and always unanimous. Just me and tight-lipped Nigel. We could do it. All we needed was lunch.

But the guy who ran the campsite was no good-natured Sam. He was a miserable old German who'd worked all his life at the Kittemat aluminium smelter and had retired to run his own laager. Short, ratty-faced, suspicious, opinionated. There was neatly cut wood in graded piles, white-painted picnic tables and furled umbrellas. A toilet block made from logs with the ends painted glossy red. The place was spotless, I had to admit, but the way he accompanied Nigel and me to the sweet-dispensing machines made it far too obvious he didn't trust us river bums. Didn't he realize that men who use birchbark canoes are there to be trusted? Didn't he know we had an Indian luck medicine hidden in the front of our boat? Nah, he wasn't even interested enough to look down at the river and see what we were going on about. I was glad there was only one oversized articulated truck of an RV parked there. 'Weekends my best time. I'm packed then,' he explained. 'Though I ain't gonna get to be a millionaire doin' this.'

Good. But we stood around, trying to make the most of the human contact.

'You wanna watch the grizzlies,' he said.

'Already seen a few.'

'You gotta gun?'

'Two-seventy Winchester.'

'Grizzly'll stand on the bank and throw rocks'll sink your boat.'

'Really?'

'I seen it happen, right down there.'

We all looked at the benign stretch of muddy bank not twenty yards from the main road to Prince George.

'I got me plenty of grizzly. Not round here but up in Alaska. Fly-ins. Biggest moose and grizzlies in the world.'

Perhaps he hoped we'd be impressed.

'You hear about that dead guy?' he rattled on.

'Yes.'

'Fuckin' idiot, they haven't found his body yet. Maybe down there. You might see him, stuck under some rocks or somethin'.'

Great. Another dead body to look out for.

'Fuckin' idiot. There was drinkin' involved, you know that?'

We didn't. Besides, the man had saved his son, that counted for something. I looked at Nigel. It was time to get moving. The campsite man continued, 'You guys English?' Then a pause. 'Pity.' He laughed. That was his idea of a joke.

'You got any smokes for sale?' I asked. He was smoking and had a full pack in his top pocket. But I knew what the answer would be.

'There's a gas station about twenty miles that way,' he snickered. 'That's where I get mine.'

Bastard. We could stand no more. He continued on his favourite theme as we walked away.

'You want to be careful in that river. It's a treacherous river. It's a real killer.'

Goodbye, you miserable bastard. No lunch except an over-priced candy bar. No smokes. And facing death by drowning. Great.

V

I only just heard Nigel's voice above the pounding noise of the waves. 'Shit ... Rob ... paddle ... broke.' We were heading at full speed towards probable death and Nigel's paddle had broken. A minute or two before, we'd whipped past two fishermen. 'Hey, guys!' they shouted and waved. 'You know what's down there, don't you?'

'Yes, no problem, we know.'

They looked relieved. If we drowned they could tell the coroner, 'Well, we told 'em, didn't we? We told 'em good, but they just went flying right on by.'

With one paddle. Shit, Nigel. Great timing. We could see the bad bit coming up. We pulled in and clung to a wet rock just in front. Nigel found another paddle. Just as well there were only two of us, these were our last two paddles. Then we were off.

In the river, right in the waves, it all looked totally different.

'Is that the island?'

'Shit. I don't know.'

'Isn't that the bit we stood on?'

'I think so.'

'As long as we stay on the left.'

The 'easier' passage next to the side looked fraught with difficulties, the least of which was getting over there without pranging ourselves on a rock. Better to stay central. Here we go. It was like going down a slope and then coming up, just like the log flume at an amusement park, splash and out and in again. Both of us paddling hard but with a growing sense of it not mattering as much as we had thought. The river had us. It called the shots, we just had to ride it until it spat us out at the other end. Just keep it straight. Skirt that hole. Just keep it straight. All our paddling seemingly symbolic. The river had us.

'Was that it?'

'No, look ahead, there's more.'

And there was. The canyon rapids went on and on, but we knew we were over the worst. And then, spat out into calm water. Done. Mackenzie would have been proud of us. Self-congratulation. Grinning like mad. We drifted on and camped on a sandy island. There was a metal tank washed up, as big as a steam-train boiler. Like two happy schoolboys Nigel and I spent a great deal of effort trying to push it down the steep beach into the river, but it just lodged in the shallows, waiting for the next flood to carry it further downstream.

VI

It was sad to be waiting. We hauled the boat out at the mouth of the Blackwater River, which was also known as the West Roads River, and waited for Lyle and the lads to turn up. It was not easy with just two to haul it out and we did more damage to the bottom, but this time it didn't matter. Lyle had agreed to look after the boat for us and a few more scratches wouldn't hurt it. It was a hot day and it took a long time to haul all our gear and the canoe to the place where the logging trail hit the river. There was a small car park and a Mackenzie Trail sign that had received a shotgun blast, a rusty spread of thumb-sized dimples.

Sadness is waiting, watching the river flow by, the great brown river on its way to the sea. We were out of it now, out of the current, our boat no longer needed. And what of the rest? Just an easy stroll – it was a trail for backpackers and Boy Scouts and was marked with little yellow trail signs just like the Pennine Way in England. This was the end of the real journey, watching that river go by, ten miles an hour, taking logs and silt and dead bodies down to the sea. Stick to the river. I knew now why Mackenzie had hesitated, had gone past this point, desperate to stay on the water at almost any cost. But then he hit the

Cottonwood Canyon further on and reluctantly gave in, and took the easy route, the Indian 'grease trail' to the ocean. It had been a hard choice to give up the canoe but in the end, 'the comparative shortness and security of such a journey, were alone sufficient to determine me.' And having decided, they still needed a guide. In desperation they kidnapped an old blind man to lead them to the start of the trail. Mackenzie shows how different he was to the later, more violent, Victorian explorers: 'I was under the very disagreeable necessity of ordering the men to carry him into the canoe; and this was the first act during my voyage, that had the semblance of violent dealing.'

The old blind man led them to more people who showed them the trail. Here 'we prepared a stage, on which the canoe was placed bottom upwards, and shaded by a covering of small trees and branches, to keep her from the sun'. A week earlier they had properly rebuilt the canoe after the hasty repairs on the Bad River and it was still on the platform when they returned from the sea. It carried them all the way back to their fort near Peace River town.

The boat becomes a part of you, it becomes your friend. The Indian medicine had protected it, and us, and now we wouldn't need it any more. Just walking. Dead easy. When the others arrived with Lyle we prolonged his departure by carving our names into *Dragonfly*. Then we hoisted our faithful canoe on to his station wagon and that was the last we saw of her.

VII

That first day we walked about two kilometres, uphill, in hot evening weather. Steve's thumb started bleeding, which was worrying. We were exhausted and demoralised but we thought we knew the reason. All those muscles developed paddling were now useless. Our legs were now having to do everything. And we had far too much kit. That night lots of gear was sacrificed, including the camping stove, several cooking pots and a tarpaulin. I ditched everything except the clothes I was wearing, a sweater, sleeping bag, raingear, Thermarest and three pairs of socks. The only thing I later regretted throwing away was a pack of cards. I cut off the bottoms of my overtrousers to make overshorts, I threw away books, a bumbag I'd used for eight years, a sweater, some English coinage, receipts I'd been inexplicably carrying since the previous year. A photocopied version of Mackenzie's journal (all the pages except the relevant ones). And even then it was too heavy.

Mackenzie explained, 'The place where the goods alone are carried is called a Decharge, and that where goods and canoes are both transported, overland, is denominated a Portage.' We were now decharge and resenting it.

Our packs weighed over a hundred pounds each because we were carrying food for eighteen days. There were other additions, all technological – Joe had his cameras, Steve had the video, Nigel had the sat phone and the tarpaulin, and I had the gun. I fixed it to my backpack and could hardly lift the bulky thing. The rifle poked up like an antenna, ready to catch on any low boughs I had to go under.

We were carrying similar weights to those hoisted by the voyageurs. Mackenzie reports the paddlers each carried 'a burden of about ninety pounds, with a gun and some ammunition. My own load, and that of Mr Mackay, consisted of twenty-two pounds of pemmican, some rice, a little sugar, etc., amounting in the whole to about seventy pounds each, besides our arms and ammunition. I had also the tube of my telescope swung across my shoulder, which was a troublesome addition to my burthen.'

Mackenzie and his men decided to 'content ourselves with two meals a day, which were regulated without difficulty, as our provisions did not require the ceremony of cooking'.

Their route inland was a Southern Carrier, or Nuxhalk Indian, 'grease trail', a major trade route at the time. The 'grease' was oolikan fish oil made in Bella Coola, our destination, and traded with the interior Indians for obsidian, nephrite for axes, copper and soapstone. The trail would have been well trodden and well maintained by constant use. Things were different two hundred years later. Though the entire trail was now designated a national path, it became obvious very quickly that it received very few visitors except at the points accessible by road. And the first thirty kilometres, where Mackenzie walked in a giant loop, received the fewest visitors of all.

It was a nightmare. Trees had fallen or been blown down every ten or so metres, turning the route into a hellish obstacle course. The dinky little trail signs, yellow rhomboids with two walkers who looked a bit like the Start-rite twins, were usually nailed to these fallen trees, as if the wind had picked them out on purpose. There was no money to keep this part of the trail open and so no one did. We blundered on, the rifle barrel jamming on branches, causing me to grovel my way much lower than the others. Bits of kit were torn off and lost for ever, including two cheap water bottles bought in Prince George. It was interesting to be having a much rougher time than Mackenzie for once – well, it was interesting for a few minutes, but hour soon followed hour in the preternatural darkness of the forest, close-spaced spruces and pines dying of pine beetle, which had been worse over the last few years owing to the warm winters.

On one log I hoisted my leg up and lost my balance. I fell backwards and then lay on the ground, as helpless as a turtle on its back. I had to be lifted up by Nigel and Steve. What if I'd been alone? Trapped for ever on my back in a damp (it was raining continuously), gloomy forest, my skeleton found pinioned by the shoulder straps I was unable to cut or shrug off ... It was after about the fiftieth time that the rifle banged into an overhead log that I decided to carry it by hand. That palled very quickly. Ten pounds of rifle and ammunition is plain murder to heft when you're constantly climbing over rotten trees and root plates ten feet high. All boyhood fantasies about the army vanished immediately. If there was a war I'd join the navy. Subs. Or better still, stay home and watch it on television. There was a growing and worrying pain in my right buttock. Every time I did a high kick to get over a downed tree it shot right through my gluteus maximus. What was worse, after my turtle fall the left pack strap had half detached and the rucksack was canted over at forty-five degrees. Now, unless I made a correction, I ended up walking off at an angle, banging into trees and devil's clubs like a drunkard. 'Only three hundred and fifty kilometres to go,' said Nigel. I didn't know if I'd last to the first camp.

But I did. We all did. Just. Far from being an easy romp it was turning out to be as severe a test as the river. And I had entered a new and invidious phase of the journey: checking out who was fittest, who was lagging, who was the gazelle leaping away at the front, and who was the warthog, struggling manfully along through the mud. I told myself a lot of comforting stuff I knew to be true but could not quite believe, not out there, resting by the stagnant, insect-infested corner of Punchaw Lake, Mackenzie's first campsite on the trail, a lake among woods, which, lacking a clear view, made it more like a big pond surrounded by rotting pines and fallen spruce. The stuff you have to tell yourself at the beginning of a big walk: 1) the first three days of a hike your body has to relearn the skill and seemingly reassign the muscles; 2) you can hit a wall after a week if you ignore this and don't take a rest after three days; 3) there is no limit to what you can throw away.

VIII

Steve and Joe sneaked off to have a joint. They thought I didn't know but I did. They were scared of me finding out. Actually, part of the pleasure of weed is knowing squares disapprove. I was stand-in for the policemen and old ladies of the real world. Would Mackenzie have permitted skunk? Would he have banned sensimilla? Would he have allowed his voyageurs a pinch of weed and a few drips of resin into their pipe bowls at night? I think not. Maybe he would have rationed it, like he did the rum. But alcohol goes with rationing, whereas drugs don't. Spliffs come with an attached ideology of freedom and excess. Rationing legitimizes the habit and seriously knocks its cool. There would be an incentive to sneak around the ration, if there was one, whereas a booze limit is actually welcomed. No one wants to drink too much, too often, because of the hangover. Spliffs exact no penalty except, possibly, a gradual evolution into an . . . addict! I had to admit my antipathy to Joe had turned me into an anti-drugs fiend. That's what I thought. In fact it was simply one symptom of a control-freakery that was extending into everything.

The next day we broke out of the nightmare of the woods on to logging roads, banked swaths of red mud with impacted shale, puddles steaming in the sudden inordinate heat of summer, mosquitoes and humidity feeding off each other. The logging road was wide and every hour or so a great twenty-wheeler carrying six or eight huge trees would thunder by, giving no quarter, honking the horn in a cloud of dust and diesel fumes.

I carried the gun again, its dead weight cradled in my arms, stooping me more and more by the hour. For rest breaks we sat back against the piled-up mud and shale on the roadside, lifting the weight off our packs. Logging roads are among the most hateful places to walk in the hot sun. The shade is never where you want to walk and the forest blocks out any kind of refreshing breeze. Add to that the danger of being run over by a monster Mack, and the tedium of walking on a flat unyielding surface (perfect for blister formation), and you see why we decided to stick to Mackenzie's easy schedule and stop for the day at Cleswuncut Lake after only four hours' walking. Everyone lay down, talk reduced to a minimum. We revived after three cups of tea. Perhaps wanting to cheer us up, Steve told some stories from his childhood: 'I got this mothball stuck up my nose once. It was terrible. I had to have it surgically removed.'

This time everyone threw stuff away. The pile was quite attractive, as long as you had no intention of walking anywhere with it. We fired the gun at several waterlogged stumps, reducing the weight of the ammunition I had to carry. In order to further justify having lugged the rifle so far I decided to loose off some more shells Saddam Hussein-style – one-handed. But what if that monstrous tyrant had really strong wrists? After a few two-handed practices I was ready. All I needed was that porkpie hat he used to wear. The kick was minimal, in fact satisfying –

one-handed rifle-shooting definitely appeals to a despotic frame of mind.

There are very few instances of Mackenzie mucking about. But he reveals one, which happened close to the start of the overland walk. His men were some distance ahead, sheltering by a log house and expecting an Indian attack (which never came) and yet Mackenzie does something understandable but rather childish – he decides to see how far he can shoot an arrow at the house: 'I thought it impossible for an arrow to reach it, having a bow and quiver in my hand, I very imprudently let fly an arrow, when, to my astonishment and infinite alarm I heard it strike a log of the house . . . when I arrived I found that the arrow had passed within a foot of one of the men.' Who were naturally not very pleased with their careless leader.

Joe and Steve had brought no medication for sore or blistered soles and their feet were fine. Nigel and I had moleskin and plasters and already had several blisters. I doctored mine using the old Foreign Legion technique I had learned years before whilst working as a van driver in London with an old Italian legionnaire who had then, oddly, become a cobbler and finally, at about fifty-five, a motorcycle courier. He was called Fred and was short and sparrow-like and not at all how one imagines a member of the Legion, but that's usually how these things are. Anyway, the method is to stitch across your blisters with a piece of thread. You leave the thread in and the holes remain open and drain fully. If you just prick them they close up and the blister keeps forming.

'What's the most important thing about being a soldier? I mean, after your feet?' I asked Fred.

'Never lose your rifle or your spoon,' he answered immediately.

I was obviously no legionnaire. By the third day I knew the gun had to go. I had rebuilt the inner frame of my rucksack to make it more rigid. I had repaired the torn stitching caused by my turtle fall. I had thrown a ton of nice things away, but still it was too heavy. We had fifteen days' worth of food on our backs and that easily added thirty pounds to the weight of each sack. We were not going to do any hunting. If a bear attacked then we would have to rely on the bangers and the bearhorn. And increasingly I worried what we would do when we reached Bella Coola – we couldn't take the rifle with us and neither could we hide it now that we no longer had a canoe to hide it in. We left the logging road and entered the bush, which is where anyone who enjoys walking rather than self-torture usually starts the trail. Here the path had been kept clear. I was looking for a fallen cedar tree. Trappers in the past stored metal traps inside cedar-wood trunks: one of its odd properties is that it even in a damp climate it helps the steel remain rust-free. I coated the rifle in gun oil and wrapped it in an oil-soaked rag. There was a tree that had fallen some way from the path and split its trunk. There was just enough room for me to slide the rifle in, leaving it hidden from view. Good for another thirty years.

Free of the odious weight of the rifle, and now walking along a ridge path that looked far down on the Blackwater, I was happy. It was an upwelling of happiness, full of the absurd good news of life. Even when it rained it was merely refreshing. We tramped up and down paths that wound through open woods, building that happiness all day long. Joe's moodiness seemed far away as we played his favourite game, which was thinking up a new career for him. When I told him he'd be silly to do anything except photography because he was obviously so talented at it, he dropped behind and then ran forward and gave me a flower, 'for having faith in me'.

I could feel my pack getting lighter and lighter as the body finally adjusted itself. 'Bougainvillaea,' said Steve, for no reason. 'I like the sound of that word, don't you?' I did. It felt like an odd kind of poetry, but appropriate to our situation, striding along shining good will on everything.

Twelve

JOE ALONE

'Mr Mackay informed me that the men had expressed their dissatisfaction to him in a very unreserved manner, and had in very strong terms declared their resolution to follow me no further in my proposed enterprise.' Alexander
Mackenzie faces a mutiny

I

Steve was ahead all that day, his legs comfortable at a faster pace than ours. Joe's ankle was still swollen and bruised but holding up in its kinky lace-up corset. Steve doctored his thumb each day and it had stopped bleeding. Slowly it was healing. About their injuries they never once complained, both as tough as Mackenzie's voyageurs, I had to admit. Nigel and I kept swapping places in the order that we walked, a sort of vaguely competitive air about it. We were in woodland, mainly big poplars, with some cedar and pine. The ground was littered with cowpats. The track had been widened by an ATV, a nasty little quad or trike, the fat sod's answer to outback freedom, I muttered to myself.

There were sections of the trail, known as moccasin trails; these avoided rocks and swamps and were centuries-old, had been designed for walking in moccasins. These alternated with cart tracks and ATV tracks, all part of the reconstructed trail that Mackenzie and his Nuxhalk Carrier guides walked. There was something marvellous about the single-line efficiency over moss of the moccasin trails. ATVs spoiled all that. I realized that walking is always best in places where vehicles can't go. It increases the necessity of it, just as canoeing is always more fun in places where powerboats can't go.

But ATVs have one benefit: by churning up the trail they often expose ancient native tools. All of us found one or two obsidian spearheads and arrowheads, beautifully crafted with hundreds of chip marks to fashion a short blade. These tools predated Mackenzie. By the time he walked the trail they already had iron, traded in bars with the coastal Indians who obtained it from European traders. He wrote, 'They fix it to an handle at right angles, which they employ as an axe. When the iron is worn down, they fabricate it into points for their arrows and spikes.'

The path had been winding through the cowpat-studded woods for hours. We had been in deep shade, it seemed, for days. It was like travelling through the jungle. Even though the maps showed items of geographical interest such as lakes and hills, you couldn't always see them because of the trees. We had a special guidebook for the walk so it would have been hard to get lost, but it often felt as though we were lost. Partly it was the deviations caused by the endless surmounting of fallen logs. Mackenzie described the trail as a 'well beaten path' though at one point he did remark, 'Our way was impeded by a considerable number of fallen trees.' 'But nothing like as impeded as ours,' said Steve when I read this out.

There was the additional frustration of crossing clear cuts, which looked like the Somme, a few years on. We'd climb and jump and trip and get snagged and get lost as the yellow trail signs disappeared, or you might find yourself looking down on one nailed to a recently slain tree, but with no indication of where the trail continued.

There had been no little yellow sign for hours and hours and all those cowpats were getting us down. This wooded area was a ranch, with cattle we could see knocking through the trees, though the ranch house was miles away, situated on a dirt road. We began to doubt whether we were on the right path. I began to doubt it. So did the others. Those rhomboid-shaped trail markers were as addictive as chocolate. But like any diet of junk food they made real nourishment unpalatable. The markers meant you could relax your navigation. Which was all very well until they disappeared, leaving you sweating like a junkie for a fix.

It started with an argument about the utility of doing a GPS fix. I argued that on a 250,000-scale map a GPS was fairly pointless unless you were way off course. I knew we weren't, it was the just the particulars that were confusing. Joe said it would make him feel better if I did a fix. My retort may have been laced with barbaric sarcasm, I may have patronized the lad with my tone and exact choice of words, I may have departed from the hog-tied deference Joe's moods exacted from us timid souls who enjoyed an easy life. Whatever tactical error I made, the results were explosive.

Things had been brewing, it was obvious.

'You're panicking, aren't you?' said Joe.

'No.'

'You are, that's why you're uptight and trying to put me down. You don't talk to the others like that, do you?'

'No, because they don't talk to me like you do.'

'They think it though.'

'But they don't say it because they're grown up and you're . . . a boy.'

The other two busied themselves in an unconvincing display of adjusting their rucksacks. Joe unslung his and made the face he always made when he was about to get rude.

'You . . . wanker!'

'Grow up.'

'WANKER!'

When the insults became repetitive Joe changed tack. 'You're panicking because you know you should have cached some food. We won't make it with what we've got.'

This was the first time any one of us had suggested it might be folly to do as Mackenzie did. There were a few ranches *en route* and other walkers had supplies flown in to be collected as they walked. It was a good idea, but not what Mackenzie did, and contrary to the spirit of the enterprise, not to mention the cost and the organization involved. And we had agreed it all in Prince George. It was the plan. We had to stick to the plan. It was like a deep groove worn into my brain: depart from the plan and everything falls apart. Joe had found my button and now he was stamping on it. Undermining the whole enterprise. Going too far. It seemed such a serious accusation to my paranoid mind that I didn't even want to debate it with him. I felt myself falling into a chasm-like generation gap. I had become the authority figure I wanted and he hated. But all I could do was fume as he ranted on, 'You're such a wanker. Wank-ker! You fucked up and you know you fucked up!'

His face got littler, his voice more shrill. I shouldered my rucksack, full of rage and a sudden insight. 'You know what?' I said, with a growing certainty. 'If you don't like it, you can sod off. Go on! Piss off, you little whiner. That logging road's only twenty kilometres back the way we came. Go on! Sod off back to the Fulham Road.'

I adjusted my pack and marched ahead. After about a mile Steve came alongside and said, 'Well, you told him all right, didn't you?' His genial face smacked of covert sympathy for me. I was surprised. I thought I was on my own.

After another mile we found one of the little yellow signs, taunting us, playing with us.

I had been right this time, but at what cost?

II

That night at the camp there was the ugly smell of unresolved argument over everything. It didn't help that we had chosen a spot next to a pile of rotting fish. We were near to an old wagon trail, well marked back to the road, a tempting invitation to split up.

I went down to the smooth lake next to our tents. In my anger-befuddled state I didn't want to mess it all up. Not now. Not after all we had been through.

Throughout the whole trip I had never felt close to Mackenzie.

His dry journal and lack of personal reflection did not encourage sympathy. But at this point, I understood him, saw him clearly. At the start of his walk, not so many miles from where I was now, he had to give a 'warm eulogium on the fortitude, patience, and perseverance' of his fellow voyageurs in order to persuade them to follow him. But he ended by saying, 'I declared, in the most solemn manner, that I would not abandon my design of reaching the sea, *if I made the attempt alone.*' I could feel his obsession crossing the centuries. I was now prepared to do the same. That's what I had meant when I told Joe to get lost. I was prepared to go alone. I had built obsession to its logical conclusion: one man, alone, oblivious to everything except his narrow goal. But this wasn't 1793 and I wasn't Mackenzie. Of course, we had to be focused, but this was going too far. I had to conclude, as the sun sat hugely over the calm lake, that I was finally losing it.

III

Every day seemed hotter than the last. Each man carried two litres of water, quickly consumed and leaving a dry mouth between the small streams where we refilled our bottles. The path joined a dirt track that went through a Kluskus Indian reserve. All the little yellow walker signs had been torn down. We didn't feel welcome. Along the whole trail, whenever there was an official metal sign with information and a picture of Mackenzie it would be peppered with bullet holes. In the last three signs Mackenzie's eyes had been carefully shot out. These signs were at places you could get to down a logging road or on the way to a ranch. They weren't everywhere, but the relief of seeing one was always tempered by the sad sight of a blind Mackenzie.

Indian activists didn't like the government. The signs were paid for by the taxpayer and were therefore government property. Plus they were very tempting, no doubt, to check the accuracy of your gun.

Along the Kluskus road, dangling from trees, were pieces of old cars. Exhaust systems, a wheel, bumpers, even bits of body-work. The metal hung in the dry trees as if it were part of a sculpture park. There was something ironic about all the bits of car junk in the trees. It was like a message to the white man: We don't really need your cars. We prefer them as jewellery for our trees. There was also something post-holocaust and vaguely sinister about the dangling metalwork, eerily blowing in the breeze like industrial windchimes.

At the Indian village, a clutch of white-painted board cabins and a big church, we saw no one. A path ran just below the village. It was open country, a series of shorn stony meadows before the forest started again. Then a white woman walked down to talk to us. The woman was young with straw-blond hair pulled tightly back. She was friendly and eager to give advice. She'd been in the village a few weeks, waiting for the school term to start – she was their teacher. Eager, idealistic, politically correct. Doing her bit to make sure the Indians learned English and maths. But like us they also need courses in birchbark-canoe building, tracking, wilderness survival, moosehide working, traditional fishing and medicine, teepee building and moccasin making. Every one of these crafts and skills can be turned into good money. She gave us the stats: ten children, fourteen houses, between fifteen and sixty residents. She said it as if it were better that more of them lived in the village. But Indians like to move around and be where they want to be. The white man calls those who live in towns 'cement Indians', as if this proves a point. Something I've observed about Indians being observed is that we want them to be 'really Indian' – no Western clothes, pick-ups and modern con-veniences. At the same time we don't like their cultural Indian-ness, their economy of words, reliance on intuition, flexibility in the face of our rigid systems. I was just the same: I preferred 'outgoing-type Indians' – those most like white men, in fact. But in a birchbark canoe, please, and wearing moccasins.

Mackenzie wrote that 'as late as 1786, when the first traders from Canada arrived on the banks of the river, the natives employed bows and snares, but at present very little use is made of the former, and the latter are no longer known'. Steel traps and rifles had arrived for good. I was constantly reminded that native people along the Peace have had modern technology and have been in contact with European peoples for over two hundred years yet still retain a completely different culture.

Leaving the village we wound our way through woods. Turning a corner a big rock, about the size of a brick, whizzed between Steve and me, missing our ears by an inch or two. 'Shit, where did that come from?' There were sounds of laughter and tittering in the trees. Then around the corner came a gaggle of Indian kids with a sturdy, blank-faced woman looking after them. The stone thrower came down from the bank above the path without a pang of guilt. The woman was uncommunicative until we remarked on the sweatlodge we'd seen a few hundred yards back. She explained how the men used it every Sunday. It had been built by one of the boys' fathers. They were OK kids but you could see the seeds of delinquency. They weren't nearly as cheerful as the kids who stoned us on the Peace.

IV

Joe and I had reached the grim but workable compromise of barely talking to each other. Then it all flared up again. This time the issue was rations. It seemed we had enough after all. Joe wanted us to slack off. I wanted to maintain the ration so that we had food in reserve. I tried to understand why I hated him. Every day there was a different reason. He walked too fast. He walked too slow. He was always up last. He put seeds in the porridge. Mere symptoms. I hated him because he was in the way. The final flowering of obsession divides the world. Those who support your tunnel vision and those who don't.

That morning when he insisted he had a right to more food I jostled him backwards and his porridge spilt on the pine-needled floor. It was like a grotesque version of *Oliver Twist*. Now I had really gone too far and Joe sensed the insanity. 'So what

375

you going to do? Kill me and hide my body out here in the bush?'

I looked around. Plenty of places to get rid of someone.

Packing up the campsite meant constantly having to skirt the vomit-like spread of porridge, which stared back, reproaching me for going mad.

V

'There are three blokes ahead,' said Steve, 'and they're stark-bollock-naked.'

We rounded some bushes in an open meadow and there were the Germans. Three of them were, it was true, bathing without clothes on in the river. The other two were tending a large blackened pot hanging over the fire. The naked bathers appeared and sheepishly covered themselves up. The oldest-looking was Norbert, their leader. 'Did you see his bollocks?' whispered Steve. 'Bloody huge. And red.'

One was called Fritz. 'There's one in every group,' he quipped. He had a bushy beard and was actually the oldest at fifty-nine.

The next day we were off through the forest first, expecting to leave them far behind. But as we rested for lunch we heard the sound of bells, cowbells and something higher, like the little tinkling bells people attach to cats' collars. It was the Germans. Rather than keep in one group (there is no recorded bear attack on a group of five or more) they decided to wear a variety of different-sized bells to scare off any bears. But, of course, this also scared off any other wildlife.

Almost every day we passed the Germans, or they passed us. In an act of generosity so characteristic of Steve he handed over to the Germans five Mars bars – his own ration for five days. We were all stunned. And ashamed. None of us could imagine giving away half his Mars-bar supply just for diplomatic reasons. But Steve was surprising like that. And after that the Germans were our pals, sharing their coffee and trailmix, and Fisherman's Friends with us. But even the Germans knew something was wrong. 'You and Joe – OK?' asked Ulie, handing me another Fisherman's Friend.

'OK,' I lied.

VI

It was early evening and we were all walking down a steep track. It was quiet and the air had that stillness you sometimes get at twilight after a summer's day, the air still warm. No wind. Lumbering up the path towards us was a shape, a black bear shape. Loping. It didn't see us immediately. Then it did. We all stopped. I fumbled for the bear banger in my shirt pocket. It was a young bear by the look of it, big enough but not one of the really heavy-looking ones. It took in all four of us, turned and with a clatter of claws climbed straight up a fir tree at the side of the trail. Right on the trail.

'Don't fancy walking under that tree with him still up it,' I said in a low voice.

'Shall we wait until he comes down?' whispered Nigel.

We all started walking backwards, but still facing the tree, giving the bear some space. The most recent scare story we'd heard had been on this trail, not far away, when two men walked into a bear at twilight. One had been mauled so badly he lost an arm.

We went back and I fingered the banger. It was like a thin party popper, orange plastic, that you screwed into a metal pen-type device. The pen had a thumb-loaded spring that fired a pin into the neck of the banger. They went *whoosh-bang*, like a mini-rocket. Should I shoot it at the tree? Over the tree? If it banged on the wrong side it could scare the bear towards us. One opinion had it that it was best to fire it at the ground in between you and the bear. Ricochets? Rebounds?

We kept backing off. The bear looked black and fat and rather comfortable up the tree. Then, almost as if we'd gone back out of his personal space, there was another clatter of claws and snapping of thin branches and he was down, and running for his life.

'Feels good to see a bear that scared of you, doesn't it?' said Nigel.

VII

Bear fear always brought us together again. Maybe we could last it out. If only there was a chance to get out of each other's company for a bit.

Nigel and I were walking together, looking for firewood.

'Joe's thinking of leaving,' he said.

'And going alone?'

'He's been asking Norbert for directions.'

'Norbert can't speak English.'

'I know, I wouldn't trust his directions myself.'

'He hasn't got any kit.'

'He found a map in that deserted fishing lodge, and he got a tarpaulin from the ruined Indian house.'

'He's welcome to try.'

But before anyone made a decision we arrived at a ranch in the middle of nowhere.

Thirteen

INTERNATIONAL HARVESTERS

*'I represent him as an object of ridicule and contempt
for his pusillanimous behaviour; though, in fact, he
was a very useful, active, and laborious man.'*
Alexander Mackenzie on crew member Beauchamp

I

'That's my baby, Rob; I want you to take real good care of her.' I
felt flattered that Dave would entrust me with his baby. His big
baby: a 1963 dull green International Harvester pick-up with
outsize tyres protruding well clear of the body.

Dave looked like a cheery French farmer, with red cheeks and
a big swept-down moustache. He ran the Euchiniko Lakes Ranch
with his wife Maureen. In return for food and wine and a
cabin and a precious break from each other we agreed to collect
firewood for them. Dave's helper, Kramer, would chop the trees
down. We would transport the logs. There were three sheds to
fill.

Kramer was laid-back, smoking a cigarette, squinting at the
sun, in no real hurry. Mostly he was a hunting guide, taking
hunters on packhorses through the hills. He also did odd-jobs.
He was skinny with small frameless glasses, like an astute
cowboy. He finished his cigarette and we were all raring to go,
keen to show we weren't slackers. The night before, Dave had
given us a winebox, food and coffee, and invited us to play
croquet with his fly-in fishing guests from Oregon. The ranch

made most of its money from guiding fishermen and providing accommodation.

We walked over to the truck in the early-morning sunlight. 'She hasn't got power steering,' explained Dave, 'or syncromesh. When you change gear ...'

'Double de-clutch.'

'Right on, Rob! The brakes don't work and the front wheelnuts have a tendency to come loose. Better check them first.'

'No brakes?'

'Hey, Rob, if you need a brake you're goin' too fast.'

'Is there a handbrake?'

Dave laughed. 'Not on this model. Just watch out for the kick from the steering wheel. I've broken a finger going over a rock before now.

'And watch out for the key. If you turn it too far the coil burns out.'

I looked over the truck and found more worrying signs of undrivability. The accelerator had lost its pad and was just a single prong. I practised moving my foot on and off the prong and it got stuck in the cleats of my boot. But where would I move my foot to anyway? The brake which didn't work? Both front wheels had loose wheelnuts which I tightened with a spanner from Dave's big concrete-floored workshop. I gave the windscreen a cursory wipe with my elbow. Steve grinned supportively. I fired her up, leaving the choke pulled well out.

Nigel went first. He drove Kramer's positively car-like pick-up along the winding mountain path that led out of the back of the ranch. The track was so narrow the wide tyres caught against the hillside. On the other side was a plunging drop. 'At least there are a few trees,' said Steve, 'to break our fall.'

'Right on, Steve!' I said and stalled the engine on a steep slope. Bloody hell, this was difficult. I pushed in the clutch and we started rolling back down the hill. Then we ran backwards into the side of the hill. Good. First lesson: drive into something before you park; that's your brake. After a lot of revving and gunning and careful key-turning we were moving again. Then we hit a big rock and the steering wheel kicked like something alive and dangerous. I got my fingers clear but my funnybone bashed against the door catch. Sickeningly painful. Second lesson: keep your elbows in.

Then I got the pick-up stuck between two trees. 'You're going too easy on her,' said Kramer, 'treatin' her too good. There's pretty much nothing you can do that'll harm that old bitch,' and he got in and revved the engine and jerked and clunked and tyre-spun the truck out from its prison.

With a load of logs on it was harder. Coming back down the hill I felt the thing sliding away at the back. I accelerated and gripped the wheel even tighter, making sure my thumbs were clear of the spokes. The slide stopped and we straightened out, losing only one log in the process. 'You're doing fine,' said Steve.

Kramer searched for trees that had been killed by the pine beetle, which threatened the whole inland forest. Kramer was philosophical. 'If it kills all the pines another tree'll grow in its place. And every now and then you find a tree that has resisted the beetle, somehow become immune to it.'

He swung his chainsaw up and down the logs, first limbing and then chopping the wood into small logs. We made a chain and loaded the trucks, enjoying the arm work of lifting and throwing; working as a team again. If only I didn't keep bashing my elbows whenever that wheel spun.

We stayed a second day and filled the sheds to the roof. It felt good to be able to do so much work. Dave and Maureen were grateful. We left the ranch walking with great strides down the rocky track through the forest. The lake was on our left, flashes of blue through the thin aspens.

That night Joe shared with me some of the wine he had bought from Dave and Maureen. I took the cup and walked off some way into the woods. He had been prepared to go it alone, with even less gear than I had. And with an injured foot. He wanted to finish this thing as much as I did. Thinking about him brought a lump to my throat. It was like having a son you despaired of. Let's just get this over with, I thought.

There were only three ranches on the trail and they were all grouped together. They all operated as fishing lodges as well as working ranches. At the second we brought in the hay crop using pitchforks and a tiny old tractor and trailer with a huge mound of dry grass piled high. As we lay on top of the massive haypile bumping through the fields Steve said, 'This is like a return to the childhood I never had.' Rob, the owner, was the son of Pan Philips, the first man to ever ranch the area, and he and his wife gave freely of their food and home-made wine. Moe, the owner of the last ranch, kindly invited us to dinner as we wandered through. A party of lawyers, doctors, dentists and a former undercover cop were staying for a fishing trip. They were all from southern California. The former undercover cop was grossly fat, with elephant legs and a belly below the belt. He had just returned from Thailand. He had been giving a seminar on security matters. 'If he was undercover,' said Steve, 'it was under a lot of covers. Imagine those Thai girls ... doing things to him.'

One chap, a dentist, trying to make small-talk, asked if we ate much roadkill. 'Where we've been,' said Nigel, 'there haven't been too many roads.'

A divorce lawyer who had been divorced twice gave me two fat cigars. He took me to his cabin and opened a waterproof Pelli-Case, the kind cameramen use to protect their kit. Inside were about fifty cigars. Hand-rolled Cubans without labels. Fifty-dollar cigars. Maybe he took pity on me. When I told him I was a writer he sort of winced and said, 'It's tough being a writer.' I suppose he meant there was less money in it than in divorce proceedings in southern California. I was grateful for the cigars but at the time felt completely distant from this well-intentioned guy and his well-fed cronies, flying into the wilderness to do a little fishing, playing poker for pennies at night – they were rich enough, why not play for real bucks? I guess some of them were richer than others, and there was the nub. They carried their values of money and status here into the bush. The fat guy who was a former cop – he couldn't walk five miles without collapsing exhausted, he was bear food, despite all the talk. I saw what I valued most about the wilderness was the way it stripped away all the bullshit impedimenta of ordinary life, all the rubbish we've persuaded ourselves we need to live with, all the symbols that show we've got more money and status than our next-door neighbour. Those games sickened me and that is why I was glad when I walked back with Joe from the log cabin where the Americans were just starting their poker game and sipping their iced bourbon for our austere campsite down by the lake with the ever-present loon calling across the water.

. Joe had been prepared to go it alone. He was part of my world not theirs. I gave him one of the symbolic cigars. I still wasn't thinking straight, except for one thing. I knew now we'd finish this journey together.

Fourteen

TO STINKING LAKE

'At about eight we got out of the river, which discharges itself by various channels into an arm of the sea.' Alexander Mackenzie reaches the Pacific Ocean

I

Ground-dwelling grouse were everywhere and rather stupid. Joe caught one by running after it, in his bare hands. 'Surprised they're not extinct already,' said Steve. It was just after breakfast when Joe caught his grouse, so we let it go. We had to get on, plucking and drawing the thing would take time. We had to catch the Germans.

We came over the mountains and pushed through the treeline. The trees got smaller and smaller and more and more densely leaved. They were midget versions of all the trees lower down. A two-foot spruce, up here on the windswept mountain moorland, might take thirty years to grow. It was tempting to uproot a few, just because every guidebook makes such a racket about protecting this dwarf foliage, but we didn't. Too tired, too stunned to be out of the forest. You climb and climb from the boggy woods, sensing the freedom of the mountains. The treeline is less of a line and more of a series of increasing gaps between ever-shortening trees, then suddenly you're there, in amongst frost-blasted scree and short turf with marmots and grouse – all the familiar sights of European mountains. Our packs were lighter than at the beginning but the climb was still hard. It wasn't very high, seven thousand feet or so, but the accumulated exhaustion, emotional and physical, made it seem harder than it should have been.

Coming out on to the open moor, we realized we'd been under cover for weeks. The forest stretched more or less from the Fraser to the Pacific. Only the mountains were clear. Our suntans had gone. We were woods dwellers emerging blinking into the light.

It was the last range before the sea. As we went through the scoured saddle that was Mackenzie Pass we expected to see the Pacific. Instead we saw what Mackenzie named 'The Stupendous Mountain', a huge snow-covered monolith ringed by other, more jagged peaks. But we knew these mountains surrounded the fjords of Bella Coola. Saltwater fjords.

By nightfall we had caught the Germans. They were camped at a small lake halfway down the mountain range on the Pacific side, just below the treeline. The next day, our last day, we hoped, it started pouring with rain before dawn. The Germans decided to wait it out, see if the weather improved. We put on our German Army waterproofs. Sadly they weren't much good; even the Germans thought they were a sad reminder of the GDR's poor army. The waterproofs had a fabric liner that wicked all water, from sweat as well as cuffs, all over the interior. This fabric didn't dry very quickly so the waterproof was soon soaked inside and out. The previous year I'd used a non-breathable police waterproof. The zip had broken but it had been excellent – sufficiently baggy for the sweat to dissipate, but also with a plastic-like inside which dried in seconds when held over a fire. I'd learned my lesson in the first year that 'breathable' garments were an expensive con, letting in water after the third or fourth hour of continuous rain.

Downhill, with heavy packs, your knees do all the work. And we would be dropping almost to sea level so we had the full seven thousand feet to go. As we passed again into the trees the foliage was all different. We had left the northern woods. Now it seemed as if we were in the tropics. Huge cedars grew every-where, as thick as rainforest trees. Rhododendrons billowed exuberantly all over the path, making it hard to see where to put your feet. My insistence on going first meant I received the first and worst dumping of water lodged in all the greenery we brushed through. I was reminded of Mackenzie 'beating the bushes' for his men as they went on, saving them from getting too wet. Would I beat the bushes for Joe? Of course I would. The first thing to start leaking were my overshorts, which, despite their natty design, overhanging my gaiters, soon sucked up enough water to render my nether regions soggy and cold. The wick-like interior absorbed all the water I kicked up and spread it all over my inner trousers, which were soon sopping wet. The coat fared little better. Branches and ferns that sprang up from underfoot discharged a load of water under it and along the fastening at the front. I was sweating, too, which didn't help. Soon my top half was soaked through. We waded through rivers and a thigh-deep lake and only wrung our socks out – might as well keep going as fast as possible now we were soaked through.

The constant streams of water running down my hood covered my glasses in water. If I extended the hood too far I also managed to get steam on the inside. I settled for just water, designing in my mind a pair of mini clip-on windscreen wipers for just such an occasion. Down and down we went, through the lush temperate rainforest vegetation, following zigzag paths endlessly. My toes were soon jammed right up at the end of the boots and my thighs ached from walking bent-kneed, taking the strain of the rucksack and the descent.

Mackenzie's actual path at this point has always been debated. He describes coming down a valley full of awful precipices. Our path, which supposedly was made later, went less directly, weaving its way down the face of the mountain rather than the river valley we kept crossing. It had been tempting to just plunge down Burnt Bridge Creek, which some believe is what Mackenzie did. Others contest he went much closer to Bella Coola and descended there. None of the direct routes is particularly easy – a recent army expedition that ascended one had to be airlifted to safety after they got stuck. Our route was as authentic as any, and by now the urge to just finish had overwhelmed any nice distinctions about route finding. No one wanted to get lost for a night in the pouring rain when it wasn't even certain that was the Big Mack's route.

But even on this well-marked path we went astray. As we

descended the winding trail through step-up and step-down stones I sensed the path must keep descending. I found myself on the earthy extremity of a buttress, a thousand feet up, looking out into a misty valley. The mist cleared and there was the road, a silver line reflecting the sun. The road. Two lanes of asphalt and divided by a line of paint. Civilization. In a sense the real end of our journey. Then the mist was back again. The rain carried on pouring down. I clambered back up to where Joe had found the correct path.

My knees now wobbled from the strain of descending at such speed. Now any slight incline was welcomed as a change from the hateful regularity of down, down, down. I had always rather enjoyed going downhill before, now it seemed loathsome. I thought every few minutes about what I would do when we reached the road. Change into my sweater and a vest, which were the only two dry items of clothing I had. Eat some dry porridge oats and that last tin of sardines. Or had I eaten it already?

We caught further glimpses of the road. Then we heard the roar of the river. There had been a native village on the Bella Coola River in Mackenzie's day and they had ferried him down the fast grey-green stream to Bella Coola itself. The Germans had arranged for a taxi to come and pick them up. We would have to rely on hitching.

After the roar of the river we heard the sound of cars zooming by, and then, with the abruptness of such things, we spilled out on to the rain-slicked highway, the coast road, wide and well made and connecting us to the world. The end of the line. Nigel kissed the tarmac. We all hugged each other. And, as the car drove by, we hooted and high-fived, all in the pouring rain. Two thousand miles. Still together, too. I shook Joe's hand and he stared me in the face earnestly as he always did. 'Couldn't have made it without you,' I said. And it was true. We were joyous in the pouring rain, and hungry. We sat down and ate every last bit of food.

EPILOGUE

'Here my voyages of discovery terminate. Their
toils and their dangers, their solicitudes and
sufferings, have not been exaggerated in my
description. On the contrary, in many instances,
language has failed me in the attempt to describe
them. I received, however, the reward of my
labours, for they were crowned with
success.' Alexander Mackenzie

I

Mackenzie, though he had reached the sea at Bella Coola, was determined to go further, if only to get a good glimpse of the horizon to take an astronomical position. He borrowed a dugout canoe from the Bella Coola Indians but travelling up the fjord he finally ran into trouble. A group of Heiltsuk Indians, less friendly than the Nuxalk of Bella Coola, intercepted him and 'examined everything we had in our canoe with an air of indifference and disdain'. Mackenzie was blamed for ill treatment by other white men (quite possibly by men from Vancouver's ship which had visited this coast only fifty days earlier). One of the natives grabbed him, though Mackenzie fought back. 'I soon disengaged myself from him; and, that he did not avail himself of the opportunity of plunging his dagger into me, I cannot conjecture. They certainly might have overpowered me, and though I should probably have killed one or two of them, I must have fallen at last.'

It was time to beat a retreat. Though 'a reconciliation took place', Mackenzie knew not to chance his luck.

II

'There's your canoe,' said the strong-looking Nuxalk Indian called Peter. Many of his family were wood carvers in Bella Coola, though he worked in logging. He had met us in town and brought us to the river to see the boat. It lay on the bank next to the green river, awash with rotting salmon, this being the end of the season for chum or dog salmon. It was the last spoon-end dugout canoe in Bella Coola. Unfortunately we were a little late. It had been hauled out and its stern sawn off. Its sides had split in the sun and the frost. Once there had been hundreds of them plying the river and the fjord. Mackenzie had taken such a canoe out to the rock in the fjord where he wrote his name. Now there were none, except for this rotting log.

'Looks a bit far gone to patch up,' said Steve, even his innate optimism blunted by the sight of the wreck.

Something had started when I went looking with John Zeitoun for that perfect tree. Now we would have to find another perfect tree to complete the journey. We were camping on the lawn of Mary, a kind lady who had picked us up in the pouring rain that day we came down the mountain to the road. She had a few huge cedars on her forty acres of land. If we stayed a bit longer, or came back the next summer, I could perhaps find another perfect tree; this one needed to be six feet across at the base and thirty feet high. One logger quoted me $5,000 for such a tree, if I could find one. A perfect tree to make a perfect canoe. The world seemed open to me then as a series of journeys, all linking, and all starting with that search for a perfect tree.

I tasted the water at Bella Coola to make sure it was salty. It was. We'd made it to the Stinking Lake. Though I had lost my urge to emulate the details of Mackenzie's trip I knew we still had to get out to the rock, his furthest point west. To have done with it. I couldn't face a plastic canoe after all that time in a real one, so we settled on the modern equivalent of a dugout, what the modern Indians used – a powered fishing boat. It took two hours to go the thirty miles to the rock, which was once the site of a settlement. We were sure of this because on the beach Nigel and Joe found some rock petroglyphs, not mentioned anywhere before, even the fisherman had never seen them. And Mackenzie, being preoccupied with hostile Indians and making an astronomical sighting, had also never seen them, or at least never thought to mention them.

Bella Coola is famous for its petroglyphs. Thor Heyerdahl studied them and pronounced them very similar to those he'd seen in the Marquesa Islands in the Pacific. It seemed another clue, another hint to continue the journey. The world was wrapped in voyages, end to end. Now we were a part of it. We didn't carve our own petroglyph. Mackenzie had already done it when he wrote in vermilion paint:

ALEXANDER MACKENZIE, FROM CANADA, BY LAND,
THE TWENTY-SECOND OF JULY,
ONE THOUSAND SEVEN HUNDRED AND NINETY-THREE